Crowd Simulation

Daniel Thalmann · Soraia Raupp Musse

Crowd Simulation

Second Edition

 Springer

Daniel Thalmann
Institute for Media Innovation
Nanyang Technological University
Singapore, Singapore
and
IC-DO
EPFL
Lausanne, Switzerland

Soraia Raupp Musse
Graduate Course in Computer Science
Pontifical Catholic University of Rio
 Grande do Sul
Porto Alegre, Rio Grande do Sul, Brazil

ISBN 978-1-4471-4449-6   ISBN 978-1-4471-4450-2 (eBook)
DOI 10.1007/978-1-4471-4450-2
Springer London Heidelberg New York Dordrecht

Library of Congress Control Number: 2012950038

© Springer-Verlag London 2007, 2013
This work is subject to copyright. All rights are reserved by the Publisher, whether the whole or part of the material is concerned, specifically the rights of translation, reprinting, reuse of illustrations, recitation, broadcasting, reproduction on microfilms or in any other physical way, and transmission or information storage and retrieval, electronic adaptation, computer software, or by similar or dissimilar methodology now known or hereafter developed. Exempted from this legal reservation are brief excerpts in connection with reviews or scholarly analysis or material supplied specifically for the purpose of being entered and executed on a computer system, for exclusive use by the purchaser of the work. Duplication of this publication or parts thereof is permitted only under the provisions of the Copyright Law of the Publisher's location, in its current version, and permission for use must always be obtained from Springer. Permissions for use may be obtained through RightsLink at the Copyright Clearance Center. Violations are liable to prosecution under the respective Copyright Law.
The use of general descriptive names, registered names, trademarks, service marks, etc. in this publication does not imply, even in the absence of a specific statement, that such names are exempt from the relevant protective laws and regulations and therefore free for general use.
While the advice and information in this book are believed to be true and accurate at the date of publication, neither the authors nor the editors nor the publisher can accept any legal responsibility for any errors or omissions that may be made. The publisher makes no warranty, express or implied, with respect to the material contained herein.

Printed on acid-free paper

Springer is part of Springer Science+Business Media (www.springer.com)

(Daniel)
To my beloved wife Nadia and beloved daughters Melanie, Vanessa, and Sabrina

(Soraia)
To my daughters Marina and Helena and husband Claudio, who enlighten my life.

Preface

This book surveys algorithms and techniques of crowd simulation, and is intended for graduate students, researchers, and professionals. In particular, computer animation researchers, developers, designers, and urban planners will greatly benefit from this book. This second edition presents new techniques and methods proposed since 2007, when we published the first edition of the book.

In 1996, when the authors started researching into crowd simulation, there was very little material available on this topic in the Computer Science literature. Daniel Thalmann supervised Soraia Raupp Musse's PhD thesis in 1997 and since then they have both extensively published in the domain. As a result, many other research groups have also started working in the area. As early pioneers in this research, the authors organized the first workshop on Crowd Simulation (V-Crowds) in 2005 in Lausanne. Today, Daniel Thalmann at the Nanyang Technological University in Singapore and Soraia Raupp Musse at PUCRS in Brazil keep working on crowds. Crowd simulation is now a popular area of research and many techniques have been developed, with the entertainment industry in particular realising the potential of crowd animation. But why is this subject so fascinating?

Aggregated motion is both beautiful and complex to contemplate. Beautiful due to the synchronisation, homogeneity and unity described in this type of motion, and complex because there are many parameters to be handled in order to provide these characteristics. History shows that there has always been interest in understanding and controlling the motion and behaviour of crowds of people. Psychologists and sociologists have studied the behaviours of groups of people for several years, primarily to study the effects that occur when people with the same goal become one entity—a crowd or a mass. When this happens, people can lose their individuality and adopt the behaviour of the crowd entity, behaving in a different way than if they were alone.

The simulation of large crowds in real time requires many instances of similar characters. We need algorithms to allow for each individual in the crowd to be unique. In this book we present some possibilities of character generation and customization. We emphasize population modelling, including shapes, sizes, and colors. We also discuss the importance of adding accessories like bags, glasses, mobile phones, and their impact on animation. This topic is very important in the sense that it provides coherent visualization of populations, as discussed in Chap. 3.

Crowd animation is fundamentally based on the animation of the individual virtual humans. Chapter 4 explains the methods used to animate these individuals especially their locomotion. We explain walking models based on methods like Principal Component Analysis. We also insist on animation variety as it is essential for realistic crowd behaviour.

Certain problems arise only when studying crowds. For instance, crowds have a certain intelligence in collective behaviors, whilst individual intelligence and behaviors can be observed at the same time. Interaction (verbal or non-verbal) among individuals, groups and crowds can be perceived in low density flow of persons. Navigation is probably the most crucial behavior for crowds that can be simulated on a computer. We discuss in detail techniques of path planning including a new hybrid approach between navigation graphs and potential-based methods. Collision avoidance problems related to a large number of individuals in the same place require different strategies in comparison with the methods used to avoid collision between individuals. In real life people can stop because they don't have enough space to walk, and unfortunately they can even die because the high density of individuals in the same space. We also introduced a new Section on gaze attention as we think it is important that individuals seem aware of the environment and other people. The relationship between people and the environment is given by some aspects such as culture, knowledge, experience, memory, etc. Computers should generate behavior patterns to achieve such levels of interaction. Chapters 4 and 5 present some aspects to contribute with this discussion.

Moreover, a crowd is not only a large group of individuals, but can also be formed by groups which in turn are related to individuals. In addition other levels of behaviour can exist when treating crowds in this hierarchical structure. The group behaviours can be used to specify the way a group moves, behaves and acts. Individual abilities can also be required in order to improve the autonomy and intelligence of crowds, for instance perception, emotional status, memory, communication, etc. However, when we consider thousands of individuals, these complex behaviours cannot be provided individually due to the hardware constraints and to computational time rates. A further problem relates to how to improve the intelligence and provide autonomy to scalable crowds, in real-time systems. In Chap. 6 we discuss the integration of crowd simulation and computer vision to bring new ground in this discussion.

Chapter 7 discusses techniques for rendering crowds especially when real time simulations are required to populate virtual environments in virtual reality systems. We introduce a complete pipeline for fast rendering including levels of details, deformable and non-deformable characters as well as impostors. A new section explains how crowd patches can be used to generate unlimited populated environments.

Crowd simulation is dependent on the environment, which means that this environment has to be modelled in a specific way. Chapter 8 discusses how to model such informed environments including terrains and buildings. It also shows how ontologies can play an essential role in crowd simulation.

The last Chapter is dedicated to applications and case studies like crowds in Virtual heritage and Safety systems. We have added a new Section on the revival of the Pompeii city and another on immersion in crowds.

Some crowd requirements along with strategies and techniques that can be adopted to deal with these, are described in this book. Some of the topics presented are related to population modelling, virtual human animation, computer vision techniques focusing on crowd control and crowd rendering, and some applications are analysed.

Acknowledgements The authors would like to thank to Springer and Matheus Ruschel for support in the text edition.

Contents

1 **Introduction** 1
   1.1 Requirements and Constraints for Crowd Modeling 2
   1.2 Crowd Simulation Areas 3
   References 4

2 **State-of-the-Art** 9
   2.1 Crowd Dynamics 10
   2.2 Sociological Models of Crowds 10
   2.3 Crowd Simulation 11
   2.4 Behavioral Animation of Groups and Crowds 12
   2.5 Crowd Management Training Systems 15
   2.6 Group Behavior in Robotics and Artificial Life 16
   2.7 Environment Modeling for Crowds 16
      2.7.1 Environment Models 16
      2.7.2 Path Planning 17
      2.7.3 Collision Avoidance 19
   2.8 Crowd Rendering 20
   2.9 Crowds in Non-real-time Productions 22
   2.10 Crowds in Games 23
   2.11 Crowd Scenario Authoring 24
   References 25

3 **Modeling of Populations** 31
   3.1 Introduction 31
   3.2 Creative Methods 32
   3.3 Body Shape Capture 33
   3.4 Interpolated Techniques 34
   3.5 A Model for Generation of Population 36
      3.5.1 Definition of the Initial Data 38
      3.5.2 Choice of a Template 38
      3.5.3 Definition of New Somatotypes 38

	3.5.4	Calculation of Influence of Sample Somatotypes	39
	3.5.5	Calculation of Mesh Variation	40
	3.5.6	Body Parts' Deformation	41
	3.5.7	Results and Discussion	43
3.6	Using Computer Vision to Generate Crowds		46
	3.6.1	A Model for Generating Crowds Based on Pictures	47
	3.6.2	Results	56
3.7	Crowd Appearance Variety		57
	3.7.1	Variety at Three Levels	58
	3.7.2	Color Variety	59
	3.7.3	Accessories	66
3.8	Final Remarks		78
References			78

4 Virtual Human Animation 81
4.1 Introduction 81
4.2 Related Work in Locomotion Modeling 82
    4.2.1 Kinematic Methods 82
    4.2.2 Physically Based Methods 83
    4.2.3 Motion Interpolation 84
    4.2.4 Statistical Models 86
4.3 Principal Component Analysis 87
    4.3.1 Motion Capture Data Process 87
    4.3.2 Full-Cycle Model 88
    4.3.3 Motion Extrapolation 90
4.4 Walking Model 93
    4.4.1 Motion Interpolation and Extrapolation 93
4.5 Motion Retargeting and Timewarping 95
4.6 Motion Generation 98
    4.6.1 Speed Control 98
    4.6.2 Type of Locomotion Control 99
    4.6.3 Personification Control 99
    4.6.4 Motion Transition 100
    4.6.5 Results 100
4.7 Animation Variety 102
    4.7.1 Accessory Movements 103
4.8 Steering 104
    4.8.1 The Need for a Fast Trajectory Control 104
    4.8.2 The Seek and Funneling Controllers 105
4.9 Final Remarks 107
References 107

5 Behavioral Animation of Crowds 111
5.1 Introduction 111
5.2 Related Work 111
5.3 Crowd Behavioral Models 114

		5.3.1	PetroSim's Behavioral Model	114
		5.3.2	A Physically Based Behavioral Model	120
	5.4	Crowds Navigation	126
		5.4.1	Robot Motion Planning	127
		5.4.2	Crowd Motion Planning	129
		5.4.3	A Decomposition Approach for Crowd Navigation	134
		5.4.4	An Hybrid Architecture Based on Regions of Interest (ROI)	142
	5.5	A Collision Avoidance Method Based on the Space Colonization Algorithm	145
		5.5.1	The Crowd Model: Biocrowds	146
		5.5.2	Experimental Results	150
	5.6	Gaze Behaviors for Virtual Crowd Characters	157
		5.6.1	Simulation of Attentional Behaviors	158
		5.6.2	Gaze Behaviors for Crowds	159
		5.6.3	Automatic Interest Point Detection	160
		5.6.4	Motion Adaptation	161
	5.7	Final Remarks	164
	References	164
6	**Relating Real Crowds with Virtual Crowds**	169
	6.1	Introduction	169
	6.2	Studying the Motion of Real Groups of People	169
		6.2.1	Crowd Characteristics	169
		6.2.2	Crowd Events	172
		6.2.3	Parameters for Simulating Virtual Crowds Using Real Crowd Information	173
		6.2.4	Simulating Real Scenes	173
	6.3	Sociological Aspects	177
	6.4	Computer Vision for Crowds	179
		6.4.1	A Brief Overview on People Tracking	179
	6.5	An Approach for Crowd Simulation Using Computer Vision	181
		6.5.1	Using Computer Vision for People Tracking	182
		6.5.2	Clustering of Coherent Trajectories	184
		6.5.3	Generation of Extrapolated Velocity Fields	185
		6.5.4	Simulation Based on Real Data	186
		6.5.5	Some Examples	188
	6.6	Final Remarks	190
	References	191
7	**Crowd Rendering**	195
	7.1	Introduction	195
	7.2	Virtual Human Representations	196
		7.2.1	Human Template	196
		7.2.2	Deformable Mesh	196
		7.2.3	Rigid Mesh	198
		7.2.4	Impostor	198

	7.3	Architecture Pipeline	199
		7.3.1	Human Data Structures	201
		7.3.2	Pipeline Stages	203
	7.4	Motion Kits	211
		7.4.1	Data Structure	211
		7.4.2	Architecture	213
	7.5	Database Management	215
	7.6	Shadows	216
	7.7	Crowd Patches	218
		7.7.1	Introduction	218
		7.7.2	Patches and Patterns	220
		7.7.3	Creating Patches	221
		7.7.4	Creating Worlds	223
		7.7.5	Applications and Results	224
	7.8	Final Remarks	226
	References	227
8	**Populated Environments**	229
	8.1	Introduction	229
	8.2	Terrain Modeling	230
		8.2.1	Plants and Lakes	232
		8.2.2	Sky and Clouds	233
	8.3	Generation of Virtual Environments	233
	8.4	A Model for Floor Plans Creation	235
		8.4.1	Treemaps and Squarified Treemaps	236
		8.4.2	The Proposed Model	238
		8.4.3	Results	243
	8.5	Informed Environment	246
		8.5.1	Data Model	249
		8.5.2	Topo Mesh	251
	8.6	Building Modeling	253
	8.7	Landing Algorithms	253
	8.8	Ontology-Based Simulation	254
		8.8.1	Using Ontology for Crowd Simulation in Normal Life Situations	256
		8.8.2	Applying Ontology to VR Environment	257
		8.8.3	The Prototype of UEM	257
		8.8.4	Simulation Results	260
	8.9	Real-Time Rendering and Visualization	261
	8.10	Implementation Aspects	263
	8.11	Final Remarks	263
	References	264
9	**Applications: Case Studies**	267
	9.1	Introduction	267
	9.2	Crowd Simulation for Virtual Heritage	267

	9.2.1	Virtual Population of Worshippers Performing Morning Namaz Prayer Inside a Virtual Mosque 268
	9.2.2	Virtual Roman Audience in the Aphrodisias Odeon 271
	9.2.3	Populating Ancient Pompeii with Crowds of Virtual Romans 275

9.3 Immersion in a Crowd 278
9.4 Crowdbrush 279
    9.4.1 Brushes 281
9.5 Safety Systems 286
9.6 Olympic Stadium 287
9.7 Final Remarks 290
References 290

Book Contribution 293

Index 295

Chapter 1
Introduction

Animation of crowds finds applications in many areas, including entertainment (e.g., animation of large numbers of people in movies and games), creation of immersive virtual environments, and evaluation of crowd management techniques (for instance, simulation of the flow of people leaving a football stadium after a match). Several techniques for modeling crowd dynamics already exist, but important aspects of crowd simulation have remained open for further research. Specifically, (i) the existing approaches are often focused on panic situations rather than usual (normal) behavior, in which people in the crowd have goals to seek; (ii) behaviors are usually individual and groups or families are not treated; (iii) separate pre-programmed techniques are usually needed to calibrate the movement of people in low or high density crowds, and to affect local and global motion planning; and (iv) existing crowd-modeling methods are often complex, and they require careful parameter tuning to obtain visually convincing results [TM07, UdHCMT06].

In the past two decades researchers from a broad range of fields such as architecture [SOHTG99, PT01, TP02], computer graphics [Rey87, HB94, BG96, MT01, TLC02b, UT02, BMB03], physics [HM95, HFV00, FHV02], robotics [PJ01], safety science [TM95a, Sti00, Sim04], training systems [Bot95, Wil95, VSMA98], and sociology [CPC92, TSM99, JPvdS01] have been creating simulations involving collections of individuals. Nevertheless, despite the apparent breadth of the crowd simulation research basis, interdisciplinary exchange of ideas is rare; researchers in one field are usually not very aware of works done in other fields.

In order to have a persuasive application using crowds in virtual environments, various aspects of the simulation have to be addressed, including behavioral animation, environment modeling, and crowd rendering. If there is no satisfactory rendering, even the best behavior model will not be very convincing. If there is no good model of a behavior, even a simulation using the best rendering method will look dumb after only a few seconds. If there is no appropriate model of the environment, characters will not behave believably, as they will perform actions in the wrong places, or not perform at all.

Most approaches were application-specific, focusing on different aspects of the collective behavior, using different modeling techniques. Employed techniques range from those that do not distinguish individuals such as flow and network models in some of the evacuation simulations [TT92], to those that represent each individual as being controlled by more or less complex rules based on physical laws [HIK96, HFV00], chaos equations [SKN98], behavioral models in training systems [Wil95], or sociological simulations [JPvdS01].

We can distinguish two broader areas of crowd simulations. The first one is focusing on a *realism of behavioral aspects* with usually simple 2D visualizations like evacuation simulators, sociological crowd models, or crowd dynamics models. In this area, a simulated behavior is usually from a very narrow, controlled range (for example, people just flying to exit or people forming ring crowd structures) with efforts to quantitatively validate correspondence of results to real-world observations of particular situations [TM95b]. Ideally, a simulation's results would then be consistent with data sets collected from field observations or video footage of real crowds either by human observers [SM99] or by some automated image processing method [MVCA98, CYC99]. Visualization is used to help understand simulation results, but it is not crucial. In most cases, a schematic representation, with crowd members represented by colored dots, or sticky figures, is enough, sometimes even preferable as it allows highlighting important information.

In the second area, a main goal is *high-quality visualization* (for example, in movie productions and computer games), but usually the realism of the behavior model is not the priority. What is important is a convincing visual result, which is achieved partly by behavior models, partly by human intervention in the production process. A virtual crowd should both look good and be animated in a believable manner, the emphasis of the research being mostly on rendering and animation methods. Crowd members are visualized as fully animated three-dimensional figures that are textured and lit to fit into the environment [DHOO05]. Here, behavior models do not necessarily aim to match quantitatively the real world; their purpose is more to alleviate the work of human animators, and to be able to respond to inputs in case of interactive applications.

1.1 Requirements and Constraints for Crowd Modeling

Real-time crowds bring different challenges compared with the systems either involving a small number of interacting characters (for example, the majority of contemporary computer games), or non-real-time applications (as crowds in movies, or visualizations of crowd evacuations after off-line model computations). In comparison with single-agent simulations, the main conceptual difference is the *need for efficient variety management* at every level, whether it is visualization, motion control, animation, or sound rendering. As everyday experiences hint, virtual humans composing a crowd should look different, move different, react different, sound different, and so forth. Even if assuming perfect simulation of a single virtual human would be possible, creating a simulation involving multiple such humans would still be a difficult and tedious task. Methods easing control of many characters are needed; however, such methods should still preserve the ability to control individual agents. Moreover, behaviors should be coherent in comparison with reality.

In comparison with non-real-time simulations, the main technical challenge is *increased demand on computational resources* whether it is general processing power, graphics performance, or memory space. One of the foremost constraining factors for real-time crowd simulations is crowd rendering. Fast and scalable methods both to compute behavior, able to take into account inputs not known in advance, and to render large and varied crowds, are needed. While non-real-time simulations are able to take advantage of knowing a full run of the simulated scenario (and therefore, for example, can run iteratively over several possible options selecting the globally best solution), real-time simulations have to react to the situation as it unfolds in the moment.

1.2 Crowd Simulation Areas

In order to create a full simulation of the crowd in the virtual environment, many issues have to be solved. The areas of relevance for crowd simulation and some associated questions include:

Generation of virtual individuals: How to generate a heterogeneous crowd? How to create a population with desired distribution of features [GKMT01, SYCGMT02, BBOM03]? Chapter 3 discusses some of these aspects.

Crowd animation: How should virtual entities move around and avoid collisions with both a static environment and dynamic objects How can a group move in a coordinated manner? [ALA*01, GKM*01, AMC03, LD04, BBM05]? Chapter 4 presents some techniques to solve these problems.

Crowd behavior generation: How should a virtual crowd respond to changes in their surroundings? How should agents respond to behaviors of other agents? What is an appropriate way of modeling perception for many agents [Rey87, TT94, HB94, BCN97, BH97, Rey99, Mus00, UT02, NG03]? Chapter 5 describes some methods used for solving these questions.

Interaction with virtual crowds: How and which information should be exchanged from real people to control virtual humans? What is the most efficient metaphor to direct crowds of virtual extras [FRMS*99, UdHCT04]? Chapter 6 presents some discussion concerning these aspects.

Virtual crowd rendering: How to display many animated characters, quickly? How to display a wide variety of appearances [ABT00, LCT01, TLC02a, WS02, dHSMT05, CM05]? Chapter 7 explains some details concerning crowd rendering.

Integration of crowds in virtual environments: Which aspects of the environment need to be modeled? Which representation of environmental objects is best suited for fast behavior computation [FBT99, BLA02a, KBT03, LMA03, PVM05]? Chapter 8 presents some discussion about these aspects.

Many of these aspects are to a greater or lesser extent intertwined. For example, efficiency of rendering constrains the possible variety of behaviors and appearances; higher-level behavior generation controls lower-level motion systems, but the behavior should also respond appropriately to collisions encountered while moving; the behavior model affects interaction possibilities; the environment representation affects possible behaviors; relating real and virtual humans allows handling of more complex behavior and environment representations and so on.

This book aims to discuss some of these aspects, organized in nine chapters, also including a state-of-the-art and presentation of some relevant applications developed by the authors.

References

[ABT00] AUBEL A., BOULIC R., THALMANN D.: Real-time display of virtual humans: Levels of detail and impostors. *IEEE Transactions on Circuits and Systems for Video Technology 10*, 2 (2000), 207–217.

[ALA*01] ASHIDA K., LEE S., ALLBECK J., SUN H., BADLER N., METAXAS D.: Pedestrians: Creating agent behaviors through statistical analysis of observation data. In *Proceedings of IEEE Computer Animation* (Seoul, Korea, 2001), pp. 84–92.

[AMC03] ANDERSON M., MCDANIEL E., CHENNEY S.: Constrained animation of flocks. In *Proc. ACM SIGGRAPH/Eurographics Symposium on Computer Animation (SCA'03)* (2003), pp. 286–297.

[BBM05] BRAUN A., BODMAN B. J., MUSSE S. R.: Simulating virtual crowds in emergency situations. In *Proceedings of ACM Symposium on Virtual Reality Software and Technology—VRST 2005* (Monterey, California, USA, 2005), ACM, New York.

[BBOM03] BRAUN A., BODMANN B. E. J., OLIVEIRA L. P. L., MUSSE S. R.: Modelling individual behavior in crowd simulation. In *Proceedings of Computer Animation and Social Agents 2003* (New Brunswick, USA, 2003), IEEE Computer Society, Los Alamitos, pp. 143–148.

[BCN97] BOUVIER E., COHEN E., NAJMAN L.: From crowd simulation to airbag deployment: Particle systems, a new paradigm of simulation. *Journal of Electrical Imaging 6*, 1 (January 1997), 94–107.

[BG96] BOUVIER E., GUILLOTEAU P.: Crowd simulation in immersive space management. In *Proc. Eurographics Workshop on Virtual Environments and Scientific Visualization'96* (1996), Springer, London, pp. 104–110.

[BH97] BROGAN D., HODGINS J.: Group behaviors for systems with significant dynamics. *Autonomous Robots 4* (1997), 137–153.

[BLA02a] BAYAZIT O. B., LIEN J.-M., AMATO N. M.: Better group behaviors in complex environments using global roadmaps. In *Proc. Artificial Life'02* (2002).

[BMB03] BRAUN A., MUSSE S., BODMANN L. O. B.: Modeling individual behaviors in crowd simulation. In *Computer Animation and Social Agents* (New Jersey, USA, May 2003), pp. 143–148.

[Bot95] BOTTACI L.: A direct manipulation interface for a user enhanceable crowd simulator. *Journal of Intelligent Systems 5*, 4 (1995), 249–272.

[CM05] COURTY N., MUSSE S. R.: Simulation of large crowds in emergency situations including gaseous phenomena. In *Proceedings of Computer Graphics International 2005* (Stony Brook, USA, 2005), IEEE Computer Society, Los Alamitos, pp. 206–212.

References

[CPC92] MCPHAIL C., POWERS W., TUCKER C.: Simulating individual and collective actions in temporary gatherings. *Social Science Computer Review 10*, 1 (Spring 1992), 1–28.

[CYC99] CHOW T. W. S., YAM J. Y.-F., CHO S.-Y.: Fast training algorithm for feedforward neural networks: Application to crowd estimation at underground stations. *Artificial Intelligence in Engineering 13* (1999), 301–307.

[DHOO05] DOBBYN S., HAMILL J., O'CONOR K., O'SULLIVAN C.: Geopostors: A real-time geometry/impostor crowd rendering system. In *SI3D'05: Proceedings of the 2005 Symposium on Interactive 3D Graphics and Games* (New York, NY, USA, 2005), ACM, New York, pp. 95–102.

[dHSMT05] DE HERAS P., SCHERTENLEIB S., MAÏM J., THALMANN D.: Real-time shader rendering for crowds in virtual heritage. In *Proc. 6th International Symposium on Virtual Reality, Archaeology and Cultural Heritage (VAST 05)* (2005).

[FBT99] FARENC N., BOULIC R., THALMANN D.: An informed environment dedicated to the simulation of virtual humans in urban context. In *Eurographics'99* (Milano, Italy, 1999), Brunet P., Scopigno R. (Eds.), vol. 18, pp. 309–318.

[FHV02] FARKAS I., HELBING D., VICSEK T.: Mexican waves in an excitable medium. *Nature 419* (2002), 131–132.

[FRMS*99] FARENC N., RAUPP MUSSE S., SCHWEISS E., KALLMANN M., AUNE O., BOULIC R., THALMANN D.: A paradigm for controlling virtual humans in urban environment simulations. *Applied Artificial Intelligence Journal—Special Issue on Intelligent Virtual Environments 14*, 1 (1999), 69–91.

[GKM*01] GOLDENSTEIN S., KARAVELAS M., METAXAS D., GUIBAS L., AARON E., GOSWAMI A.: Scalable nonlinear dynamical systems for agent steering and crowd simulation. *Computers & Graphics 25*, 6 (2001), 983–998.

[GKMT01] GOTO T., KSHIRSAGAR S., MAGNENAT-THALMANN N.: Automatic face cloning and animation. *IEEE Signal Processing Magazine 18*, 3 (2001), 17–25.

[HB94] HODGINS J., BROGAN D.: Robot herds: Group behaviors for systems with significant dynamics. In *Proc. Artificial Life IV* (1994), pp. 319–324.

[HFV00] HELBING D., FARKAS I., VICSEK T.: Simulating dynamical features of escape panic. *Nature 407* (2000), 487–490.

[HIK96] HOSOI M., ISHIJIMA S., KOJIMA A.: Dynamical model of a pedestrian in a crowd. In *Proc. IEEE International Workshop on Robot and Human Communication'96* (1996).

[HM95] HELBING D., MOLNAR P.: Social force model for pedestrian dynamics. *Physical Review E 51* (1995), 4282–4286.

[JPvdS01] JAGER W., POPPING R., VAN DE SANDE H.: Clustering and fighting in two-party crowds: Simulating the approach-avoidance conflict. *Journal of Artificial Societies and Social Simulation 4*, 3 (2001).

[KBT03] KALLMANN M., BIERI H., THALMANN D.: Fully dynamic constrained Delaunay triangulations. In *Geometric Modelling for Scientific Visualization* (2003), Brunnett G., Hamann B., Mueller H., Linsen L. (Eds.), Springer, Berlin, pp. 241–257.

[LCT01] LOSCOS C., CHRYSANTHOU Y., TECCHIA F.: Real-time shadows for animated crowds in virtual cities. In *Proceedings of the ACM Symposium on Virtual Reality Software and Technology (VRST'01)* (New York, 2001), Shaw C., Wang W. (Eds.), ACM, New York, pp. 85–92.

[LD04] LAMARCHE F., DONIKIAN S.: Crowds of virtual humans: A new approach for real time navigation in complex and structured environments. *Computer Graphics Forum 23*, 3 (September 2004), 509–518.

[LMA03] LOSCOS C., MARCHAL D., MEYER A.: Intuitive crowd behavior in dense urban environments using local laws. In *Proc. Theory and Practice of Computer Graphics (TPCG'03)* (2003).

[MT01] MUSSE S. R., THALMANN D.: A hierarchical model for real time simulation of virtual human crowds. *IEEE Transactions on Visualization and Computer Graph-*

ics 7, 2 (April–June 2001), 152–164.

[Mus00] MUSSE S. R.: *Human Crowd Modelling with Various Levels of Behaviour Control.* PhD thesis, EPFL, Lausanne, 2000.

[MVCA98] MARANA A. N., VELASTIN S. A., COSTA L. F., LOTUFO R. A.: Automatic estimation of crowd density using texture. *Safety Science 28*, 3 (1998), 165–175.

[NG03] NIEDERBERGER C., GROSS M.: Hierarchical and heterogenous reactive agents for real-time applications. *Computer Graphics Forum 22*, 3 (2003), 323–331. (Proc. Eurographics'03.)

[PJ01] MOLNAR P., STARKE J.: Control of distributed autonomous robotic systems using principles of pattern formation in nature and pedestrian behavior. *IEEE Transactions on Systems, Man and Cybernetics B 31*, 3 (June 2001), 433–436.

[PT01] PENN A., TURNER A.: Space syntax based agent simulation. In *Pedestrian and Evacuation Dynamics* (2001), Schreckenberg M., Sharma S. (Eds.), Springer, Berlin.

[PVM05] PAIVA D. C., VIEIRA R., MUSSE S. R.: Ontology-based crowd simulation for normal life situations. In *Proceedings of Computer Graphics International 2005* (Stony Brook, USA, 2005), IEEE Computer Society, Los Alamitos.

[Rey87] REYNOLDS C. W.: Flocks, herds and schools: A distributed behavioral model. In *Proceedings of the Annual Conference on Computer Graphics and Interactive Techniques (SIGGRAPH'87)* (New York, NY, USA, 1987), ACM, New York, pp. 25–34.

[Rey99] REYNOLDS C. W.: Steering behaviors for autonomous characters. In *Game Developers Conference* (San Jose, California, USA, 1999), pp. 763–782.

[Sim04] Simulex, 2004. Evacuation modeling software, product information, http://www.ies4d.com.

[SKN98] SAIWAKI N., KOMATSU T., NISHIDA S.: Automatic generation of moving crowds in the virtual environments. In *Proc. AMCP'98* (1998).

[SM99] SCHWEINGRUBER D., MCPHAIL C.: A method for systematically observing and recording collective action. *Sociological Methods & Research 27*, 4 (May 1999), 451–498.

[SOHTG99] SCHELHORN T., O'SULLIVAN D., HAKLAY M., THURSTAIN-GOODWIN M.: Streets: An agent-based pedestrian model. In *Proc. Computers in Urban Planning and Urban Management* (1999).

[Sti00] STILL G.: *Crowd Dynamics.* PhD thesis, Warwick University, 2000.

[SYCGMT02] SEO H., YAHIA-CHERIF L., GOTO T., MAGNENAT-THALMANN N.: Genesis: Generation of e-population based on statistical information. In *Proc. Computer Animation'02* (2002), IEEE Press, New York.

[TLC02a] TECCHIA F., LOSCOS C., CHRYSANTHOU Y.: Image-based crowd rendering. *IEEE Computer Graphics and Applications 22*, 2 (March–April 2002), 36–43.

[TLC02b] TECCHIA F., LOSCOS C., CHRYSANTHOU Y.: Visualizing crowds in real-time. *Computer Graphics Forum 21*, 4 (December 2002), 753–765.

[TM95a] THOMPSON P., MARCHANT E.: A computer-model for the evacuation of large building population. *Fire Safety Journal 24*, 2 (1995), 131–148.

[TM95b] THOMPSON P., MARCHANT E.: Testing and application of the computer model 'simulex'. *Fire Safety Journal 24*, 2 (1995), 149–166.

[TM07] THALMANN D., MUSSE S. R.: *Crowd Simulation.* Springer, London, 2007.

[TP02] TURNER A., PENN A.: Encoding natural movement as an agent-based system: An investigation into human pedestrian behaviour in the built environment. *Environment and Planning B: Planning and Design 29* (2002), 473–490.

[TSM99] TUCKER C., SCHWEINGRUBER D., MCPHAIL C.: Simulating arcs and rings in temporary gatherings. *International Journal of Human–Computer Systems 50* (1999), 581–588.

[TT92] TAKAHASHI T. S. H.: Behavior simulation by network model. *Memoirs of Kougakuin University 73* (1992), 213–220.

References

[TT94] TU X., TERZOPOULOS D.: Artificial fishes: Physics, locomotion, perception, behavior. In *Computer Graphics (ACM SIGGRAPH'94 Conference Proceedings)* (Orlando, USA, July 1994), vol. 28, ACM, New York, pp. 43–50.

[UdHCMT06] ULICNY B., DE HERAS CIECHOMSKI P., MUSSE S. R., THALMANN D.: EG 2006 course on populating virtual environments with crowds. In *Eurographics 2006* (2006), ch. State-of-the-art: Real-time crowd simulation.

[UdHCT04] ULICNY B., DE HERAS CIECHOMSKI P., THALMANN D.: Crowdbrush: Interactive authoring of real-time crowd scenes. In *Proc. ACM SIGGRAPH/Eurographics Symposium on Computer Animation (SCA'04)* (2004), pp. 243–252.

[UT02] ULICNY B., THALMANN D.: Towards interactive real-time crowd behavior simulation. *Computer Graphics Forum 21*, 4 (Dec. 2002), 767–775.

[VSMA98] VARNER D., SCOTT D., MICHELETTI J., AICELLA G.: UMSC small unit leader non-lethal trainer. In *Proc. ITEC'98* (1998).

[Wil95] WILLIAMS J.: *A Simulation Environment to Support Training for Large Scale Command and Control Tasks*. PhD thesis, University of Leeds, 1995.

[WS02] WAND M., STRASSER W.: Multi-resolution rendering of complex animated scenes. *Computer Graphics Forum 21*, 3 (2002), 483–491. (Proc. Eurographics'02.)

Chapter 2
State-of-the-Art

One of the largest areas where crowd behaviors have been modeled is the domain of safety science and architecture with the dominant application of crowd evacuation simulators. Such systems model movements of a large number of people in usually closed and well-defined spaces like inner areas of buildings [TM95a, BBM05], subways [Har00], ships [KMKWS00], or airplanes [OGLF98]. Their goal is to help designers to understand the *relation between the organization of space and human behavior* [OM93].

The most common use of evacuation simulators is the modeling of crowd behavior in case of forced evacuation from a confined environment due to some threat like fire or smoke. In such a situation, a number of people have to evacuate the given area, usually through a relatively small number of fixed exits. Simulations are trying to help answer questions like: Can the area be evacuated within a prescribed time? Where do the holdups in the flow of people occur? Where are the likely areas for a crowd surge to produce unacceptable crushing pressure [Rob99]? The most common modeling approach in this area is the use of cellular automata serving both as a representation of individuals and as a representation of the environment.

Simulex [TM95a, TM95b] is a computer model simulating the escape movement of persons through large, geometrically complex building spaces defined by 2D floor plans and connecting staircases. Each individual has attributes such as position, body size, angle of orientation, and walking speed. Various algorithms as distance mapping, way finding, overtaking, route deviation, and adjustment of individual speeds due to proximity of crowd members are used to compute egress simulation, where individual building occupants walk toward and through the exits.

G. Still developed a collection of programs named *Legion* for simulation and analysis of the crowd dynamics in evacuation from constrained and complex environments like stadiums [Sti00]. Dynamics of crowd motion is modeled by mobile cellular automata. Every person in the crowd is treated as an individual, calculating its position by scanning its local environment and choosing an appropriate action.

Helbing et al. [HM95, HFV00, WH03] proposed a model based on physics and sociopsychological forces in order to describe the human crowd behavior in panic situations. The model is set up by a particle system where each particle i of mass m_i

has a predefined speed v_i^0, i.e., the desired velocity, in a certain direction $\mathbf{e}_i^0$ to which it tends to adapt its instantaneous velocity $\mathbf{v_i}$ within a certain time interval τ (for 1st term of Eq. (2.1)). Simultaneously, the particles try to keep a velocity-dependent distance from other entities j and walls w controlled by interaction forces $\mathbf{f}_{ij}$ and $\mathbf{f}_{iw}$ (second and third terms of Eq. (2.1)), respectively. The change of velocity with time t is given by the dynamical equation:

$$m_i \frac{dv_i}{dt} = F_i^{(H)} = m_i \frac{v_i^0 \mathbf{e}_i^0 - \mathbf{v}_i(t)}{\tau_i} + \sum_{j \neq i} \mathbf{f}_{ij} + \sum_w \mathbf{f}_{iw} \qquad (2.1)$$

Braun et al. [BMB03, BBM05] extended the Helbing Model ($F_i^{(H)}$) in order to deal with different individuals and group behaviors, and also with complex environments. In this work, the agents' population can be composed heterogeneously by individuals with different attributes.

This chapter presents several works on crowd domain, as crowd dynamics and simulation.

2.1 Crowd Dynamics

The behavior of real crowds was analyzed in [Hen71, Hen74, Fru71, Hel97, Sti00]; results of their analysis provide a useful reference for simulation and animation of crowds. Two important aspects that guide the motion of real people are: goal seeking, reflecting the target destination of each individual; and the least-effort strategy, reflecting the tendency of people to reach the goal along a path requiring the least effort [Sti00]. According to these strategies, people travel along smooth trajectories, since this requires less energy than frequent changes of direction or speed. In particular, adjustments of direction and speed, required to avoid collisions, are minimized. Further consequences of the least-effort strategy are the formation of lanes and the speed reduction effect. The first term refers to the tendency of people walking in the same directions to reduce their effort by closely following each other, while the second one refers to the reduction of speed in dense crowds.

The concept of personal space, the subject of study of interpersonal interactions in a spatial context (proxemics) [Hal59], also plays an important role in population dynamics. Personal space can be thought of as an area with invisible boundaries, surrounding each individual, which should not be penetrated by other individuals in order for interpersonal interactions to occur comfortably. The size of this zone depends on the environment as well as the people culture, and decreases as the crowd density gets higher. In the context of simulations, the personal space determines the minimum distance that should be maintained among the agents.

2.2 Sociological Models of Crowds

Despite being a field primarily interested in studying collective behavior, only a relatively small number of works on crowd simulations have been done in sociology.

McPhail et al. [CPC92] studied individual and collective actions in temporary gatherings. Their model of the crowd is based on perception control theory [Pow73] where each separate individual is trying to control his or her experience in order to maintain a particular relationship to others: in this case it is a spatial relationship with others in a group. The simulation program *GATHERING* graphically shows movement, milling, and structural emergence in crowds. The same simulation system was later used by Schweingruber [Sch95] to study the effects of reference signals common to coordination of collective behavior and by Tucker et al. [TSM99] to study formation of arcs and rings in temporary gatherings.

Jager et al. [JPvdS01] modeled clustering and fighting in two-party crowds. A crowd is modeled by a multi agent simulation using cellular automata with rules defining approach–avoidance conflict. The simulation consists of two groups of agents of three different kinds: hardcore, hangers-on, and bystanders, the difference between them consisting in the frequency with which they scan their surroundings. The goal of the simulation was to study effects of group size, size symmetry, and group composition on clustering, and "fights".

2.3 Crowd Simulation

Virtual crowds are usually modeled as collections of interacting agents, although treating a crowd as a continuum (for example, obeying laws of fluid dynamics) is also possible [TCP06]. In *behavioral models*, movements of a group of agents are an emergent property of individual agents, which are both influenced by and influencing their neighbors. These individual behaviors are defined using sets of simple goal-oriented rules, such as "move with the average speed of your neighbors" or "keep an optimal distance to your neighbors". Behavioral animation was pioneered by Reynolds [Rey87], who simulated flocks of birds and schools of fish assuming that each agent has direct access to the motion characteristics (position and velocity) of other agents. Tu and Terzopoulos [TT94] improved the conceptual realism of this work by endowing artificial fish with synthetic vision and perception of the environment. Both the original results of Reynolds and the models of Tu and Terzopoulos were confined to relatively small, low-density groups of animals.

To control human crowds, Musse and Thalmann [MT01] proposed a hierarchical crowd organization with groups of different levels of autonomy. In a related work, Ulicny and Thalmann [UT01] proposed a model that provided agent control at the level of an individual, a group, and the crowd.

The rules governing the movements of agents in behavioral models may be viewed as an abstract representation of the "psychology" of modeled individuals. In contrast, in *force-field models*, interactions among agents (in this case, often referred to as particles) are based on analogies with physics. For example, Bouvier et al. [BCN97] modeled individuals in a high-density crowd as charges moving in electric fields. Helbing et al. [HM97, HFV00] introduced abstract attraction and repulsion forces to simulate groups of people in panic situations. Braun et al. [BMB03] extended this model by endowing agents with individual characteristics and including the concept of groups, which improved the realism of simulations.

In *data-driven models*, the motion of real crowds is used to calibrate simulations. For example, Musse et al. [MJJB07] used computer vision techniques to track individual agents in images obtained using a video camera, then applied the resulting statistics to drive a physically-based simulator, while Lee et al. [LCHL07] used aerial images for a similar purpose. Lerner and collaborators [LCL07] proposed a model for collision avoidance using a manually-built database of videos of pedestrians. The goal of this work was to improve the realism of collisions treatment using real-world data.

Hybrid methods have also been proposed. For instance, the approaches presented by [PAB07] and [vdBPS*08] integrate behavioral and force-fields techniques in order to improve crowd control, aiming to minimize the drawbacks of both technologies. However, the negative aspect of these methods is the increase in complexity of the implementation.

Each category of models presents a tradeoff. Behavioral models are suited for an individualized specification of agents, but global crowd control is more difficult to achieve because of the emergent character of the motions. In contrast, force-field models offer good global crowd control in high-density situations, but tend to generate less realistic motions of individual characters, which reflect their simplistic physical basis. Finally, data-driven models make it possible to improve the realism of simulations, but the acquisition and interpretation of real-life data is often difficult. This sets the stage for our method, in which crowds of agents obeying simple behavioral rules can be globally controlled and relatively realistic motions can be obtained without tedious parametrization as emergent properties of the model.

2.4 Behavioral Animation of Groups and Crowds

Human beings are arguably the most complex known creatures, therefore they are also the most complex creatures to simulate. A behavioral animation of human (and humanoid) crowds is based on foundations of group simulations of much more simple entities, notably flocks of birds [Rey87, GA90] and schools of fish [TT94]. The first procedural animation of flocks of virtual birds was shown in the movie by Amkraut, Girard, and Karl called Eurhythmy, for which the first concept [AGK85] was presented at The Electronic Theater at SIGGRAPH in 1985 (final version was presented at Ars Electronica in 1989). The flock motion was achieved by a global vector force $_eld$ guiding a ow of flocks [GA90].

In his pioneering work, Reynolds [Rey87] described a distributed behavioral model for simulating aggregate motion of a flock of birds. The technical paper was accompanied by an animated short movie called "Stanley and Stella in: Breaking the Ice" shown at the Electronic Theater at SIGGRAPH'87. The revolutionary idea was that a complex behavior of a group of actors can be obtained by simple local rules for members of the group instead of some enforced global condition. The flock is simulated as a complex particle system, with the simulated birds (called boids) being the particles. Each boid is implemented as an independent agent that navigates according to its local perception of the environment, the laws of simulated physics, and the set of behaviors. The boids try to avoid collisions with one another and with other objects in their environment, match velocities with nearby flock mates, and move toward a center of the flock. The aggregate motion of the simulated flock is the result of the interaction of these relatively simple behaviors of the individual simulated birds. Reynolds later extended his work by including various steering behaviors as goal seeking, obstacle avoidance, path following, or fleeing [Rey99], and introduced a simple finite-state machines behavior controller and spatial queries optimizations for real-time interaction with groups of characters [Rey00].

Tu and Terzopoulos proposed a framework for animation of artificial fishes [TT94]. Besides complex individual behaviors based on perception of the environment, virtual fishes have been exhibiting unscripted collective motions as schooling and predator evading behaviors analogous to flocking of boids. An approach similar to boids was used by Bouvier et al. [BG96, BCN97] to simulate human crowds. They used a combination of particle systems and transition networks to model crowds for the visualization of urban spaces. At the lower level, attractive and repulsive forces, analogous to physical electric ones, enable people to move around the environment. Goals generate attractive forces, obstacles generate repulsive force fields. Higher level behavior is modeled by transition networks with transitions depending on time, visiting of certain points, changes of local population densities, and global events.

Brogan and Hodgins [HB94, BH97] simulated group behaviors for systems with significant dynamics. Compared to boids, a more realistic motion is achieved by taking into account physical properties of motion, such as momentum or balance. Their algorithm for controlling the movements of creatures proceeds in two steps: first, a perception model determines the creatures and obstacles visible to each individual, and then a placement algorithm determines the desired position for each individual given the locations and velocities of perceived creatures and obstacles. Simulated systems included groups of one-legged robots, bicycle riders, and point-mass systems. Musse and Thalmann [Mus00, MT01] presented a hierarchical model for real-time simulation of virtual human crowds. Their model is based on groups, instead of individuals: groups are more intelligent structures, where individuals follow the groups specification. Groups can be controlled with different levels of autonomy: guided crowds follow orders (as go to a certain place or play a particular animation) given by the user in run-time; programmed crowds follow a scripted behavior; and autonomous crowds use events and reactions to create more complex behaviors. The environment comprises a set of interest points, which signify goals and way points; and a set of action points, which are goals that have some actions associated. Agents move between way points following Bezier curves.

Recently, another work was exploring group modeling based on hierarchies. Niederberger and Gross [NG03] proposed an architecture of hierarchical and heterogeneous agents for real-time applications. Behaviors are defined through specialization of existing behavior types and weighted multiple inheritance for creation of new types. Groups are defined through recursive and modulo based patterns. The behavior engine allows for the specification of a maximal amount of time per run in order to guarantee a minimal and constant frame rate.

Ulicny and Thalmann [UT01, UT02] presented a crowd behavior simulation with a modular architecture for multiagent system allowing autonomous and scripted behavior of agents supporting variety. In their system, the behavior is computed in layers, where decisions are made by behavioral rules and execution is handled by hierarchical finite-state machines. Most recently, a real-time crowd model based on continuum dynamics has been proposed by [TCP06]. In their model, a dynamic potential field integrates global navigation with moving obstacles, efficiently solving for the motion of large crowds without the need for explicit collision avoidance. Perceived complexity of the crowd simulation can be increased by using levels of detail (LOD). O'Sullivan et al. [OCV*02] described a simulation of crowds and groups with level of details for geometry, motion, and behavior. At the geometrical level, subdivision techniques are used to achieve smooth rendering LOD changes. At the motion level, the movements are simulated using adaptive levels of detail. Animation subsystems with different complexities, as a keyframe player or a real-time reaching module, are activated and deactivated based on heuristics. For the behavior, LOD is employed to reduce the computational costs of updating the behavior of characters that are less important. More complex characters behave according to their motivations and roles, less complex ones just play random keyframes. The behavior of autonomous characters has been widely studied in the area of crowd simulation during the past few years. Most crowd simulation models obtain plausible macroscopic behaviors but have a limited ability to manage behavioral autonomy. Decision systems are generally applied to simple reactive behaviors such as collision avoidance because of the computational cost of implementing existing rational models with a crowd of virtual people. To address these challenges, Paris and Donikian [PD09] proposed a crowd simulation cognitive model that can be used to develop complex goal-oriented behaviors for numerous virtual people in real time. The model integrates a decision process that provides a full bidirectional link between four layers, biomechanical, reactive, cognitive, and rational (see Allen Newell's Unified Theories of Cognition). Each layer informs the layer directly above it of specific information on imposed constraints and controls the layer directly underneath it. Each layer is built independently and exchanges only a set of identified data.

Shao and Terzopoulos artificial life approach [ST07] integrates motor, perceptual, behavioral, and cognitive components within a comprehensive model of pedestrians as individuals. They claimed that the model can yield results of unprecedented fidelity and complexity for fully autonomous multi-human simulation in a large urban environment. Following Tu and Terzopoulos [TT94], they adopted a bottom-up strategy that uses primitive reactive behaviors as building blocks that in turn support more complex motivational behaviors, all controlled by an action selection mechanism. The behavioral model consists of basic reactive behaviors, navigational behaviors, motivational behaviors, mental state and action selection. Realistic behavioral modeling, whose purpose is to link perception to appropriate actions, is a big challenge in the case of autonomous virtual humans. Even for 3 pedestrians, the complexity of any substantive behavioral repertoire is high. Except computer graphics, many relevant studies in psychology, ethology, artificial intelligence, robotics, and artificial life are devoted to this subject. With these behavioral models, virtual humans can be interacted with in some situations. Here the behavioral models are limited to the applications of pedestrians. The cognitive and perceptual components are also helpful in improving the plausibility of crowd simulation, e.g. the problem of local collision can be avoided by behavioral modeling. However, complex behavioral models are usually too expensive to be used in real-time massive crowd simulation. For the interactive crowd simulation, a behavioral model is necessary, and we have to face the tradeoff between precision of the behavioral the model and the computing time.

2.5 Crowd Management Training Systems

The modeling of crowds has also been essential in police and military simulator systems used for training in how to deal with mass gatherings of people.

CACTUS [Wil95] is a system developed to assist in planning and training for public order incidents such as large demonstrations and marches. The software designs are based on a world model in which crowd groups and police units are placed on a digitized map and have probabilistic rules for their interactive behavior. The simulation model represents small groups of people as discrete objects. The behavioral descriptions are in the form of a directed graph where the nodes describe behavioral states (to which correspond actions and exhibited emotions) and transitions represent plausible changes between these states. The transitions depend on environmental conditions and probability weightings. The simulation runs as a decision making exercise that can include pre-event logistic planning, incident management, and debriefing evaluation.

Small Unit Leader Non-Lethal Training System [VSMA98] is a simulator for training U.S. Marines Corps in decision making with respect to the use of non-lethal munitions in peacekeeping and crowd control operations. Trainees learn rules of engagement, the procedures for dealing with crowds and mobs, and the ability to make decisions about the appropriate level of force needed to control, contain, or disperse crowds and mobs. Crowds move within a simulated urban environment along instructor-predefined pathways and respond both to actions of a trainee and to actions of other simulated crowds. Each crowd is characterized by a crowd profile—series of attributes like fanaticism, arousal state, prior experience with nonlethal munitions, or attitude toward Marines. During an exercise, the crowd behavior computer model operates in real time and responds to trainee actions (and inactions) with appropriate simulated behaviors such as loitering, celebrating, demonstrating, rioting, and dispersing according to a set of Boolean relationships defined by experts.

2.6 Group Behavior in Robotics and Artificial Life

Researchers working in the field of artificial life are interested in exploring how group behavior emerges from local behavioral rules [Gil95]. Software models and groups of robots were designed and experimented with in order to understand how complex behaviors can arise in systems guided by simple rules. The main source of inspiration is nature, where, for example, social insects efficiently solve problems such as finding food, building nests, or division of labor among nestmates by simple interacting individuals without an overseeing global controller. One of the important mechanisms contributing to a distributed control of the behavior is *stigmergy*, indirect interactions among individuals through modifications of the environment [BDT99].

Dorigo introduced *ant systems* inspired by behaviors of real ant colonies [Dor92]. Ant algorithms have been successfully used to solve a variety of discrete optimization problems including the traveling salesman problem, sequential ordering, graph coloring, or network routing [BDT00]. Besides insects, groups of more complex organisms such as flocks of birds, herds of animals, and schools of fish have been studied in order to understand principles of their organization. Recently, Couzin et al. presented a model of how animals that forage or travel in groups can make decisions even with a small number of informed individuals [CKFL05].

Principles from biological systems were also used to design behavior controllers for autonomous groups of robots. Mataric studied behavior-based control for a group of robots, experimenting with a herd of 20 robots whose behavioral repertoire included safe wandering, following, aggregation, dispersion, and homing [Mat97]. Molnar and Starke have been working on assignment of robotic units to targets in a manufacturing environment using a pattern formation inspired by pedestrian behavior [PJ01]. Martinoli applied swarm intelligence principles to autonomous collective robotics, performing experiments with robots that were gathering scattered objects and cooperating to pull sticks out of the ground [A.99]. Holland and Melhuish experimented with a group of robots doing sorting of objects based on ant behaviors where ants sort larvae and cocoons [HM99]. In an interesting work using a robot to control animal behavior, Vaughan et al. developed a mobile robot that gathers a flock of real ducks and maneuvers them safely to a specified goal position [VSH*00].

2.7 Environment Modeling for Crowds

2.7.1 Environment Models

Environment modeling is closely related to behavioral animation. The purpose of the models of the environment is to facilitate simulation of entities dwelling in their surrounding environments. Believability of virtual creatures can be greatly enhanced if they behave in accordance with their surroundings. On the contrary, the suspense of disbelief can be immediately destroyed if they perform something not expected or

2.7 Environment Modeling for Crowds

not permitted in the real world, such as passing through the wall or walking on water. The greatest efforts have therefore been directed to representations and algorithms preventing forbidden behaviors from occurring; until quite recently the two major artificial intelligence issues concerning game development industry were collision avoidance and path-planning [Woo99, DeL00]. The majority of the population in the developed world lives in cities; it is there that most human activities take place nowadays. Accordingly, most of the research has been done for modeling of virtual cities. Farenc et al. [FRMS*99] introduced an informed environment dedicated to the simulation of virtual humans in the urban context. The informed environment is a database integrating semantic and geometrical information about a virtual city. It is based on a hierarchical decomposition of an urban scene into environment entities, like quarters, blocks, junctions, streets, and so on. Entities can contain a description of the behaviors that are appropriate for agents located on them; for example, a sidewalk tells that it should be walked on, or a bench tells that it should be sat on. Furthermore, the environment database can be used for a path-finding that is customized according to the type of client requesting the path, so that, for example, a pedestrian will get paths using sidewalks, but a car will get paths going through roads.

Another model of a virtual city for a behavioral animation was presented by Thomas and Donikian [TD00]. Their model is designed with the main emphasis on traffic simulation of vehicles and pedestrians. The environment database is split into two parts—a hierarchical structure containing a tree of polygonal regions, similar to the informed environment database; and a topological structure with a graph of a road network. Regions contain information on directions of circulation, including possible route changes at intersections. The agents then use the database to navigate through the city. In a recent work, Sung et al. [SGC04] presented a new approach to control the behavior of a crowd by storing behavioral information into the environment using structures called situations. Compared with previous approaches, environmental structures (situations) can overlap; behaviors corresponding to such overlapping situations are then composed using probability distributions. Behavior functions define probabilities of state transitions (triggering motion clips) depending on the state of the environment features or on the past state of the agent.

2.7.2 Path Planning

Path planning is an important and challenging task in crowd simulation, which helps each agent to find the path to its individual goal. The path planning problem has been widely explored by the robotics community. Although the multiple-agent path planning has been addressed for cooperative tasks of multiple robots, it is still a challenge to solve the path planning problem for large crowds in real time, especially for large-scale crowds. Because the methods used for robots are usually exponential in the number of robots, which are too expensive to be adopted in crowd simulation.

Benefit from motion planning algorithms in robotics, geometric representation of probabilistic roadmaps (PRM) can also be used for path planning in crowd simulation. PRM was applied to solve the problem of determining a collision-free path between a starting configuration of the robot and a goal configuration [KSLO96]. Arikan et al. [ACF01] used the visibility graph for the path planning for large numbers of virtual agents. The visibility graph connects together vertices of the environment if and only if they see each other. The PRM-based approaches were improved by being integrated with other techniques [BLA02a, BLA02b, SKG05]. Kallmann et al. [KBT03] proposed a fast path-planning algorithm based on a fully dynamic constrained Delaunay triangulation. Bayazit et al. [BLA02a] used global roadmaps to improve group behaviors in geometrically complex environments. Groups of creatures exhibited behaviors such as homing, goal searching, covering, or shepherding, by using rules embedded both in individual flock members and in roadmaps. Tang et al. [TWP03] used a modified A* algorithm working on a grid overlaid over a height-map generated terrain. Other approaches of geometric representation of environments have been explored specially for the path planning of multi-agent systems. Lamarche and Donikian [LD04] built an accurate hierarchical topological structure from geometric database of a virtual environment. They performed the following steps for the final navigation: spatial subdivision, topology abstraction, roadmap generation, and triangulation construction. It is reported that this approach can allow the navigation of several hundreds of agents in real time. Kamphuis and Overmars defined a walkable corridor that ensured sufficient clearance to allow a given group of units to pass [KO04]. The Voronoi diagram can be used to subdivide a free space based on a set of points, from which edges are generated to produce the roadmap. Sud et al. [SAC*08] proposed a new data structure based on Voronoi diagrams, which is used to perform path planning and proximity computations for each agent in real time. Inspired from Voronoi diagrams, Pettré et al. [PLT05, PdHCM*06, PGT08] presented a novel approach to automatically extract a topology from a scene geometry and handle path planning using a navigation graph. The environment is usually discretized into a fine regular grid in the potential field method. Kapadia et al. [KSHF09] introduced a discretization method of egocentric fields with variable resolution information representation. Helbing's social force model [HM95] is one of the most influential models in agent-based motion planning. This model considers each agent as a particle subject to long-ranged forces induced by the social behavior of individuals. The movement of agents can be described with a main function which determines the physical and social forces, similar to Newtonian mechanics. The social force model is capable of describing the self-organization of several observed collective effects of pedestrian behavior. Nevertheless, due to lack of anticipation and pre-diction, the characters interact when they get sufficiently close. Consequently, the resulting motions tend to look unnatural and contain undesirable oscillations. The problem becomes more obvious in large and cluttered environments. This model was extended to achieve more realistic crowd behaviors [HBJW05, LKF05]. Karamouzas et al. [KHBO09] introduced the evasive force to improve the social force model. Their approach is based on the hypothesis that an individual adapts its route as early as possible, trying to minimize the amount of interactions with others and the energy required to solve these interactions. With this model, the agents do not repel each other, but rather anticipate future situations avoiding collisions long in advance and with minimal effort. However, the applications of social force model are limited by the calculation efficiency because of its complex rules. Treuille et al. [TCP06] proposed realistic motion planning for crowds, making an analogy with potential fields. Their method produces a potential field from the addition of a static field (goal) and a dynamic field (modeling other people). Each pedestrian then moves against the gradient towards the next suitable position in space (a waypoint) and thus avoids all obstacles. Compared to agent-based approaches, these techniques allow simulating thousands of pedestrians in real time, and are also able to show emergent behaviors. However, they produce less believable results, because they require assumptions that prevent treating each pedestrian with individual characteristics. For instance, only a limited number of goals can be defined and assigned to sets of pedestrians. The resulting performance depends on the size of the grid cells and the number of sets. Hybrid architectures have also been explored to get advantages from different approaches. Pelechano et al. [PAB07] combined psychological, physiological, and geometrical rules with physical forces to simulate dense crowds of autonomous agents. Morini et al. [MYMT08] proposed a hybrid architecture to handle the path planning of thousands of pedestrians in real time, while ensuring dynamic collision avoidance. This method is detailed in Sect. 5.4.4. To address regions of varied interest, motion planning is ruled by different algorithms. Hybrid path planning should be deliberately designed to ensure agent motion continuity when switching between different algorithms.

2.7.3 Collision Avoidance

Except the topological model of the environment and path planning, collision avoidance is another challenging problem to be addressed. The collision avoidance techniques should be efficient enough to prevent a large number of agents from bumping into each other in real time. The greatest difficulty of collision avoidance is from the absence of other agents current velocities. Furthermore, the agents are not able to communicate to coordinate their navigation. A common solution to this problem is to assume that the other agents are dynamic obstacles whose future motions are predicted as linear extrapolations of their current velocities. The agent then selects a velocity that avoids collisions with the extrapolated trajectories of other agents. This is the idea of Velocity Obstacle. Considering the case in which each agent navigates independently without explicit communication with other agents, van den Berg et al. [vdBPS*08] propose a new concept the "Reciprocal Velocity Obstacle", which takes into account the reactive behavior of the other agents by implicitly assuming that the other agents make a similar collision avoidance reasoning. This concept can be applied to navigation of hundreds of agents in densely populated environments containing both static and moving obstacles for real-time simulation.

Ondrej et al. [OPOD10] explored a novel vision-based approach of collision avoidance between walkers that fits the requirements of interactive crowd simulation. By simulating humans based on cognitive science results, visual stimuli is used to detect future collisions as well as the level of danger. The motor-response is twofold: a reorientation strategy prevents future collision, whereas a deceleration strategy prevents imminent collisions. Several simulation results show that the emergence of self-organized patterns of walkers is reinforced using this approach. The overall efficiency of the walkers' traffic is improved and improbable locking situations is avoided.

2.8 Crowd Rendering

Real-time rendering of a large number of 3D characters is a considerable challenge; it is able to exhaust system resources quickly even for state-of-the-art systems with extensive memory resources, fast processors, and powerful graphic cards. "Bruteforce" approaches that are feasible for a few characters do not scale up for hundreds, thousands, or more of them. Several works have been trying to circumvent such limitations by clever use of graphics accelerator capabilities, and by employing methods profiting from the fact that our perception of the scene as a whole is limited.

We can perceive in full detail only a relatively small part of a large collection of characters. A simple calculation shows that to treat every crowd member as equal is rather wasteful. Modern screens can display around 2 million pixels at the same time, where a fairly complex character can contain approximately 10,000 triangles. Even if assuming that every triangle were be projected to a single pixel, and that there would be no overlap of characters, the screen fully covered by a crowd would contain only around 200 simultaneously visible characters. Of course, in reality the number would be much smaller; a more reasonable estimate is around a few dozen fully visible characters, with the rest of the crowd either being hidden behind these prominent characters or taking significantly less screen space. Therefore, it makes sense to take full care only of the foremost agents, and to replace the others with some less complex approximations. Level of details techniques then switch visualizations according to position and orientation of the observer. In the recent work of Hamill et al. [HMDO05] they pursue psychophysics, a discipline to decide perceptual limitations to the human vision system for example. Doing tests on how motion affects the perception of a human represented by an impostor or by a geometric structure, they were able to define distances of least noticeable switching between models.

Billboarded impostors are one of the methods used to speed up crowd rendering. Impostors are partially transparent textured polygons that contain a snapshot of a full 3D character and are always facing the camera. Aubel et al. [ABT00] introduced dynamically generated impostors to render animated virtual humans. In their approach, an impostor creating process is running in parallel to full 3D simulations, taking snapshots of rendered 3D characters. These cached snapshots are then used

2.8 Crowd Rendering

over several frames instead of the full geometry until a sufficient movement of either camera or a character will trigger another snapshot, refreshing the impostor texture.

In another major work using impostors, Tecchia et al. [TLC02a] proposed a method for real-time rendering of an animated crowd in a virtual city. Compared with the previous method, impostors are not computed dynamically, but are created in a preprocessing step. Snapshots are sampled from viewpoints distributed in the sphere around the character. This process is repeated for every frame of the animation. In run-time, images taken from viewpoints closest to the actual camera position are then used for texturing of the billboard. Additionally, the silhouettes of the impostors are used as shadows projected to a ground surface. Multitexturing is used to add variety by modulating colors of the impostors. In a later work they added lighting using normal maps [TLC02b]. Their method using precomputed impostors is faster than dynamical impostors, but it is very demanding on texture memory, which leads to lower image quality as size of textures per character and per animation frame have to be kept small.

A different possibility for a fast crowd display is to use *point-based rendering techniques*. Wand and Strasser [WS02] presented a multiresolution rendering approach which unifies image based and polygonal rendering. They create a view-dependent octree representation of every keyframe of animation, where nodes store either a polygon or a point. These representations are also able to interpolate linearly from one tree to another so that in-between frames can be calculated. When the viewer is at a long distance, the human is rendered using point rendering; when zoomed in, using polygonal techniques; and when in between, a mix of the two.

An approach that has been getting new life is that of *geometry baking*. By taking snapshots of vertex positions and normals, complete mesh descriptions are stored for each frame of animation as in the work of Ulicny et al. [UdHCT04]. Since current desktop PCs have large memories, many such frames can be stored and replayed. A hybrid approach of both baked geometry and billboarding was presented at I3d, where only a few actors are fully geometrical while the vast number of actors are made up of billboards [DHOO05]. A similar approach can be found in [CLM05]. A more recent approach to crowd rendering using geometry is through *dynamic meshes* as presented in the work of de Heras et al. [dHSMT05], where dynamic meshes use systems of caches to reuse skeletal updates which are typically costly. A hybrid of dynamic and baked meshes is found in [YMdHC*05] where the graphics programming unit (GPU) is used to its fullest.

What is common to all approaches is instancing of template humans, by changing the texture or color, size, orientation, animation, animation style, and position. This is carefully taken care of to smoothly transition from one representation to another so as not to create pops in representation styles. In the billboarding scenario this is done by applying different colors on entire zones such as torso, head, legs, and arms. This way the texture memory is used more efficiently as the templates are more flexible. For the geometrical approaches these kinds of differences are usually represented using entirely different textures as the humans are too close just to change basic color for an entire zone [UdHCT04].

2.9 Crowds in Non-real-time Productions

One of the domains with the fastest growth of crowd simulations in recent years is special effects. While only 10 years ago, there were no digital crowds at all, nowadays almost every blockbuster has some, with music videos, television series, and advertisements starting to follow. In comparison with crowds of real extras, virtual crowds allow one to significantly reduce costs of production of massively populated scenes and allow for bigger creative freedom because of their flexibility. Different techniques, as replications of real crowd video footage, particle systems, or behavioral animation, have been employed to add crowds of virtual extras to shots in a broad range of movies, from historical dramas,[1,2,3] through fantasy and science fiction stories,[4,5,6] to animated cartoons.[7,8,9]

The main factors determining the choice of techniques are the required visual quality and the production costs allowed for the project [Leh02]. It is common to use different techniques even in a single shot in order to achieve the best visuals; for example, characters in the front plane are usually real actors, with 3D characters taking secondary roles in the background.

Although a considerable amount of work was done on crowds in movies, only relatively little information is available, especially concerning more technical details. Most knowledge comes from disparate sources, for example, from "making-of" documentary features, interviews with special effects crew or industry journalist accounts. For big budget productions, the most common approach is *in-house development* of *custom tools* or suites of tools which are used for a particular movie. As the quality of the animation is paramount, large libraries of motion clips are usually used, produced mainly by motion capture of live performers. All production is centered around shots, most of the times only a few seconds long. In contrast to real-time simulations, there is little need for continuity of the simulation over longer periods of the time. It is common that different teams of people work on parts of the shots which are then composited in postprocessing.

The most advanced crowd animation system for non-real-time productions is *Massive*; used to create battle scenes for *The Lord of the Rings* movie trilogy.[10] In *Massive*, every agent makes decisions about its actions depending on its sensory inputs using a brain composed of thousands of logic nodes [Koe02]. According

---

[1] http://www.titanicmovie.com.

[2] http://www.dreamworks.com.

[3] http://troymovie.warnerbros.com.

[4] http://www.starwars.com/.

[5] http://www.lordoftherings.net.

[6] http://whatisthematrix.warnerbros.com.

[7] http://www.pixar.com/featurefilms/abl.

[8] http://disney.go.com/disneyvideos/animatedfilms/lionking.

[9] http://www.shrek2.com.

[10] http://www.massivesoftware.com.

to the brain's decision, the motion is selected from an extensive library of motion captured clips with precomputed transitions. For example, in the second part of the trilogy over 12 million motion captured frames (equivalent to 55 hours of animation) were used. *Massive* also uses rigid body dynamics, a physics-based approach to facilitating realistic stunt motion such as falling, or animation of accessories. For example, a combination of physics-based simulation and custom motion capture clips was used to create the scene of "The Flooding of Isengard" where orcs are fleeing from a wall of water and falling down the precipice [Sco03].

In comparison with real-time application, the quality of motion and visuals in non real-time productions is far superior, but it comes at a great cost. For example, for *The Lord of the Rings: The Two Towers*, rendering of all digital characters took 10 months of computations on a strong render farm with thousands of computers [Doy03].

2.10 Crowds in Games

In current computer games, virtual crowds are still relatively rare. The main reason is that crowds are inherently costly, both in terms of real-time resource requirements and for costs of a production. Nevertheless, the situation is starting to change, with the real-time strategy genre leading the way as increase of sizes of involved armies has a direct effect on gameplay [Rom04, The04].

The main concern for games is the *speed of both rendering and behavior computation*. In comparison with non-real-time productions, the quality of both motion and rendering is often sacrificed in a trade-off for fluidity. Similarly to movie production, computer games often inject realism into virtual worlds from the real world by using large libraries of animations, which are mostly motion captured. The rendering uses level-of-detail techniques, with some titles employing animated impostors [Med02].

To improve costs of behavior computations for games that involve a large number of simulated entities, simulation level-of-detail techniques have been employed [Bro02, Rep03]. In such techniques, behavior is computed only for characters that are visible or soon to be visible. Characters are created in a space around the player with parameters set according to some expected statistical distributions, the player lives in a "simulation bubble". However, handling simulation LOD is much more complex than handling rendering LOD. It is perfectly correct not to compute visualization for agents that are not visible, but not computing behaviors for hidden agents can lead to an incoherent world. In some games it is common that the player causes some significant situation (for example, traffic jam), looks away, and then after looking back, the situation is changed in an unexpected way (a traffic jam is "magically" resolved).

In case the scenario deals with hundreds or thousands of entities, many times the selectable unit with distinct behavior is a formation of troops, not individual soldiers. What appears to be many entities on the screen is indeed only one unit being rendered as several visually separated parts[11] [Med02].[12]

A special case are sport titles such as various football, basketball, or hockey simulations, where there is a large spectator crowd, but only of very low details. In most cases there is not even a single polygon for every crowd member (compared with individual impostors in strategy games). A majority of the crowd is just texture with transparency applied to stadium rows, or to a collection of rows, and only a few crowd members, close to the camera, are 3D models.

2.11 Crowd Scenario Authoring

Regardless of the quality of crowd rendering or the behavioral model, a virtual crowd simulation is not very useful if it is too difficult to produce content for it. The authoring possibilities are an important factor influencing the usability, of a crowd simulation system, especially when going beyond a limited number of "proof-of-concept" scenarios. When increasing the number of involved individuals, it becomes more difficult to create unique and varied content of scenarios with a large number of entities. Solving one set of problems for crowd simulation (such as fast rendering and behavior computation for large crowds) creates a new problem of how to create content for crowd scenarios in an efficient manner.

Only recently have researchers started to explore ways of how to author crowd scenes. Anderson et al. [AMC03] achieved interesting results for a particular case of flocking animation following constraints. Their method can be used, for instance, to create and animate flocks moving in shapes. Their algorithm generates a constrained flocking motion by iterating the simulation forwards and backwards. Nevertheless, their algorithm can get very costly when increasing the number of entities and simulation time.

Ulicny et al. [UdHCT04] proposed a method to create complex crowd scenes in an intuitive way using a Crowdbrush tool. By employing a brush metaphor, analogous to the tools used in image manipulation programs, the user can distribute, modify, and control crowd members in realtime with immediate visual feedback. This approach works well for creation and modification of spatial features; however, the authoring of temporal aspects of the scenario is limited.

Sung et al. [SGC04] used a situation-based distributed control mechanism that gives each agent in a crowd specific details about how to react at any given moment based on its local environment. A painting interface allows one to specify situations easily by drawing their regions on the environment directly like drawing a picture on the canvas. Compared with previous work where the user adds, modifies, and deletes crowd members, here the interface operates on the environment.

---

[11] http://www.totalwar.com.

[12] http://praetorians.pyrostudios.com.

Chenney [Che04] presented a novel technique for representing and designing velocity fields using flow tiles. He applied his method on a city model with tiles defining the flow of people through the city streets. Flow tiles drive the crowd using the velocity to define the direction of travel for each member. The use of divergence-free flows to define crowd motion ensures that, under reasonable conditions, the agents do not require any form of collision detection.

References

[A.99] MARTINOLI A.: *Swarm Intelligence in Autonomous Collective Robotics: From Tools to the Analysis and Synthesis of Distributed Collective Strategies*. PhD thesis, EPFL, Lausanne, 1999.

[ABT00] AUBEL A., BOULIC R., THALMANN D.: Real-time display of virtual humans: Levels of detail and impostors. *IEEE Transactions on Circuits and Systems for Video Technology 10*, 2 (2000), 207–217.

[ACF01] ARIKAN O., CHENNEY S., FORSYTH D. A.: Efficient multi-agent path planning. In *Proceedings of the Eurographic Workshop on Computer Animation and Simulation* (New York, NY, USA, 2001), Springer, New York, pp. 151–162.

[AGK85] AMKRAUT S., GIRARD M., KARL G.: Motion studies for a work in progress entitled "Eurythmy". *SIGGRAPH Video Review*, 21 (1985) (second item, time code 3:58 to 7:35).

[AMC03] ANDERSON M., MCDANIEL E., CHENNEY S.: Constrained animation of flocks. In *Proc. ACM SIGGRAPH/Eurographics Symposium on Computer Animation (SCA'03)* (2003), pp. 286–297.

[BBM05] BRAUN A., BODMAN B. J., MUSSE S. R.: Simulating virtual crowds in emergency situations. In *Proceedings of ACM Symposium on Virtual Reality Software and Technology—VRST 2005* (Monterey, California, USA, 2005), ACM, New York.

[BCN97] BOUVIER E., COHEN E., NAJMAN L.: From crowd simulation to airbag deployment: Particle systems, a new paradigm of simulation. *Journal of Electrical Imaging 6*, 1 (January 1997), 94–107.

[BDT99] BONABEAU E., DORIGO M., THERAULAZ G.: *Swarm Intelligence: From Natural to Artificial Systems*. Oxford University Press, London, 1999.

[BDT00] BONABEAU E., DORIGO M., THERAULAZ G.: Inspiration for optimization from social insect behaviour. *Nature 406* (2000), 39–42.

[BG96] BOUVIER E., GUILLOTEAU P.: Crowd simulation in immersive space management. In *Proc. Eurographics Workshop on Virtual Environments and Scientific Visualization'96* (1996), Springer, London, pp. 104–110.

[BH97] BROGAN D., HODGINS J.: Group behaviors for systems with significant dynamics. *Autonomous Robots 4* (1997), 137–153.

[BLA02a] BAYAZIT O. B., LIEN J.-M., AMATO N. M.: Better group behaviors in complex environments using global roadmaps. In *Proc. Artificial Life'02* (2002).

[BLA02b] BAYAZIT O. B., LIEN J.-M., AMATO N. M.: Roadmap-based flocking for complex environments. In *Proceedings of the 10th Pacific Conference on Computer Graphics and Applications, PG'02* (Washington, DC, USA, 2002), IEEE Computer Society, Los Alamitos, pp. 104–113.

[BMB03] BRAUN A., MUSSE S., BODMANN L. O. B.: Modeling individual behaviors in crowd simulation. In *Computer Animation and Social Agents* (New Jersey, USA, May 2003), pp. 143–148.

[Bro02] BROCKINGTON M.: Level-of-detail AI for a large role-playing game. In *AI Game Programming Wisdom* (2002), Rabin S. (Ed.), Charles River Media, Hingham.

[Che04] CHENNEY S.: Flow tiles. In *Proc. ACM SIGGRAPH/Eurographics Symposium on Computer Animation (SCA'04)* (2004), pp. 233–245.

[CKFL05] COUZIN I. D., KRAUSE J., FRANKS N. R., LEVIN S. A.: Effective leadership and decision-making in animal groups on the move. *Nature 433* (2005), 513–516.

[CLM05] COIC J.-M., LOSCOS C., MEYER A.: *Three LOD for the Realistic and Real-Time Rendering of Crowds with Dynamic Lighting*. Research report, LIRIS, France, 2005.

[CPC92] MCPHAIL C., POWERS W., TUCKER C.: Simulating individual and collective actions in temporary gatherings. *Social Science Computer Review 10*, 1 (Spring 1992), 1–28.

[DeL00] DELOURA M. (Ed.): *Game Programming Gems*. Charles River Media, Hingham, 2000.

[DHOO05] DOBBYN S., HAMILL J., O'CONOR K., O'SULLIVAN C.: Geopostors: A real-time geometry/impostor crowd rendering system. In *SI3D'05: Proceedings of the 2005 Symposium on Interactive 3D Graphics and Games* (New York, NY, USA, 2005), ACM, New York, pp. 95–102.

[dHSMT05] DE HERAS P., SCHERTENLEIB S., MAÏM J., THALMANN D.: Real-time shader rendering for crowds in virtual heritage. In *Proc. 6th International Symposium on Virtual Reality, Archaeology and Cultural Heritage (VAST 05)* (2005).

[Dor92] DORIGO M.: *Optimization, Learning and Natural Algorithms*. PhD thesis, Politecnico di Milano, Italy, 1992.

[Doy03] DOYLE A.: The two towers. *Computer Graphics World* (February 2003).

[FRMS*99] FARENC N., RAUPP MUSSE S., SCHWEISS E., KALLMANN M., AUNE O., BOULIC R., THALMANN D.: A paradigm for controlling virtual humans in urban environment simulations. *Applied Artificial Intelligence Journal—Special Issue on Intelligent Virtual Environments 14*, 1 (1999), 69–91.

[Fru71] FRUIN J. J.: *Pedestrian and Planning Design*. Metropolitan Association of Urban Designers and Environmental Planners, New York, 1971.

[GA90] GIRARD M., AMKRAUT S.: Eurhythmy: Concept and process. *The Journal of Visualization and Computer Animation 1*, 1 (1990), 15–17. Presented at The Electronic Theater at SIGGRAPH'85.

[Gil95] GILBERT N.: Simulation: An emergent perspective. In *New Technologies in the Social Sciences* (Bournemouth, UK, 27–29 Oct. 1995).

[Hal59] HALL E. T.: *The Silent Language*. Doubleday, Garden City, 1959.

[Har00] HAREESH P.: Evacuation simulation: Visualisation using virtual humans in a distributed multi-user immersive VR system. In *Proc. VSMM'00* (2000).

[HB94] HODGINS J., BROGAN D.: Robot herds: Group behaviors for systems with significant dynamics. In *Proc. Artificial Life IV* (1994), pp. 319–324.

[HBJW05] HELBING D., BUZNA L., JOHANSSON A., WERNER T.: Self-organized pedestrian crowd dynamics: Experiments, simulations, and design solutions. *Transportation Science 39*, 1 (Feb. 2005), 1–24.

[Hel97] HELBING D.: Pedestrian dynamics and trail formation. In *Traffic and Granular Flow'97* (Singapore, 1997), Schreckenberg M., Wolf D. E. (Eds.), Springer, Berlin, pp. 21–36.

[Hen71] HENDERSON L. F.: The statistics of crowd fluids. *Nature 229*, 5284 (1971), 381–383.

[Hen74] HENDERSON L. F.: On the fluid mechanic of human crowd motions. *Transportation Research 8*, 6 (1974), 509–515.

[HFV00] HELBING D., FARKAS I., VICSEK T.: Simulating dynamical features of escape panic. *Nature 407* (2000), 487–490.

[HM95] HELBING D., MOLNAR P.: Social force model for pedestrian dynamics. *Physical Review E 51* (1995), 4282–4286.

[HM97] HELBING D., MOLNAR P.: Self-organization phenomena in pedestrian crowds. In *Self-Organization of Complex Structures: From Individual to Collective Dynamics*

References

(1997), Gordon & Breach, London, pp. 569–577.
[HM99] HOLLAND O. E., MELHUISH C.: Stigmergy, self-organisation, and sorting in collective robotics. *Artificial Life 5* (1999), 173–202.
[HMDO05] HAMILL J., MCDONNEL R., DOBBYN S., O'SULLIVAN C.: Perceptual evaluation of impostor representations for virtual humans and buildings. *Computer Graphics Forum 24*, 3 (September 2005), 581–590.
[JPvdS01] JAGER W., POPPING R., VAN DE SANDE H.: Clustering and fighting in two-party crowds: Simulating the approach-avoidance conflict. *Journal of Artificial Societies and Social Simulation 4*, 3 (2001).
[KBT03] KALLMANN M., BIERI H., THALMANN D.: Fully dynamic constrained Delaunay triangulations. In *Geometric Modelling for Scientific Visualization* (2003), Brunnett G., Hamann B., Mueller H., Linsen L. (Eds.), Springer, Berlin, pp. 241–257.
[KHBO09] KARAMOUZAS I., HEIL P., BEEK P., OVERMARS M. H.: A predictive collision avoidance model for pedestrian simulation. In *Proceedings of the 2nd International Workshop on Motion in Games, MIG'09* (2009), Springer, Berlin, pp. 41–52.
[KMKWS00] KLÜPFEL H., MEYER-KÖNIG M., WAHLE J., SCHRECKENBERG M.: Microscopic simulation of evacuation processes on passenger ships. In *Theoretical and Practical Issues on Cellular Automata* (2000), Bandini S., Worsch T. (Eds.), Springer, London, pp. 63–71.
[KO04] KAMPHUIS A., OVERMARS M.: Finding paths for coherent groups using clearance. In *SCA'04: Proceedings of the ACM SIGGRAPH/Eurographics Symposium on Computer Animation* (2004), pp. 19–28.
[Koe02] KOEPPEL D.: Massive attack. *Popular Science* (November 2002).
[KSHF09] KAPADIA M., SINGH S., HEWLETT W., FALOUTSOS P.: Egocentric affordance fields in pedestrian steering. In *Proceedings of the 2009 Symposium on Interactive 3D Graphics and Games, I3D'09* (New York, NY, USA, 2009), ACM, New York, pp. 118–127.
[KSLO96] KAVRAKI L., SVESTKA P., LATOMBE J., OVERMARS M.: *Probabilistic Roadmaps for Path Planning in High-Dimensional Configuration Spaces*. Technical Report 12, Stanford, CA, USA, 1996.
[LCHL07] LEE K. H., CHOI M. G., HONG Q., LEE J.: Group behavior from video: A data-driven approach to crowd simulation. In *Proceedings of ACM SIGGRAPH/Eurographics Symposium on Computer Animation (SCA'07)* (Aire-la-Ville, Switzerland, 2007), Eurographics Association, Geneve, pp. 109–118.
[LCL07] LERNER A., CHRYSANTHOU Y., LISCHINSKI D.: Crowds by example. *Computer Graphics Forum 26*, 3 (2007), 655–664.
[LD04] LAMARCHE F., DONIKIAN S.: Crowds of virtual humans: A new approach for real time navigation in complex and structured environments. *Computer Graphics Forum 23*, 3 (September 2004), 509–518.
[Leh02] LEHANE S.: Digital extras. *Film and Video Magazine* (July 2002).
[LKF05] LAKOBA T. I., KAUP D. J., FINKELSTEIN N. M.: Modifications of the Helbing–Molnár–Farkas–Vicsek social force model for pedestrian evolution. *Simulation 81*, 5 (May 2005), 339–352.
[Mat97] MATARIC M.: Behavior-based control: Examples from navigation, learning, and group behavior. *Journal of Experimental and Theoretical Artificial Intelligence 9*, 2–3 (1997), 323–336.
[Med02] Medieval: Total War, 2002. Game homepage, http://www.totalwar.com.
[MJJB07] MUSSE S. R., JUNG C. R., JULIO C. S. J. JR, BRAUN A.: Using computer vision to simulate the motion of virtual agents. *Computer Animation and Virtual Worlds 18*, 2 (2007), 83–93.
[MT01] MUSSE S. R., THALMANN D.: A hierarchical model for real time simulation of virtual human crowds. *IEEE Transactions on Visualization and Computer Graphics 7*, 2 (April–June 2001), 152–164.

[Mus00] MUSSE S. R.: *Human Crowd Modelling with Various Levels of Behaviour Control.* PhD thesis, EPFL, Lausanne, 2000.

[MYMT08] MORINI F., YERSIN B., MAÏM J., THALMANN D.: Real-time scalable motion planning for crowds. *The Visual Computer 24* (2008), 859–870.

[NG03] NIEDERBERGER C., GROSS M.: Hierarchical and heterogenous reactive agents for real-time applications. *Computer Graphics Forum 22*, 3 (2003), 323–331. (Proc. Eurographics'03.)

[OCV*02] O'SULLIVAN C., CASSELL J., VILHJÁLMSSON H., DINGLIANA J., DOBBYN S., MCNAMEE B., PETERS C., GIANG T.: Levels of detail for crowds and groups. *Computer Graphics Forum 21*, 4 (Nov. 2002), 733–741.

[OGLF98] OWEN M., GALEA E. R., LAWRENCE P. J., FILIPPIDIS L.: The numerical simulation of aircraft evacuation and its application to aircraft design and certification. *The Aeronautical Journal 102*, 1016 (1998), 301–312.

[OM93] OKAZAKI S., MATSUSHITA S.: A study of simulation model for pedestrian movement with evacuation and queuing. In *Proc. International Conference on Engineering for Crowd Safety'93* (1993).

[OPOD10] ONDŘEJ J., PETTRÉ J., OLIVIER A.-H., DONIKIAN S.: A synthetic-vision based steering approach for crowd simulation. *ACM Transactions on Graphics 29* (July 2010), 123:1–123:9.

[PAB07] PELECHANO N., ALLBECK J. M., BADLER N. I.: Controlling individual agents in high-density crowd simulation. In *Proceedings of the 2007 ACM SIGGRAPH/Eurographics Symposium on Computer Animation, SCA'07* (Aire-la-Ville, Switzerland, 2007), Eurographics Association, Geneve, pp. 99–108.

[PD09] PARIS S., DONIKIAN S.: Activity-driven populace: A cognitive approach to crowd simulation. *IEEE Compututer Graphics and Applications 29*, 4 (July 2009), 34–43.

[PdHCM*06] PETTRÉ J., DE HERAS CIECHOMSKI P., MAÏM J., YERSIN B., LAUMOND J.-P., THALMANN D.: Real-time navigating crowds: scalable simulation and rendering: Research articles. *Computer Animation and Virtual Worlds 17*, 3–4 (2006), 445–455.

[PGT08] PETTRÉ J., GRILLON H., THALMANN D.: Crowds of moving objects: Navigation planning and simulation. In *ACM SIGGRAPH 2008 Classes, SIGGRAPH'08* (New York, NY, USA, 2008), ACM, New York, pp. 54:1–54:7.

[PJ01] MOLNAR P., STARKE J.: Control of distributed autonomous robotic systems using principles of pattern formation in nature and pedestrian behavior. *IEEE Transactions in Systems, Man and Cybernetics B 31*, 3 (June 2001), 433–436.

[PLT05] PETTRÉ J., LAUMOND J. P., THALMANN D.: A navigation graph for real-time crowd animation on multilayered and uneven terrain. In *First International Workshop on Crowd Simulation (V-CROWDS'05)* (2005), pp. 81–89.

[Pow73] POWERS W. T.: *The Control of Perception.* Aldine, Chicago, 1973.

[Rep03] Republic: The Revolution, 2003. Game homepage, http://www.elixir-studios.co.uk/nonflash/republic/republic.htm.

[Rey87] REYNOLDS C. W.: Flocks, herds and schools: A distributed behavioral model. In *Proceedings of the Annual Conference on Computer Graphics and Interactive Techniques (SIGGRAPH'87)* (New York, NY, USA, 1987), ACM, New York, pp. 25–34.

[Rey99] REYNOLDS C. W.: Steering behaviors for autonomous characters. In *Game Developers Conference* (San Jose, California, USA, 1999), pp. 763–782.

[Rey00] REYNOLDS C. W.: Interaction with groups of autonomous characters. In *Proc. Game Developers Conference'00* (2000), pp. 449–460.

[Rob99] ROBBINS C.: Computer simulation of crowd behaviour and evacuation. *ECMI Newsletter*, 25 (March 1999).

[Rom04] Rome: Total War, 2004. Game homepage, http://www.totalwar.com.

[SAC*08] SUD A., ANDERSEN E., CURTIS S., LIN M. C., MANOCHA D.: Real-time path planning in dynamic virtual environments using multiagent navigation graphs.

References

[Sch95] SCHWEINGRUBER D.: A computer simulation of a sociological experiment. *Social Science Computer Review 13*, 3 (1995), 351–359.

[Sco03] SCOTT R.: Sparking life: Notes on the performance capture sessions for 'The Lord of the Rings: The Two Towers'. *ACM SIGGRAPH Computer Graphics 37*, 4 (2003), 17–21.

[SGC04] SUNG M., GLEICHER M., CHENNEY S.: Scalable behaviors for crowd simulation. *Computer Graphics Forum 3*, 23 (2004), 519–528.

[SKG05] SUNG M., KOVAR L., GLEICHER M.: Fast and accurate goal-directed motion synthesis for crowds. In *Proceedings of the 2005 ACM SIGGRAPH/Eurographics Symposium on Computer Animation, SCA'05* (New York, NY, USA, 2005), ACM, New York, pp. 291–300.

[ST07] SHAO W., TERZOPOULOS D.: Autonomous pedestrians. *Graphical Models 69*, 5–6 (Sept. 2007), 246–274.

[Sti00] STILL G.: *Crowd Dynamics*. PhD thesis, Warwick University, 2000.

[TCP06] TREUILLE A., COOPER S., POPOVIĆ Z.: Continuum crowds. *ACM Transactions on Graphics 25*, 3 (July 2006), 1160–1168.

[TD00] THOMAS G., DONIKIAN S.: Modeling virtual cities dedicated to behavioural animation. In *Eurographics'00* (Interlaken, Switzerland, 2000), Gross M., Hopgood F. (Eds.), vol. 19, pp. C71–C79.

[The04] The Lord of the Rings, The Battle for Middle Earth, 2004. Game homepage, http://www.eagames.com/pccd/lotr_bfme.

[TLC02a] TECCHIA F., LOSCOS C., CHRYSANTHOU Y.: Image-based crowd rendering. *IEEE Computer Graphics and Applications 22*, 2 (March–April 2002), 36–43.

[TLC02b] TECCHIA F., LOSCOS C., CHRYSANTHOU Y.: Visualizing crowds in real-time. *Computer Graphics Forum 21*, 4 (December 2002), 753–765.

[TM95a] THOMPSON P., MARCHANT E.: A computer-model for the evacuation of large building population. *Fire Safety Journal 24*, 2 (1995), 131–148.

[TM95b] THOMPSON P., MARCHANT E.: Testing and application of the computer model 'simulex'. *Fire Safety Journal 24*, 2 (1995), 149–166.

[TSM99] TUCKER C., SCHWEINGRUBER D., MCPHAIL C.: Simulating arcs and rings in temporary gatherings. *International Journal of Human–Computer Systems 50* (1999), 581–588.

[TT94] TU X., TERZOPOULOS D.: Artificial fishes: Physics, locomotion, perception, behavior. In *Computer Graphics (ACM SIGGRAPH'94 Conference Proceedings)* (Orlando, USA, July 1994), vol. 28, ACM, New York, pp. 43–50.

[TWP03] TANG W., WAN T. R., PATEL S.: Real-time crowd movement on large scale terrains. In *Proc. Theory and Practice of Computer Graphics* (2003), IEEE Computer Society, Los Alamitos.

[UdHCT04] ULICNY B., DE HERAS CIECHOMSKI P., THALMANN D.: Crowdbrush: Interactive authoring of real-time crowd scenes. In *Proc. ACM SIGGRAPH/Eurographics Symposium on Computer Animation (SCA'04)* (2004), pp. 243–252.

[UT01] ULICNY B., THALMANN D.: Crowd simulation for interactive virtual environments and VR training systems. In *Proceedings of the Eurographic Workshop on Computer Animation and Simulation* (New York, NY, USA, 2001), Springer, New York, pp. 163–170.

[UT02] ULICNY B., THALMANN D.: Towards interactive real-time crowd behavior simulation. *Computer Graphics Forum 21*, 4 (Dec. 2002), 767–775.

[vdBPS*08] VAN DEN BERG J., PATIL S., SEWALL J., MANOCHA D., LIN M.: Interactive navigation of multiple agents in crowded environments. In *Proceedings of the 2008 Symposium on Interactive 3D Graphics and Games, I3D'08* (New York, NY, USA, 2008), ACM, New York, pp. 139–147.

[VSH*00] VAUGHAN R. T., SUMPTER N., HENDERSON J., FROST A., CAMERON S.: Experiments in automatic flock control. *Robotics and Autonomous Systems 31* (2000), 109–177.

[VSMA98] VARNER D., SCOTT D., MICHELETTI J., AICELLA G.: UMSC small unit leader non-lethal trainer. In *Proc. ITEC'98* (1998).

[WH03] WERNER T., HELBING D.: The social force pedestrian model applied to real life scenarios. In *Proc. Pedestrian and Evacuation Dynamics'03* (2003), Galea E. (Ed.).

[Wil95] WILLIAMS J.: *A Simulation Environment to Support Training for Large Scale Command and Control Tasks*. PhD thesis, University of Leeds, 1995.

[Woo99] WOODCOCK S.: Game AI: The state of the industry. *Game Developer Magazine* (August 1999).

[WS02] WAND M., STRASSER W.: Multi-resolution rendering of complex animated scenes. *Computer Graphics Forum 21*, 3 (2002), 483–491. (Proc. Eurographics'02.)

[YMdHC*05] YERSIN B., MAÏM J., DE HERAS CIECHOMSKI P., SCHERTENLEIB S., THALMANN D.: Steering a virtual crowd based on a semantically augmented navigation graph. In *First International Workshop on Crowd Simulation (VCROWDS'05)* (2005).

Chapter 3
Modeling of Populations

3.1 Introduction

Virtual human models are becoming widespread in computer graphics applications such as virtual reality applications, simulations, and games. Usually, due to the complexity of human bodies, realistic shapes are built by means of an exhaustive and long process of graphic design. In addition, if an application requires the presence of groups and crowds of characters, a diversity of shapes and types of animations is necessary to realistically populate a virtual environment. As a consequence, the artists involved should manually create such multiplicity, increasing both the complexity of their task and the time needed to accomplish it.

This chapter does not intend to be a guide for teaching artists how to model characters but it shows techniques in the area of creating large quantities of realistic virtual humans. The main goal of those works is to generate simultaneously a large number of virtual characters different from each other regarding the geometric model of their bodies.

We present some of the main works related to the modeling of virtual humans for crowds. Magnenat-Thalmann et al. [MTSC03] classified the methodologies for modeling virtual people into three major categories: creative, reconstructive, and interpolated. Geometric models created by artists such as anatomically based models fall into the first approach. The second category built 3D virtual human's geometry by capturing existing shape from 3D scanners, images, and even video sequences. Interpolated modeling uses sets of example models with an interpolation scheme to reconstruct new geometric models.

Below we review modeling techniques of virtual humans. First we look for methods that manually generate virtual characters. Section 3.3 presents techniques for shape capture of real people. Methods for modeling the variety of human body shapes are previewed in Sect. 3.4. Section 3.5 is devoted to presenting a model that generates a great amount of secondary characters in a simple and fast way for use in virtual reality applications, games, and real-time simulations. The creation process of the population diversity uses the body type classification model called somatotype, generating characters with realistic appearance. Section 3.6 illustrates an approach for generating virtual humans based on single and spontaneous images. Finally, Sect. 3.7 shows how to create materials, textures, and accessories in order to provide a greater visual diversity.

3.2 Creative Methods

The most traditional techniques for manually modeling characters are subdivision modeling and patch modeling. Subdivision modeling is a procedure for creating smooth models while keeping the total polygon count at a low level. The sculpting process is less confusing due to small point counts. Objects are made from a simple object such as a cube that is subdivided and deformed several times to reach the desired form. Patch modeling can be accomplished by creating points, polygons, splines, or Nurbs (Non-Uniform Rational B-Splines) and converting them to a polygon object.

In this case, a surface model is either a polygonal mesh or a set of surface patches, whose deformation is driven only by the motion of an underlying hierarchical structure or skeleton. This technique assigns each vertex point to one or more skeleton joints. Deformation is then implemented as a function of joint angle.

Other works aim at mimicking more closely the actual anatomy of humans or animals. The multilayered (or musculoskeletal) models contain the skeleton layer, intermediate layers to simulate the body volume (muscles, fat, bones, and so on), and the skin layer.

Wilhelms and Gelder [WG97] developed an interactive tool for designing and animating animals. In their system, ellipsoids or triangular meshes represent bones and muscle. Each muscle is a generalized cylinder made up of a certain number of cross sections that consist in turn of a certain number of points. The muscles show a relative incompressibility when deformed. A veralization is used for extracting the skin mesh initially. It includes a filtering stage whose purpose is to blur the approximating muscles, and a decay that moves the subsurface at some distance from the underlying components. Afterwards, a spring mesh is constructed from the skin mesh. Each edge spring's stiffness is related to the adjacent triangles' areas while the skin vertices are elastically anchored to underlying components. A relaxation procedure is performed for each animation frame. The number of iterations can be quite low, even for large motions, according to the authors.

Scheepers et al. [SPCM97] stressed the role of underlying components (muscles, tendons, etc.) on the form, in their work on anatomically modeling the human musculature. They use three volume-preserving geometric primitives for three different types of muscles: ellipsoids are used for rendering fusiform muscles; multi-belly muscles are represented by a set of ellipsoids positioned along two spline curves; tubularly-shaped biscuit patches provide a general muscle model. Isometric contraction is handled by introducing scaling factors and tension parameters. The skin is obtained by fitting biscuit patches to an implicit surface created from the geometric primitives. The musculature of the shoulder and upper arm is detailed as an example and they achieve good results.

3.3 Body Shape Capture

An easier and more natural way for an artist to work in 3D is to sculpt the clay models of a character. Some works rebuild the geometric model from 3D scanners, photos, or video of real people. This method is efficient in the creation of geometric models of virtual humans with realistic appearance, but the modification of the final model is not trivial.

Since the advent of 3D scanners, there has been a great deal of interest in the application of that technology to reconstructing human bodies. A 3D scanner is a device that analyzes a real-world object to collect data on its shape and possibly color. The collected data can then be used to construct digital, three dimensional models that are used in a wide variety of applications. These devices are used by industry in the production of virtual characters for movies and video games.

For many years, the goal has been to develop techniques to convert the scanned data into complete, readily animatable models. Apart from solving the classical problems such as hole filling and noise reduction, the internal skeleton hierarchy should be appropriately estimated in order to make them move. Accordingly, several approaches have been under active development to endow semantic structure to the scan data. Dekker [Dek00] used a series of meaningful anatomical assumptions in order to optimize, clean, and segment data from a Hamamelis whole body range scanner in order to generate quad mesh representations of human bodies and build applications for the clothing industry.

Recently, the development of technologies especially for human body modeling has become a popular area. To recover the degrees of freedom associated with the shape and motion of a moving human body, most of the existing approaches introduce simplifications by using a model-based approach. Kakadiaris and Metaxas [KM95] use 2D images from three mutually orthogonal views to fit a deformable model to approximate the different body size of subjects. The model then can be segmented to different body parts as the subject moves. Plänkers et al. [PFD99] also use video cameras with stereo pair for the model acquisition of body parts. A person's movements such as walking or raising arms are recorded to several video sequences and the program automatically extracts range information and tracks outline of the body. The problem to be solved is twofold: First, robustly extract silhouette information from the images; second, fit the reference models to the extracted information. The data were used to instantiate the models, and the models, augmented by our knowledge of the human body and its possible range of motions, are in turn used to constrain the feature extraction. They focus, however, more on the tracking of movement and the extraction of a subject's model is considered as the initial part of a tracking process.

Recently, more sophisticated models were introduced and their aims limited to the construction of a realistic human model. Hilton et al. [HBG*99] developed a technique that involves the extraction of body silhouettes from a number of 2D views (front, side, and back) and the subsequent deformation of a 3D template to fit the silhouettes. The 3D views are then mapped as texture onto the deformed model to enhance realism. Similarly, Lee et al. [LGMT00] proposed a feature-based approach where silhouette information from three orthogonal images is used to deform a generic model to produce a personalized animated model.

Based on adding details or features to an existing generic model, these approaches concern mainly the individualized shape and visual realism using high quality textures. While they are effective and visually convincing in the cloning aspect, these approaches hardly give any control to the user, i.e., it is very difficult to modify these meshes to a different shape as the user intends. These approaches have the drawback that they must deal with special cases using ad hoc techniques.

3.4 Interpolated Techniques

In the literature, a considerable amount of work has been reported with respect to editing existing models and blending between more than two examples to generate new ones.

Azuola et al. [ABH*94] present the Jack platform to properly generate and animate scaled human models. Human factors engineering uses Jack as a design tool that supports testing a product for human usability. For example, in airplane cockpit design, one may be concerned with the pilot's visibility and access to controls. The system creates a standardized human model based on the given statistically processed population data or, alternatively, a given person's dimension can be directly used in the creation of a virtual human model. In the former case, it automatically generates dimensions of each segment of a human figure based population data supplied as input. Their initial virtual human was composed of 31 segments, of which 24 had a geometrical representation. For each segment or body structure with geometrical representation, three measurements were considered, namely, the segment length, width, and depth or thickness. Their Spreadsheet Anthropometry Scaling System (SASS) enables the user to create properly scaled human models that can be manipulated in Jack. The SASS is a spreadsheet-like system which allows interactive access to all anthropometric variables needed to size a virtual human figure.

Lewis [Lew00, LP00] describes a system implemented as a plug-in to Maya by using Maya's embedded script language. It aims to generate geometric models of virtual human bodies by using genetic algorithms. His paper shows some body samples selectable by the user, whose choices are used to define the fitness function. This function is finally used to produce a new body model. In order to create a wide diversity of body shapes, some random changes are made in the genotypes of the baseline models. All the used geometric models in this work have the same hierarchy. Thus, the genotypes are made of strings with the dimensions of each body part.

Modesto et al. [MGR01] present how PDI/Dreamworks produced many different secondary characters in crowd scenes for *Shrek*. They create some generic characters (six body types for guards and five body types for the other characters) that are uniformly scaled to produce new ones. After character creation, the designers

3.4 Interpolated Techniques

select what is visually acceptable or not, since the system can create some shapes which are aesthetically unpleasant. To increase the variety of characters, they model different heads, hats, and hairs to each original model.

More recently, novel interpolation methods that start with range scan data and use data interpolation to generate controllable diversity of appearance in human face and body models have been introduced. Arguably, the captured geometry of real people provides the best available resource to model and estimate correlations between measurements and the shape.

The automatic modeling approach introduced by Seo and Magnenat-Thalmann [SMT03] is aimed at realistic human models whose sizes are controllable by a number of anthropometric parameters. Instead of statistically analyzed form of anthropometric data, they make direct use of captured sizes and shapes of real people from range scanners to determine the shape in relation to the given measurements. The body geometry is represented as a vector of fixed size (i.e., the topology is known a priori) by deforming the template model onto each scanned model. A compact vector representation was adopted by using principal component analysis (PCA). A new desired physique is obtained by deformation of the template model, which is considered to have two distinct entities—rigid and elastic deformation. The rigid deformation is represented by the corresponding joint parameters, which will determine the linear approximation of the physique. The elastic deformation is essentially vertex displacements, which, when added to the rigid deformation, depict the detail shape of the body. Using the prepared dataset from scanners, interpolators are formulated for both deformations. Given a new arbitrary set of measurements at runtime, the joint parameters as well as the displacements to be applied on the template model are evaluated from the interpolators. And since an individual can simply be modeled by providing a number of parameters to the system, modeling a population is reduced to the problem of automatically generating a parameter set. The resulting models exhibit a visual fidelity, and the performance and robustness of the implementation.

Allen et al. [ACP03] present a method for fitting scanned models of the human body to high-resolution template meshes. Once the correspondence is established for all example models, a mapping function is found by solving a transformation that maps body features, such as height and weight, formed by PCA. This function can then be used to create new different bodies by modifying their weight or height.

The model presented in the next section is based on a variation of a template similar to Azuola's framework. However, in this work there are no constraints related to the number of segments and the hierarchy of the geometric models, as existent in Azuola's method, since the technique presented here makes use of the geometric model's skeleton defined in the specified template. Furthermore, a wide variety of body shapes with reliable dimensions and realistic appearance can be created due to the use of the somatotype body type classification model to create the required diversity.

3.5 A Model for Generation of Population

Due to the growing use of 3D virtual humans, the amount of research being carried out for automatic generation of geometric models is increasing. However, few works have considered the aesthetically accepted (visual quality of results) and the association of the geometric model to a skeleton to provide animations in the generation of virtual humans. Thus, we propose the modeling of virtual humans in their possible shapes based on a classical classification of real human body forms, in order to employ a coherent way to generate the largest number of realistic virtual characters possible. From all the methods presented for the classification of real human body types, the somatotype model is the most consolidated of them. This concept has direct application in medicine and physical education and helps to understand human development within contexts of growth, exercise, performance, and nutrition. It was introduced by Sheldon [She40] and later modified by Heath and Carter [HC90]. Sheldon determined that there are three basic elements which, when put together, defined all physical types. He nominated the three basic elements as endomorphy, mesomorphy, and ectomorphy, is relation to the three embryonic layers (endoderm, mesoderm, and ectoderm).

To Sheldon, endomorphy is centered in the abdomen and all the digestive system, mesomorphy is centered in the muscles, and ectomorphy is related to the brain and the nervous system. According to Sheldon, the body shape of each person is composed of these three elements. Nobody is exclusively endomorph, not presenting at the same time some portion of mesomorphy and ectomorphy. In fact, everyone carries these components in different quantities. The somatotype is then expressed as a three-number ratio representing the endomorphy, mesomorphy, and ectomorphy components, respectively, always following this order. Endomorphy is the relative fatness, mesomorphy is the relative musculoskeletal robustness, and ectomorphy is the relative linearity or slenderness of a physique.

The simplest way to imagine the variety of forms of human bodies is to examine their extremities. In accordance with Sheldon's method, a body of somatotype 7-1-1 is an extreme endomorph with minimum mesomorphy and ectomorphy. This type of body is distinguished from others due to characteristics such as mass concentration in the abdominal area, soft skin, soft body contours, nonprominent bones, and spherical head. The body shape of an extreme mesomorph, or 1-7-1, is characterized by having well-developed and defined muscles, wide bones, predomination of the chest area over the abdominal region, salient muscles on both sides of the neck, and well-developed thighs and arms. The physical form of a extreme ectomorph, or 1-1-7, is one of fragile and delicate appearance with weak musculature. In contrast to the other two extremes, he or she has a lank aspect. To determine all the body types and to locate possible corporal forms, Sheldon defined a diagram. Figure 3.1 shows the extreme body forms.

Indeed, the somatotype model is originally used to classify real human bodies. We propose a computational model where somatotype classification is used to generate virtual human bodies. However, it is important to recognize that the somatotype method is a general descriptor of physics and does not define the specific

3.5 A Model for Generation of Population

Fig. 3.1 The three extreme somatotypes [Arr88]

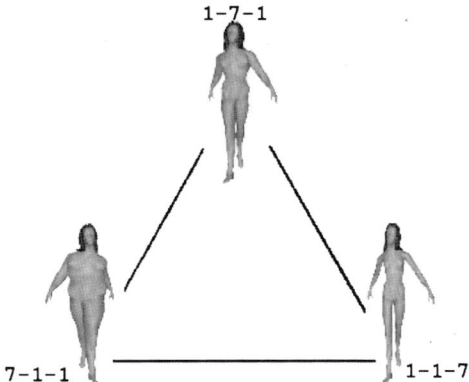

dimensions of each body part. Thus, by using some examples of body forms with their respective somatotype values, we can generate a multiplicity of visually valid shapes.

The geometric modeling of virtual characters in our approach is based on two input data: (i) the input character templates and (ii) the intended characteristics of the population to be created. The templates in our model consist of the geometric model and a set of information such as: gender, minimum and maximum age, dimensions of each part of the body defined for the geometric model's skeleton, dimensions for samples of extreme somatotypes (endomorph, mesomorph, and ectomorph), animation files, and a further set of materials (to provide better visual variations). This information will be detailed in the current and next sections. As soon as the input data are gathered, the generation of characters' geometry starts. Briefly, the steps for the generation of a population of virtual characters are:

1. *Definition of the initial data*: Statistical distributions of population data specified by the user.
2. *Selection of a template*: The templates are selected according to the informed population characteristics. This selection takes into account the template's gender and age, by searching the template that best fits the population requirements.
3. *Definition of new somatotypes*: A somatotype value is defined for each new character to be created.
4. *Calculation of influence of sample somatotypes*: Once a somatotype value is defined for each character to be created, we compute the contribution of each extreme somatotype contained in the initial template. Consequently, the generation of a new character is a function of three extreme somatotype contributions.
5. *Calculation of mesh variation*: The contribution calculated in step 4 is used to define the shape of the new body to be generated. The variations are then calculated to each of the body parts of the geometric model that will be deformed to reach the defined shape.
6. *Body parts' deformation*: The geometric model's vertices are deformed to generate the new shape applied to the new character.

The definition of initial data can be used either for a specific individual or for a population. Results generated by this model are shown in Sect. 3.5.7. Each of the previous steps is specified in the next sections.

3.5.1 Definition of the Initial Data

The geometric modeling of the virtual characters is established according to two pieces of information: the templates and the physical characteristics of the population to be created. The physical characteristics of the population to be created are: name and number of characters to be generated, percentage of female and male characters, age, height, and weight averages besides standard deviations. The population will be created according to the given statistical distribution. First, a number of male and female models are created by using the informed values of quantity and percentages of females and males to create the new population.

Then, for each character to be created, values of age, height, and weight are defined regarding the informed distribution. The creation of only one character is also possible by defining accurate values for sex, age, height, and weight. A user interface is used to inform these values individually for each character to be created. This information is used to create the geometric model of the new virtual humans, as explained in the next sections.

3.5.2 Choice of a Template

A template is selected to each new character according to data defined in Sect. 3.5.1. This selection takes into account the template's gender and age by searching the template that best fits the population requirements. The gender information must coincide with the gender of the template, and the age must range from the minimum to the maximum values informed in the template. The number of templates to be used is not limited and can be specified by the user depending on the purpose of the simulation. We use only two templates: one male adult (aged between 15 and 80) and one female adult (aged between 15 and 80).

3.5.3 Definition of New Somatotypes

There are three ways to obtain the somatotype ratio of a person: the *anthropometric plus photoscopic* method, which combines values of anthropometry and ratios provided by a photograph; the *photoscopic* method, in which the ratios are gathered from standardized photographs; and the *anthropometric* method, in which the anthropometry is used to establish the somatotype criterion.

3.5 A Model for Generation of Population

Due to the fact that most people do not have the opportunity to collect the ratio criterion through the photographic method, the anthropometric system is the most usual. Also, it requires a smaller amount of resources, such as photographic equipment and calculation. As mentioned before, the somatotype is composed of three components. In anthropometric systems, the endomorphic factor is estimated by the measurement of skinfolds, the mesomorphic factor is obtained by the measurement of the body dimensions, and the ectomorphic factor is computed considering the height divided by the cube root of weight (HWR):

$$HWR = \frac{height}{\sqrt[3]{weight}} \quad (3.1)$$

When the system generates the somatotype of the new character, the ectomorphic factor is calculated through its height and weight values. Later, values for mesomorphy and endomorphy are specified according to user definition. If one wants to generate diversity in population model, the system can choose mesomorphy and endomorphy randomly. On the other hand, if the user wants to provide a range of values for such factors, the system will generate people coherently with data specification. And finally, it is determined whether the new somatotype calculated is valid or not (according to [NO96]). If the new somatotype ratio is invalid, new values for mesomorphy and endomorphy are defined by the system. Indeed, the correlation between the three components is presented in Eq. (3.2), where k is a constant used as metric for validating the generated somatotype.

$$Ectomorphy + Mesomorphy + Endomorphy = k \quad (3.2)$$

We empirically observed that the sum of three somatotype components results in a value of k in the range [9;13] for measurements of in people two books [HC90, NO96]. In results given in Sect. 3.5.7 we use the k in this specific range; however, it can be changed, if desired. The creation of only one individual is also possible and this is accomplished by the input of specific somatotype values. In the prototype implemented in this work, the ectomorphy component is automatically calculated through the values of height and weight. The user, through an interface, specifies values for mesomorphy and endomorphy.

3.5.4 Calculation of Influence of Sample Somatotypes

To determine the dimensions of a new character, this model should have an example of each extreme somatotype (endomorph, mesomorph, and ectomorph). The initial templates contain tables of sample dimensions of extreme somatotypes for each body part defined in the geometric model's skeleton. The influence of each of the dimensions sampled (extreme somatotypes) is calculated as a function of the dimensions of the extreme somatotypes, the new somatotype associated with the character, and the dimensions of the chosen template.

In real life, people do not put on weight or increase their musculature in the same way. They differ from one another, since there are people in many different forms. For example, some people put on weight uniformly while others do so more noticeably in the abdominal area, and others in the pelvis, buttocks, and thighs. For example, athletes engaged in different sport modalities increase or reduce their musculature in a particular way, depending on their physical activity. To achieve a larger diversity of body forms, it is possible to inform more than one table of dimensions for each of the extreme somatotypes. For instance, tables can be created to measure a body presenting a bulky abdomen, and another type of table can be created for a body with big buttocks and thighs for samples of endomorph. In this case, a table of dimensions can be specifically chosen for each extreme somatotype (endomorph, mesomorph, and ectomorph), called $S1$, $S2$, and $S3$, where $S1_{endo}$, $S1_{meso}$, and $S1_{ecto}$ are the three components of extreme somatotype $S1$ (equivalent to $S2$ and $S3$). If more than one dimension table is available for each somatotype and the user requires great diversity, a somatotype table can be randomly chosen from existing ones.

To calculate the influence (weight W) of each of the sample somatotypes (W_{S1}, W_{S2}, and W_{S3}), the product of the composed matrix of the three sample somatotypes ($S1$, $S2$, and $S3$) by the desired weight (W) is equal to the value of new somatotype (NS), as shown in Eqs. (3.3) and (3.4).

$$\begin{bmatrix} S1_{endo} & S2_{endo} & S3_{endo} \\ S1_{meso} & S2_{meso} & S3_{meso} \\ S1_{ecto} & S2_{ecto} & S3_{ecto} \end{bmatrix} \cdot \begin{bmatrix} W_{S1} \\ W_{S2} \\ W_{S3} \end{bmatrix} = \begin{bmatrix} NS_{endo} \\ NS_{meso} \\ NS_{ecto} \end{bmatrix} \quad (3.3)$$

$$\begin{cases} NS_{endo} = S1_{endo} \cdot W_{S1} + S2_{endo} \cdot W_{S2} + S3_{endo} \cdot W_{S3} \\ NS_{meso} = S1_{meso} \cdot W_{S1} + S2_{meso} \cdot W_{S2} + S3_{meso} \cdot W_{S3} \\ NS_{ecto} = S1_{ecto} \cdot W_{S1} + S2_{ecto} \cdot W_{S2} + S3_{ecto} \cdot W_{S3} \end{cases} \quad (3.4)$$

Equation (3.4) calculates the contribution of each of the extreme somatotypes solved through a simple linear equation system solver with three variables. The corresponding weight for each somatotype (W_{S1}, W_{S2}, and W_{S3}) is used in the variation of the body parts, as presented in the next section.

3.5.5 Calculation of Mesh Variation

The geometric model deformation is done in an approach similar to Azuola's method; except for the number of body parts which is not fixed in this method, the generated body follows the specification of the skeleton of the template's geometric model. In this work, the template's geometric model or the skeleton have no restrictions related either to the topology or to the number of vertices. The artist is free to shape the geometric models as he/she pleases.

The tables of body dimensions contained in the template are used to define the dimensions of each of the body parts of the new character in each direction (height,

3.5 A Model for Generation of Population

width, and depth). The body dimensions and the weights associated with the three extreme somatotypes are used as a linear combination to determine the corporal form of the character. First, the new dimension (*ND*) of each body part p is calculated as a function of the part size (*PS*) of sample somatotypes (*S1*, *S2*, and *S3*) and their associated weight (computed in Sect. 3.5.4). The new dimension in each of the body part directions i (height, width, and depth) is the sum of the products between the calculated weight (Eq. (3.4)) and the dimensions of each sample somatotype in the same body part, as shown in the equation below:

$$ND_{p_i} = W_{S1_{p_i}} \cdot PS_{S1_{p_i}} + W_{S2_{p_i}} \cdot PS_{S2_{p_i}} + W_{S3_{p_i}} \cdot PS_{S3_{p_i}} \quad (3.5)$$

When creating new characters, the shape of the template's body varies according to the combination of sample somatotypes chosen. Thus, if there are more tables of dimensions to each extreme somatotype, different body shapes will be created using the same somatotype ratio, generating a greater crowd diversity. After the new dimension (ND_{p_i}) of each part is defined, the variation (*Variation*) that should be applied in the template's geometric model is computed, indicating the growth factor in each of the directions i of each body part. The template contains a table of dimensions of the base geometric model that will be used to modify its form. The variation in each part of the body (p) is determined through the division of the new calculated dimension by the base geometric model dimension (*BD*). Moreover, a small random value (*rand*), computed between [−0.1 and 0.1], is also added to increase the diversity of the generated geometric models. The main objective of this random number is to prevent the creation of identical models using the same somatotype ratio and the same sample dimension tables. This equation is applied to each direction i, and calculates the variation in each body part p:

$$Variation_{p_i} = \frac{ND_{p_i}}{BD_{p_i}} + rand \quad (3.6)$$

After calculating the variation that will be applied to the template's geometric model in each of its parts ($Variation_{p_i}$), the vertices that compose the mesh of the geometric model are deformed in order to create the new character, as described in the next section.

3.5.6 Body Parts' Deformation

First, the geometric model base is entirely scaled to reach the desired height. This scale is made uniformly so that no deformation is produced in the geometric model. If the geometric model were scaled only in the height (stretched), some body parts would be deformed (the head would be elongated thus changing the face, for instance). To determine the scale to be applied to the new geometric model, the height ratio (*HR*) between the template height (*TH*) and the new character height (*CH*) is calculated as follows: $HR = CH/TH$. Thus, each mesh vertex of the new geometric model is multiplied by HR in order to reach the desired height.

After the entire body is uniformly deformed, each body part will be scaled differently to reach the desired shape of the new character. To calculate the new position of each vertex v of the geometric model, the previously computed variations of the body part p in the direction i (*Variation*$_{p_i}$) are used with the influence (*Influence*) of the skeleton bone of the body part p in the vertex v:

$$v = v \cdot \sum_p \mathit{Variation}_{p_i} \cdot \mathit{Influence}[p_v] \qquad (3.7)$$

The influence of each vertex in a body part (p_v) indicates how this vertex will vary when the skeleton moves. Thus, besides the different body parts varying differently and nonuniformly scaled, no discontinuity will be generated between the parts in the geometric model of the new character. These influences are acquired from the geometric model, exported by an artist through a modeling program (3D Studio or Maya, for instance) and taken into account in this model.

The new characters are created through the variation in the vertices that compose the template's geometric model. The effects suffered by the vertices due to the animation of each skeleton bone are the same. Thus, the rigging (association between skeleton and geometric mesh), one of the most complex and difficult tasks of a designer in order to animate a virtual human, does not need to be performed for the new characters in our model. The skeleton is not modified either. Thus, the animations created for the geometric model defined in the template are directly applied to the geometric model of the new characters. In addition, template models can contain a set of materials or textures in order to provide a greater visual diversity. Each character created is defined through a texture contained in the template, which is randomly chosen. Based on input data, the model is capable of simultaneously generating a wide variety of characters, by applying the same skeleton of a chosen template. The model presented in this work has no restrictions regarding the topology, number of vertices or hierarchy. The model is capable of manipulating geometric models with any hierarchic structure or skeleton, since the tables of dimensions are generated in accordance with the skeleton of the template. In Sect. 3.5.7 some results with different hierarchies as well as different numbers of polygons will be presented.

The expected quality of the results obtained from the use of this method depends on the application to which it is addressed. For example, when the artists shape a main character for the production of movies, they are interested in the details and peculiarities of the specific model, which will probably not be based on templates. However, the objective of this model is to generate characters that can be directly applied in virtual reality applications, games, real-time simulations, and even secondary characters for movie production.

3.5 A Model for Generation of Population

3.5.7 Results and Discussion

In this section, some results obtained by the implemented prototype will be examined. The first point concerns the following question: Do the shapes of our created characters look realistic? In the first section of this chapter, we argued that our work allows the creation of aesthetically acceptable characters. Then, we proposed a model consisting of templates and anthropometric data based on real people somatotypes to create a variety of characters. In this section, we propose to answer the above question through the use of two metrics that will indicate whether a body appearance is realistic or not. Such assessment is performed from two points of view: first, we consider the microscopic information, i.e., checking if the appearance of a specific character looks as it should according to its input data compared with real life, and second, the macroscopic analysis, i.e., whether a population simultaneously generated attains a required diversity of shapes. The following subsections describe both standpoints.

Microscopic Analysis

This subsection describes details about the generation of specific characters, showing some geometric models along with parameters informed for their creation. Thus, we can verify whether the generation of new geometric models respects the input data and whether the shape of a character looks coherent with such data. Further, images of real people will be presented in order to provide a comparison between them and generated characters. The criterion used to accomplish the microscopic analysis was to visually compare pictures of real people with images of the generated geometric models by using the same values of height, weight, and somatotype. The body form of real people and the generated geometric models should not differ significantly.

Images of male and female characters created by the model proposed in this work follow, which are displayed and compared with images of real people, reproduced from [HC90]. The tool that creates a single character is fed with the same information of height, weight, and somatotype obtained from the person pictured. This information is presented for each figure. For the male models, only one sample dimension table of the extreme somatotypes for each one was used. Figure 3.2 illustrates some examples of bodies created with only three dimension tables. Figure 3.2(a) shows a body of a robust man and the image of its corresponding geometric model (b), i.e., it was generated with the same values regarding height, weight, and somatotype. If the mesomorphy and endomorphy ratings of this man were reduced, his body would look like an average person's one, as shown in Fig. 3.2(c).

There are different ways in which people can gain or lose weight, due to different metabolic and hormonal characteristics. These different forms can be defined, in this work, by setting more than one dimension table to a sample somatotype in the template. To illustrate this aspect, two dimension tables for extreme endomorphs have been used in a female template: the first one was created to generate bodies whose

Fig. 3.2 Picture (**a**) and generated character (**b**) of a fat and strong man (height: 171.5 cm; weight: 100.5 kg; somatotype: 4-8-$\frac{1}{2}$). (**c**) Geometric model of a virtual human with an average body (height: 171.5 cm; weight: 63.8 kg; somatotype: 4-4-3)

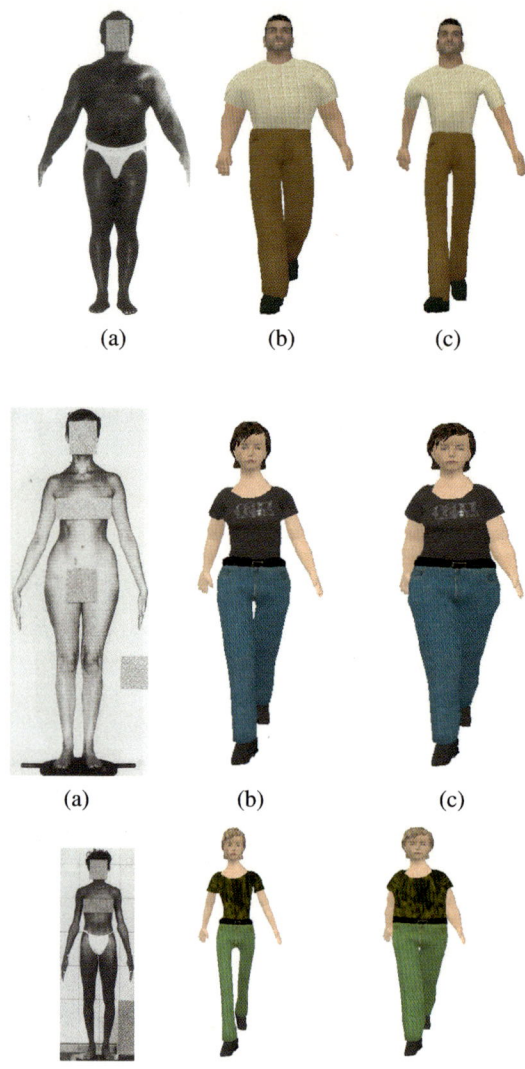

Fig. 3.3 Picture (**a**) and generated character (**b**) of an average woman (height: 168.2 cm; weight: 56.5 kg; somatotype: $4\frac{1}{2}$-$2\frac{1}{2}$-$3\frac{1}{2}$). Geometric model (**c**) of a fat woman (height: 168.2 cm; weight: 79.0 kg; somatotype: $8\frac{1}{2}$-2-$\frac{1}{2}$). Picture (**d**) and generated character (**e**) of a thin woman (height: 176.1 cm; weight: 55.4 kg; somatotype: $1\frac{1}{2}$-$3\frac{1}{2}$-$5\frac{1}{2}$). Geometric model (**f**) of a fat woman (height: 176.1 cm; weight: 70.0 kg; somatotype: $8\frac{1}{2}$-2-$\frac{1}{2}$)

parts showing more fat are located in the hips, buttocks, and thighs, and another dimension table to define the body form of a woman who put on weight uniformly over her whole body. Dimension tables for other body types could be used, but we can demonstrate the results obtained with a minimal set of parameters. Figure 3.3(a) presents a body of an average woman whose possible bigger tendency is to put on weight in the hips, buttocks, and thighs. Figure 3.3(b) shows the geometric model generated by using the dimension table (for extreme endomorph) that represents this same body form. If she puts on weight, her probable body form would be as shown in Fig. 3.3(c). Figure 3.3(d) presents a body of a thin woman and the geometric

3.5 A Model for Generation of Population

Fig. 3.4 Low resolution characters

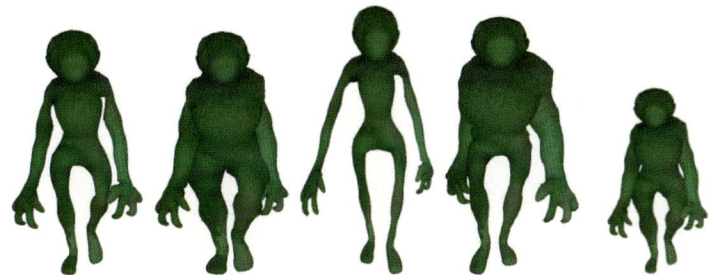

Fig. 3.5 Non-human characters

model (e) created by using the same values for height, weight, and somatotype. The geometric model shown in Fig. 3.3(f) is generated by using the same somatotype from Fig. 3.3(c), but now with the dimension table for uniform fattening.

Figure 3.4 shows examples of results obtained from the use of this model with very low resolution characters (270 polygons). The first figure shows the original model, and the others present the results achieved for endomorph, ectomorph, and mesomorph body types, respectively. These models were not created for this work, showing it is generic enough to enable the use of characters which contain a varied number of polygons.

Many virtual environments, games, and movies make use of crowds of non-human-like characters. In such cases, geometric models with similar appearances are created to avoid shaping these characters one by one. Sometimes the same geometric model, with just a few changes, is used to show a crowd of virtual characters. Since the aim of this work is the creation of population diversity, it is useful that the model is capable of generating nonhuman characters too.

In order to verify the generality and robustness of this model and to extend its use, populations of nonhuman characters have been created. Figure 3.5 shows some characters created from the same geometric model. The first shape on the left is the original model; the others present the results achieved showing examples of endomorph, ectomorph, mesomorph, and a little character, respectively.

Although somatotype concerns a method for human body form classification, it was verified that, through the use of this model, the creation of nonhuman characters is also possible.

Fig. 3.6 Population generated using four templates

Table 3.1 Time (seconds) for generating virtual characters

Number of Characters	Total Number of Vertices	Time (s) with I/O	Time (s) without I/O
1,000	8,672,000	26	12
5,000	43,360,000	128	61
10,000	86,720,000	256	176
50,000	433,600,000	1,274	596

Macroscopic Analysis

This subsection aims to visually evaluate a large population from a macroscopic point of view. As seen in Fig. 3.6, the results are acceptable since the characters do not look aesthetically "strange". Thus, this represents a verification as to whether the purpose of an automatic creation of populational diversity with visual consistency has been attained. Figure 3.6 presents the geometric models generated using four templates.

Table 3.1 presents the execution time of various numbers of created characters, using a computer with a Pentium 4 3 GHz processor and 1 GB RAM, which shows execution times with and without disk recording. The male adult template, with 8672 vertices, was used for this time measurement. In addition, the used memory is 341 kB for this character.

3.6 Using Computer Vision to Generate Crowds

The reconstruction of virtual humans (VHs) is important for several applications, such as games and simulations. Lately, the game industry has achieved a large number of players around the world, pushing game developers to create new gameplay experiences. One of these new experiences is to allow the player to use her/his own appearance-like avatar while playing, which is already present in several Electronic Arts sports games (http://www.ea.com/games). However, in order to generate such virtual humans, artists usually spend a large amount of time modeling the characters.

Other applications for VH reconstruction include Collaborative Virtual Environments (CVEs) and Virtual Reality (VR) scenarios. In some cases, there are manual interfaces for character customization. One can imagine that such interfaces could be replaced by a semi-automatic approach, where users could just choose a picture for customizing their avatars instead of doing it manually. This approach could also be employed to avoid the work of generating several different characters in games and real-time applications. However, some challenges arise in VH reconstruction based on a single and spontaneous image. Firstly, 2D human segmentation in images is still an open research problem, mainly due to clutter background, varying illumination conditions, and a wide variety of human postures. Secondly, the 3D human pose in the picture should be known in order to build the virtual human coherently using spontaneous pictures. Finally, textures and animations can be applied to the generated VH.

This section presents a model for the reconstruction of animatable virtual humans using information processed in pictures (human segmentation), 3D pose and silhouette data (extracted from the picture containing width values for the human parts). This technique generates an articulated 3D model of a character that can be further animated.

3.6.1 A Model for Generating Crowds Based on Pictures

We propose a semi-automatic pipeline to generate a VH based on single and spontaneous images. By spontaneous images we mean pictures of human subjects taken under usual circumstances, which may contain a variety of poses of the person to be reconstructed, more than one people in the picture as well as heterogeneous background. Our approach is semi-automatic, since the user must provide a few clicks locating joints of the human structure. All the rest of process is automatic, except for the gender selection, which happens in the graphical interface to generate the VH.

The pipeline is formed by four main processes, as illustrated in Fig. 3.7. These processes together generate all information required to build the VH, namely: XML files containing the 3D pose, the sizes of the body parts computed trough the silhouette, and files containing the original, segmented and binary images.

The Virtual Human Reconstruction step is responsible for the VH generation. Firstly a template (female or male) is chosen by the user. Then, the 3D pose in the picture is taken into account to provide the VH posture, coherently with the original image. This step is followed by the reconstruction process. Finally, pieces of the segmented image, which are automatically extracted based on body parts clicked by the user, are processed to generate textures that are applied to the VH. This last phase can present better performance if post-processed by artists, and it should be

Fig. 3.7 Overview of our model for virtual humans reconstruction

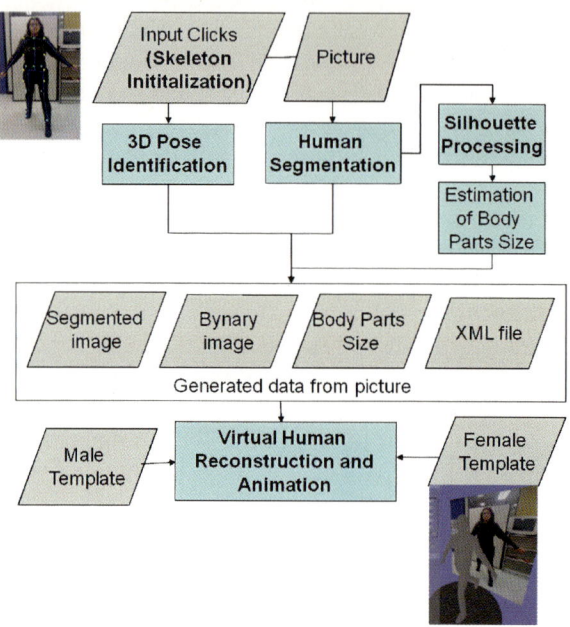

noticed that texture processing is not included in the main scope of this model. The next sections describe details of the main parts of our model.

Skeleton Initialization

Detecting humans in images is a challenging task, due to their variable appearance and the wide range of poses that they can adopt [DT05]. As related by Hornung et al. [HDK07], interactive 2D human posture acquisition presents some advantages when compared to automatic procedures, since manual intervention usually takes just a few minutes to complete and leads to superior results in poses that are ambiguous for automatic human-pose estimators, or that are difficult to estimate due to occlusions, for example. For these reasons we also initialize our skeleton model of a human being using manual interventions—the user informs the height of the person (in pixels) and the positions of the joints (in image coordinates).

In this work, the skeleton model is composed by nineteen bones and twenty joints, as illustrated in Fig. 3.8. All these bones have initial 3D lengths and widths, both parametrized as a function of the height h of an average person based on anthropometric values [Til02]. More precisely, for a certain body part with label i, the corresponding length l_i and width w_i are given by

$$l_i = h f_{li}, \qquad w_i = h f_{wi}, \qquad (3.8)$$

where the proportionality factors f_{li} and f_{wi} are derived from [Til02]. Table 3.2 presents all body parts used in this work, along with the corresponding values for

3.6 Using Computer Vision to Generate Crowds

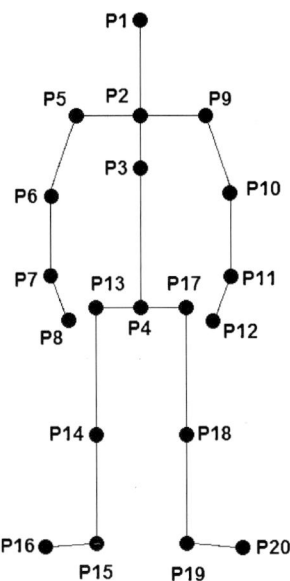

Fig. 3.8 The adopted skeleton model

f_{li} and f_{wi}. The initial bone lengths are used mainly in the image segmentation stage and in the 3D pose estimation procedure. The estimated width of each body part is used in the segmentation stage.

There are two different ways to obtain the height of the person through manual intervention. When the person is standing in the photograph and the full body is visible, the user simply clicks on the top of the head and on the bottom of the feet, obtaining the height directly. In any other situation (e.g. if the person is sitting down), his/her height can be estimated based on any bone the user selects to be used as reference (including the face), and the height can be estimated based on Table 3.2. Since the camera parameters are not known, it is advisable to select a bone that is parallel to the image plane, to reduce the influence of perspective issues. For instance, if the user choose to use the face size as reference, the user clicks on the top of the head and on the tip of the chin, to compute the height of the face h_f. The height of the person is then estimated by $h = h_f/0.125$, where 0.125 is a weight derived from anthropometric values [Til02].

Image Segmentation

This section describes the proposed approach to segment human subjects in a semi-automatic way, similarly to the automatic method described in [JDJ*10]. Although the approach in [JDJ*10] estimates each body part (from the upper body only) automatically, it is prone to errors in more complex poses, as most automatic models. In this case, we explore manually informed data about the joints (and, consequently, body parts) to achieve better accuracy, and also to handle with lower body parts. This approach can be divided in two main steps: (i) skeleton initialization and (ii) object

Table 3.2 In the first column: the body part index; in the second column: the body part (bone); in the third column: the two joints that form each bone; in the fourth column: the weights used to compute each bone length; and in the fifth column: the weights used to compute each bone width

i	Bone	Joints	f_{li}	f_{wi}
0	Head	(P1–P2)	0.20	0.0883
1	Chest	(P2–P3)	0.098	0.1751
2	Abdomen	(P3–P4)	0.172	0.1751
3	Right Shoulder	(P2–P5)	0.102	not used
4	Right Arm	(P5–P6)	0.159	0.0608
5	Right Forearm	(P6–P7)	0.146	0.0492
6	Right Hand	(P7–P8)	0.108	0.0593
7	Left Shoulder	(P2–P9)	0.102	not used
8	Left Arm	(P9–P10)	0.159	0.0608
9	Left Forearm	(P10–P11)	0.146	0.0492
10	Left Hand	(P11–P12)	0.108	0.0593
11	Right Hip	(P4–P13)	0.050	not used
12	Right Thigh	(P13–P14)	0.241	0.0912
13	Right Calf	(P14–P15)	0.240	0.0608
14	Right Feet	(P15–P16)	0.123	0.0564
15	Left Hip	(P4–P17)	0.050	not used
16	Left Thigh	(P17–P18)	0.241	0.0912
17	Left Calf	(P18–P19)	0.240	0.0608
18	Left Feet	(P19–P20)	0.123	0.0564

segmentation. The skeleton initialization is done manually, while the object segmentation is done automatically and it is briefly described next. Yet, it is important to mention that any other method of people segmentation can be used (e.g. based on graph or grab cuts [RKB04, BJ01]). We develop a method that could be used with the same input that posture estimation instead of having any other intervention in the image.

Learning the Color Model

We propose a method to segment human body parts in images, based on dominant colors. To do this, we firstly create a color model for each body part, and estimate a search region. Basically fourteen body parts are segmented given their joints (head, chest and abdomen as only one body part, right and left arms, right and left forearms, right and left hands, right and left thighs, right and left calf, and finally, right and left foot). It is important to mention that this method is mainly focused on dominant colors, consequently textured parts of the body may not be segmented correctly.

We initially define a region Tr_i around the corresponding bone that will be used to learn the dominant color(s) of each body part. The selected region is a rectangle,

3.6 Using Computer Vision to Generate Crowds

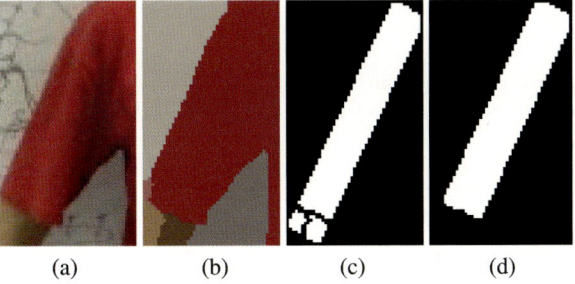

Fig. 3.9 Illustration of the initial segmentation adopted in the color model learning stage. From left to right: (**a**) input image, (**b**) initial segmentation, (**c**) segments, and (**d**) retrieved segments

which central axis coincides with the corresponding bone, and that should ideally contain only pixels related to the corresponding body part. In the proposed approach, the length of the rectangle is exactly the length of the bone as clicked by the user, and the width is a fraction s_1 (set experimentally to 0.4) of the expected width of the corresponding body part w_i, given in Table 3.2. It is important to note that the 3D length l_i of each body part is used instead of the 2D distance (that could be computed directly from the corresponding joints in image coordinates). In fact, assuming that each body part is approximately cylindrical, the width of the 2D projection is not affected significantly by perspective issues. On the other hand, the 2D–3D correspondence of the bone length may change significantly depending on the pose of the body part (e.g. arms parallel to the ground).

To obtain the dominant color(s) of each body part, the unsupervised color-based segmentation algorithm [Jun07] is initially applied to obtain the main regions within Tr_i, as illustrated in Fig. 3.9. In most cases, the largest of these regions is related to the dominant color. However, there are some common situations (shirts with writings, illustrations, shadows, etc.) in which the largest segmented region does not correspond to the dominant color. To cope with this issue, the N largest segmented regions within Tr_i, with area larger than a threshold T_a are retrieved (we experimentally set $N = 3$ and $T_a = 0.1 \# Tr_i$, where $\# Tr_i$ is the area of Tr_i).

For a given body part i, let us consider the $N_i \leq N$ largest segmented regions that satisfy the minimum area criterion. The color distribution within each region is represented as a multivariate Gaussian model, which requires the computation of the mean vector ($\boldsymbol{\mu}_{ij}$) and covariance matrix ($\boldsymbol{C}_{ij}$), where $1 \leq j \leq N_i$ relates to a different color model for the body part.

Finding the Silhouette

To find the pixels that are related to body part i, search region Te_i (also rectangular) is defined. Unlike the training search region Tr_i, this test region should be large enough to comprise all pixels related to the body part. The length of the search region is the length of Tr_i increased by a multiplicative factor (set experimentally to 1.15), and the width of Te_i is based on the estimated value of the corresponding (body part given in Table 3.2) increased by another multiplicative factor (set

Fig. 3.10 Illustration of the region used to learn and search the dominant colors. The *blue line* is the informed bone; the *green rectangle* is the estimated region for learning; and the *black rectangle* is the estimated region for searching

experimentally to 2). This means that body parts as wide as twice the average anthropometrical width may be detected using the proposed approach.

Figure 3.10 illustrates a clicked bone (the blue line), the training region Tr_i used to learn the dominant color models (green rectangle), and the test region Te_i used to find pixels coherent with the N_i learned models. To compute such coherence within Te_i, the squared Mahalanobis distance $D_{ij}(c)$ for each pixel with color c and retrieved segment j is obtained through

$$D_{ij}^2(c) = (c - \mu_{ij})^T C_{ij}^{-1} (c - \mu_{ij}), \quad 1 \leq j \leq N_i, \qquad (3.9)$$

and a threshold T_{ij} is computed for each dominant color j automatically, based on the peaks and valleys of the histogram of $D_{ij}^2(c)$ (see [JDJ*10] for more details). Then, a given pixel with color c is aggregated to body part i if for at least one dominant color j the relationship $D_{ij}^2(c) \leq T_{ij}$ is satisfied.

The color-based approach described so far provides an initial estimate of each body part. However, noise, varying illumination, texture, and non-uniform regions may generate spurious responses and/or holes in the segmented regions. Morphological operators are then used to remove residual noise and fill small holes. More precisely, a sequence of an opening and a closing operator with a 3×3 cross-shaped structuring element is applied. The opening removes isolated responses, but may separate regions that are connected by narrow bridges. The subsequent closing operator intends to connect disjoint regions that are sufficiently close to each other (including those separated by the initial opening). Then, a hold filling operator is used to complete possible holes in the interior of the binary images (particularly in the chest regions, due to possible text and/or images in the shirt).

Figure 3.11 illustrates the final segmentation procedure, where each body part is shown with a different color. Interceptions of different body parts are also shown in a different color (i.e., the thigh and calf are painted using two different colors, as they interception—probably the knee). The union of all detected body parts compose a binary silhouette of the person, as shown in Fig. 3.12(a). However, since the detected individual body parts overlap, a separate procedure is used to estimate the width of body part, which is required to reconstruct the VH.

3.6 Using Computer Vision to Generate Crowds

Fig. 3.11 Illustration of the final segmentation result

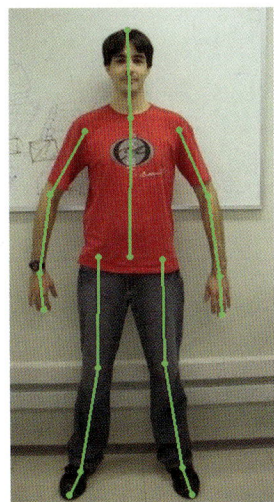

Silhouette Processing

Given the binary silhouette of the person and the 2D clicked joints, we estimate the width of each body part. The main idea is to compute the length of line segments connecting a bone and the boundary of the silhouette, and then combining these measurements robustly to estimate the corresponding width.

For each body part i, the central part of the bone (clicked by the user) is retrieved, as shown in Fig. 3.12(c). Along this portion of the bone, line segments are traced perpendicularly to its corresponding bone to both sides, until a silhouette contour

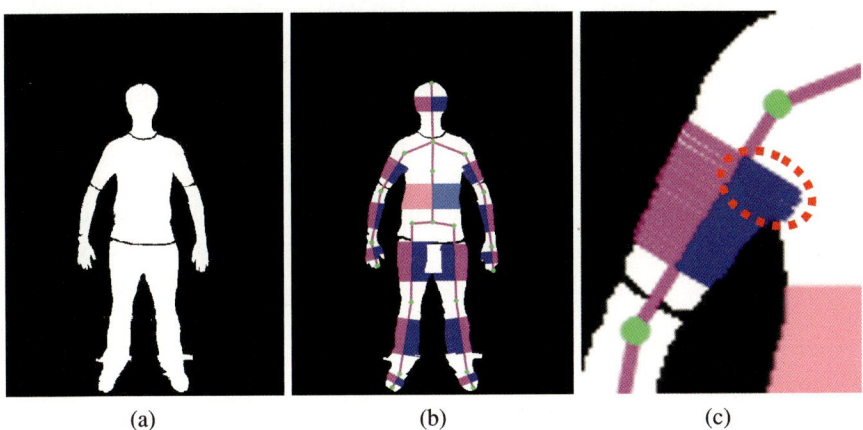

Fig. 3.12 (a) Silhouette obtained from the segmentation process using Fig. 3.11. (b) Found widths for each interested body part. (c) Zoom given at right arm. The *dotted area* shows an place were a left edge was not found, so the measurement of the right side of the bone was replicated to the left side

point is reached. Ideally, the lengths ls_{ik} of those segments should be close to $w_i/2$ (half the standard width of the body part, computed through Eq. (3.8)). However, due to segmentation errors, some of these segments may be significantly smaller or larger than w_i. To cope with this problem, a range of valid possible lengths is created, and modified lengths ls'_{ik} are computed through:

$$ls'_{ik} = \min\{\max\{L_{low}, ls_{ik}\}, L_{high}\}, \qquad (3.10)$$

where $L_{low} = 0.5w_i$ and $L_{high} = 2w_i$ define the limits of valid lengths, so that body parts between half and twice the average anthropometrical value can be detected.

Given the set of modified length values ls'_{ik}, the estimated width of body segment i is given by

$$ew_i = 2_k\{ls'_{ik}\}. \qquad (3.11)$$

3D Pose Identification

The problem of estimating the 3D pose of a person from image data has received a special attention in the computer vision literature. This is, in part, due to the fact that solutions to this problem could be employed in a wide range of applications. According to Taylor [Tay00], most of the research in this area has focused on the problem of tracking a human actor through an image sequence, and less attention has been directed to the problem of determining an individuals posture based on a single picture. Indeed, this problem is challenging because 2D image constraints are often not sufficient to determine 3D poses of an articulated object. Our solution to this problem is based on Taylor's work [Tay00], which presents a method for recovering information about the configuration of articulated objects from a single image.

According to Taylor, if we have a line segment of known length l in the image under scaled orthographic projection, the two 3D end points (x_1, y_1, z_1) and (x_2, y_2, z_2) are projected to (u_1, v_1) and (u_2, v_2), respectively. If the scale factor s of the projection model is known, it would be a simple matter to compute the relative depth of the two endpoints, denoted by $\Delta z = z_1 - z_2$, using the following equation [Tay00]:

$$\Delta z^2 = l^2 - \frac{(u_1 - u_2)^2 + (v_1 - v_2)^2}{s^2}. \qquad (3.12)$$

Such formulation generates ambiguities for each segment, since the sign of Δz can not be determined (i.e., we may have $z_1 > z_2$ or $z_2 > z_1$). If the skeleton has twenty joints, there are 2^{20} possible postures in the worst scenario. Despite the generation of ambiguities, this approach is very simple to implement, requiring only a straightforward sequence of computations. To minimize the problem of ambiguity,

3.6 Using Computer Vision to Generate Crowds

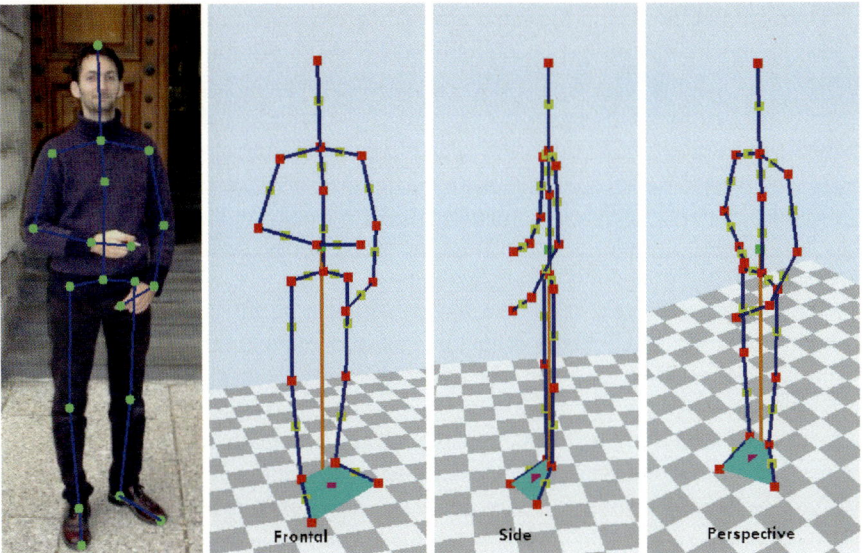

Fig. 3.13 Illustration shows three different views of a 3D pose obtained with our model

we firstly consider $z1 > z2$, and then the user can change it by using a tool we implemented, where the user can easily correct the generated pose, if necessary (see Fig. 3.13[1]).

Virtual Human Reconstruction

This section describes our approach proposed to reconstruct the VH based on two templates (male and female), but any other human-like templates are possible (e.g. children). Given the gender of the person (manually informed), the corresponding template is deformed to match the silhouette processing information saved in the XML file. There are three steps required to transform the initial template into the final VH, briefly described next.

The first step is to adequate the posture of the template to match the posture estimated from the image. The XML file generated by the posture detector contains a set of labeled joints, as well as the corresponding 3D positions. From this set of points, it is easy to obtain the orientation of each bone, or the rotation angle at each joint. The rotation angles at each joint are then used to modify the posture of a generic VH, which assumes the posture of the person being analyzed in the photograph.

---

[1] Image used from 'INRIA', dataset containing 1805 64 × 128 images of humans cropped from a varied set of personal photos. The database is available from http://lear.inrialpes.fr/data for research purposes.

Once we put the VH in the same pose of the character in the picture, it is necessary to match dimensions of each individual body part of the template (e.g. arms, thorax, thighs, forearms and etc.) to the dimensions (namely, length and width) computed from the image. Since each body part of the generic VH (template) presents predefined length tl_i and width tw_i, a simple linear scaling applied to both dimensions (length and width) can be used to obtain the desired dimensions of each body part in the final VH model. It is important to emphasize that the simple linear scale has been chosen in order to reconstruct the VH in a easy and fast way, making it applicable to games and mobile applications.

Finally, the geometric 3D model of the VH must be filled with color and texture. In our work, small pieces of textures are generated automatically (in regions defined as bones when clicked by the user) during the segmentation process, and in this phase they are used to provide textured body shapes. Since this process is automatic, we avoid using textures of faces and hands, which could include problems (e.g. when face picture is not frontal). It is also important to note that post-processed textures by artists (mainly for faces and hands) are recommended in order to improve the quality of mapped textures, but the scope of this paper is mostly focused on posture and geometry.

3.6.2 Results

Our pipeline is organized in two prototypes. Firstly, the prototype responsible for manual 2D clicks, segmentation, pose estimation and silhouette processing, which generates an XML file containing all information required to model the virtual human. For VH rendering and animation, our prototype uses Irrlicht Engine (http://irrlicht.sourceforge.net/) and Cal3D (http://gna.org/projects/cal3d/), respectively. Results discussed in this section were obtained using an Intel Xeon E405 equipped with a NVidia Quadro FX 4800 graphic card. The creation of the two generic templates (male and female, containing 4825 and 4872 vertices, respectively) were made with Autodesk 3D Studio MAX 9 (http://usa.autodesk.com).

All examples presented in this section have been automatically processed (except the manual intervention to inform the joints, the height of the person and the gender), as described previously in the paper. Occasionally, another manual intervention can be to improve the generated 3D posture. Also, when the face is completely frontal in the picture, the texture mapping is more likely to work, since the 3D model has always frontal orientation for the face. This is one of aspects that should be improved in future works. The images shown in Fig. 3.14 present results obtained by using the proposed approach. The same VH model is shown in Fig. 3.15 including the face texture. Also, it is possible to export (in CAL3D format) the VH generated in our model, and subsequently import it in another tool or animation Engine. In case of Fig. 3.15, we animated the VH in the Irrlicht engine, using a predefined animation file.

3.7 Crowd Appearance Variety

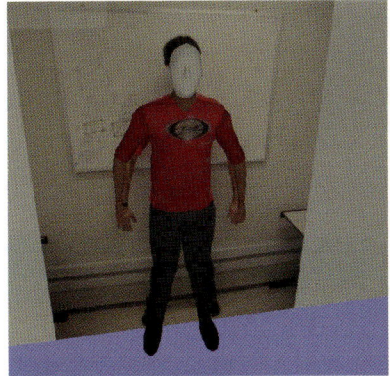

(a) Generated virtual human.   (b) Another point of view from the same scene.

Fig. 3.14 Results from our model illustrating the VH and the picture used as input

Fig. 3.15 Results from VH model imported and animated using Irrlicht engine

3.7 Crowd Appearance Variety

When simulating a small group of virtual humans, it is easy to make them look singularly different: one can use several meshes and textures for each virtual human present in the scene, and assign them different animations. However, when the group extends to a crowd of thousands of people, this solution becomes unfeasible. First, in terms of design, it is unimaginable to create one mesh and series of animations per individual. Moreover, the memory space required to store all the data would be far too demanding. Unfortunately, there is no direct solution to this problem. It is, however, possible to achieve good results by multiplying the levels where variety can be introduced.

First, several human templates can be used. Second, for each template, several textures can be designed. Third, the color of each part of a texture can be varied so that two virtual humans issued from the same template and sharing the same texture do not have the same clothes/skin/hair color. Finally, we also develop the idea of accessories, which allows a human mesh to be "augmented" with various objects such as a hat, watch, backpack, glasses, etc.

Variety can also be achieved through animation. We mainly concentrate on the locomotion domain, where we vary the movements of the virtual humans in two ways. First, we generate in a preprocess several locomotion cycles (walk and run) at different speeds, which are then played by the virtual humans online. Second, we use offline inverse kinematics to enhance the animation sequences with particular movements, like having a hand in a pocket, or at the ear as if making a phone call. The methodology is discussed in more details in Chap. 4.

In the following sections, we further develop each necessary step to vary a crowd in appearance: in Sect. 3.7.1, we show the three levels where variety can be achieved. In Sect. 3.7.2, we detail how we segment the texture of a virtual human in order to apply varied colors to each identified body part. Finally, accessories are fully explained in Sect. 3.7.3. More details may be found in [MYT09].

3.7.1 Variety at Three Levels

When referring to appearance variety, we mean how we modulate the rendering aspect of each individual of a crowd. This term is completely independent of the animation sequences played, the navigation, or the behavior of the virtual humans.

First, let us recall that a human template is a data structure containing:

1. A skeleton, defining what and where its joints are,
2. A set of meshes, representing its different levels of detail,
3. Several appearance sets, i.e., textures and their corresponding segmentation maps,
4. A set of animation sequences that can only be played by this human template.

For further indications on the human template structure, the reader is directed to Chap. 7.

We apply appearance variety at three different levels. The first, coarsest level is simply the number of human templates used. It seems obvious that the more human templates there are, the greater the variety. In Fig. 3.16, we show five different human templates to illustrate this. The main issue when designing many human templates is the time required. Indeed, such templates necessitate hours of work, and thus their number is limited. In order to mitigate this problem, we further vary the human templates by creating several textures and segmentation map sets for each of them. For simplification, we designate a texture and its associated segmentation maps as an appearance set.

The second level of variety is represented by the texture of an appearance set. Indeed, once an instance of a human template is provided with an appearance set, it automatically assumes the appearance of the corresponding texture. Of course,

3.7 Crowd Appearance Variety

Fig. 3.16 Five different human templates

Fig. 3.17 Five different textures of a single human template

changing the appearance set, and thus the texture, does not change the shape of the human template. For instance, if its mesh contains a ponytail, it will remain whatever the texture applied. However, it can impressively modify the appearance of the human template. In Fig. 3.17, we show five different textures applied to the same human template.

Finally, at the third level, we can play with color variety on each body part of the texture, thanks to the segmentation maps of the appearance set. Section 3.7.2 is devoted to this particular level. In Fig. 3.18, we show several color modulated instances of a single mesh and appearance set.

3.7.2 Color Variety

Human templates possess several textures, improving the sense of variety. But too often, characters sharing the same texture, i.e., looking exactly the same, appear in the vicinity of the camera, breaking the feeling of uniqueness of the spectator. Dif-

Fig. 3.18 Several color modulated instances of a single mesh and texture

ferentiating character body parts and then applying a unique combination of colors to each of them is a way to obtain variation inside a single texture.

Principles of the Method

Previous work on increasing the variety in color appearance for the characters composing a crowd share the common idea of storing the segmentation of body parts in a single alpha layer, i.e., each of them is represented by a specific level of gray. Tecchia et al. [TLC02a] use multipass rendering and the alpha channel to select parts to render for billboards. Dobbyn et al. [DHOO05] and de Heras et al. [dHSMT05] avoid multipass rendering by using programmable graphics hardware. They also extend the method for use on 3D virtual humans too. Figure 3.19 depicts a typical texture and its associated alpha zone map. The method is based on texture color

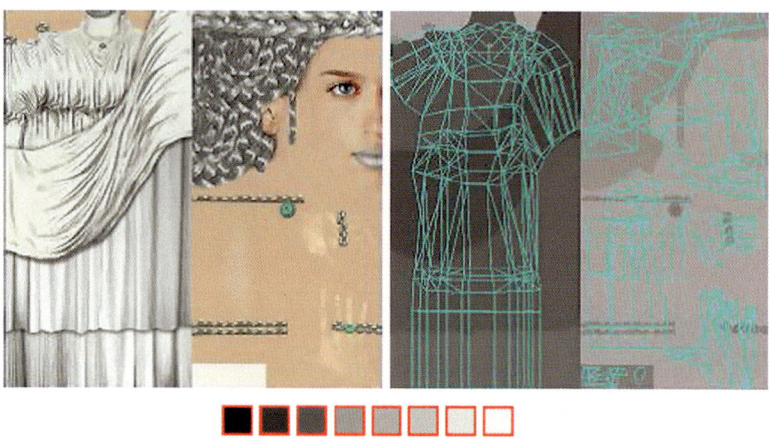

Fig. 3.19 Typical RGBA image used for color variety. The RGB part composes the texture and the alpha the segmentation map

3.7 Crowd Appearance Variety

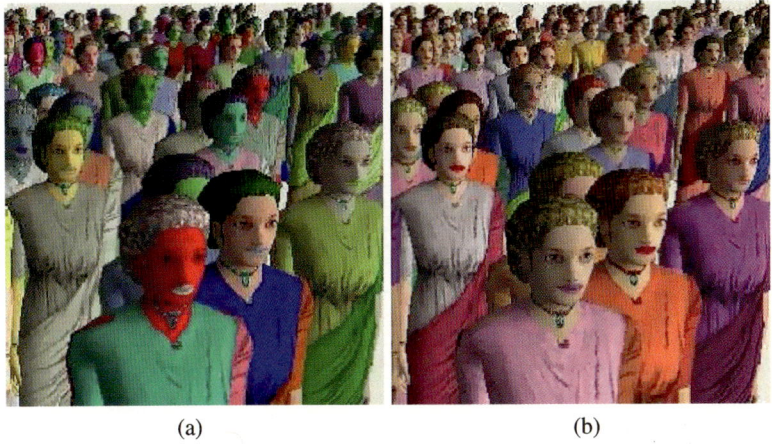

Fig. 3.20 Random color system (**a**) versus HSB control (**b**)

modulation: the final color C_b of each body part is a modulation of its texture color C_t by a random color C_r:

$$C_b = C_t C_r \qquad (3.13)$$

Colors C_b, C_t, and C_r can take values between 0.0 and 1.0. In order to have a large panel of reachable colors, C_t should be as light as possible, i.e., near 1.0. Indeed, if C_t is too dark, the modulation by C_r will give only dark colors. On the other hand, if C_t is a light color, the modulation by C_r will provide not only light colors, but also dark ones. This explains why part of the texture has to be reduced to a light luminance, i.e., the shading information and the roughness of the material. The drawback of passing the main parts of the texture to luminance is that funky colors can be generated, i.e., characters are dressed in colors that do not match. Some constraints have to be added when modulating colors randomly.

HSB Color Spaces

The standard RGB color model representing additive color primaries of red, green, and blue is mainly used for specifying color on computer screens. With this system, it is hard to constrain colors effectively (see Fig. 3.20).

In order to quantify and control the color parameters applied to the crowd, a user-friendly color is used. Smith [Smi78] proposed a model that deals with everyday life color concepts, i.e., hue, saturation, and brightness, which are more linked to the human color perception than the RGB system. This system is called the HSB (or HSV) color model (see Figs. 3.20(b) and 3.21):

1. The hue defines the specific shade of color, as a value between 0 and 360 degrees.

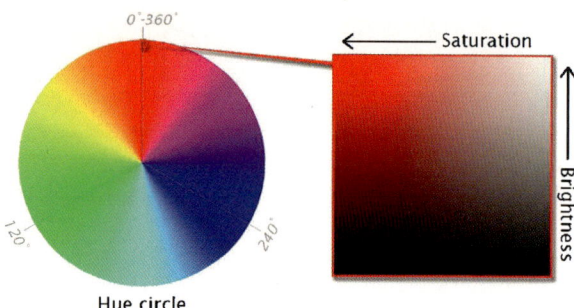

Fig. 3.21 HSB color space. Hue is represented by a *circular region*. A separate *square region* may be used to represent saturation and brightness, i.e., the *vertical axis of the square* indicates brightness, while the *horizontal axis* corresponds to saturation

2. The saturation denotes the purity of the color, i.e., highly saturated colors are vivid while low saturated colors are washed-out, like pastels. Saturation can take values between 0 and 100.
3. The brightness measures how light or dark a color is, as a value between 0 and 100.

In the process of designing virtual human color variety, localized constraints are dealt with: some body parts need very specific colors. For instance, skin colors are taken from a specific range of unsaturated shades with red and yellow dominance, almost deprived of blue and green. Eyes are described as a range from brown to green and blue with different levels of brightness. These simple examples show that one cannot use a random color generator as is. The HSB color model enables control of color variety in an intuitive and flexible manner. Indeed, as shown in Fig. 3.22, by specifying a range for each of the three parameters, it is possible to define a 3D color space, called the HSB map.

The Need for Better Color Variety

The method presented above is perfectly adequate when viewing crowds at far distances. However, when some individuals are close to the camera, the method tends to

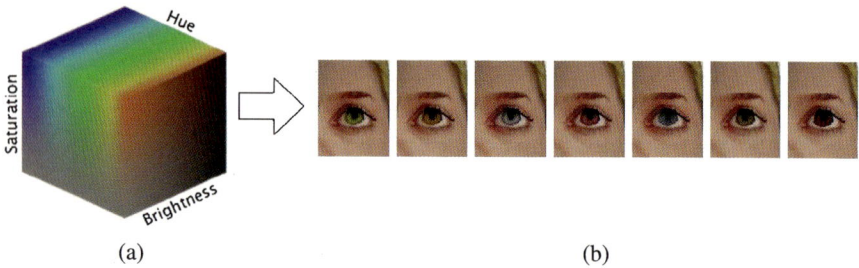

Fig. 3.22 The HSB space is constrained to a three-dimensional color space with the following parameters (**a**): hue from 20 to 250, saturation from 30 to 80, and brightness from 40 to 100. Colors are then randomly chosen inside this space to add variety on the eyes texture of a character (**b**)

3.7 Crowd Appearance Variety

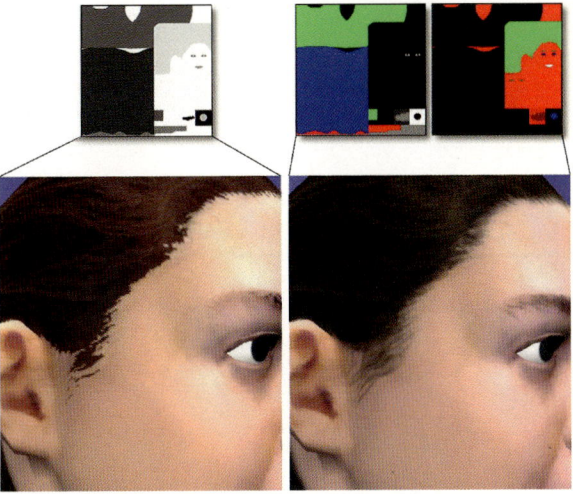

Fig. 3.23 Closeup of the transition between skin and hair: artifacts in previous methods when segmenting body parts in a single alpha layer (*left*), smooth transitions between parts with our method (*right*)

have too sharp transitions between body parts. There is no smooth blending between different parts, e.g., the transition between skin and hair, as depicted in Fig. 3.23.

Also, character closeups reveal the need for a new method capable of handling detailed color variety, for instance, subtle makeup effects for female characters. Moreover, at short distances, materials should be illuminated differently to obtain realistic characters at the forefront.

To obtain a detailed color variety method, we propose, for each appearance set, to use segmentation maps, as detailed in the next section.

Segmentation Maps

Principles of Segmentation A segmentation map is a four channel image, delimiting four body parts (one per channel) and sharing the same parametrization as the texture of the appearance set. The intensity of each body part is thus defined throughout the whole body of each character, i.e., 256 levels of intensity are possible for each part, 0 meaning it is not present at this location, and 255 meaning it is fully present. For our virtual humans, we have made experiments with eight body parts, i.e., two RGBA segmentation maps per appearance set. The results are satisfying for our specific needs, but the method can be used with more segmentation maps if more parts are needed. For instance, it would be possible to use the method for adding color variety to a city by creating segmentation maps for buildings.

Using segmentation maps to efficiently distinguish body parts also provides two advantages over previous methods:

1. Possibility to apply different illumination models to each body part. With previous methods, achieving such effects requires costly fragment shader branching.
2. Possible mipmapping activation and use of linear filtering, which greatly reduce aliasing. Since previous methods use the alpha channel of the texture to segment

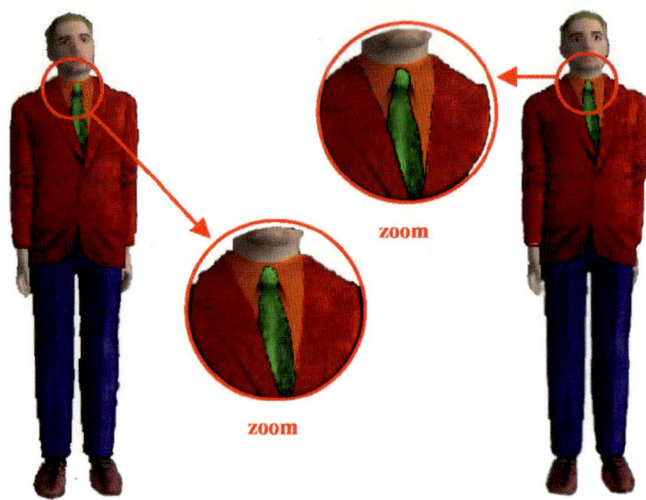

Fig. 3.24 Bilinear filtering artifacts in the alpha layer can be seen in the *right zoomed-in version*, near the borders of the *orange shirt*, the *green tie*, and the *red vest* [Mau05]

their body parts, they cannot benefit from this algorithm, which causes the appearance of artifacts at body part seams (see Fig. 3.24).

Figure 3.25 depicts the different effects achievable with our color variety method: makeup, texture, localized specular parameters.

The segmentation maps are designed manually. Ideally, for a given pixel, we wish the sum of the intensity of each body part to reach 255. When designing the segmentation maps with software like Adobe Photoshop,[2] unwanted artifacts may later appear within the smooth transitions between body parts. Indeed, some pixel sums of intensity levels may not reach 255. For instance, imagine the transition between the hair and the skin of a virtual human. A pixel of the segmentation map may reach a contribution of 100 for the skin part, while the hair part contribution is 120. Their sum is 220. Although this is not an issue while designing the segmented body parts in Photoshop, it leads to problems when trying to normalize the contributions in the application. Indeed, with simple normalization, such pixels compensate the incomplete sum with a black contribution, thus producing a final color much darker than expected. This is illustrated in Fig. 3.26. The proposed solution is to compensate this lack with white instead of black, to get a real smooth transition without unwanted dark zones.

The results obtained with our three levels of appearance variety are illustrated in Fig. 3.27, where several instances of a single human template are displayed, taking full advantage of all available appearance sets and color variety.

---

[2]http://www.adobe.com/fr/products/photoshop.

3.7 Crowd Appearance Variety

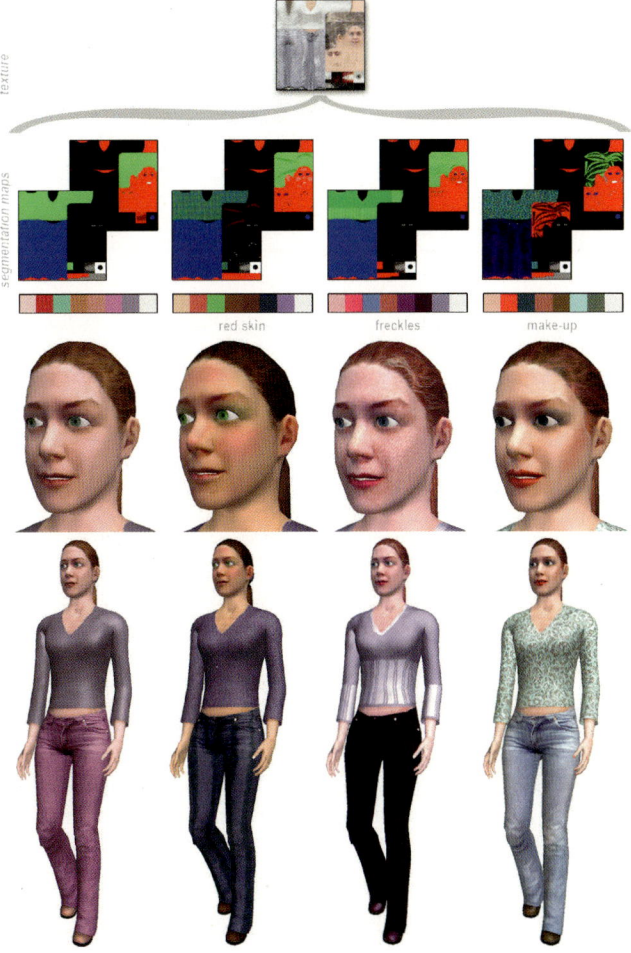

Fig. 3.25 Examples of achievable effects through appearance sets (makeup, freckles, clothes design, etc.), and per body part specular parameters (shiny shoes, glossy lips, etc.)

Color Variety Storage Each segmentation map of a human template is divided into four different body parts. Each of these parts has a specific color range, and specularity parameters. The eight body parts we need are designed in two different segmentation maps, i.e., two RGBA images, each containing four channels and thus four body parts. At its birth, each character is assigned a unique set of eight random colors from the constrained color spaces, similarly to de Heras et al. [dHSMT05]. These eight colors are stored in eight contiguous RGB texels, starting at the top left of a 1024 × 1024 image, called color look up table (CLUT). We show an illustration of a CLUT in Fig. 3.28.

Fig. 3.26 A blue-to-red gradient. (**a**) The sum of the red and blue contributions does not reach 255 in some pixels, causing the gradient to suffer from an unwanted black contribution. (**b**) A white contribution is added so that the sum of contributions is always 255

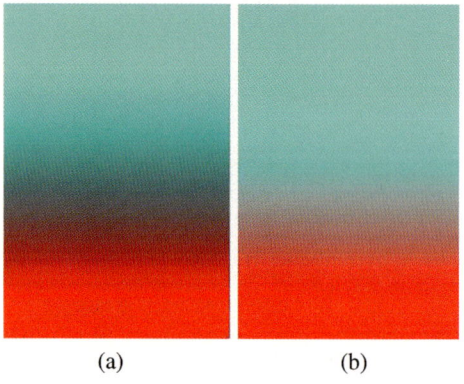

(a) (b)

Therefore, if a 1024 × 1024 image is used for storing the CLUT, it is possible to store a set of up to:

$$1024 \cdot 1024 \div 8 = 131{,}072 \qquad (3.14)$$

unique combinations of colors. Note that illumination parameters are set per body part and thus not saved within the CLUT, but directly sent to the GPU.

3.7.3 Accessories

We have already described how to obtain varied clothes and skin colors by using several appearance sets. Unfortunately, even with these techniques, the feeling of watching the same person is not completely overcome. The main reason is the lack

Fig. 3.27 Several instances of a single human template, exploiting all its appearance sets and color variety

3.7 Crowd Appearance Variety

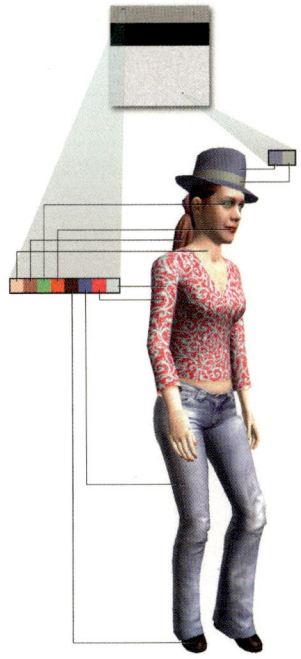

Fig. 3.28 A CLUT image used to store the color of each virtual human body part and accessory

of variety in the meshes used. Indeed, very often the same mesh (or a small number of them) is used for the whole crowd, resulting in large groups of similarly shaped humans. We cannot increase too much the number of meshes, because it requires a lot of work for a designer: create the mesh, its textures, its skinning, its different levels of detail, etc.

However, in real life, people have different haircuts, they wear hats or glasses, carry bags, etc. These particularities may look like details, but it is with the sum of those details that we are able to distinguish anyone. In this section, we first explain what exactly accessories are. Then, we show from a technical point of view the different kinds of accessories we have identified, and how to develop each of them in a crowd application.

An accessory is a simple mesh representing any element that can be added to the original mesh of a virtual human. It can be a hat as well as a handbag, or glasses, a clown nose, a wig, an umbrella, a cell phone, etc. Accessories have two main purposes: First, they allow one to easily add appearance variety to virtual humans. Second, they make characters look more believable: even without intelligent behavior, a virtual human walking around with a shopping bag or a cell phone looks more realistic than one just walking around. The addition of accessories allows a spectator to identify himself to a virtual human, because it performs actions that the spectator himself does every day.

We basically distinguish two different kinds of accessories that are incrementally complex to develop. The first group is composed of accessories that do not influence the movements of a virtual human. For instance, whether someone wears a hat or

Fig. 3.29 Two human templates wearing the same hat, in their default posture. The *pink*, *yellow* and *blue points* represent the position and orientation of the root, the head joint ($m1$), and the hat accessory ($m2$), respectively

not will not influence the way he walks. The second group gathers the accessories requiring a small variation in the animation clip played, e.g., a virtual human moving with an umbrella or with a bag still walks the same way, but the arm in contact with the accessory needs an adapted animation sequence.

Simple Accessories

The first group of accessories does not necessitate any particular modification of the animation clips played. They simply need to be correctly "placed" on a virtual human. Each accessory can be represented as a simple mesh, independent of any virtual human.

First, let us lay the problem for a single character. The issue is to render the accessory at the correct position and orientation, according to the movements of the character. To achieve this, we can "attach" the accessory to a specific joint of the virtual human. Let us take a real example to illustrate our idea: imagine a person wearing a hat and walking in a street. Supposing that the hat has the correct size and does not slide, it basically has the same movement as the head of the person as he walks. Technically, this means that the series of matrices representing the head movement are the same for the hat movement. However, the hat is not placed at the exact position of the head. It usually is on top of the head and can be oriented in different ways, as shown in Fig. 3.29.

Thus, we also need the correct displacement between the head joint position and the ideal hat position on top of it. In summary, to create a simple accessory, our needs are the following:

1. For each accessory:

3.7 Crowd Appearance Variety

    a. A mesh (vertices, normals, texture coordinates),
    b. A texture,
2. For each human template/accessory couple:
    a. The joint to which it must be attached,
    b. A matrix representing the displacement of the accessory, relative to the joint.

Note that the matrix representing the displacement of the accessory is not only specific to one accessory, but specific to each human template/accessory couple. This allows us to vary the position, the size, and the orientation of the hat depending on which virtual human mesh we are working with. This is depicted in Fig. 3.29, where the same hat is worn differently by two human templates. It is also important to note that the joint to which the accessory is attached is also dependent on the human template. This was not the case at first: a single joint was specified for each accessory, independent of the human templates. However, we have noticed that depending on the size of a virtual human, some accessories may have to be attached to different joints. For instance, a backpack is not attached to the same vertebra if it is for a child or a grownup template. Finally, with this information, we are able to assign each human template a different set of accessories, increasing greatly the feeling of variety.

Complex Accessories

The second group of accessories we have identified is the one that requires slight modifications of the animation sequences played. Concerning the rendering of the accessory, we still keep the idea of attaching it to a specific joint of the virtual human. The additional difficulty is the modification of the animation clips to make the action realistic. For instance, if we want to add a cellphone accessory, we also need the animation clips allowing the virtual human to make a phone call.

We focus only on locomotion animation sequences. Our raw material is a database of motion captured walk and run cycles that can be applied to the virtual humans. From each animation clip, an adjustment of the arm motion is performed in order to obtain a new animation clip integrating the wanted movement, e.g., hand close to the ear. These animation modifications can be generalized to other movements that are independent from any accessory, for instance, hands in the pockets. This is why we fully detail the animation adaptation process in this chapter.

Additional steps are required to constrain the character's animation. At initialization, the designer specifies which joints will be constrained and in which way, i.e., a joint can be frozen in a given orientation, or its movement can be limited within a given range of angles. Then, in real-time during simulation, joints are first updated as usual. Once the skeleton posture is fully updated, the joints that need special treatment are either overwritten, or clamped. Typically, for carrying a bunch of flowers, the shoulder movement is limited to a chosen angle range, while the elbow is completely frozen at an angle of about 90 degrees.

For each complex accessory, we have to define which joint to constrain and how to constrain it. There are two possibilities:

Fig. 3.30 (**a**) Clamping joints. (**b**) Freezing joint

1. The motion is restricted, in this case, we clamp the joints defining the limits of the joint angle (minAngle, maxAngle) (see Fig. 3.30(a))
2. The motion is blocked and the angle is frozen to a certain value (Freezing Angle) (see Fig. 3.30(b)).

At runtime, the animation is updated as usual, the frozen joints are overwritten, and we use exponential maps to clamp joints.

Loading and Initialization

In this section, we focus on the architectural aspect of accessories, and how to assign them to all virtual humans. First, each accessory has a type, e.g., "hat" or "backpack". We differentiate seven different types, but this number is arbitrary. In order to avoid the attribution of, for instance, a cowboy hat and a cap on the same head, we never allow a character to wear more than one accessory of each type. To distribute accessories to the whole crowd, we need to extend the following data structures:

1. *Human template*: each human template is provided with a list of accessory ids, sorted by type. Thus, we know which template can wear which accessory. This process is necessary, since all human templates cannot wear all accessories. For instance, a school bag would suit the template of a child, but for an adult template, it would look much less believable.
2. *Body entity*: each body entity possesses one accessory slot per existing type. This allows one to later add up to seven accessories (one of each type) to the same virtual human.

We also create two data structures to make the accessory distribution process efficient:

1. *Accessory entity*: each accessory itself possesses a list of body ids, representing the virtual humans wearing it. They are sorted by human template.

3.7 Crowd Appearance Variety

Algorithm 3.1: Simulation loop

```
1  begin
2    for each accessory in database: do
3        load its data contained in the database
4        create its vertex buffer (for later rendering)
5        insert it into the accessory repository (sorted by type)
6    end
7    for each human template h: do
8        for each accessory a suitable to h: do
9            insert a's id into h's list l (sorted by type)
10       end
11   end
12   for each body b: do
13       get human template h of b
14       get accessory id list l of h
15       for each accessory type t in l do
16           choose randomly an accessory a of type t
17           assign a to the correct accessory slot of b
18           push b's id in a's body id list (sorted by human template)
19       end
20   end
21 end
```

2. *Accessory repository*: an empty repository is created to receive all accessories loaded from the database. They are sorted by type.

At initialization, the previous data structures are filled. We detail this process in the pseudo-code in Algorithm 3.1.

The process of filling these data structures is done only once at initialization, because we assume that once specific accessories have been assigned to a virtual human, they never change. However, it would be easy to change online the accessories worn, through a call to the last loop. Note that a single vertex buffer is created for each loaded accessory, independently of the number of virtual humans wearing it.

Rendering

Since the lists introduced in the previous section are all sorted according to our needs, the rendering of accessories is much facilitated. We show in the pseudo-code in Algorithm 3.2 our pipeline.

Although this pseudo-code may seem complex at first sight, it is quite simple and well optimized to minimize state switches. First, at line (3), each accessory has

Algorithm 3.2: Pipeline of execution

```
 1  begin
 2      for each accessory type t of the repository do
 3          for each accessory a of type t do
 4              bind vertex buffer of a
 5              send a's appearance parameters to the GPU
 6              get a's list l of body ids (sorted by human template)
 7              for each human template h in l do
 8                  get the joint j of h to which a is attached
 9                  get the original position matrix m1 of j
10                  get the displacement matrix m2 of couple [a,h]
11                  for For each body b of h do
12                      get matrix m3 of b's current position
13                      get matrix m4 of j's current deformation for b
14                      multiply current modelview matrix by mi (i=1..4)
15                      call to vertex buffer rendering
16                  end
17              end
18          end
19      end
20  end
```

its vertex buffer boundary. We can process this way, independently of the bodies, because an accessory never changes its shape or texture. Then, we process through each accessory's body id list (5). This list is sorted by human template (6), allowing us to retrieve information common to all its instances, i.e., the joint j to which is attached the accessory (7), along with its original position matrix m1 in the skeleton (8), and the original displacement matrix m2 between m1 and the desired position of the accessory (9). An example with a hat attached to the head joint of 2 human templates is illustrated in Fig. 3.29.

Once the human template data are retrieved, we iterate over each body wearing the accessory (10). A body entity also has specific data that are required: its position for the current frame (11), and the displacement of its joint, relatively to its original position, depending on the animation played (12). Figure 3.31 illustrates the transformation represented by these matrices.

Finally, by multiplying the matrices extracted from the human template and body data, we are able to define the exact position and orientation of the accessory (13). The rendering of the vertex buffer is then called and the accessory is displayed correctly (14).

3.7 Crowd Appearance Variety

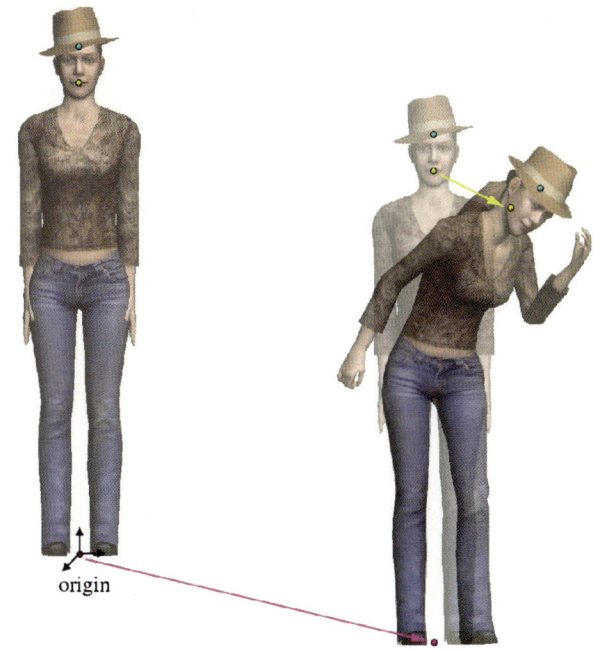

Fig. 3.31 *Left*: a human template in default posture. *Right*: the same human template playing an animation clip. The displacement of the body, relatively to the origin ($m3$), is depicted in *pink*, the displacement of the head joint due to the animation clip ($m4$) in *yellow*

Empty Accessories

We have identified seven different accessory types. And, through the accessory attribution pipeline, we assign seven accessories per virtual human. This number is important and the results obtained can be unsatisfying: indeed, if all characters wear a hat, glasses, jewelry, backpack, etc., they look more like Christmas trees than believable people. We need the possibility of having people without accessories too. To allow for this, we could simply randomly choose for each body accessory slot, whether it is used or not. This solution works, but a more efficient one can be considered. Indeed, at the rendering phase of a large crowd, testing each slot of each body to know whether it is used or not implies useless code branching, i.e., precious computation time. We therefore propose a faster solution to this problem by creating empty accessories. An empty accessory is a fake one, possessing no geometry or vertex buffer. It only possesses a unique id, similarly to all other accessories.

At initialization, before loading the real accessories from the database, the pseudo-code in Algorithm 3.3 is executed.

The second loop over human templates is necessary in order to make all empty accessories compatible with all human templates. Once this preprocess is done, the loading and attribution of accessories is achieved as detailed in Sect. 3.7.3. This fore introduction of empty accessories causes later their possible insertion in some of the accessory slots of the bodies. Note that if, for instance, a body entity gets an empty accessory for hat, reciprocally, the id of this body will be added to the empty accessory's body id list. This is illustrated with an example in Fig. 3.32.

Algorithm 3.3: Pseudo-code of initialization

```
1 begin
2    for each accessory type t do
3        create one empty accessory e of type t
4        put e in the accessory repository (sorted by type)
5        for each human template h: do
6            put e's id in h's accessory id list
7        end
8    end
9 end
```

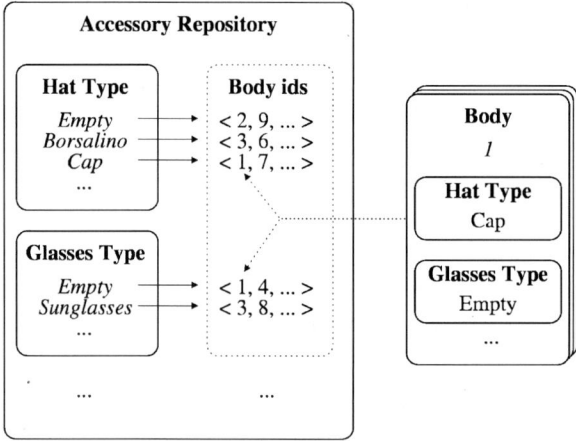

Fig. 3.32 *Left*: a representation of the accessory repository, sorted by type. Each accessory possesses its own list of body ids. Reciprocally, all bodies possess slots filled with their assigned accessories. *Right*: illustrated example of the accessory slots for body with id 1

One may wonder how the rendering is achieved. If keeping the same pipeline as detailed in Algorithm 3.2 in Sect. 3.7.3, we meet trouble when attempting to render an empty accessory. Moreover, some useless matrix computation would be done. Our solution is simple. Since the empty accessories are the first ones to be inserted into the accessory repository (sorted by type), we only need to skip the first element of each type to avoid their computation and rendering. The pseudo-code given in Sect. 3.7.3 only needs a supplementary line, which is:

```
1b skip first element of t.
```

With this solution, we take full advantage of accessories, obtaining varied people, not only through the vast choice of accessories, but also through the possibility of not wearing them. And there is no need for expensive tests within the rendering

3.7 Crowd Appearance Variety

Fig. 3.33 Several instances of a single human template, varied through the appearance sets, color variety, and accessories

loop. In Fig. 3.33, we show the results obtained when using accessories in addition to the appearance variety detailed in Sect. 3.7.2.

Color Variety Storage

In Sect. 3.7.2, we detail how to apply color variety to the different body parts of a texture. The same method can be applied to the accessories. A human texture is segmented in eight body parts, each having its specific color range. At initialization, for each instantiated virtual human and each body part, a color is randomly chosen in a range to modulate the original color of the texture. Since accessories are smaller and less complex than virtual humans, we only allow for four different parts, i.e., one segmentation map per appearance set. Then, similarly to the characters, each instance of each accessory is randomly assigned four colors within the HSB ranges defined for each part. These four random colors also have to be stored. We reemploy the CLUT used for storing the virtual humans color variety to save the colors of the accessories. In order not to confuse the color variety of the body parts and those of the accessories, we store the latter contiguously from the bottom right of the CLUT (see Fig. 3.28). Each character thus needs 8 texels for its own color variety and 7×4 other texels for all its potential accessories. This sums up to 36 texels per character. A 1024×1024 CLUT is therefore able to roughly store more than 29,000 unique color variety sets.

Scalability

We can simulate a high number of virtual humans, thanks to our different representations. It is important to note that the above description of accessories solves

Algorithm 3.4: Accessories information

1 **begin**
2   **for** *each rigid animation* **do**
3   **for** *each keyframe* **do**
4   **for** *each vertex of the accessory* **do**
5   save its new position which is found through the animation matrices
6   save its corresponding normal, which is found through the animation matrices
7   **end**
8   **end**
9   **end**
10 **end**

only the case of dynamically animated virtual characters, i.e., deformable meshes. However, if we want to ensure continuity when switching from one representation to another, it is important to also find a solution for the accessories: a hat on the head of a virtual human walking away from the camera cannot suddenly disappear when the virtual human is switching to a lower representation. We develop here how to make accessories scalable.

First, let us detail how accessories can be scaled to fit rigid meshes. An accessory has an animation clip of its own, similar to the animation of a particular joint of a virtual human. If we wanted to simply apply the rigid mesh principle (see Chap. 6) to accessories, we would have to store an important quantity of information (see Algorithm 3.4).

As one can see, this pipeline corresponds to the one used to store the vertices and normals of a rigid mesh at each keyframe of a defined animation clip. If we analyze this pipeline, we can observe that there is a clear redundancy in the information stored: first, an accessory is never deformed, which means that its vertices do not move, relatively to each other. They can be considered as a single group transformed by the animation matrices. The same applies to the normals of the accessory. Second, as detailed in Chap. 6 it is impossible to store in a database a rigid and an impostor animation clip for each existing skeletal animation. It follows that creating all the rigid/impostor versions of an animation clip for each possible accessory cannot be considered.

In order to drastically diminish the information to store for an accessory in a rigid animation, we propose a solution in two steps: First, as previously detailed, there is no need to store all the vertices and all the normals at each keyframe of an animation sequence, since the mesh is not deformed. It is sufficient to keep a single animation matrix per keyframe, valid for all vertices. Then, at runtime, the original mesh representing the accessory is transformed by the stored animation matrices. Second, we can regroup all accessories depending on the joint they are attached to. For instance, all hats and all glasses are attached to the head. Thus, basically, they all have the

3.7 Crowd Appearance Variety

Algorithm 3.5: Process the joints

1 **begin**
2   **for** *each rigid animation* **do**
3   **for** *each keyframe* **do**
4   **for** *each joint using an accessory* **do**
5   a single matrix representing
6   the transformation of the joint at this keyframe
7   **end**
8   **end**
9   **end**
10 **end**

Algorithm 3.6: Process the accessories

1 **begin**
2   **for** *each human template/accessory couple (independent of the animation)* **do**
3   a matrix representing the accessory's displacement
4   relatively to the joint
5   **end**
6 **end**

same animation. The only difference between a pair of glasses and a hat is the position where they are rendered, relatively to the head position (the hat is above the head, the glasses in front of it). So, we only need to keep this specific displacement for each accessory relatively to its joint. This corresponds to a single matrix per human template/accessory couple, which is completely independent of the animation clip played. In summary, with this solution, we only need Algorithms 3.5 and 3.6.

Scaling the accessory principle to impostors proves to be complicated. Once again, a naive approach would be as in Algorithm 3.7.

One can quickly imagine the explosion the memory would endure, even when starting with only a few original impostor animations. We cannot afford to generate one impostor animation for each possible combination of accessories. The first possible simplification is to let the unnoticeable accessories disappear. Indeed, impostors are usually employed when the virtual humans are far from the camera, and thus, small details, taking only a few pixels, can be ignored. Such accessories would be watches, jewelry, and others. Of course, it is also dependent on the distance from the camera where the impostors are used, and whether such disappearances are noticeable or not. As for larger accessories, like hats or bags, we have no finite solution to expose.

Algorithm 3.7: Process the impostors with accessories

```
1  begin
2    for each original impostor animation (without accessories) do
3      for all possible combinations of accessories do
4        create a similar impostor animation directly
5        containing these accessories
6      end
7    end
8  end
```

3.8 Final Remarks

This chapter presented some useful techniques in order to create large quantities of realistic virtual humans. We discussed a possible strategy to generate virtual humans based on single images. The main goal of methods described here is to generate simultaneously a large number of virtual characters different from each other, regarding several attributes like colors, materials, texture, and geometric model of virtual human bodies.

References

[ABH*94] AZUOLA F., BADLER N. L., HO P.-H., KAKADIARIS I., METAXAS D., TING B.-J.: Building anthropometry-based virtual human models. In *Proceedings of IMAGE Conf.* (1994), ACM, New York.

[ACP03] ALLEN B., CURLESS B., POPOVIĆ Z.: The space of all body shapes: Reconstruction and parametrization from range scans. In *Proceedings of ACM SIGGRAPH 2003* (2003), ACM Press, New York.

[Arr88] ARRAJ J.: *Tracking the Elusive Human, Volume 1: A Practical Guide to C.G. Jung's Psychological Types, W.H. Sheldon's Body and Temperament Types and Their Integration.* Inner Growth Books, Chiloquin, 1988.

[BJ01] BOYKOV Y. Y., JOLLY M. P.: Interactive graph cuts for optimal boundary & region segmentation of objects in n-d images. In *Proceedings of the Eighth IEEE International Conference on Computer Vision. ICCV 2001* (2001), vol. 1, pp. 105–112.

[Dek00] DEKKER L.: *3D Human Body Modeling from Range Data.* PhD thesis, University College London, 2000.

[DHOO05] DOBBYN S., HAMILL J., O'CONOR K., O'SULLIVAN C.: Geopostors: A real-time geometry/impostor crowd rendering system. In *SI3D'05: Proceedings of the 2005 Symposium on Interactive 3D Graphics and Games* (New York, NY, USA, 2005), ACM, New York, pp. 95–102.

[dHSMT05] DE HERAS P., SCHERTENLEIB S., MAÏM J., THALMANN D.: Real-time shader rendering for crowds in virtual heritage. In *Proc. 6th International Symposium on Virtual Reality, Archaeology and Cultural Heritage (VAST 05)* (2005).

[DT05] DALAL N., TRIGGS B.: Histograms of oriented gradients for human detection. In *IEEE Computer Society Conference on Computer Vision and Pattern Recognition. CVPR 2005* (2005), vol. 1, pp. 886–893.

References

[HBG*99] HILTON A., BERESFORD D., GENTILS T., SMITH R., SUN W.: Virtual people: Capturing human models to populate virtual worlds. In *Proceedings of Computer Animation* (1999), ACM, New York, pp. 174–185.

[HC90] HEATH B. H., CARTER J. E. L.: *Somatotyping—Development and Application*. Cambridge University Press, New York, 1990.

[HDK07] HORNUNG A., DEKKERS E., KOBBELT L.: Character animation from 2d pictures and 3d motion data. *ACM Transactions on Graphics 26* (2007), 1–9.

[JDJ*10] JACQUES J. C. S. JR., DIHL L., JUNG C. R., THIELO M. R., KESHET R., MUSSE S. R.: Human upper body identification from images. In *IEEE International Conference on Image Processing* (2010), pp. 1–4.

[Jun07] JUNG C. R.: Unsupervised multiscale segmentation of color images. *Pattern Recognition Letters 28*, 4 (March 2007), 523–533.

[KM95] KAKADIARIS I., METAXAS D.: 3d human body model acquisition from multiple views. In *Proceedings of the Fifth International Conference on Computer Vision* (1995), pp. 618–623.

[Lew00] LEWIS M.: *Evolving Human Figure Geometry*. Technical Report OSU-ACCAD-5/00-TR1, ACCAD, The Ohio State University, May 2000.

[LGMT00] LEE W., GU J., MAGNENAT-THALMANN N.: Generating animatable 3d virtual humans from photographs. In *Proceedings of Eurographics* (2000), ACM, New York, pp. 1–10.

[LP00] LEWIS M., PARENT R.: *An Implicit Surface Prototype for Evolving Human Figure Geometry*. Technical Report OSU-ACCAD-11/00-TR2, ACCAD, The Ohio State University, 2000.

[Mau05] MAUPU D.: Creating variety a crowd creator tool. Semester project at Swiss Federal Institute of Technology—EPFL, VRLab, 2005.

[MGR01] MODESTO L., RANGARAJU V.: Generic character variations, "Shrek" the story behind the screen. In *ACM SIGGRAPH 2001* (Los Angeles 2001), conference lecture.

[MTSC03] MAGNENAT-THALMANN N., SEO H., CORDIER F.: Automatic modeling of virtual humans and body clothing. In *Proceedings of SIGGRAPH* (2003), ACM Press, New York, pp. 19–26.

[MYT09] MAÏM J., YERSIN B., THALMANN D.: Unique character instances for crowds. *IEEE Computer Graphics and Applications 29*, 6 (Nov. 2009), 82–90.

[NO96] NORTON K., OLDS T.: *Anthropometrica*. University of New South Wales Press, Sydney, 1996.

[PFD99] PLÄNKERS R., FUA P., D'APUZZO N.: Automated body modeling from video sequences. In *Proceedings of ICCV Workshop on Modeling People* (September 1999).

[RKB04] ROTHER C., KOLMOGOROV V., BLAKE A.: Grabcut: Interactive foreground extraction using iterated graph cuts. *ACM Transactions on Graphics 23* (August 2004), 309–314.

[She40] SHELDON W. H.: *The Varieties of Human Physique*. Harper and Brothers, New York, 1940.

[Smi78] SMITH A. R.: Color gamut transform pairs. In *Proceedings of ACM SIGGRAPH* (1978), ACM, New York, pp. 12–19.

[SMT03] SEO H., MAGNENAT-THALMAN N.: An automatic modelling of human bodies from sizing parameters. In *Proceedings of ACM SIGGRAPH/Eurographics Symposium on Computer Animation* (2003), ACM, New York.

[SPCM97] SCHEEPERS F., PARENT R. E., CARLSON W. E., MAY S. F.: Anatomy-based modeling of the human musculature. In *Proceedings of the 24th Annual Conference on Computer Graphics and Interactive Techniques (SIGGRAPH'97)* (1997), ACM Press, New York, pp. 163–172.

[Tay00] TAYLOR C. J.: Reconstruction of articulated objects from point correspondences in a single uncalibrated image. *Computer Vision and Image Understanding 80*, 3 (2000), 349–363.

[Til02] TILLEY A. R.: *The Measure of Man and Woman—Human Factors in Design*. Wiley, New York, 2002.

[TLC02a] TECCHIA F., LOSCOS C., CHRYSANTHOU Y.: Image-based crowd rendering. *IEEE Computer Graphics and Applications 22*, 2 (March–April 2002), 36–43.

[WG97] WILHELMS J., GELDER A. V.: Anatomically based modeling. In *Proceedings of the 24th Annual Conference on Computer Graphics and Interactive Techniques* (1997), pp. 173–180.

Chapter 4
Virtual Human Animation

4.1 Introduction

While designing an animation engine usable in crowd simulations, several criteria have to be taken into account: animation computation should be efficient and scalable, it should allow for variability, and it should be compatible with levels of detail. To understand the problems, let us take the most important animation pattern used in crowd simulation, as well as games, i.e., locomotion, basically composed of walking and running motions.

The first idea that comes to mind is to generate different locomotion cycles online for each individual. Unfortunately, even though the engine could be very fast, we cannot afford spending so much computation time for such a task. Moreover, some rendering techniques such as billboards or rigid meshes even request an offline animation stage to prepare the appropriate data structures.

A second approach is to use an animation database. In the present chapter we focus on the walking pattern with varying speeds. We wish not only to allow any virtual human to walk with a different speed but also to break the uniformity of the standard walking pattern by compositing it with secondary movements such as using one's cell phone or having both hands in the pockets. The first step toward this goal is to constitute a database of walking cycles that will be exploited optimally with the GPU at runtime.

To create such a database, we generate offline many different locomotion cycles, with varying parameters (e.g., speed and style). Procedural modeling is one general approach achieving this goal by explicitly linking high-level parameters (e.g., speed) to the animation parameters (i.e., the skeleton joint values). This method requires a careful analysis of several real patterns performed with various sets of qualitative and quantitative motion characterizations. One of the major difficulties is to find sufficient data, e.g., within the biomechanics literature, and to compose them to create complex coordinated walking [BUT04] or running motions.

An alternate approach is to conduct a motion capture campaign to systematically record locomotion cycles with a dense speed sampling for walking and running and for multiple subjects. Using such raw captured movements is possible for building the database for crowd animation (once transformed in joint trajectories). However, we are limited to the captured speeds and to the style of the original movement performers. It is worth building a statistical model out of this mass of data to offer a generic locomotion engine driven by one or more high-level continuous variables. A typical example of statistically based motion generation method was introduced by Glardon et al. [GBT04]. The method exploits the PCA (Principal Component Analysis) technique on MOCAP (Motion Capture) data to yield a reduced dimension space controlled by a quantitative speed parameter where both interpolation and extrapolation are possible. Moreover, with proper normalization and time warping methods, the engine is generic and can produce walking motions with continuously varying human height and speed. However, despite its good performances (i.e., around 1 ms/cycle of 25 frames on a 1.5 GHz CPU), its cost is still too important for animating a large crowd. Nevertheless, it is a very flexible tool for the offline creation of locomotion databases for any character size, speed, and blend of walking and running.

The remaining part of the present chapter first provides a state of the art in locomotion modeling prior to describing a PCA model of locomotion [GBT04]. We then explain how the standard walking cycle can be enriched to introduce more lifelike variety. The chapter ends by providing some elements about the steering control to produce arbitrary trajectory in the plane.

4.2 Related Work in Locomotion Modeling

Walking motion synthesis is a central problem due to its strategic importance in crowd animation. Similarly to [MFCG*99], we have grouped the various methods into four families.

4.2.1 Kinematic Methods

Most of the kinematic approaches rely on biomechanical knowledge, and combine direct and inverse kinematics. They do not necessarily preserve physical laws and focus on the kinematics attached to a skeleton (positions, speeds and acceleration of the rigid body parts). During the 1980s, methods were developed to generate locomotion patterns, driven by high-level parameters such as step length and frequency. Zeltzer in [Zel82, Zel83] defined finite state machines to control the synthesized human gait. The states represent bundle of key-frames which are interpolated to produce a desired walking motion. Boulic et al. [BTM90, BUT04] proposed a walking engine built from experimental data on a wide range of normalized speed. It allows one to animate virtual humans of any size driven by two high-level parameters: the linear and angular speed. Other kinematic approaches aim at ensuring that the feet do not penetrate into the ground such as [GM85, Gir87, BT92, BC93] for walking

4.2 Related Work in Locomotion Modeling 83

and [BC96] for running motions. In [CH99], the foot position of the support leg is controlled prior to the swing leg. In addition, a collision avoidance module is used to generate stair climbing walking. More sophisticated methods offer other motion controls. The method presented in [SM01] adapts the walk to uneven terrain by deforming original motion generated in a 2D space of step length and step height parameters. The original motions are represented in the sagittal plane whose orientation is progressively modified according to the locomotion direction. Tsumara et al. [TYNN01] proposed a locomotion well adapted for brisk direction changes, by handling the next footprint positions. However, the speed cannot be controlled by the user. Kulpa et al. have proposed a normalized representation of movement that allows the inverse kinematic retargeting of locomotion sequences on various characters and terrains [KMA05].

One of the main drawbacks of these methods concerns their lack of motion realism. Therefore, physical models improve upon those negative aspects.

4.2.2 Physically Based Methods

The pioneer work of [RH91] exploited the dynamic control of legged robots to animate simple legged figures. However, it was not able to animate the full body of a complex character. Controllers have therefore been used in order to provide the forces and torques to apply to the body parts, according to given constraints. Hodgins et al. [HWBO95] proposed control algorithms based on finite state machines to describe a particular motion (running, bicycling, vaulting), and on Proportional Derivative (PD) servos to compute the joint forces and torques. This method has been improved by Wooten et al. [WH96, WH00] allowing the switch from one to another controller for generating transitions between jump and landing motions, while preserving balance. In [FvdPT01], the balance is also controlled to generate motions recovering from a fall. Ko and Badler [KB96] proposed a method which first generates a locomotion sequence using kinematics. Then dynamics rules are enforced to improve the animation realism, notably by maintaining balance with respect to human strength limits. The use of dynamics to control the motion of an articulated figure is very difficult. On the one hand, controlling an n DOF body dynamically means controlling n actuators; this is at least as difficult as, and much less intuitive than, controlling n joints directly. On the other hand, once a controller has successfully been created, one can attempt to adapt it to a new context. For example, Hodgins and Pollard in [HP97] introduced a technique for adapting physical controllers to different morphologies and skeleton types. For cyclic motion like walking, Laszlo et al. [LvdPF96] improved the motion stability in a dynamic environment by adding a closed-loop control to an open-loop system. The closed-loop control is based on forcing the gait motion back to a stable limit cycle after a perturbation is applied. The control is achieved by manipulating hip pitch and roll. Finally, Faloutsos et al. [FvdPT01] proposed a method allowing the composition of different controllers in order to generate, still realistic, but more complex motions by using simpler controllers. The composition can be performed manually or determined automatically through learning methods like Support Vector Machine (SVM).

However, the controllers provide at present a relatively narrow range of realistic motions. Therefore, complex composite controllers have to be designed, capable of synthesizing a full spectrum of human like motor behaviors. In addition, physically based methods demand too much user assistance with a high parameter dimension, inappropriate for human animation systems.

4.2.3 Motion Interpolation

The next research direction encompasses techniques combining preexisting motion data, obtained either through the above-cited methods or through motion capture. In [UAT95], a motion representation based on Fourier series is used to compare and quantify a characteristic (tiredness, sadness, joy) between similar movements. For example, the parameter "briskness" is obtained by the subtraction of a "normal" walk from a "brisk" walk expressed in the Fourier domain. Guo and Robergé [GR96] presented another pioneering work which combines up to four widely differing locomotion cycles, from walk to run with differing stride lengths, tagged with key events such as "heel-strike" and "toe-off." New sequences are generated by linear combinations of locally time-warped postures within each of the successive subintervals defined by the key-events.

Other approaches allow a multidimensional motion interpolation over a wide range of scattered input data. Rose et al. [RCB98] chose an interpolation scheme based on RBF (Radial Basis Function) to produce parametrized motions. Input motions are first manually classified by activities ("verbs") and characterized by a parameter vector. The motion data are then represented by B-spline control points which model the DOF functions over time. In addition, the motions attached to a given verb are structurally aligned by using a time warping process based on [BW95]. To generate a new motion, a combination of RBF and polynomials is selected and provides the B-spline coefficients corresponding to the requested parametrized motion. The polynomial function provides an overall approximation of the example motion space, while the RBF locally adjusts the polynomial so as to get the exact example motion when the user gives its corresponding parameter vector. Sloan et al. [SRC01] adopted cardinal basis functions for further performance improvements. This RBF-based technique is incorporated in [PSS02] for online locomotion synthesis and provides weights to be assigned to the example input motions. New motions are then generated by performing a weighted linear combination of the example data, using a multiple quaternion interpolation scheme. Recently, Mukai and Kuriyama [MK05] improved the RBF construction described in [RCB98] by defining a specific kernel function for each input motion according to its characteristics. This approach is based on geostatistics which takes into account the correlation between spatial distances and corresponding control parameters. It results in a more accurate motion interpolation.

4.2 Related Work in Locomotion Modeling

Even efficient enough to perform real-time motion synthesis, the above scattered data interpolation approaches force each input motion to contribute to the generated motion. On the one hand, it induces a computational efficiency which is dependent on the number of example motions. On the other hand, the method provides rough results when the user requests parameters far from the examples as interpolation weights are based purely on the linear approximation.

Therefore, other methods propose to parametrize motions with fewer examples. Pettré and Laumond [PL05] proposed to represent motion captured data into the frequency domain, similar to [UAT95]. The authors use walking cycles characterized with two parameters: linear and angular speeds. The original motions, expressed with Fourier coefficients, are projected into this 2D parameter space, and a Delaunay triangulation is performed. This approach is also analogous to the one described in [SM01] where, according to a given parameter pair, the three nearest neighboring motions can be selected to perform a weighted linear interpolation between them. In [KG03], a more general motion interpolation method is proposed, by addressing the time-warping issue among other problems. A new data-structure, referred to as registration curve, is introduced. This concept ensures automatically a consistent time-warping and an alignment of the humanoid root node for all input motions. In addition, physical constraints of the input motions are appropriately interpolated. To obtain a new motion, the user sets weights on manually selected motion examples. Their attached registration curve allows one to perform a consistent interpolation, based on the technique explained in [PSS02].

For motion interpolation, the selection of the necessary example motions over the entire input dataset can be performed automatically. The general strategy of sampling the space of interpolation was originally introduced in [WH97], leading to grids of regular samplings in the parameter space. According to a given parameter combination, a region can be determined in the parameter space and the interpolation is performed between the motions only included in this area. Other works are based on this strategy. Zordan and Hodgins [ZH02] generate dense sets of example motions as an aid for inverse kinematics tasks, while Rose et al. [RSC01] improve the accuracy of the resulting motions by adding additional samples to parameter space.

Another alternative method has been proposed in [KG04] to select the example motions. Given a segment of the motion dataset ("query"), the method locates and extracts motion segments that are similar, representing the same action or sequence of actions. This search is performed repeatedly, by taking the extracted segments as new queries. This process finished, the extracted segments are applied to perform a k-nearest-neighbor interpolation, as suggested in [ACP02]. This allows one to explicitly constrain interpolation weights to reasonable values and to project points outside the accessible region of parameter space back onto it. The animation methods based on scatter data interpolation [RCB98, PSS02] produce rough results when the user parameters are far from original input data as the interpolation is purely based on the linear approximation.

4.2.4 Statistical Models

Some statistical methods have been explicitly exploited for the motion parametrization problem. For articulated character animation, Brand and Hertzmann [BH00] used hidden Markov models along with an entropy minimization procedure to learn and synthesize motions with particular style. Their appealing method computes automatically structural correspondences and extracts style between motion sequences. This approach, although impressive, suffers from a complex mathematical framework which is dependent on a specific parametrization. In addition, the animations are not generated in real time.

PCA is another statistical method used in many fields for decades. This method is employed as a data compression technique to identify the significant variations in the data and eliminate the redundancy in the representation. Recently, PCA has been applied to computer graphics topics. Alexa and Mueller [AM00] applied PCA to represent geometric key-frame animations allowing an adaptive compression. Special attention has to be drawn for the motion data representation applied to PCA. When data are 3D joint positions, velocities, or accelerations, PCA can be directly applied, as used in [AFO03] to reduce the dimension of motion feature vectors. For joint angle measurements which have a non-Euclidean geometry, it is necessary to approximate them into the Euclidean space by the use of the exponential maps for example [Gra98]. In [LT02], PCA is first used to compress these data and then motion parametrization is performed on the reduced space using the RBF interpolation technique from [RCB98]. The main interest of this approach is that each motion example is considered as a point in the PCA space. The synthesis of idle motions in [EMMT04] is also based on PCA to facilitate operations such as blending and fitting of motions. This allows the production of small posture variations and personalized change of balance. Safonova et al. [SHP04] reduced the input data dimension using PCA so as to perform physically based motion synthesis more efficiently. Troje [Tro02] presented an approach to parametrized walking motions, represented by 3D marker positions, with attributes like gender or mood. The method consists in first applying PCA to each captured datum and then representing it by temporal sine functions. Finally, a second PCA is applied to all of these dimensionally reduced motions producing a new space where discriminant functions are used for determining the contribution of each dimension with respect to attributes. Despite interesting results, this approach is limited for motion synthesis application. First, the data are not represented into the joint angle spaces, inducing length modification for the body limbs. Second, an attribute change implies undesired consequences like the locomotion speed modification. A method [GMHP04] based on Scaled Gaussian Process Latent Variable Model (SGPLVM) allows the mapping from a low-dimensional space (latent space) to a feature space which characterizes motions (joint angles, velocities, and accelerations). Hence, a kernel function maps the correlation between postures according to their corresponding representations in the latent space. Similarly to the approach in [MK05], the method generalizes RBF interpolation, providing an automatic learning of all RBF parameters. However, the

4.3 Principal Component Analysis

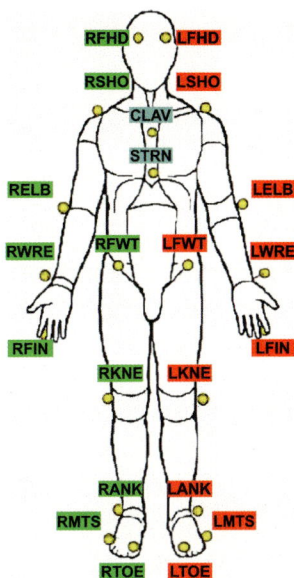

Fig. 4.1 Front view of the marker set used

SGPLVM technique requires some tuning and optimizations for its use in real-time motion synthesis based on large motion capture databases.

To summarize, the works discussed above suffer from a number of limitations, such as a poor capacity of motion extrapolation. To alleviate this problem, the input motions have to be separated into clusters, according to their parameters. Hence, the motion interpolation and extrapolation are precisely performed on those separated clusters, with intuitive and quantitative high-level parameters, like locomotion speed. Another limitation of the previous work concerns the motion adaptation to any kind of virtual character. In the next section, we describe a framework allowing the production of generic locomotion animations, applicable for various character sizes [GBT04].

4.3 Principal Component Analysis

4.3.1 Motion Capture Data Process

In this section, we propose a PCA space built from angular input data, where modifying a parameter does not influence other motion characteristics. We first describe the acquisition process of motion data and then the creation of a reduced dimension space composed of these data.

As a practical example, our method is explained here using a popular commercial optical motion capture system[1] with a set of 37 markers, illustrated in Fig. 4.1.

---

[1] Vicon Motion Systems. www.vicon.com, 2004.

Regarding the convention of skeleton modeling, we use the H-ANIM standard[2] that defines common default joint orientations and a flexible topology for the hierarchical structure (any subset respecting the parent–child relation is valid). The mapping of marker positions to joint angles is achieved by applying the method described in [MBT99].

4.3.2 Full-Cycle Model

In this section, we introduce our full-cycle model allowing efficient generation of a whole locomotion sequence only at each high-level parameter update. To illustrate our methodology, we use two examples of locomotion: walking and running.

Input Data

To create a motion database, we used a Vicon™ optical motion capture system and a treadmill to record five subjects differing in age and gender (two women and three men). The physical parameter speed of the various sequences varies from 3.0 km/h to 7.0 km/h, by increments of 0.5 km/h, in the case of walking, and from 6.0 km/h to 12.0 km/h, by increments of 1.0 km/h, for running. The sequences were then segmented into cycles (one cycle includes two steps, starting at right heel strike), and four of them have been selected.

These cycles are aligned to an identical locomotion direction, converted to joint angle space (represented by exponential maps) and finally normalized, so that each sequence is represented by the same number of samples. In addition, a standing (neutral) position sequence of each subject has been inserted to represent the speed value 0 km/h. Consequently, the database is composed of 180 walking cycles and 140 running cycles.

Main PCA

In practice, a person's posture, or body pose, can be defined by the position and orientation of a root node and a vector of joint angles. A motion can then be represented by an angular motion vector θ, which is a set of such joint angle vectors measured at regularly sampled intervals.

As computing the entire locomotion sequence is time consuming, the PCA technique is applied, drastically reducing the dimension of the input motion capture data space. The resulting space, referred to as the main PCA, is computed with the input motion matrix M composed of all motion vectors θ from our database with

---

[2]H-ANIM. Humanoid Animation Working Group. www.hanim.org.

4.3 Principal Component Analysis

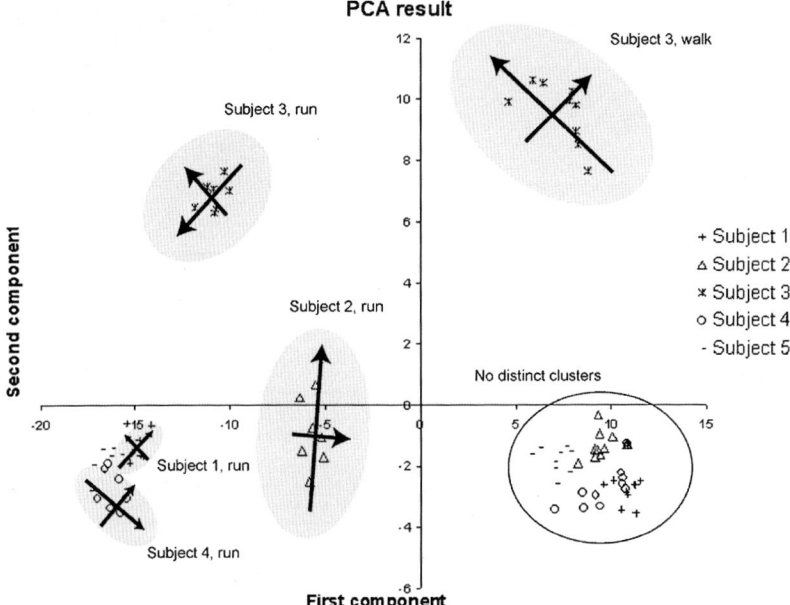

Fig. 4.2 The motion database in the first two PCs of the main PCA

k subjects. To center this space with respect to the whole dataset, we define θ_0 as an average vector of all n motion vectors. The basis vectors describing this space are the m first orthogonal PCs (Principal Components) necessary to compute an approximation of the original data. Letting $\alpha = (\alpha_1, \alpha_2, \ldots, \alpha_m)$ be a coefficient vector and $E = (e_1, e_2, \ldots, e_m)$ a vector matrix of the first PCs (or eigenvectors) of M, a motion θ can be expressed as

$$\theta \cong \theta_0 + \sum_{i=1}^{m} \alpha_i e_i = \theta_0 + \alpha E \quad (4.1)$$

Figure 4.2 depicts the first two α_i components of the original walking, running and standing motions. Note that each point represents the mean motion of the four cycles for a captured speed. This representation is used for all other graphs presented in this section.

As mentioned, the purpose of this PCA is to reduce the dimensionality of the input data. To generate a new and entire motion, a blending technique could be applied on various α, according to three high-level parameters: personification vector p, where p_i is the weight for subject I, type of locomotion T (walk or run), and speed S. The fact that original data are mostly nonlinear (exponential map) is not a problem in practice as the limb movements occur mostly within the sagittal plane (i.e., with 1D rotations), therefore allowing linear interpolation. However, blending is not appropriate for motion extrapolation. The next subsection examines how to address this issue.

Fig. 4.3 Polynomial/RBF extrapolation (*yellow*) and our method (*blue*)

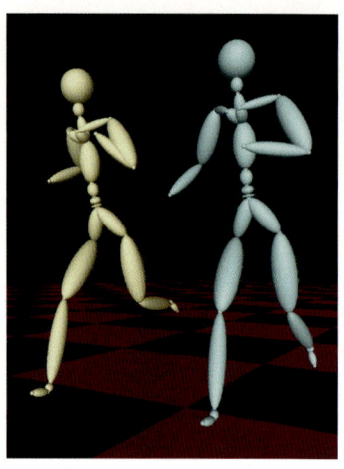

4.3.3 Motion Extrapolation

Here, we present a hierarchical structure of PCA spaces allowing extrapolation in an efficient way for the generation of full-cycle-based locomotion.

Many works [SRC01] use RBF to perform multidimensional scattered data interpolation. Weights of the example motions for a given parameter vector are computed via a polynomial and RBF functions. RBF functions ensure that for a given parameter vector corresponding to an example motion, the method effectively returns the example motion. The polynomial functions allow motion extrapolation, and are based on a linear least-squares method.

However, this method presents a negative aspect: all motions are implied in the computation of a new locomotion. Actually, even if the user desired to blend only a selected group of example motions, no example motion gets a zero weight, which costs computation time. Moreover, the extrapolation of the speed parameter for an existing subject with a locomotion type produces undesired results, due to the influence of other subjects' examples. Figure 4.3 illustrates limitations of the extrapolation, by comparing the method of [RCB98] and ours, for a running posture at 16 km/h. Note the difference at the elbows.

Concretely, our method treats the speed extrapolation individually for each subject and for each type of locomotion. Thus, all example motions α_i have to be treated by group of similarities (subject, type of locomotion) and then linear least squares can be applied to get the corresponding coefficient vector α for a given speed S. Here we describe a hierarchical structure of PCA spaces that first helps to classify the motions, and second allows a linear least squares in a very low dimension, instead of in the main PCA space.

4.3 Principal Component Analysis

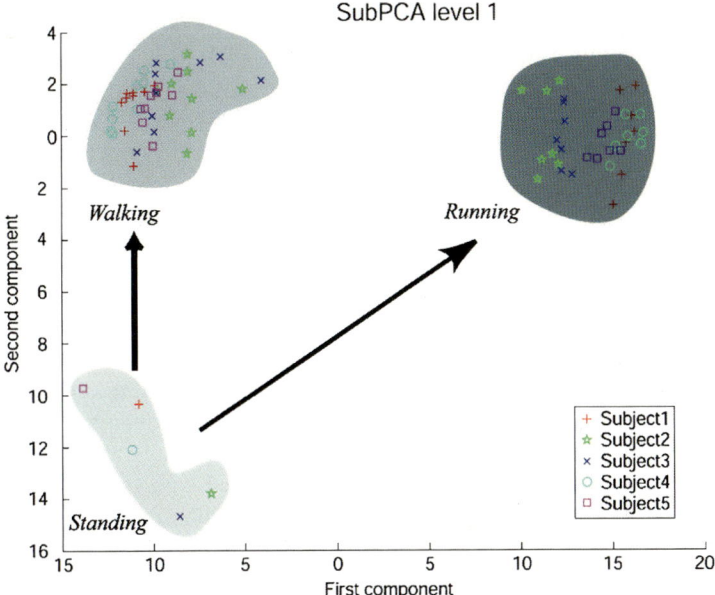

Fig. 4.4 The first two values of the β's for all subjects in the sub-PCA level 1

Second PCA Level (Sub-PCA Level 1)

The main PCA, as Fig. 4.2 depicts, shows relatively compact clusters related to subjects and type of locomotion. Therefore, simple clustering methods like k-means can be applied to separate the different subjects. These coefficient vectors α, computed in the main PCA and grouped by subject, are used to apply a second PCA algorithm step, leading to new PCA spaces, called sub-PCA level 1. Therefore, a coefficient vector α relative to a specific subject v can be decomposed following the formula in Eq. (4.1), leading to

$$\alpha \cong \alpha_0 + \sum_{i=1}^{b} \beta_i f_i = \alpha_0 + \beta F_v \quad (4.2)$$

where $\beta = (\beta_1, \beta_2, \ldots, \beta_b)$ represents the new coefficient vector and $F_v = (f_1, f_2, \ldots, f_b)$ the b first eigenvectors of the new basis F_v, with b being smaller than the number of sequences for this subject. The vector α_0 represents the average of all coefficient vectors α for a subject v. By plotting the first two coefficient values of all β relative to a subject v in F_v, three distinct clusters clearly emerge, one for each locomotion type. As Fig. 4.4 depicts, for all subjects (they do not have the same PCA space), the first PC separates data from walking and running, while the standing posture is more considered a special case of walking. Here a visualization in the first two PCs is sufficient, as their eigenvalues explain the most significant variation between the β.

These sub-PCA level 1 spaces are well-suited to extract the high-level parameter T. The standing posture is integrated in both types of locomotion in order to give a lower bound (where the speed is null) for the generation of new motion. Here, interpolation based on blending techniques can be performed on both types of locomotion, for a subject v.

Third PCA Level (Sub-PCA Level 2)

Again, a PCA algorithm is applied on the coefficient vector â of a subject v, now relative to a type of locomotion, leading to a new space, called sub-PCAs level 2. For every type of locomotion, two sub-PCAs level 2 are needed in order to avoid giving too much importance to the neutral posture. Indeed, as illustrated in Fig. 4.4, the distance between this neutral posture and the walking (or running) cluster is proportionally much bigger than the distance between the various walking (or running) motions. Therefore, a first sub-PCA space is computed with coefficient vectors β relative to the standing motions and to a motion type with minimal speed value (in this case PCA is similar to linear interpolation), and a second sub-PCA space with coefficient vectors β relative to all motions of the same locomotion type. Thus, a walking motion β belonging to the second subspace is defined as follows:

$$\beta \cong \beta_0 + \sum_{i=1}^{t} \gamma_i g_i = \beta_0 + \gamma G \qquad (4.3)$$

where $\gamma = (\gamma_1, \gamma_2, \ldots, \gamma_c)$ is the new coefficient vector and $G = (g_1, g_2, \ldots, g_c)$ the c first eigenvectors of the new basis G. The vector γ_0 represents the average of all coefficient vectors γ for a specific subject with a certain type of locomotion.

This third hierarchy level allows one to determine a relationship between a coefficient vector ã and its corresponding speed value. Comparing the coefficient vector values and their corresponding speed values, as shown in Fig. 4.5 for walking motions and Fig. 4.6 for running, a linear relation can be observed.

A linear least-squares fit is performed on the coupled coefficient vector and speed value S. We want to find a linear approximation function $A(S) = \gamma = aS + b$ by minimizing the sum of the square distances between the effective coefficient values γ_i and the approximated coefficient values $\hat{\gamma}_i$, for a given speed. Equation (4.4) describes this fitting for the p PC over w distinct motions, differing in speed values:

$$\min \sum_{i=1}^{w} (\gamma_{pi} - \hat{\gamma}_{pi}) = \min \sum_{i=1}^{c} (\gamma_{pi} - a_p S_i - b_p)^2 \qquad (4.4)$$

Thus, a function $A(S)$ is attached to every sub-PCA level 2, allowing one to generate a coefficient vector γ with speed values S inside and outside the domain of input data. Figure 4.7 illustrates the result of fitting the data of a subject for walking and running motions having speed values starting at the captured minimal speed data (walking 3.0 km/h, running 6.0 km/h). Due to the previous successively applied PCA algorithms, the computation of Eq. (4.4) is performed in a single dimension, leading to vector a of one dimension.

4.4 Walking Model

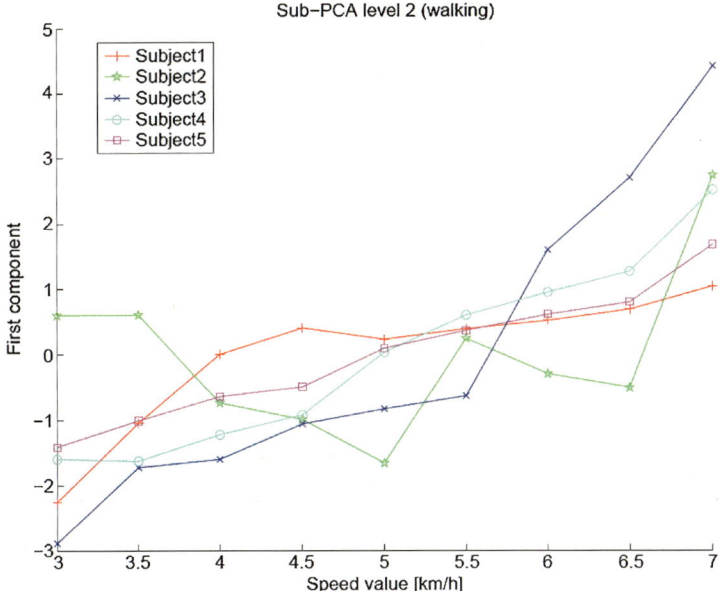

Fig. 4.5 Speed and the first coefficient vectors γ for all subjects (walking case)

4.4 Walking Model

Our walking engine is driven by two high-level parameters: speed and human size. First, interpolation and extrapolation are achieved in the PCA spaces of each subject to generate a motion according to a speed value. Second, a timewarping method allows one to handle the human height parameter.

4.4.1 Motion Interpolation and Extrapolation

As the walking motions that compose a PCA space differ only at the speed parameter level, its PCs tend to express the most variance between slow and fast motions. Therefore, a relationship between a coefficient vector α and its corresponding speed value is determined in order to allow motion interpolation and extrapolation.

First the number m of PCs that significantly influence the motion is specified by taking the first PCs representing 80% of the motion information. Indeed, as Fig. 4.8 illustrates, the contribution of the PCs beyond this percentage value is small compared to the first m, and probably does not provide a relevant relation to speed values. Moreover, this percentage represents an important dimension reduction factor of the space, appropriated for our real-time specifics.

Then, the various captured speed values are compared to their corresponding coefficient vectors α, for each dimension of the PCA space. The resulting graphs,

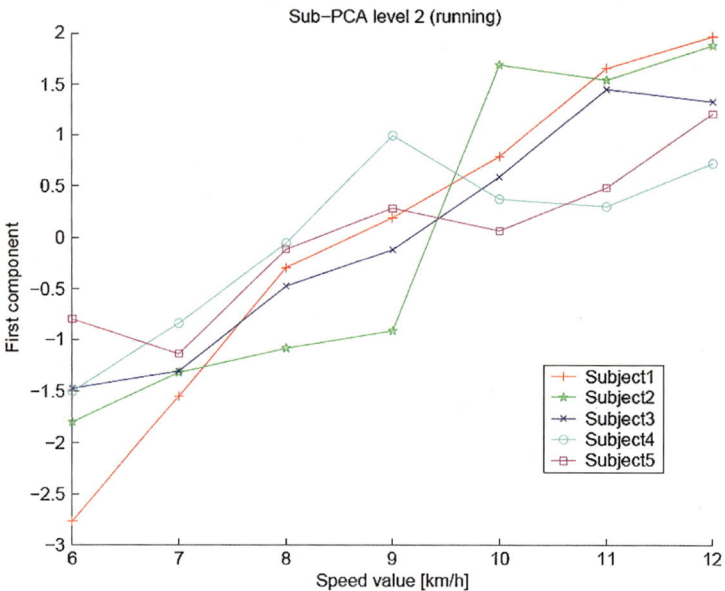

Fig. 4.6 Speed and the first coefficient vectors γ for all subjects (running case)

depicted in Figs. 4.9 and 4.10, clearly show a linear relationship between motions having speed values greater than zero, whereas the standing posture cancels this linearity. The fitting of a polynomial curve to these motions is unfortunately unadapted in practice, especially for motion extrapolation. Hence, two linear functions are constructed and attached to each dimension.

The first function is a linear least-squares fit performed on the pairs of coefficient vectors α and their corresponding speed values S, excluding the speed value zero. Thus, for a given iPC, a linear approximation function $A_i(S)$ can be $A_i = m_i S + b_i$ over the j increasing speed values is computed by minimizing the sum of the square distances between the actual coefficient values α_{ij} and the approximated coefficient value d_{ij}, as follows:

$$\sum_{j=1}^{nbS}(\alpha_{ij} - d_{ij})^2 = \sum_{j=1}^{nbS}(\alpha_{ij} - m_i S_i - b_i)^2 \tag{4.5}$$

where nbS is the number of speed values. The second function is a simple linear interpolation between the coefficient vector at null speed value α_{ij} and the function A_i evaluated at the minimal captured speed value ($j = 2$). Figure 4.11 illustrates the result of the two fitting functions on a subject.

Therefore, applying the two described approximation functions, it is now possible not only to interpolate, but also to extrapolate walking motions for a given speed value. Actually, these functions return a coefficient vector α that has to be inserted into Eq. (4.1) to compute the new generated walking motion.

4.5 Motion Retargeting and Timewarping

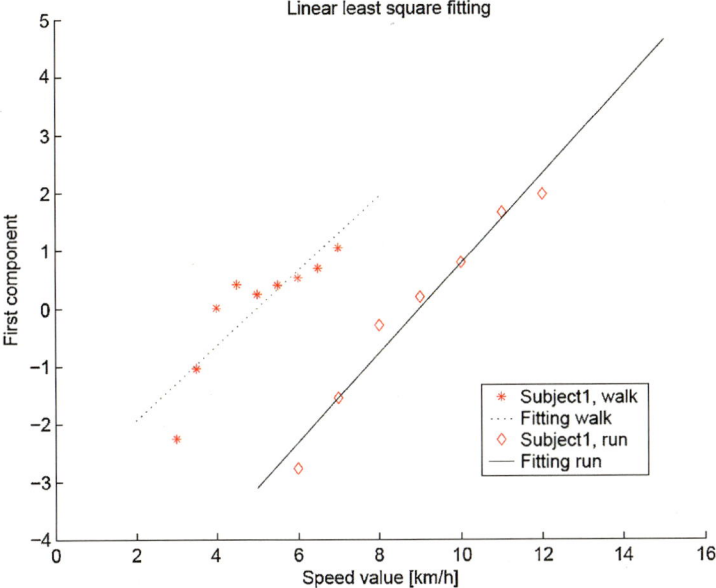

Fig. 4.7 Fitting of the coefficient from sub-PCA level 2 (walking and running, one subject)

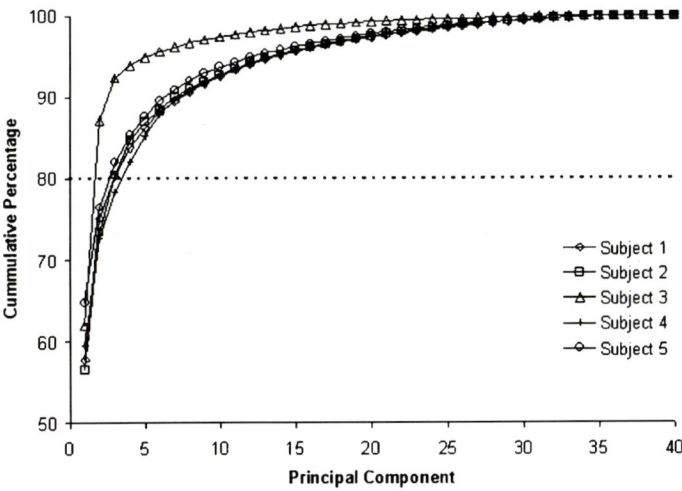

Fig. 4.8 The cumulative percentage of the PCs for the five subjects of our database

4.5 Motion Retargeting and Timewarping

This section explains how the data are retargeted to different human sizes from those captured, and presents a process, based on motion analysis, to unwarp the normalized data.

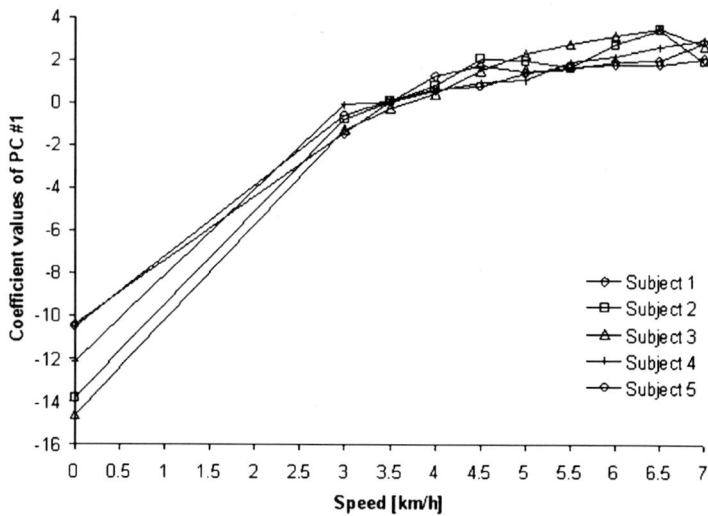

Fig. 4.9 Comparison between the speed values and the coefficient values of the first PC, for five subjects

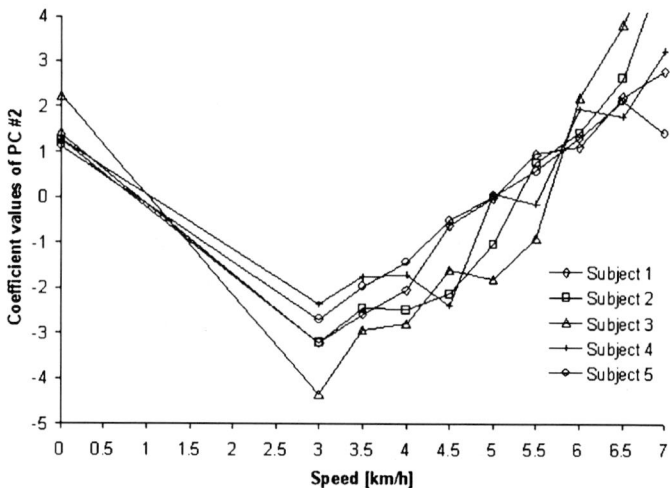

Fig. 4.10 Comparison between the speed values and the coefficient values of the second PC, for five subjects

To produce animation adaptable to any kind of virtual humans, the generalization of the heterogeneous input data we used is an important aspect. Indeed, we captured various subjects, not only with differences in the style of motion, but also, and more importantly, differences in size.

First, all 3D positions (i.e., the humanoid root joint) of the motion vectors è are divided by the leg length of the captured subject. Murray [Mur67] has shown that

4.5 Motion Retargeting and Timewarping

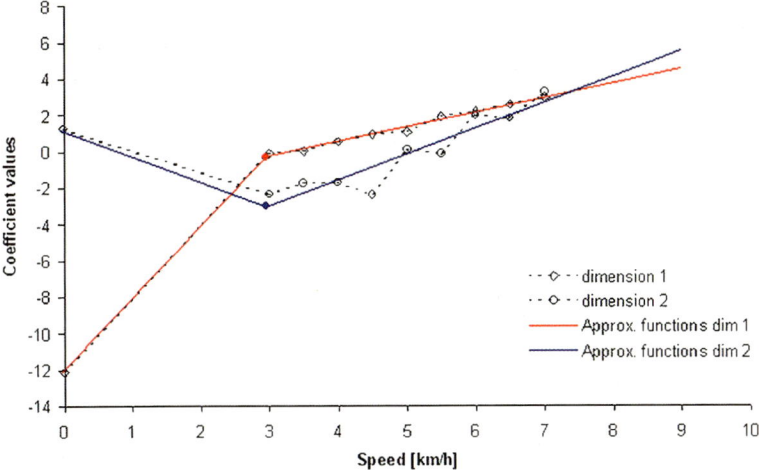

Fig. 4.11 The approximation functions (linear interpolation and A_i) relative to the first two PCs

all the leg flexion-extension angles in the sagittal plane (hip, knee, ankle) show very similar trajectories for all adult men for the same value of *normalized speed V*, obtained by dividing the walking velocity v (in m/s) by the hip joint height H (i.e., the leg length in meters). We generalize this statement to the running motion too.

Every input locomotion sequence and also each generated sequence contains a fixed number of frames, due to the normalization step performed during preprocessing. The induced timewarp is handled using a walking cycle frequency function f that links the given normalized speed V to the cycle frequency f, called the Inman law [IRT81]. We adapted this law to our observations, performed on a treadmill, and extended it to the case of running motion. We fit the data to an approximation function of the form axb, similar to the Inman law. Figure 4.12 illustrates the evolution of the frequencies with respect to normalized speed, for five subjects captured during walking and running motion. The resulting frequency functions are described by the equation

$$f(V) = 0.85 V^{0.4} \tag{4.6}$$

for walking motions, and by the equation:

$$f(V) = 1.07 V^{0.24} \tag{4.7}$$

for running motions.

Therefore, the animation engine is able to continuously vary the speed and compute the phase φ update as in the walking engine in [BTM90, BUT04], where the phase varies between $[0 \ldots 1]$ and the phase update is computed with the equation

$$\Delta \varphi = \Delta t f(V) \tag{4.8}$$

where Δt is the elapsed time between two posture updates and V the normalized speed. The phase φ multiplied by the number of frames in the normalized sequences returns the frame to display.

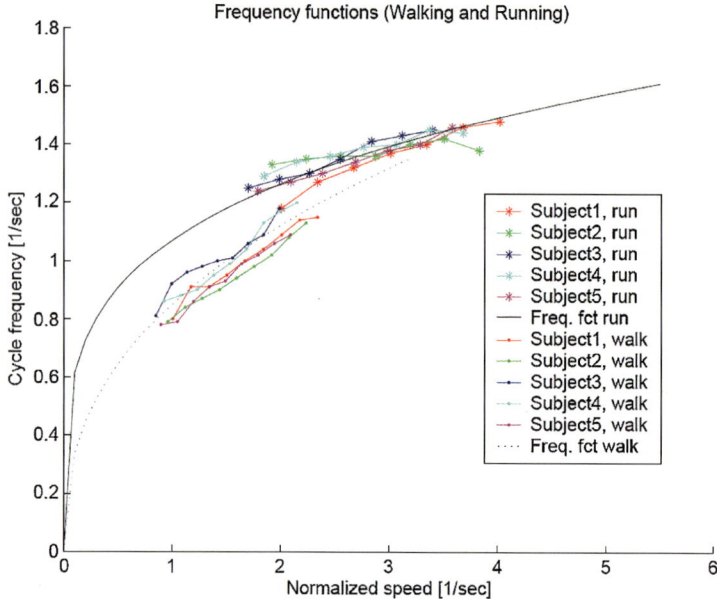

Fig. 4.12 Approximation of frequency functions for walking and running

4.6 Motion Generation

The goal of our full-cycle method is to allow the end-user to set some high-level parameters: a personification vector p composed of weights assigned to each subject, the type of locomotion T, the speed S, and the human size (i.e., the leg size H).

After the preprocessing work, consisting in the construction of all hierarchical PCA spaces, the input data are structured as follows. First the main PCA space is computed with the motion database M. Second, n sub-PCA spaces level 1 are formed for the n subjects expressed in the first PCA space. Finally, for each type of locomotion in the n subspaces, two new PCA level 2 subspaces are created, one containing the standing posture, and the other with motions captured at various speeds. Figure 4.13 illustrates this structure. This hierarchical data structure helps us to generate new motion according to the three high-level (or end-user) parameters: S, T, and p. This process is explained in the next subsections.

4.6.1 Speed Control

We start with the lowest level of our hierarchy, namely, sub-PCA level 2 spaces where a function $A(S)$ maps speed S onto coefficient vectors γ, allowing extrapolation. For each subject, the sub-PCA level 2 spaces including the S value return a coefficient vector β. In our case, two vectors β, one for walking and one for running, characterize each subject for the same (normalized) speed.

4.6 Motion Generation

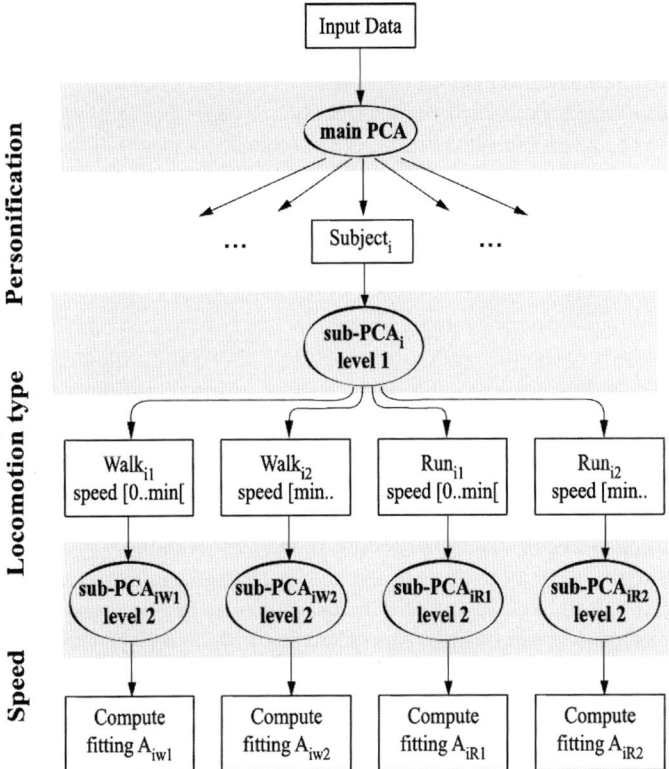

Fig. 4.13 Diagram of the hierarchical structure of the PCA spaces

4.6.2 Type of Locomotion Control

After setting the speed S, the type of locomotion parameter T has to be taken into account. This parameter varies from 0 (pure walking type) to 1 (pure running type), allowing the end-user to generate hybrid motion between walking and running. For each subject, a linear interpolation between both coefficient vectors β (computed in child PCA level) is performed, with respect to the parameter T. This interpolation is possible because both vectors are expressed in the same sub-PCA level 1 space. Then, this vector is computed in the main PCA space, to get a coefficient vector α that corresponds to a specific speed and type of locomotion for a given subject.

4.6.3 Personification Control

The last high-level parameter, the personification vector p, lets the user assign weights to the various input subjects, to produce a new generated motion with different style characteristics. For this purpose, the subject's coefficient vectors α are interpolated with normalized weights p_i and the motion vector θ can finally be computed. In addition, the translation of root joint is scaled according to the leg size, and is added to a global horizontal translation.

This motion generation scheme clearly encompasses motions that are only concerned with the given high-level parameters. Indeed, for a $p_i = 0$, its corresponding subject is ignored by the computation process.

4.6.4 Motion Transition

The transition between different motions is an important problem in computer animation. We do not need to capture motion transition as presented in [PhKS03]. In our case, the difficulty has been solved as follows: the basic idea is to perform a transition between two motions having a different type of locomotion, but the same speed, as our hierarchical PCA structure operates. Moreover, as the motions are normalized, cut into cycles and have similarities in postures (family of cyclic locomotion), we ensure that, at a specific frame i for walking, the nearest frame is also i for running. Therefore, it is possible to perform seamless transitions between different types of locomotion, where the user gives a specific transition duration in seconds. Additionally we linearly interpolate the walking and the running frequency, according to the T variable.

In practice, any change in a high-level parameter leads to a recomputation, as described above. To optimize this process, the interpolation parameter relative to each high-level parameter are combined in the lowest PCA level, whose dimension is strongly reduced compared with other spaces. Then, for upper levels, only additions between data are needed, eliminating the multiplication of interpolation parameters. Moreover, if one of the interpolation parameters is null, no addition is made, improving the performance when many weights p_i are null.

4.6.5 Results

We apply our hierarchical PCA method to our walking and running motion database. The sequences have been recorded at 120 Hz and normalized to 100 frames containing animations of 78 DOFs. The total size of the database is 25 MB. The first PCA is composed of the first 10 PCs (from over 380 PCs, coming from the 17 different motions in four examples, for the five subjects) representing 97% of all the information data. Next, each subject determines a sub-PCA level 1, with the first two PCs, representing on average 95% of the data information. Finally, sub-PCAs level 2 are computed, leading to a space of one dimension, as summarized in Table 4.1. The resulting size of data required to recompute a motion is 1 MB, therefore compressed with a factor of 25. Additionally, the approximation functions that fit normalized speed to coefficients of the sub-PCA level 2 spaces are computed, as well as the frequency functions for walking and running. All the operations described above are

4.6 Motion Generation

Table 4.1 Dimension of the PCAs

PCAs Name	#PCs	Data%	Reduction Factor
Main PCA	10	97%	38
Sub-PCAs level 1	2	95%	5
Sub-PCAs level 2	1	95%	2

computed in a preprocessing phase. In the execution phase, a human skeleton based on the H-ANIM hierarchy is animated according to the high-level parameter values, which the user can change in real time: the different weights for personification, speed, type of locomotion, and leg length.

Extrapolation and interpolation of walking motion can be performed from 0 km/h up to 15 km/h, as shown in Fig. 4.14(right). Beyond this value, undesired behavior occurs at the skeleton level, especially when the arms reach the head level. Another effect is that the double support phase is no longer ensured. Running motions can be generated with speed from 0 km/h until 20 km/h, illustrated in Fig. 4.14(left). Beyond this value, other effects occur, which are different from those met in the case of walking. Indeed, the feet are sliding on the floor, although it is difficult for the human eye to catch this effect at such speed values. But this problem can be solved by introducing constraints at the feet joints.

Transitions between walking and running (and inversely) are smooth, changing the dynamics of the movements and the arms trajectories, which are higher in running. Personification is less easy to exploit, as we only captured natural walking motions and not exaggerated ones such as lazy, happy, or impulsive.

Personification can be obtained by mixing the different weights associated with the captured subjects. The new stylized motion is preserved over the speed range and locomotion type because the hierarchical PCA structure decouples speed, type of locomotion, and style control along mutually orthogonal dimensions.

In terms of performance, 13 seconds is necessary for the preprocessing phase. During the animation using the described data (i.e., 360 cycles composed of 100 frames), the updating for the generation of a new motion is interactive, with a computation time within 1.5 ms on a CPU 1.8 GHz machine. As our full-cycle method computes the entire cycle at each update, one frame is updated in 15 ms. If the

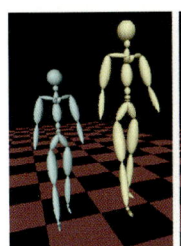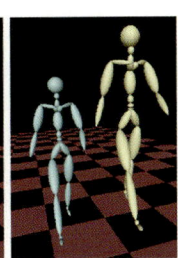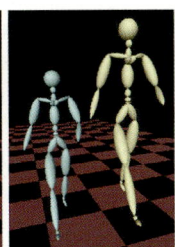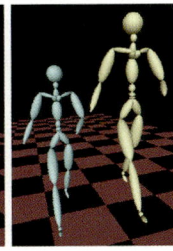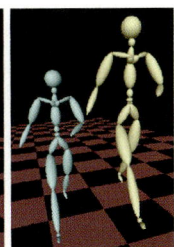

Fig. 4.14 Postures at identical moment in the walk cycle, with two different skeleton sizes. From left to right: 2.0, 4.0, 6.0, 8.0, and 10.0 km/h

Table 4.2 PCA space information for each subject

Subject ID	#PCSs for 80% of Whole Data	Reduction Factor
1	3	13
2	3	13
3	2	20
4	4	10
5	3	13

weight vector is set for one subject only, the update per cycle decreases to 1.3 ms. We tested our method with sparse data on two subjects each having three walking and two running motions (i.e., 40 cycles). The input data being very low, the update time is 0.7 ms. These values are similar to other existing methods based on frame-by-frame generation.

Scaling the human size directly influences the cycle frequency in order to preserve motion properties. In the case of two humans of different heights, the smaller one walks with a higher frequency for an identical motion speed.

This engine allows generating locomotion cycles, parametrized by a few user-defined values as shown in Table 4.2:

1. Speed: the speed at which the human moves,
2. Style: a value between 0 and 1, 0 being a walk motion, 1 being a run motion,
3. Personification: a weight to blend between the five different locomotion styles of five different motion captured people.

Note that when such a engine is fully integrated into a crowd framework, it is possible to generate many different locomotion cycles by simply varying the above parameters, thus making each individual unique. This engine has been extended for handling curved walking [GBT06b] and dynamic obstacle avoidance [GBT06a].

4.7 Animation Variety

We have used the PCA locomotion engine described in the previous section to generate over 100 different locomotion cycles per human template exploited in the crowd. For each of them, we sample walk cycles at speeds varying from 0.5 m/s up to 2 m/s and similarly for the run cycles between 1.5 m/s and 3 m/s. Each human template is also assigned a particular personification weight so that it has its own style. With such a high number of animations, we are already able to perceive a sense of variety in the way the crowd is moving. Virtual humans walking together with different locomotion styles and speeds add to the realism of the simulation. Once provided with a large set of animation clips, the issue becomes to store and use them in an efficient way. Chapter 7 presents details as to how the whole data are managed.

Fig. 4.15 Examples of accessory movements (hand in the pocket, phone call, hand on hip)

4.7.1 Accessory Movements

Variety in movement is one necessary condition for achieving believable synthetic crowds as individuals are seldom unrolling the sole locomotion cycle while moving from one place to another. The upper limb movements not being compulsory in locomotion, hands are most of the time exploited for accessory activities such as holding an object (cell phone, bag, umbrella, etc.) or are simply protected by remaining in the pocket of some clothing (see Fig. 4.15). These activities constitute alternate coordinated movements that have to match the continuously changing constraints issued from the primary locomotion movement. Indeed, constantly reusing the same arm posture through the locomotion cycle leads to a loss of a believability; for example, a hand "in the pocket" should follow the pelvis forward–backward movement when large steps are performed. For these reasons, a specific animation cycle has to be defined also for an accessory movement that is to be exploited with locomotion.

We achieve the accessory movement design stage after the design of the individual locomotion cycles for a set of discretized speeds. We exploit a Prioritized Inverse Kinematics solver that allows combining various constraints with a priority level if necessary. The required input is:

1. The set of locomotion cycles,
2. One "first guess" posture of the hand and arm, possibly with the clavicle, designed with the skinned target character,
3. The set of "effector" points to be constrained on the hand or arm (see Fig. 4.16, the three colored cubes on the hand),
4. For each effector, its corresponding target goal location expressed in other local frames of the body; for example, relative to the head for a cell-phone conversation, or to the pelvis and thigh for a hand in a trousers' pocket (see Fig. 4.16, the three corresponding colored cubes attached to the pelvis),
5. If an effector is more important than the others, the user can associate it with a greater priority level. Our solver ensures that the achievement of other effectors' goals does not perturb the high-priority one [BB04].

Fig. 4.16 Set of controlled effectors attached to the hand (*A*) and corresponding goal positions attached to the pelvis (*B*)

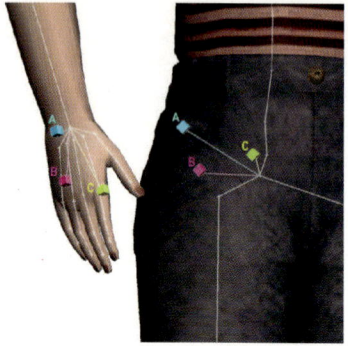

All the additional elements to the original locomotion cycles can be specified by an animator by locating them on the target character mesh in a standard animation software. The resulting set of parameters can be saved in a configuration file for the second stage of running the Inverse Kinematics adjustment of the posture for all frames of the locomotion cycles (Fig. 4.17). The resulting accessorized locomotion cycles are saved in files for a further storage optimization stage described in Chap. 7. Figure 4.18 shows successive postures from such a movement.

4.8 Steering

4.8.1 The Need for a Fast Trajectory Control

Steering is the capacity to alter the linear and angular speed over time to achieve various types of trajectory control (e.g., seek, avoid, group movements, etc.). This is an essential function for the management of displacements in complex environments. A prior theoretical work has demonstrated that the shortest path to an oriented goal

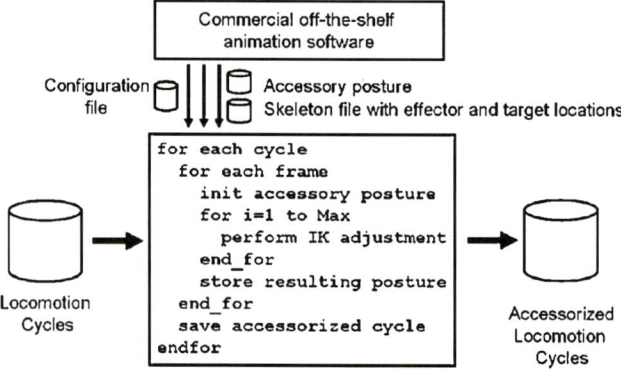

Fig. 4.17 Overview of the two-stage process for producing accessorized locomotion cycles

4.8 Steering

Fig. 4.18 Example of posture from an accessorized locomotion cycle

is made out of linear segments and angular arcs [Dub57]. However, such an approach leads to discontinuities in curvature that are not acceptable for human locomotion trajectories. Other approaches have exploited Bezier curves [MT01, PLS03] or more elaborated continuous trajectories [LL01, FS04]. However, this comes with a significant cost that precludes their application to a significant number of moving entities. On the other hand, alternate approaches rely on an instantaneous update of the linear and angular speeds without evaluating the trajectory up to the goal. For example, the major steering behaviors of generic mobile entities have been described in detail by Reynolds [Rey99] in a general game context. Some other studies have focused on specific applications with mobile robots [AOM03], exploited potential fields [HM95, BJ03, MH04], or relied on precomputed data [Bou05b, Bou05a] or trajectory segments in [GTK06]. More elaborate planning approaches exist (e.g., [CK04, GBT06a]) but they are not compatible with the low computing cost requirement addressed in this section. We now recall the seek behavior and how it can be extended to achieve a desired orientation at the goal location (funneling control).

4.8.2 The Seek and Funneling Controllers

The seek controller simply ensures reaching a desired target position without a prescribed orientation at that position (Fig. 4.19(left)). One way to proceed is to progressively cancel the angle α made between the forward direction and the radial direction that points to the target. In other words, the radial direction can be considered as the heading direction for the seek controller. Our control scheme differs from [Rey99] in the sense that we only allow bounded accelerations and speeds. The two PD controllers exploited in the seek mode are:

1. The *angular speed controller* drives the scalar angular acceleration aiming to align the forward direction with the heading direction (Fig. 4.19(right)). The acceleration is proportional to the direction error α; a damping term smoothens high-frequency variations.
2. The *forward speed controller* has an implicit lower priority compared with the angular control; it controls the scalar forward acceleration aiming to achieve the

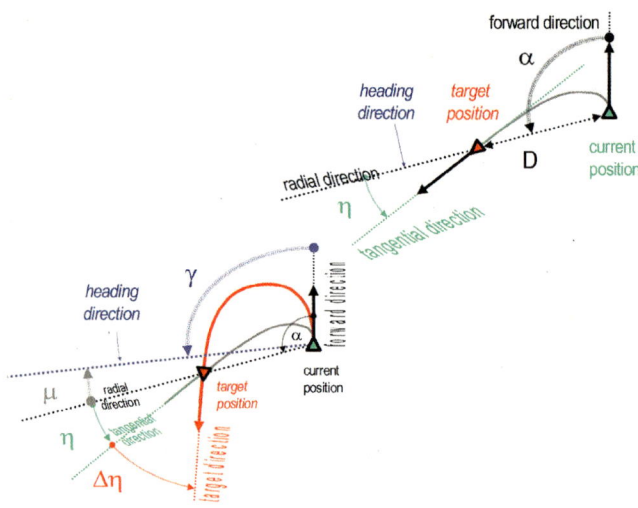

Fig. 4.19 The radial-tangential seek angle α is the angle made by the seek trajectory with the radial direction at the target position

Fig. 4.20 Funneling control of 42 mobile entities that have all started simultaneously on the left side with the same initial linear speed (no collision management). The relative position and orientation of the *lower left* goal leads to a different type of access trajectory

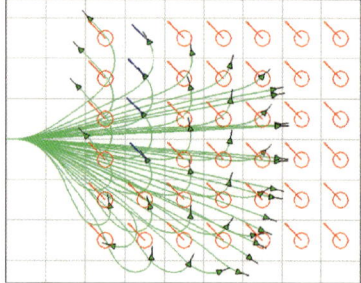

relaxed desired forward speed compatible with a given maximum normal acceleration [Bou05a].

In the seek mode, when the mobile entity reaches the target, one can easily observe the angle η made by the tangent at the target with the initial radial direction (Fig. 4.19(left)). This angle is called the *tangential-radial angle*. The main characteristic of the funneling controller is to *modulate* the heading direction so that a desired final orientation is achieved at the target position (Fig. 4.19(right)). The modulation is a function of the angular difference $\Delta\eta$ between the *desired* direction and the *tangential* direction that would be obtained with the simple seek controller. Each update of the control requests only to estimate the η angle and to derive the heading direction modulation μ (Fig. 4.19(right)). This makes the method extremely fast and flexible if the angle η is precomputed for a sufficiently dense sampling of goal positions in the mobile entity coordinate system. For example, [Bou05b] evaluates this angle for goals expressed in polar coordinates (10 distances D × 10 angles α per side hemisphere) and for a reasonable sampling of the current speed (9 angular speeds × 8 linear speeds) and the desired linear speed (6 levels). Altogether 43,200 η angles are stored in a 5-entry table noted $T\eta$ for a storage cost of 0.5 MB. A *reachability* Boolean is also stored in the same table to characterize the difficulty of reaching each goal.

The funneling control exploiting such a table $T\eta$ is detailed in [Bou05b]. One control update cost is reasonably low with 12 ms on average on a Pentium IV, even for a moving goal. The resulting trajectories have a coherent curvature behavior in the neighborhood of the goal as opposed to Bezier curves where the curvature increases when the distance increases (while keeping the same tangent lengths) [Bou05a]. Figure 4.20 illustrates the trajectories obtained for 42 mobile entities starting from the same point on the left side and that have to walk through individual oriented targets with a desired linear speed. Each target can have a different position tolerance (red circle) and orientation tolerance (small triangle). The trajectories are smooth and display a plausible local curvature near the goal.

4.9 Final Remarks

This chapter provided discussions concerning methods for animation of virtual humans in the contexts of crowds. In order to deal correctly with crowd animation, we should analyze it in the perspective of human animation and locomotion. Several methods have been discussed in order to propose solutions to this important challenge.

References

[ACP02] ALLEN B., CURLESS B., POPOVIC Z.: Articulated body deformation from range scan data. *ACM Transactions on Graphics 21*, 3 (2002), 612–619.

[AFO03] ARIKAN O., FORSYTH D., O'BRIEN J.: Motion synthesis from annotations. In *Proceedings of ACM SIGGRAPH* (2003), pp. 402–408.

[AM00] ALEXA M., MUELLER W.: Representing animations by principal components. In *Proceedings of EG Eurographics* (2000), pp. 411–426.

[AOM03] AMOR H. B., OBST O., MURRAY J.: *Fast, Neat and Under Control: Inverse Steering Behaviors for Physical Autonomous Agents*. Research report, Institut für Informatik, Universität Koblenz-Landau, 2003.

[BB04] BAERLOCHER P., BOULIC R.: An inverse kinematic architecture enforcing an arbitrary number of strict priority levels. *The Visual Computer 6*, 20 (2004), 402–417.

[BC93] BRUDERLIN A., CALVERT T.: Interactive animation of personalized human locomotion. In *Proceedings of Graphics Interface* (1993), pp. 17–23.

[BC96] BRUDERLIN A., CALVERT T.: Knowledge-driven, interactive animation of human running. In *Graphics Interface'96* (1996), pp. 213–221.

[BH00] BRAND M., HERTZMANN A.: Style machines. In *Proceedings of ACM SIGGRAPH* (2000), pp. 183–192.

[BJ03] BROGAN D. C., JOHNSON N. L.: Realistic human walking paths. In *Proceedings of Computer Animation and Social Agents 2003* (2003), IEEE Computer Society, Los Alamitos, pp. 94–101.

[Bou05a] BOULIC R.: Proactive steering toward oriented targets. In *Proc. of EG Eurographics'05* (2005).
[Bou05b] BOULIC R.: Reaching oriented targets with funnelling trajectories. In *Proc. of V-CROWDS'05* (2005).
[BT92] BOULIC R., THALMANN D.: Combined direct and inverse kinematic control for articulated figure motion editing. *Computer Graphics Forum 2*, 4 (1992), 189–202.
[BTM90] BOULIC R., THALMANN D., MAGNENAT-THALMANN N.: A global human walking model with real time kinematic personification. *The Visual Computer 6*, 6 (1990), 344–358.
[BUT04] BOULIC R., ULICNY B., THALMANN D.: Versatile walk engine. *Journal of Game Development 1*, 1 (2004), 29–52.
[BW95] BRUDERLIN A., WILLIAMS L.: Motion signal processing. In *Proceedings of ACM SIGGRAPH* (1995), pp. 97–104.
[CH99] CHUNG S., HAHN J.: Animation of human walking in virtual environments. In *Proceedings of Computer Animation* (1999).
[CK04] CHESTNUTT J., KUFFNER J.: A tiered planning strategy for biped navigation. In *Proc. of IEEE Int. Conf. on Humanoid Robotics (Humanoids'04)* (2004).
[Dub57] DUBINS L.: On curves of minimal length with a constrain on average curvature and with prescribed initial and terminal positions and tangents. *American Journal of Mathematics 79*, 3 (1957), 497–516.
[EMMT04] EGGES A., MOLET T., MAGNENAT-THALMANN N.: Personalised real-time idle motion synthesis. In *Proceedings of Pacific Graphics* (2004).
[FS04] FRAICHARD T., SCHEUER A.: From Reeds and Shepp's to continuous-curvature paths. *IEEE TRA 6*, 20 (2004), 1025–1035.
[FvdPT01] FALOUTSOS P., VAN DE PANNE M., TERZOPOULOS D.: The virtual stuntman: Dynamic characters with a repertoire of autonomous motor skills. *Computers & Graphics 6*, 25 (2001), 933–953.
[GBT04] GLARDON P., BOULIC R., THALMANN D.: Pca-based walking engine using motion capture data. In *Proc. Computer Graphics International* (2004), pp. 292–298.
[GBT06a] GLARDON P., BOULIC R., THALMANN D.: Dynamic obstacle clearing for real-time character animation. *The Visual Computer 6*, 22 (2006), 399–414.
[GBT06b] GLARDON P., BOULIC R., THALMANN D.: Robust on-line adaptive footplant detection and enforcement for locomotion. *The Visual Computer 3*, 22 (2006), 194–209.
[Gir87] GIRARD M.: Interactive design of 3-d computer-animated legged animal motion. In *Proc. of ACM Symposium on Interactive 3D Graphics* (1987), pp. 131–150.
[GM85] GIRARD M., MACIEJEWSKI A.: Computational modeling for the computer animation of legged figures. In *Proc. of ACM SIGGRAPH* (1985), pp. 263–270.
[GMHP04] GROCHOW K., MARTIN S., HERTZMANN A., POPOVIC Z.: Style-based inverse kinematics. In *Proceedings of ACM SIGGRAPH* (2004).
[GR96] GUO S., ROBERGÉ J.: A high-level control mechanism for human locomotion based on parametric frame space interpolation. In *Proceedings of Eurographics Workshop on Computer Animation and Simulation 96* (1996), pp. 95–107.
[Gra98] GRASSIA F.: Practical parameterization of rotations using the exponential map. *The Journal of Graphics Tools 3*, 3 (1998), 29–48.
[GTK06] GO J., THUC V., KUFFNER J.: Autonomous behaviors for interactive vehicle animations. *Graphical Models 68*, 2 (2006), 90–112.
[HM95] HELBING D., MOLNAR P.: Social force model for pedestrian dynamics. *Physical Review E 51* (1995), 4282–4286.
[HP97] HODGINS J., POLLARD N.: Adapting simulated behaviors for new characters. In *Proceedings of ACM SIGGRAPH* (1997), pp. 153–162.
[HWBO95] HODGINS J., WOOTEN W., BROGAN D., O'BRIEN J.: Animating human athletics. In *SIGGRAPH'95: Proceedings of the 22nd Annual Conference on Computer Graphics and Interactive Techniques 29* (1995), pp. 71–78.

References

[IRT81] INMANN V., RALSTON H., TODD F.: *Human Walking*. Williams & Wilkins, Baltimore, 1981.

[KB96] KO H., BADLER N.: Animating human locomotion with inverse dynamics. *IEEE Computer Graphics and Applications 2*, 16 (1996), 50–58.

[KG03] KOVAR T., GLEICHER M.: Flexible automatic motion blending with registration curves. In *Proceedings of ACM SIGGRAPH/Eurographics Symposium on Computer Animation* (2003), pp. 214–224.

[KG04] KOVAR L., GLEICHER M.: Automated extraction and parameterization of motions in large data sets. *ACM Transactions on Graphics 23*, 3 (2004), 559–568.

[KMA05] KULPA R., MULTON F., ARNALDI B.: Morphology-independent representation of motions for interactive human-like animations. In *Proceedings of ACM SIGGRAPH* (2005).

[LL01] LAMIRAUX F., LAUMOND J.: Smooth motion planning for car-like vehicle. *IEEE TRA 4*, 17 (2001), 498–502.

[LT02] LIM I., THALMANN D.: Construction of animation models out of captured data. In *Proceedings of IEEE Conference Multimedia and Expo* (2002).

[LvdPF96] LASZLO J., VAN DE PANNE M., FIUME E.: Limit cycle control and its application to the animation of balancing and walking. In *Proceedings of ACM SIGGRAPH* (1996), pp. 153–162.

[MBT99] MOLET T., BOULIC R., THALMANN D.: Human motion capture driven by orientation measurements. *Presence 8* (1999), 187–203.

[MFCG*99] MULTON F., FRANCE L., CANI-GASCUEL M.-P., DEBUNNE G.: Computer animation of human walking: A survey. *The Journal of Visualization and Computer Animation 1*, 10 (1999), 39–54.

[MH04] METOYER R., HODGINS J.: Reactive pedestrian navigation from examples. *The Visual Computer 10*, 20 (2004), 635–649.

[MK05] MUKAI T., KURIYAMA S.: Geostatistical motion interpolation. In *Proceedings of ACM SIGGRAPH* (2005), pp. 1062–1070.

[MT01] MUSSE S. R., THALMANN D.: A hierarchical model for real time simulation of virtual human crowds. *IEEE Transactions on Visualization and Computer Graphics 7*, 2 (April–June 2001), 152–164.

[Mur67] MURRAY M. P.: Gait as a total pattern of movement. *American Journal of Physical Medicine 1*, 46 (1967), 290–333.

[PhKS03] PARK S., HOON KIM T., SHIN S. Y.: *On-line Motion Blending for Real-Time Locomotion Generation*. Technical report, Computer Science Department, KAIST, 2003.

[PL05] PETTRÉ J., LAUMOND J.-P.: A motion capture based control-space approach for walking mannequins. *Computer Animation and Virtual Worlds 1*, 16 (2005), 1–18.

[PLS03] PETTRÉ J., LAUMOND J. P., SIMÉON T.: A 2-stages locomotion planner for digital actors. In *SCA'03: Proceedings of the ACM SIGGRAPH/Eurographics Symposium on Computer Animation* (2003), pp. 258–264.

[PSS02] PARK S., SHIN H., SHIN S.: On-line locomotion generation based on motion blending. In *Proceedings of ACM SIGGRAPH/Eurographics Symposium on Computer Animation* (2002).

[RCB98] ROSE C., COHEN M., BODENHEIMER B.: Verbs and adverbs: Multidimensional motion interpolation. *IEEE Computer Graphics and Applications 5*, 18 (1998), 32–41.

[Rey99] REYNOLDS C. W.: Steering behaviors for autonomous characters. In *Game Developers Conference* (San Jose, California, USA, 1999), pp. 763–782.

[RH91] RAIBERT M. H., HODGINS J. K.: Animation of dynamic legged locomotion. In *Proceedings of ACM SIGGRAPH* (New York, NY, USA, 1991), ACM Press, New York, pp. 349–358.

[RSC01] ROSE C., SLOAN P.-P., COHEN M.: Artist-directed inverse-kinematics using radial basis function interpolation. In *Proceedings of EG Eurographics* (2001).

[SHP04] SAFONOVA A., HODGINS J., POLLARD N.: Synthesizing physically realistic human motion in low-dimensional, behavior-specific spaces. In *Proceedings of ACM SIGGRAPH* (2004).
[SM01] SUN H., METAXAS D.: Automating gait generation. In *Proceedings of ACM SIGGRAPH* (2001), pp. 213–221.
[SRC01] SLOAN P.-P. J., ROSE C. F., COHEN M. F.: Shape by example. In *Symposium on Interactive 3D Graphics* (2001), pp. 135–144.
[Tro02] TROJE N.: Decomposing biological motion: A framework for analysis and synthesis of human gait patterns. *Journal of Vision 2*, 5 (2002), 371–387.
[TYNN01] TSUMURA T., YOSHIZUKA T., NOJIRINO T., NOMA T.: T4: A motion-capture-based goal directed real-time responsive locomotion engine. In *Proceedings of Computer Animation* (2001), pp. 52–60.
[UAT95] UNUMA M., ANJYO K., TAKEUCHI R.: Fourier principles for emotion-based human figure. In *Proceedings of ACM SIGGRAPH* (1995), pp. 91–96.
[WH96] WOOTEN W., HODGINS J.: Animation of human diving. *Computer Graphics Forum 1*, 15 (1996), 3–13.
[WH97] WILEY D., HAHN J.: Interpolation synthesis of articulated figure motion. *IEEE Computer Graphics and Applications 6*, 17 (1997), 39–45.
[WH00] WOOTEN W., HODGINS J.: Simulating leaping, tumbling, landing and balancing humans. In *Proceedings of IEEE International Conference on Robotics and Automation* (2000).
[Zel82] ZELTZER D.: Motor control techniques for figure animation. *IEEE Computer Graphics and Applications 2*, 9 (1982), 53–59.
[Zel83] ZELTZER D.: Knowledge-based animation. In *ACM SIGGRAPH/SIGART, Workshop on Motion* (1983), pp. 187–192.
[ZH02] ZORDAN V., HODGINS J.: Motion capture-driven simulations that hit and react. In *Proceedings of ACM SIGGRAPH/Eurographics Symposium on Computer Animation* (2002), pp. 89–96.

Chapter 5
Behavioral Animation of Crowds

5.1 Introduction

One of the important characteristics of behavioral animation is its ability to reduce the workload on the animators. This is achieved by letting a behavioral model automatically take care of the low-level details of the animation, freeing the animator to concentrate on the big picture. Freeing the animator from low-level animation details is even more important when dealing with crowds. An animator manually creating a crowd animation is overwhelmed not only by the large number of animated entities, but also by the interactions between them.

For instance, manually animating ten human characters walking in a room requires more than ten times the work of animating a single character walking in a room, because the animator must deal with new problems like the possibility of collisions between characters. This observation reinforces the importance of research on behavioral animation models for crowds. Indeed, the entire field of behavioral animation has its origins strongly connected to crowds. This can be seen in the next section, where a review of the field is presented. Section 5.3 describes two behavioral models for crowds that have been successfully used in crowd simulations. Then, Sect. 5.4 discusses crowds navigation, which is one of the most important behaviors for crowd simulations.

5.2 Related Work

The seminal work by Reynolds [Rey87] is considered by many the first one in the field of behavioral animation. It presented a method to animate large groups of entities called *boids*, which present behaviors similar to those observed in flocks of birds and schools of fishes. Reynolds started from the premise that the group behavior is just the result of the interaction between the individual behavior of the group members. Therefore, it would suffice to simulate the reasonably simple boids individually, and the more complex flocking behavior would emerge from the interaction between them.

The boid model proposed by Reynolds consisted of three simple rules: (i) avoiding collisions with other boids, (ii) matching the velocity of nearby boids, and (iii) flying toward the center of the flock. Results presented by the author demonstrated that, as he originally expected, the interaction between creatures whose behavior was governed by these three simple rules leads to the emergence of a much more complex flocklike behavior.

Tu and Terzopoulos [TT94] created a realistically rich environment inhabited by artificial fishes. The complexity of the undersea life, including interactions between fishes like predators hunting preys, mating, and schooling, was obtained by modeling the behavior of individual fishes: group behaviors emerged as the individuals interacted. In this sense, this work is similar to the work by Reynolds discussed in the previous paragraphs.

It must be emphasized, though, that the artificial fishes created by Tu and Terzopoulos are much more complex than the boids created by Reynolds. The body of each fish, for instance, is modeled as a spring–mass system. Some of the springs represent muscles, which can be contracted in order to produce movements like a swinging tail. The fishes locomotion is the result of a hydrodynamics model that takes into account, for example, the volume of water displaced as the artificial fish swings its tail. Fishes' sensing capabilities include models of vision and temperature sensing.

Concerning the behavioral model, the simulated fishes are also much more complex than the boids. Their internal state includes variables hunger, libido, and fear, and also some "habit parameters," indicating whether they prefer, for instance, cold or warmth. The fishes' intentions are generated by an algorithm that uses all these aspects (in addition to senses) to produce its output. The actual execution of the generated intentions in the virtual environment is performed by "behavior routines," which specify which low-level actions must be executed by the fish in order to fulfill its intention.

Going even further in the direction of using more realistic models of the simulated entities, Brogan and Hodgins [BH97] described an algorithm to control the movements of entities with "significant dynamics" that travel in groups. By "significant dynamics," the authors mean that the work is focused on simulating systems whose dynamics are complex enough to have a strong impact on the motion of the simulated entities. For example, one of the case studies presented by the authors simulates the dynamics of one-legged robots, which move by jumping. These robots have "significant dynamics" because they cannot intentionally change their velocity during a jump, while they are not in contact with the ground. Besides the one-legged robots, the authors also present results with simulations involving bicyclists modeled as a hierarchy of rigid bodies connected by joints, and a simple point-mass system. Unlike the other two studied systems, the point-mass system does not have complex dynamics, and was added to the experiments in order to help in the understanding of the impact of dynamics in the performance of the algorithm.

The algorithm for group behaviors described in this work is divided in two parts: perception and placement. Perception works by allowing a simulated entity to sense the relative position and velocity of the entities near it, and also static obstacles.

5.2 Related Work

Fig. 5.1 Crowd simulation in a train station [MT01]

The placement part of the algorithm works by computing a desired position for an entity, given the other visible entities and obstacles. This high-level perception and placement algorithm is common among all three simulated systems, but the lower-level details differ: each of them has a specific control system, which translates the desired position to a desired velocity, and actuates in order to achieve this desired velocity in the most efficient way that obeys the dynamics of the simulated entity.

Crowds of human agents simulated in real time were explored by Musse and Thalmann [MT01], in a work that addressed both crowd structure and crowd behavior. The crowd is structured in a hierarchy with three levels: the crowd itself, groups, and individuals. Some crowd parameters can be set at higher levels of the hierarchy and are inherited to lower levels. It is possible, though, to redefine these parameters for some specific structure at a lower level. This enables, for instance, to easily create a simulation scenario in which there exists a single sad group in a happy crowd: it just requires setting the emotional status of the crowd to "happy," and redefining the emotional status of the desired group to "sad."

The adoption of groups in the model also allowed optimizing the system so that real-time performance could be achieved with large crowds. In fact, groups are the most complex structure in the model: group members share the decision process (and most of the information necessary for the decision process) that is used to define the actions performed during the simulation. Optionally, groups can have sociological effects enabled. If this is the case, more complex behaviors like group splitting and changes of the group leader can arise during the simulation.

Regarding crowd behavior, the authors proposed a model with three different levels of autonomy: autonomous, scripted, and guided. An autonomous group behaves responding to events, according to behavioral rules written by the animator. Scripted groups behave according to scripts that explicitly define the actions to be performed during the simulation. Finally, guided groups are interactively guided by the user as the simulation runs. Figure 5.1 shows a snapshot of a simulation based on this model.

Another model for simulating crowds of virtual humans was presented by Ulicny and Thalmann [UT02]. Unlike the previously described model, this one focuses on individual agents, instead of groups. The behavioral model is composed of three levels. The highest level is composed of a set of rules. Each rule has an antecedent part (that specifies which agents are allowed to use the rule and under which circumstances) and a consequent part (that describes the effects of firing the rule). Ex-

Fig. 5.2 Crowd entering a mosque [UT02]

ecution of rules can change the current agent behavior, change the agent attributes, or trigger events.

The current agent behavior is performed at an intermediate level, in which every possible behavior is implemented as a finite state machine (FSM) that drives the low-level actions for the virtual human. Finally, path-planning and collision avoidance are performed in the lower model level. A screenshot of a simulation based on this model is shown in Fig. 5.2.

5.3 Crowd Behavioral Models

Ideally, a behavioral model for crowds should be both realistic and efficient, that is, it should be able to simulate crowds with a very large number of agents efficiently enough to cause just a minor impact in the application's frame rate. In practice, however, there is usually a trade-off between realism and efficiency, and hence the characteristics of behavioral models for crowds vary greatly depending on their intended application.

In this section, two behavioral models that have been successfully used to simulate crowds are described. The first one was developed for a real-time, interactive application that imposed strong performance constraints. Thus, the model strives to be efficient, while still being realistic enough for the purposes of its application. The second model presented is physically based, requiring a great deal of computational resources to run. This makes the model unsuitable for simulating large crowds in real time with current hardware.

5.3.1 PetroSim's Behavioral Model

PetroSim [BdSM04] is a system for simulation of evacuations of outdoor urban areas in real time. It was developed in cooperation with Petrobras, the Brazilian

5.3 Crowd Behavioral Models

Petroleum Company, which has installations near inhabited areas. PetroSim was designed as a tool to help safety engineers in tasks like the improvement of existing evacuation plans and the evaluation of the safest place to build new potentially dangerous installations in populated areas. The nature of PetroSim required its behavioral model to be able to simulate the common behaviors found in emergency situations, yet be efficient enough to allow the simulation (and visualization) of crowds of hundreds of agents.

In order to simplify the simulated agents, most of the geographic knowledge necessary during the simulation is stored in the environment itself, and can be queried by agents as needed. Every simulated agent is an autonomous entity, described as triple of information containing knowledge, status, and intentions. The agent modeling and the decision process are detailed below.

Knowledge

The knowledge of an agent is composed by information computed in real time or obtained from the environment:

- *Environmental information* obtained from the environment. This includes the location of important places (like refuges or crowded locations) and possible paths between different places.
- *Perception of nearby agents*: position and status.
- *Perception of regions affected by an accident*, i.e., regions that should normally be avoided.

Agent's perception (of other agents and the accident) is computed in real time. Everything within a perception radius is perceived.

Status

The agent status contains information that is predefined before the beginning of the simulation and can change as a consequence of triggered events (e.g., an agent can get injured by the accident). The following items are part of the status:

- *Agent profile*, which defines the different behavioral profiles that can be observed in emergency situations. Three profiles were used in PetroSim: (i) *normal* agents, which are mental and physically capable of evacuating a region in the event of an accident; (ii) *leaders*, which try to help other agents during dangerous situations; and (iii) *dependent* agents, which cannot walk long distances without the help of another agent.
- *Consequences of accident*, which measures the degree of injury an agent has suffered.
- *Situation*, which can be "normal life," "danger," or "safe," which represent the periods before, during, and after the dangerous situation.

Intentions and Decision Process

An intention is a high-level goal that an agent is committed to achieve. The intentions of an agent are generated from its knowledge and status. A premise of PetroSim is that an agent has exactly one intention at any given time. As explained later in this section, this premise is assured to be respected by the use of finite state machines (FSMs) to model the behavior of agents.

The behavioral architecture should provide means to express that certain sequences of intentions are natural under certain circumstances. A leader, for instance, could start with the LOOK FOR PEOPLE NEEDING HELP intention. After gathering some dependents, the leader is expected to eventually change its intention to GO TO SAFE PLACE. And, just after arriving at the safe place, the leader's intention should change to LEAVE DEPENDENTS ON SAFE PLACE.

It turns out that the decision-making process cannot be entirely linear as just described. For instance, after leaving the dependents on the safe place, two different intentions could be allowed: STAY ON SAFE PLACE or, again, LOOK FOR PEOPLE NEEDING HELP.

As stated before, in this model an agent has exactly one intention at any given time. This allows one to represent the decision-making process as an FSM where each state corresponds to an intention. Transitions between states are triggered by verifying if certain conditions (based on the knowledge and status of an agent) hold. A concrete example of an FSM used in PetroSim is given in Sect. 5.3.1.

Because intentions are high-level goals, they must be translated to low-level actions that can be executed by an agent. Therefore, we describe an intention by three components: movement, animation, and interaction (collectively, MAI).

Movement specifies locomotion from the agent's current location to another place. The possible movements are NONE, GO TO SAFE PLACE, GO TO CROWDED PLACE, FOLLOW LEADER, GO TO PLACE NEAR ACCIDENT, GO TO RANDOM PLACE, and GO TO PLACE INDICATED BY LEADER. Definitions of which places are considered "safe" or "crowded" are obtained from the environment.

The implementation of movements is based on Reynolds's steering behaviors [Rey99]. Data like typical walking speeds were based on Fruin's work [Fru87].

Animation describes some visual indication of the current actions of an agent. This is passed directly to the visualization module, which is responsible for displaying it. NONE, SHOUT, WAVE, CALL, LOOK AROUND, and FALL are the valid animations.

Interaction specifies any kind of behavior that involves other agents. The possible interactions are LEAVE DEPENDENTS (e.g., if a leader successfully led a group of dependents to a safe place), GATHER DEPENDENTS (e.g., if a leader is searching for people needing help), START FOLLOWING, and STOP FOLLOWING.

Each intention is associated with a set of MAIs. This reflects the fact that there may be various distinct ways to execute a given intention. Whenever an agent decides to execute an intention, it randomly chooses one of the MAIs associated with it. This feature is an easy way to add diversity to the simulation.

Consider, for example, the intention LOOK FOR DEPENDENTS, which is typically performed by leaders trying to locate people needing help. It could be described

5.3 Crowd Behavioral Models

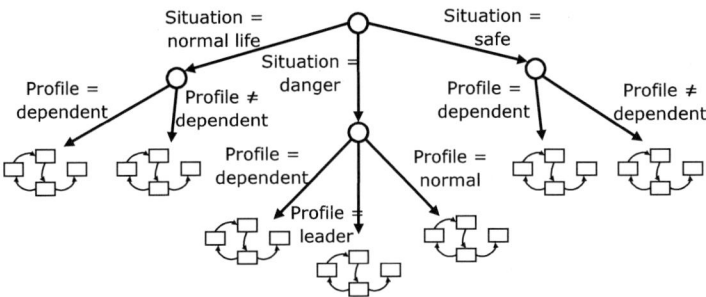

Fig. 5.3 The decision tree used to select an FSM. *Leaves* represent the FSMs used to model the behavior of agents

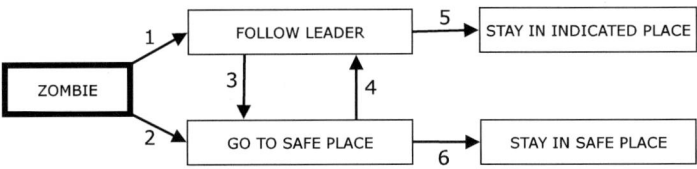

Fig. 5.4 The FSM used by normal agents when the situation is "danger." States (i.e., intentions) are represented as *rectangles*; the initial state has a *thicker border*; *arrows* indicate possible state transitions (i.e., changes in the agent intention)

by ⟨GO TO CROWDED PLACE, WAVE, GATHER DEPENDENTS⟩, ⟨GO TO CROWDED PLACE, SHOUT, GATHER DEPENDENTS⟩, and ⟨GO TO PLACE NEAR ACCIDENT, SHOUT, GATHER DEPENDENTS⟩, among others.

Simplifying the FSMs

It is certainly possible to design a single, large FSM capable of representing all possible intentions for all possible agents. Such FSM, though, would be difficult to understand and modify. The solution to this problem is to use several simpler FSMs.

The two factors with most relevance to the behavior in PetroSim are the agent situation (normal life, danger, or safe) and its profile. Based on these two attributes (situation and profile), we defined a decision tree (shown in Fig. 5.3) whose task is to select which FSM shall be used for a given agent. Other implementations of this model can use different decision trees.

An Example of FSM

As a concrete example, we now describe the FSM used by agents with the "normal" profile when the situation is "danger." This FSM is represented in Fig. 5.4.

The initial state, ZOMBIE, does not represent a real intention. It is just an artifice used to create an FSM with a single initial state when two or more intentions can be considered sensible initial intentions. At any time, at least one of the transitions leaving the state ZOMBIE is guaranteed to be active. Therefore, an agent leaves this state as soon as possible and enters a state representing a real intention.

In this example, a normal agent entering a danger situation can have two different intentions: it can follow a leader or seek a safe place alone. These two possibilities correspond, respectively, to the states FOLLOW LEADER and GO TO SAFE PLACE. Depending on the occurrence of certain events (discussed later in this section), an agent can change from one of these states to the other one. In a successful evacuation, a leader will eventually indicate a safe place where its followers are expected to stay. The intention to go to this meeting point and stay there is represented by the state STAY IN INDICATED PLACE. Similarly, a normal agent heading to a safe place without the help of a leader will eventually arrive on the refuge. Once there, its intention will be to stay there. The state STAY IN SAFE PLACE represents this.

Each transition between states is implemented as an expression that can be true or false depending on the status and the knowledge of the agent in question. When deciding the next intention for a given agent, we sequentially evaluate the expressions corresponding to the transitions leaving the current state. This sequence of evaluations is stopped when the first expression with a true value is found. In this case, the transition is executed and the FSM changes its current state (that is, the agent changes its intention). If all expressions evaluate to false, the agent remains with the same intention.

Concerning what can be used to construct these expressions, each agent has a set of flags that can be directly accessed in the expressions. These flags, which reflect aspects of the agent's status and knowledge, are listed below:

- LEADER PERCEIVED: is true when at least one agent with the leader profile is being perceived.
- DEPENDENT PERCEIVED: is true when at least one agent with the dependent profile is being perceived.
- LEADER INDICATED PLACE: is true if the leader that was being followed indicated a place to the agent stay.
- ABANDONED BY LEADER: is true if the leader that was being followed "abandoned" the agent. As implemented, this happens only if the leader dies as a consequence of the accident.
- AT SAFE PLACE: is true if the agent is currently at a safe place.
- AT GOAL: is true if the agent is currently at the end of the path it was following.

Apart from these flags, the only information used in the expressions are the constant "true," the connectives AND and OR, and the RandBool(p) function, which returns true with probability p and false otherwise.

In the FSM used as example, the following expressions are used (the numbers correspond to the labels of the transitions in Fig. 5.4):

1. LEADER PERCEIVED AND RandBool(0.1)

5.3 Crowd Behavioral Models

Fig. 5.5 Evacuation simulation in PetroSim

2. True[1]
3. ABANDONED BY LEADER
4. LEADER PERCEIVED AND RandBool(0.01)
5. LEADER INDICATED PLACE
6. AT SAFE PLACE

Results

PetroSim was tested running simulations in the village of São José, in the state of Rio Grande do Norte, Brazil, where about 350 people live near Petrobras installations. The behavioral model was capable of generating the behaviors expected during evacuations, and the simulations allowed verification, for instance, of the impact of adding more trained leaders to help the population during an emergency. A snapshot of running simulation is shown in Fig. 5.5.

To evaluate the performance of the behavioral model, two sets of simulations were run, using various numbers of agents. The first set of simulations used the complete PetroSim system, that is, both behavior and visualization were enabled. The second set of simulations had only visualization enabled. Comparing the two sets of simulations allows inferring the performance of the behavioral model. These experiments are summarized in Fig. 5.6.

---

[1] Recall that, at any given time, at least one of the transitions leaving the ZOMBIE state must be true. If transition 1 is not used (because its expression evaluated to false), transition 2 is certainly going to be used.

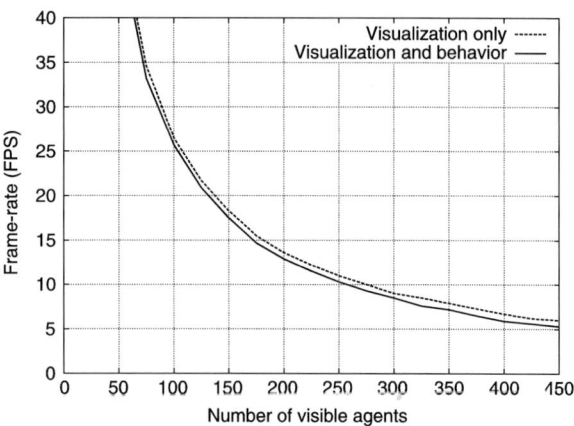

Fig. 5.6 Graphics showing PetroSim's performance on a system based on a Pentium 4 processor at 3 GHz, with 1 GB of RAM and a GeForce FX 5900 GPU

5.3.2 A Physically Based Behavioral Model

Our second example of behavioral model was proposed by Braun et al. [BMB03, BBM05]. It is designed as a parametric model for simulation of crowd evacuations from internal environments including several rooms and obstacles, in which a hazardous event such as smoke or fire propagates. This model is based on the model originally described by Helbing et al. [HM95, HFV00], and already discussed in Chap. 2.

Helbing's model represents the humans as a homogeneous particle system, i.e., they do not take into account any agent individuality. The model presented here starts by allowing the population to be composed heterogeneously by individuals with different attributes. More specifically, the following attributes (related to agent i) are used:

- $IdFamily_i$—Identifier of the family. A family is a predefined group formed by some agents who know each other.
- M_i—Mobility level of the agent represented by a value in the interval $[0, 1]$, which mimics the ability of moving without help.
- A_i—Altruism level of the individual, represented by a value in the interval $[0, 1]$. It represents the tendency of helping another agent. For simplicity, we consider altruism existent between members of the same family only, i.e., agents with high altruism try to rescue dependent agents of the same family.

In order to model the effect of the mobility parameter in the individual velocity, the desired velocity v_i^0 is computed as a function of M_i and maximum velocity v^m by

$$v_i^0 = M_i v^m \tag{5.1}$$

If agent i is totally dependent ($M_i = 0$), v_i^0 will be equal to zero, which is typical for disabled people, small children, etc. In the case of $M = 1$ for all agents, one recovers Helbing's original model.

5.3 Crowd Behavioral Models

An altruism force is used to allow members of the same family to group and head together for the exit of the virtual environment. The altruism force that attracts an agent i to an agent j (both of the same family) is computed by

$$\mathbf{fa}_{ij} = KA_i(1 - M_j)|\mathbf{d}_{ij} - \mathbf{d}_{ip}|\mathbf{e}_{ij} \qquad (5.2)$$

where K is a constant,[2] $\mathbf{d}_{ij}$ represents the distance between agents i and j (with origin at agent i), $\mathbf{d}_{ip}$ is the distance vector from agent i to its current goal, and $\mathbf{e}_{ij}$ is a unit vector with origin on agent i and pointing to agent j.

In this extended model, the equation by Helbing et al. [HM95, HFV00] is rewritten as

$$m_i \frac{d\mathbf{v}_i}{dt} = F_i^{(H)} + \sum_{j \neq i} \mathbf{fa}_{ij} + \sum_{e} \mathbf{f}_{ie} \qquad (5.3)$$

where $F_i^{(H)}$ is the resulting force of agent i modeled according to the original model, $\sum_{j \neq i} \mathbf{fa}_{ij}$ is the resulting force due to the altruism forces, and $\sum_e \mathbf{f}_{ie}$ is the resulting force between the agent i and the hazard event e. The next sections show details of the extended model.

Interaction with Environment

In Helbing's model [HFV00], the authors only considered simple environments like rooms and corridors. However, one of the main applications of the model described here is to allow safety engineers and architects to specify different simulation scenarios in realistic environments. For this reason, dealing with more complex virtual environments is one of paramount importance. In real life, there are shopping centers, schools, buildings, among others, that include rooms and internal corridors which can interfere in the flow of pedestrians. Moreover, the physical space normally has several types of obstacles (for instance, furniture, columns, and plants).

This model introduces the concept of *context* in the virtual environment, which relates to a known physical space that can be populated. *Context* represents a geometrical environment limited by walls and exits and is defined by convex polygons. Each context is specified by the user in order to describe the following attributes:

1. A group of walls limits of the room. Each wall is specified as two points that indicate its limits.
2. Interest points (IPs) define locations where agents can go to [MT01]. They can be located in the exits and represent the desired goals of agents in Helbing's model. The agents' goals are defined by the IPs, which may change during the simulation (details will be explained later).
3. A level number (n) representing the hierarchy in the environment. More internal rooms correspond to higher levels than the ones which communicate directly with the exterior. During the evacuation, the agents are able to change contexts.

---

[2] Authors have used values from 500 to 2000.

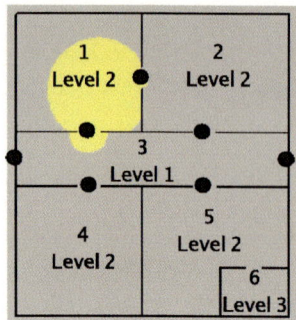

Fig. 5.7 2D representation of an environment with six contexts. Context *3* is associated with *level 1* because of its direct communication with the exterior; contexts *1*, *2*, *4*, and *5* have *level 2* and context *6* has *level 3*. The *points in the exits* represent IPs

Normally, agents leave a higher-level context to enter another one of equal or lower level. However, it can be changed as a function of agents' adopted behaviors. Figure 5.7 shows an environment with six contexts and their respective levels.

4. The hazardous events represent the accidents causing evacuation, such as fire, explosion, smoke, etc. The treatment of these events will be detailed later. A hazardous event is described as its starting position, its propagation speed (s) and its danger level (L).

Each context contains a list of agents inside it. These agents can only interact with walls, events, and other agents from the same context. The only exception is that agents of a determined context avoid collision with agents of the neighbor contexts, in order to prevent problems on the interface between two contexts when the agents pass through doors. During the evacuation, the agents go to the contexts' exits defined by IPs. When agents change contexts, they are able to perceive all the next context attributes. The possibility of having more than one exit in the context is very plausible and can be dealt with in our model, as illustrated in Fig. 5.7 and explained in more detail later.

Agents' Perception

In Helbing's model, the perception of the accident is assumed to be immediate: all agents perceive the accident at the same time. However, in real situations (especially when more complex environments are involved), people are not likely to perceive the emergency situation simultaneously, except if a global alarm system exists.

In order to deal with this kind of situation, the agents can be endowed with one of three different perception skills: (i) the skill to perceive a global alarm (all agents of a simulated environment take simultaneous notice of the event); (ii) the skill to perceive that a hazard event enters into the current context (all agents from the same context perceive the event); (iii) the skill to perceive the intention of other agents who already know about the hazard event and are evacuating from the environment. This skill imitates the communication ability.

5.3 Crowd Behavioral Models

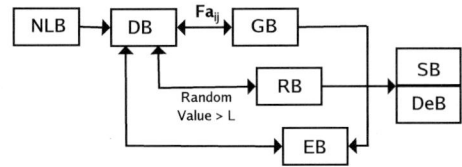

Fig. 5.8 Execution flow of simulation

The evacuation process starts if the hazard event is triggered and also if agents perceive such event. The user can configure the perception skill to be applied by agents. This gives the user options to define different scenarios and public space configurations.

In order to consider these distinct scenarios, a simplified model for the hazardous event propagation was defined. The user informs its starting location (x, y, z), the speed of propagation, and a danger level (L), which can be interpreted as the type of event: gas, fire, flooding, explosion, etc. In this simplified model, the hazard propagates with a uniform speed from the starting point specified, until reaching the exits of a current context and entering a new one. At this moment, a new event in the next context is initiated and its initial position is the IP. The danger level is constant in the area occupied by the event.

Once the agent perceives the emergency event (depending on its skills), it must decide whether to abandon the place immediately or to help others. This decision depends on the agent's individualities (altruism forces, discussed above) and on the agent's perception skills. According to these two aspects, the agents can adopt different behaviors. Below the agent's decision module, implemented using an FSM, is described.

Agents' Decision and Action

Depending on events that happen during the simulation, agents adopt one of several possible behaviors. The possible behaviors are organized in an FSM, as illustrated in Fig. 5.8. Each of these possible behaviors, and the rules that trigger behavior changes are explained below.

- *Normal Life Behavior* (NLB): The agent does not know about the hazard event: In this case, the agent walks randomly inside the current context avoiding collisions with obstacles and interpenetration with walls and other agents. This represents a normal life situation and the agents remain in this state until they perceive the hazard event. The first term on the right-hand side of Eq. (5.3) describes NLB. An agent leaves this state (and transitions to DB) when it perceives a hazard event.
- *Decision Behavior* (DB): This state models the behavior of an agent that perceived the hazard event and has to decide what to do next. Its options are grouping with other agents (GB), trying to escape (EB), or taking the risk of trespassing the area affected by the hazard event (RB).
- *Group Behavior* (GB): The agent groups with other agents of the same family, using the altruism forces discussed above (Eq. (5.2)).

- *Escape Behavior* (EB): The agent tries to evacuate from the environment escaping from the hazard event-occupied area. The Escape Behavior is described using force fields which are implemented through a repulsive force that depends on the danger level (L) assigned to the event. This force is similar to the repulsive force between agents proposed by Helbing, except for the inclusion of a factor L which describes the event danger level. The greater the danger level of the hazard event is, the stronger must be the repulsion suffered by the agent. R_{ie} is the sum of agent i's radius and event e's radius, d_{ie} is the distance between agent i and event e's initial position, and $\mathbf{n}_{ie}$ is the normalized vector, pointing from event e to agent i. A and B are constants as presented in Helbing's work [HFV00].

$$\mathbf{F} = LA \exp\left[(R_{ie} - d_{ie})/B\right]\mathbf{n}_{ie} \tag{5.4}$$

When new information is perceived by the agents, new decisions shall be taken, which implies alterations in their action. For example, the escape trajectory can be modified if the initially desired path becomes dangerous. Therefore, the system must allow new decisions, since the simulation environment is dynamic. In this sense, the system must reevaluate the choice of the IPs of each agent with a given frequency. In order to select the best IP to be followed by an agent to evacuate a context, we attributed a weight to each IP considering two criteria: distance between IP and agent and danger existent in the IP, with the weight of each IP given by

$$W_{total_{IP}} = W_{distance_{iIP}} + 2 W_{danger_{IP}}$$

The larger the total weight of an IP, the larger is the probability for this IP to be chosen for the agent. According to the danger criterion, IPs free of danger receive weight 1, while the other IPs receive weight equal to $1 - L$, where $0 \leq L \leq 1$ is the event's danger level. This way, the higher the danger level of an event, the lesser is its weight in the danger criterion. The weight related to the danger criterion is multiplied by 2, because most people will prefer to take a larger path if it is safer than the others.
- *Risk Behavior* (RB): If an agent decides to take a risk, it enters the danger area, trying to leave the environment. This simulates people who decide to make their way through the occupied area instead of running to get away from danger. The probability of making this choice depends on the event's danger level. We evaluate this probability through the generation of a random number between 0 and 1. If this number is larger than the danger level of the event, then the agent decides to dive into the danger area. In this case, the force described by Eq. (5.4) disappears since the agent no longer escapes from the event but enters the danger zone. For example, if the danger level is equal to 0.9 (representing a highly dangerous event), there is only 10% possibility for the agent to enter the danger area. If agent i is in the region affected by the event, its mobility level (M_i) decreases with time as a function of the danger level of the event (L), as shown in Eq. (5.5).

Consequently, its desired speed decreases since the mobility decreases too (according to Eq. (5.1)). The mobility of agents as well as their desired speed are modified in order to simulate effects like debilitation or injuries.

$$M_i(t) = M_i(t - \Delta t) - L \Delta t \tag{5.5}$$

5.3 Crowd Behavioral Models

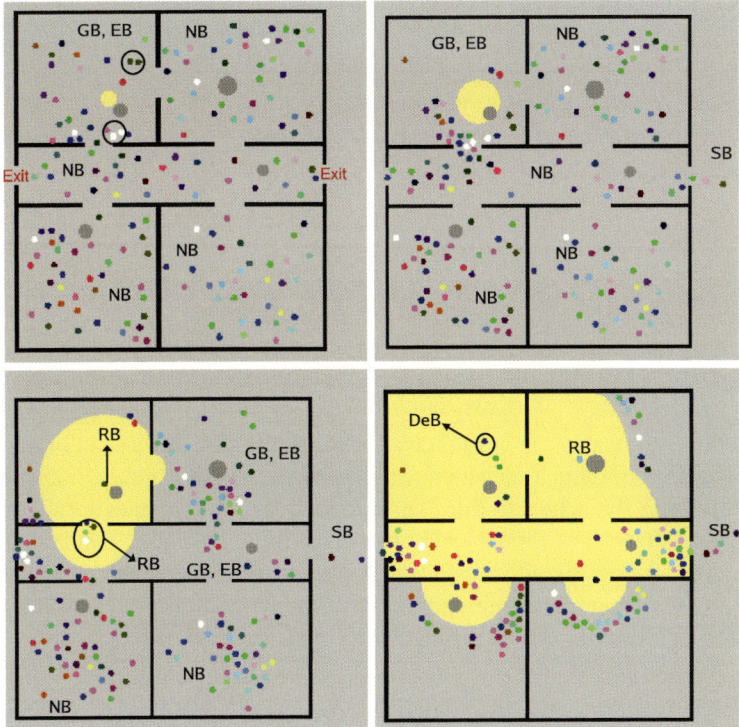

Fig. 5.9 Sequence of images showing the adopted behaviors of agents. The environment has five contexts (four rooms and a corridor) and the area occupied by the event is represented in *yellow*. The biggest *circles* (in *gray*) represent obstacles

- *Safe Behavior* (SB): Agents evacuated successfully the environment. Agents keep walking.
- *Dead Behavior* (DeB): Agents' mobility is equal to 0. Agents stop moving.

In order to illustrate the effects of the decision module on agent's behavior, Fig. 5.9 shows a sequence of images which describes the agents' adopted behaviors.

Results

The extension to Helbing's model described here has been able to simulate evacuations with good accuracy. One of the experiments performed consisted of simulating an evacuation of a four-store building and comparing the results to the ones obtained during a real drill. The results of this comparison are shown in Table 5.1.

Table 5.1 Comparison between measured data on the drill and results of simulation

Criterion	Measure on Drill	Simulation Result
Mean velocity on corridors without traffic jams	1.25 m/s	1.27 m/s
Mean velocity on corridors with traffic jams	0.5 m/s	1.19 m/s
Mean velocity on stairs without traffic jams	0.6 m/s	0.6 m/s
Mean velocity on stairs with traffic jams	0.5 m/s	0.47 m/s
Highest density	2.3 people/m^2	2.4 people/m^2
Global evacuation time	190 s	192 s

5.4 Crowds Navigation

Navigation is probably the most crucial behavior for crowds that can be simulated on a computer. Building evacuation simulations for security studies, improvements of public places for architecture design, army moves in video games are all examples of scenarios that can be formulated as crowd navigation planning problems.

However, previously cited applications have specific needs and dedicated techniques were elaborated accordingly to solve the navigation problem. Three main classes of applications can be distinguished: first, those related to Security and Architecture, second, the ones related to Entertainment such as video games or the cinematographic industry, and third, applications to Virtual Reality, such as immersing a spectator into large populated virtual places for cyber-exploration.

Security and Architecture applications need exact simulations: the way a crowd navigates must correspond to reality. The objective is to check the design of buildings or public spaces before their construction or modification. Simulations potentially handle huge populations of thousands of pedestrians in large scenes—from malls, stadiums, or stations to entire parts of cities. The simulation setup varies—pedestrians initial states and goals, and the environment digital mock-up—and results are then compared. Generally, neither interactivity nor real-time output is needed given that resulting data are analyzed at a postprocessing time.

For Entertainment applications, such as video games, interactivity is probably the most important criterion. A typical example is a real-time strategy game where the user controls an army in order to fight another army (controlled by the computer or not). The player selects large groups of units and gives strategic orders, mainly some navigation tasks; units must react interactively, even though the computer is also running other tasks (rendering, computer enemy AI, etc.). Thus, in such applications, the navigation problem has to be solved online in an efficient manner.

Finally, Virtual Reality applications require believability. The main objective is to immerse a spectator in a populated place and let him navigate, explore, and observe the virtual scene as he wants. Pedestrians moving in front of him must look natural: their appearance, but also the way they act, and in our specific case the way they navigate. Performance is a crucial point as a great part of computing resources are dedicated to the rendering of the scene and of the pedestrians while the crowd

5.4 Crowds Navigation

simulation runs. As a result, navigation is planned so that the simulation needs as few resources as possible while believability is preserved.

In any of the previous cases, the crowd navigation problem can be formulated as a motion planning problem. Given the pedestrians' initial state, the desired final state, and the geometrical description of the environment, how to compute a path joining these states while avoiding collisions with obstacles?

Robotics studied the motion planning problem to give robots' autonomy of motion: the next subsection gives an overview of the major classes of solutions to be found in the literature. Then, a description of the solutions dedicated to the crowd navigation problem will be given. Section 5.4.3 is devoted to the "Navigation Graphs" approach [PdHCM*06].

5.4.1 Robot Motion Planning

Motion planning techniques allow one to compute collision-free paths between desired destinations in an environment made of obstacles. Robotics addressed this problem in order to give robots the autonomy of motion. The main approaches developed by the robotics field are not directly applicable to the crowd navigation problem; however, dedicated methods are based on similar principles. This section offers an overview of different classes of motion planning techniques, exhaustive descriptions are to be found in [Lat91, Lau98, Lav06].

It should be noticed that most of the motion planning solutions exploit the Configuration Space abstraction instead of the 3D geometrical world. This abstraction was first introduced by Lozano-Pérez in the early 1980s [LP83], and is generally denoted $\mathcal{C}_{space}$. $\mathcal{C}_{space}$ can be seen as the state space of the transformations applicable to a robot: each point of this space corresponds to a unique configuration of the robot. It is n-dimensional, with n the number of degrees of freedom of the robot. Planning the motion of an articulated system in the 3D Euclidean world is equivalent to planning the motion for a point in $\mathcal{C}_{space}$.

Discrete Motion Planning

Discrete methods are probably the most popular and simple in practice. The basic idea is to use a discrete representation of the environment: a 2D grid lying on the floor of an environment for navigation planning, or a discretization of $\mathcal{C}_{space}$ for articulated systems. Then, a state variable is associated with each grid cell in order to describe the world: basically, a cell is free or occupied by an obstacle. Motion is allowed between adjacent free cells: the problem of reaching a given goal is reduced to a search using, for example, a forward-search technique. A-star or Dijkstra's algorithm [Dij59] allows to one compute optimal paths, but optimality is no more guaranteed in the exact definition of the world.

In order to get discrete representations of the environment that are as close as possible to reality, an adequate precision (the grid step size) must be used. In case of tight problems (large environments with narrow passages for example), memory needs and search times make the solution impractical. This limitation can be partially solved by using a hierarchical discretization: adjacent free cells are packed as a single free zone at a higher hierarchical level. As a result, the geometry of the environment is captured at the lowest levels of the hierarchy while topology is captured at the highest levels. The problem is first solved at the higher level, and lower levels are then explored to refine the solution.

Exact Motion Planning

This class of methods exploits an exact geometrical representation of the world. For this reason, they are generally limited to specific cases (e.g., polygonal worlds). Cell-decomposition techniques belong to this class [Cha87]. The basic idea is to compute a complete partition of the free space into a finite set of regions called *cells*. Cells are often convex in order to ease the navigation of a mobile into a given cell. Cell adjacency is captured into a graph in order to represent the connectivity of the free space (and, by deduction, its topology). The planning problem is then reduced to a graph search again, as in the previous case of discrete motion planning.

Maximum clearance is another exact approach (also known as generalized Voronoï diagrams [For97] or retraction method [OY82]). Here, the key idea is to remain as far as possible from obstacles in order to execute safely navigation tasks. A clearance map provides the distance to the nearest obstacle for any point of the world. The union of local maximums of this map forms the maximum clearance map. The maximum clearance map appears like a skeleton capturing the free space topology. This approach is popular in the robotics field because maximum clearance paths correspond to the safest ones in order to avoid collisions.

Sampling-Based Methods

Exact and discrete methods model the entirety of C_{space} to search for solutions. In case of complex obstacles and mechanical systems (number of degrees of freedom), the induced complexity may render such methods impractical. Then, a solution is to sample partially and randomly C_{space}.

Two pioneer approaches are to be found in the literature: Probabilistic Roadmap Method (PRM) [KSLO96] and Rapid Random Trees (RRT) [KL00]. The first one constructs a reusable data structure in order to solve multiple motion planning queries, whereas the second one builds a temporary structure to answer as fast as possible a single query. However, their principle is similar.

The method searches for collision-free configurations, and attempts to connect them by paths computed with a steering method. Collisions are then checked for these paths. Valid paths and configurations form respectively the edges and the nodes of a graph or a tree (a roadmap for PRM and a tree for RRT). Solutions to navigation queries are searched into this structure.

This randomized approach is general, and fits many classes of problems. It has been popular the last 15 years, and hundreds of variants appeared in the literature: specific metrics and pseudo-random sampling techniques [Kuf04b], heuristics or strategies to build a roadmap [SLN00], optimization techniques, adaptations to time-varying problems (dynamic environments), etc.

Reactive Methods

Previous methods provide a full path leading to the prescribed goal, whereas reactive methods only consider the problem locally. From a local observation of the environment, a new action is computed each step. Reactive methods are generally simple to implement, but, as the environment is considered locally, may result in deadlocks. For that reason, they can also be used as a feedback control law only: a full path is computed while the reactive method is only used to track the path. Such a use of reactive methods enables, for example, the consideration of dynamic environments (with moving objects).

Potential fields [Kha86] is a reactive method. In such an approach, obstacles are repulsive whereas the goal is attractive. By following the gradient of the resulting vector field, the mobile entity moves toward the goal.

Multiple Robots

Two major approaches were developed to address the motion planning problem for several robots at the same time: the *coordinated* ones and the *prioritized* ones [BO05]. Coordinated approaches can be *centralized* or *decoupled* [SL02]. Briefly, centralized approaches consider the different robots as a single articulated mechanism, and the solution combines the $\mathcal{C}_{space}$ of each independent robot into a single composite one in which the motion is planned. In decoupled approaches, the robots' motions are planned independently, and then are coordinated to avoid collisions. Finally, in prioritized approaches, each robot is assigned a priority and processed sequentially. The robots having a planned trajectory become moving obstacles for the resting one.

5.4.2 Crowd Motion Planning

The crowd motion planning problem was solved in many different manners in the literature, with respect to the constraints met: size of considered crowd and environment, objectives (realism, interactivity, believability), etc. The robot motion planning techniques were used as a basis for the solutions developed, with adaptations to the crowd problem specificities.

Models for Safety Applications

Pedestrians simulator for safety applications appeared during the past 30 years, and [SA05] provides an excellent overview of the different existing commercial softwares. The main goal of these softwares is to provide exact results: evacuation times, detection of panic situations, etc. For this reason, calibration of models and comparisons with real data are crucial, and thus, navigation planning is often a secondary problem. Three major classes of approaches are distinguished: flow-based models, agent-based models, and cellular automata.

Flow-based models address the crowd simulation problem from a global point of view: pedestrians are not modeled as individual entities, but as being part of a flow. The model defines the physical properties of the flow and of the environment in evacuation scenarios. EVACNET4 [KFN98] is an example of flow-based model. The environment is represented as a network of nodes. Nodes are bounded parts of the environment such as rooms, corridors, lobbies, etc. The state of a node is described by high-level parameters such as occupancy, average interperson spacing, or other qualitative descriptions. A gateway between two parts of the environment is modeled by an arc linking the two corresponding nodes. The user must define the flow capacity of each arc as well as the required traversal time. In order to set up a simulation, the user defines the nodes' initial states (number of people in each node, and other parameters conditioning the node state), as well as some destination nodes (evacuation exits). One can observe that the model does not describe the environment geometry explicitly, but only implicitly using a network of nodes. As a result, the path planning problem on a geometric perspective is not to be addressed. EVACNET4 searches for a minimal evacuation time, and an advanced network flow transshipment algorithm is in charge to find a solution. EESCAPE and FireWind are other examples of flow-based models.

In *cellular automata* approaches, the environment is modeled as a grid of cells. Cells are occupied by pedestrians, and local density, flow, or speed are taken into account to compute how pedestrians move from cell to cell. Note that any discrete motion planning technique (presented previously) is applicable in such a framework. AEA EGRESS [Tec] is an example of a cell-based approach. EGRESS uses hexagonal cells to get a better estimation of the direction of motion—indeed, the error is higher using square cells. Some cells are defined as attractive goals, others are occupied by obstacles. At a preliminary step, a distance map is computed: distance from any cell to the nearest goal-cell is computed. The simulation starts from the initial positions of the persons, then, at each time step, each person chooses an action to execute among four possible ones: move closer to the exit, move farther from the exit, move to a cell the same distance from the exit, or do not move. A probability is associated with each action in order to determine which one is chosen.

Simulex [TM94] also uses distance maps on 2D grids generated from CAD files to guide pedestrians, but Simulex belong to the *agent-based models* class. Several maps may exist to assign different goals to pedestrians. Distance map is a discrete vector field, and pedestrians follow the gradient to reach their goal. Pedestrian motion models (walk speed, accelerations, and interactions) are calibrated from observations of real humans.

5.4 Crowds Navigation

One of the most popular approaches is Helbing's model [HM95] known as the "social force model." A sum of forces influence the locomotion. Some are attractive, others are repulsive so that a pedestrian can follow a desired direction, respect a desired displacement speed, consider the presence of other pedestrians and static obstacles. This model was reused and refined in many other approaches, like the one described in Sect. 5.3.2.

Legion™ is also a pedestrian traffic simulator belonging to the class of agent-based models. It was mainly developed from Still's works [Sti00] (Crowds Dynamics Ltd.). Environments are modeled in a specific manner (*iSpace*). Agents and environment communicate: for example, an agent asks for a move direction given its objective, but also, agents inform the environment about the facts they previously observed: this mechanism allows information propagation between agents via the environment. Unhappily, the method used to plan pedestrian paths is not presented in detail because of a commercial nondisclosure agreement. However, the solution is globally based on the least effort algorithm, which searches for the best (optimality is not guaranteed) path satisfying a set of constraints (speed distribution, assigned destination, collision). Paths' costs are computed according to their length, required travel time, and effort.

The Fire Safety Engineering Group of the University of Greenwich also developed an agent-based evacuation simulator, EXODUS, first introduced in [GG93]. The pedestrian model integrates many psychological factors to simulate evacuations. The way-finding system is dedicated to evacuation application. Indeed, given the level of knowledge about the environment where they navigate, pedestrians know their itinerary, or react to signage or to indications from other agents. The navigation task is done using a rule-based system.

Models for Entertainment Applications

The primary need of the entertainment field is *interactivity*. However, the need for interactivity has to be interpreted in different ways from a specific application to another. The cinematographic industry uses crowds simulations to obtain impressive scenes involving thousands of virtual actors. The simulation is generally computed offline, but has to be fast enough to allow multiple trials and editions: the user interacts as a real choreographer. The user both acts at a high level, to design global crowd motions, and at the lowest level, to control precisely some elements of the crowd, the timing of their successive actions, etc.

Massive Software [Sof] was designed to answer the cinematographic industry needs. The software combines several navigation techniques in order to allow a user to author the crowd motion via an ergonomic interface. The more the user drives the crowd, the less agents have to be autonomous. Consequently, at the lowest level, basic techniques are used to control agents such as potential fields to create motion flows. However, agents are equipped with artificial intelligence (*brain*) to execute navigation tasks in an autonomous manner, so that they can react to the presence of obstacles or other agents. They are able to roam endlessly in a crowded

3D environment using a synthetic vision to detect static or dynamic obstacles and simple fuzzy rules to determine the appropriate reaction.

Another way to author crowd motion is by definition of constraints: action timing, coordination: the approach proposed by Sung et al. [SKG05] allows one to satisfy precisely such constraints. In particular, virtual characters are able to meet somewhere or execute an action at given times. A PRM (Sect. 5.4.1) is computed to help the collision-free navigation in the environment: the roadmap is dense enough to provide quite optimal paths using a Dijkstra's search without any further optimization. A specific animation technique transforms the planned paths into trajectories (i.e., with time properties that are now known for the resting operations). Collisions between pedestrians are anticipated directly at the planning stage. Characters are processed sequentially. A character whose motion is planned becomes a moving obstacle for the following ones (as for prioritized motion planning approaches in robotics described in Sect. 5.4.1).

For video games applications such as real-time strategy games involving huge armies, interactivity is also crucial. But, in this case, the computation time is the most restrictive constraint in order to obtain real-time performance. The player must observe immediately the reaction to his orders without discontinuity in the game.

The work by Reynolds [Rey87], already discussed in Sect. 5.2, demonstrated how a crowd behavior could emerge from an efficient agent-based simulation. More recent works extended the set of agent behaviors [Rey99] that can be simulated, and provided solutions to typical player queries (seeking, fleeing, pursuit, evasion, avoidance, flocking, path or wall following, etc.).

In [LK06], a technique was developed to address online path planning for a large number of pedestrians (up to 150) in a highly dynamic environment. In this approach, the environment is modeled as a 2D grid whose cells are occupied or not by an obstacle. Given the goal of each pedestrian, a dedicated search algorithm [Kuf04a] computes a global solution path. A subgoal is selected from the solutions found by running a Runtime Path Finding algorithm. Indeed, it is able to handle the presence of other characters, dynamic on specialized obstacles (forcing the character to jump over or pass under). A motion synthesis system is used at this stage in order to plan directly believable motions. Note that this approach is an extension of [LK05] where a prioritized motion planner was used to solve collision between pedestrians and other pedestrians as well as between pedestrians and mobile obstacles (for which the trajectory has to be completely known before the search).

In [TCP06], Treuille et al. model crowds as a particle system. The environment is modeled as a 2D grid which is able to map an uneven terrain. The evolution of a crowd state of the world is computed by superposing grids capturing different information: the density grid (people's locations), goal grids (where they go), boundary grids (the environment itself), etc. The superposition results in a potential field, whose gradient is followed by pedestrians.

Kamphuis and Overmars [KO04] specialized their motion planner in order to consider groups of pedestrians. The main idea is to plan the motion for a deformable shape containing all the members of the same group. The surface covered by the

5.4 Crowds Navigation

shape remains identical so that people always have enough room to move while remaining grouped. The shape is deformable so that narrow passages can be crossed, as well as large places.

Models for Virtual Reality Applications

Solutions to simulate crowds are at the crossroads of the previous models' requirements. They combine realism and performance in order to immerse an observer in a virtual crowd. Real-time simulation is required to allow interactivity with the user while believable results are required to maintain the suspension of disbelief.

To satisfy these needs, Musse and Thalmann introduced the idea of scalability in crowd simulation in [MT01]. The way collisions are detected and avoided differs with respect to the distance from the spectator's point of view. The crowd is simulated using an agent-based model. Agents group together when having compatible sociological factors. Emotional status of each agent evolves when he meets other agents.

In [TLC02a], Tecchia et al. use a succession of layers (maps) to control the behavior of pedestrians. Given the current location of the pedestrian, the method looks up successively in each layer for information in order to update the pedestrian position. One is dedicated to collision detection (between pedestrians and static obstacles), one is dedicated to intercollision detection (between pedestrians), one to define local behaviors or tasks to achieve in given locations, and one to define the attraction areas (goals). According to the authors, the combination of these four layers is sufficient to produce believable crowd behaviors.

The solution presented by Lamarche and Donikian [LD04] starts from the mesh of an environment, for which a flat walking surface is specified. A 2-m-high slice of obstacles is projected onto the walk surface to create a blueprint of the environment. The resulting 2D map is then analyzed using a 2D cell-decomposition technique: the resulting triangulation—after optimization and organization into a hierarchy to enhance path searches—is captured into a graph. A navigation planning query is solved by graph search for a path joining the desired cells (note that paths are precomputed to enhance computation times). The resulting navigation plan is a sequence of cells (free areas) and portals (segments of lines, which are the mutual boundaries of adjacent cells) to go through. A reactive technique is used to execute the plan while taking into account the presence of several pedestrians simultaneously in a cell. The way portals are crossed depends on the angle formed by the pedestrian view direction and the portal, a free-space is preserved around the pedestrians, and trajectories are linearly extrapolated to anticipate and avoid collisions.

In [ST05], Shao and Terzopoulos model the environment as a hierarchical collection of maps. At the lowest level, some specialized objects and their properties are described (seat, waiting line, etc.). At a middle level, the geometry of the environment is described using grid maps and quadtree maps. At the same level, perception maps store the list of stationary objects present in the corresponding area as well as the identifiers of the pedestrians currently there. Finally, at the top level, the environment is modeled as a set of bounded 3D volumes (such as rooms or corridors) as well as their interconnections, resulting in a graph capturing the environment topology. Pedestrians are equipped with a set of basic reactive behaviors allowing them to execute basic tasks (e.g., walk along a direction) while avoiding collision with other mobile objects, such as other pedestrians. The set of reactive behaviors allows one to consider densely populated areas or highly dynamic scenes. The topological map allows the achievement of higher-level tasks such as reaching a far destination. A global path is found which is a succession of bounded places to cross (as the nodes of this map are 3D bounded volumes). The path is then refined using the grid maps describing geometrically each node of the topological map. Performance of the solution allows 1400 pedestrians to be simulated at an average rate of 12.3 frames per second.

VR applications often require one to define and run different scenarios during experiments. Ulicny et al. designed a dedicated tool, called *Crowdbrush*, as illustrated in Fig. 5.10 easing such tasks. Among many other functionalities, Crowdbrush allows one to design sequences of places of variable size to go, defining paths. Crowdbrush also allows one to assign pedestrians to paths. No motion planning method is involved as paths are hand-designed. Helbing's social forces [HM95] are used to avoid intercollisions between virtual humans.

Finally, Dobbyn et al. [DHOO05] use a simple navigation map, stored as a texture on the graphics hardware to distinguish navigable areas from obstacles. Recently, Allen et al. also proposed the concept of polite agents for traversing dense crowds [AMTT12].

5.4.3 A Decomposition Approach for Crowd Navigation

Navigation Graphs is a novel approach to the crowd navigation problem. The next section describes the goals and objectives of Navigation Graphs. Then, the data structure supporting the solution is detailed as well as a method for computing it. The principles of two tools based on Navigation Graphs, a crowd navigation planner and a crowd navigation simulator, are then exposed.

Objectives

The main goal of Navigation Graphs is to allow the cyber-exploration of large inhabited virtual worlds, where the population activity is limited to navigation tasks. Two main problems need addressing to reach such a goal: the design of a virtual population and the simulation of navigation tasks.

Concerning the population design, the main objective is to ease the process: a few minutes and some mouse clicks are sufficient to populate a virtual world using our technique, with coherent and believable results. The second objective is to allow

5.4 Crowds Navigation

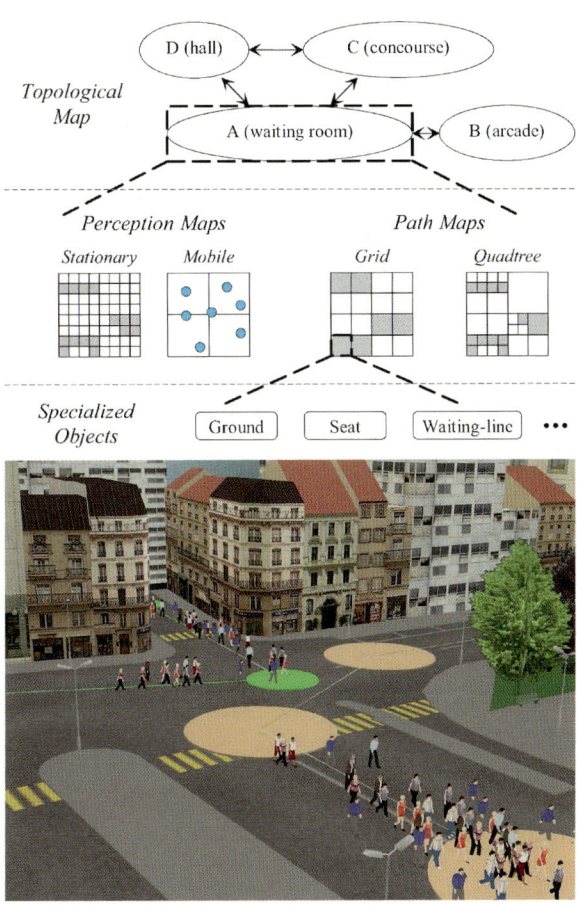

Fig. 5.10 Virtual reality

interactivity: the user is able to observe immediately the design operations' results, and to edit the configuration until he is satisfied with the resulting simulation. Finally, the solution is able to handle a large class of environments (cities, landscapes, natural scenes, buildings, etc.) and various population sizes, up to tens of thousands of pedestrians.

To reach such objectives, the Navigation Graphs-based *crowd planner* allows a user to attribute goals to pedestrians. To quicken the design process, groups of pedestrians are processed simultaneously. To increase the realism, each pedestrian has a personalized solution to reach its goal destination, which eventually varies with time with respect to the context. The proposed crowd navigation planner solves *navigation flows* queries formulated as follow: "n people are wanted to navigate between A and B with $x\%$ scattering." Its main principles are presented later in this section with technical details.

The main goal of the *crowd navigation simulator* is to provide the most believable experience to the cyber-explorer immersed in the populated virtual world. As a large crowd is simulated in real time, a distribution of the available computational resources is required in order to preserve high refresh rates. These resources should be mainly concentrated where the cyber-explorer look focuses: the way pedestrians are steered to follow their itinerary is the best there, whereas simplifications are progressively done in more distant areas. As a result, the simulation should be scalable.

Navigation Graphs ease the scaling of a crowd simulation. They maintain relationships between navigating pedestrians and the environment. They also enable the distribution of *Levels of Simulation*—LoS, which indicates the required quality of simulation at a given place and time—in an efficient manner. More details are given later in this section.

This set of objectives makes the Navigation Graphs-based planner and simulator ideal for VR and entertainment applications: different simulation setups can be rapidly created, and the immersion experience is rich thanks to the optimum quality of the simulation in the focus area of the spectator.

Navigation Graphs

Navigation Graphs is a data structure capturing the topology and the geometry of the navigable space of a given environment. This structure is inspired by cell-decomposition techniques from the robotics field; however, the decomposition is not complete. For a given environment, the navigable space is composed by the surfaces free of obstacles and flat enough to allow navigation. Navigation Graphs decompose the navigable space in a set of circles. Intersecting circles are adjacent navigable areas, and thus connected by an edge in Navigation Graphs. Figure 5.11 illustrates Navigation Graphs in an academic example (top image), and on a test environment (bottom images). The academic example shows that the graph vertices are placed in a specific manner: centered on the maximum clearance path (generalized Voronoï diagram), and each separated with a minimum distance in order to provide a trade-off between the complexity of the graph and the quality of its coverage. Geometrically, edges are segments of line joining the circles intersection. They delimit gates that pedestrians must cross to go from a navigable area to another. The two bottom images illustrate an example of Navigation Graphs computed for a test outdoor environment. Vertices and Edges are displayed separately. This example illustrates the ability of Navigation Graphs to consider uneven and multilayered environments.

The inputs of the Navigation Graphs computation technique are the mesh of the environment and a few user-defined parameters. These parameters are, first, the size of the pedestrians (maximum width and height h of people in the crowd), second, the slope angle they are capable to cross, and finally, a computational precision.

A method for computing Navigation Graphs using graphics hardware is presented in [PLT05]. It uses an intermediate grid to ease the computation. The major method steps are:

1. *Environment Mesh Sampling*: The mesh is sampled at the user-defined precision and stored as a multi-elevation map (horizontal coordinates refer to one or more elevations).

5.4 Crowds Navigation

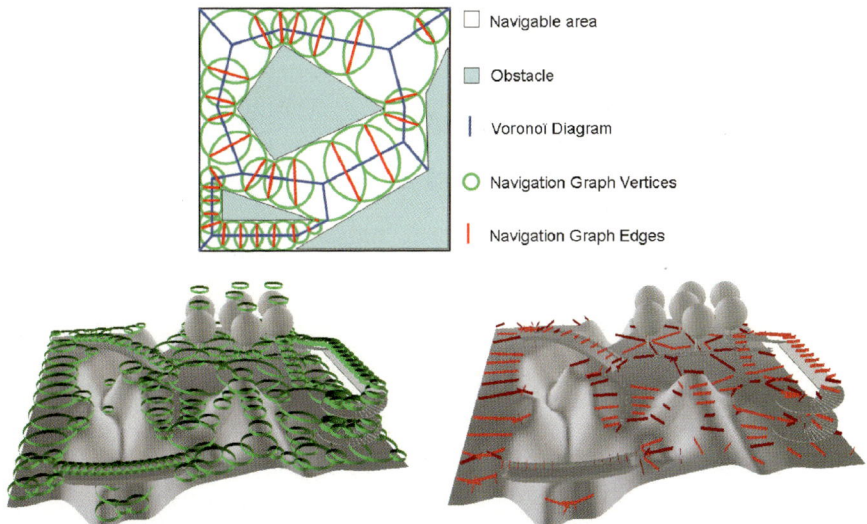

Fig. 5.11 Navigation Graphs principles. *Top*: example of a Navigation Graph in a 2D academic example. *Bottom*: Vertices (*left*) and Edges (*right*) of a Navigation Graph computed for a natural scene

2. *Map Filtering*: superposed points separated by a vertical distance below the user-defined height h are filtered. The lowest point is deleted.
3. *Map Points Connection*: The map points are then interconnected. Each point is potentially connected to its four side neighbors. Each connection between two points is done under the following conditions: no obstacle stands in-between and the slope is limited to the user-defined max slope angle.
4. *Clearance*: The distance from every point of the map to the nearest obstacle or impassable slope is computed.
5. *Navigation Graph Vertices*: Vertices are created from a set of selected elevation map points. Their characteristics are directly deduced from previous computation: circles are centered on the selected points and their radius equals the corresponding clearance.
6. *Navigation Graph Edges*: Edges are computed and created between overlapping vertices.

Navigation Graphs are computed only once for each environment. They are stored for future reuses. An advantage of Navigation Graphs is to provide a memory-saving representation of the environment (the description of a set of circles and segments of lines). No expertise is required to compute Navigation Graphs, the required input parameters can be simply deduced from the environment characteristics (size of the scene and of passages). However, a little expertise allows a user to add some optional parameters in order to find trade-offs between complexity and quality of the resulting graph.

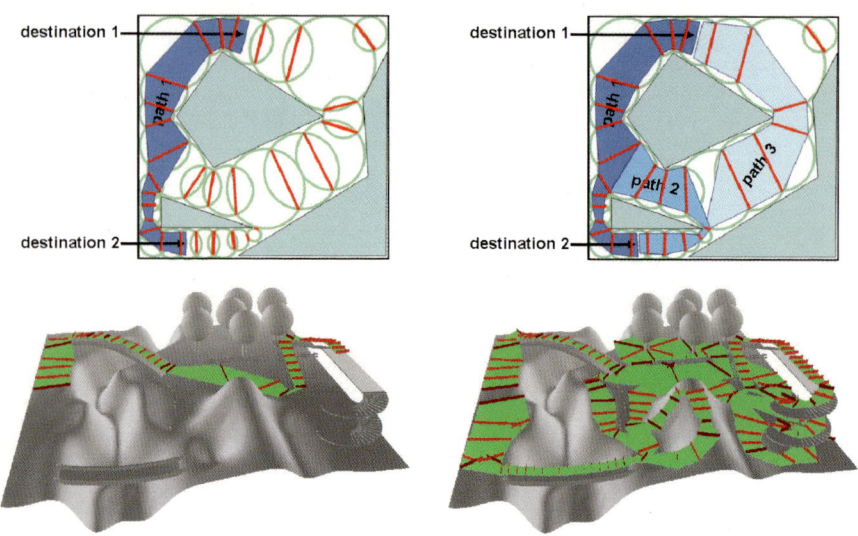

Fig. 5.12 Navigation planning principles. *Top images*: Academic environment with a navigation path (*left*) and a navigation flow (*right*) between two desired destinations. *Bottom images*: Natural environment with a navigation path (*left*) and a navigation flow (*right*) between two desired destinations

Path Planning with Variety

Navigation Flow queries—previously defined as "n people between locations A and B with x a scattering factor"—are solved by planning paths between two desired locations. As for other cell-decomposition based approaches, a graph search algorithm is used: Dijkstra's search provides the optimal solution. Given the Navigation Graphs structure, solution paths are set of gates to cross. Gates delimit polygonal corridors inside which a collision-free navigation with static obstacles is guaranteed. Pedestrians avoid each other while remaining inside corridors to accomplish their navigation goal. An example of such a path is presented in Fig. 5.12, for the academic environment (top-left image) as well as for the garden example (bottom-left image).

The corridors' width provides a first level of variety for the pedestrians' trajectories. However, congestion points may appear where the gates composing the solution are thin. For this reason, alternative solutions are searched, which provide a second level of variety. Alternative paths are found by modifying the edge costs of Navigation Graphs and running graph searches again. The deepness of the search for alternative paths depends on the desired scattering parameter x. The set of solution paths (solution and alternative ones) compose a navigation flow (right images of Fig. 5.12).

Variety is an important factor. Indeed, if pedestrians get individualized trajectories directly at the planning stage, the number of potential interactions (intercollisions) is reduced. Scattering people thus saves computation time during the sim-

5.4 Crowds Navigation

Algorithm 5.1: Navigation flow query

Data: locations A and B, Nav. Graph $\mathcal{NG}$, scattering factor x
Result: a navigation Flow F_{sol} set of solution paths $\{P_{ref}, P_{sol_1}, \ldots, P_{sol_n}\}$

```
 1  begin
 2    v_A ← the NG vertex including A
 3    v_B ← the NG vertex including B
 4    E_inc ← {}
 5    P_ref ← Dijkstra(v_A, v_B, NG)
 6    F_sol ← {P_ref}
 7    while true do
 8      P_sol_i ← Dijkstra(v_A, v_B, NG)
 9      if P_sol_i ∉ F_sol then
10        if length(P_sol_i) < x × length(P_ref) then
11          F_sol ← F_sol ∪ {P_sol_i}
12        end
13        else return F_sol
14      end
15      if ∃e \ e ← Thinnest({e | e ∈ P_sol ∧ e ∉ E_inc}) then
16        e_cost = e_cost × 10
17        E_inc ← E_inc ∪ {e}
18      end
19      else return F_sol
20    end
21  end
```

ulation. Moreover, it allows us to scale more efficiently the simulation: at far distances, where intercollisions are hardly (or even no more) detectable by a spectator, the avoidance system can be disabled, and pedestrians still get naturally scattered, which is required for believable simulations. In other approaches, variations in behaviors often result only from interactions between people (especially when goals and initial conditions are identical for several pedestrians). Finally, the simulation setup may be reduced: Navigation Flows allow the navigation planning stage for a batch of pedestrians.

A Navigation Flow query is solved using Algorithm 5.1: it puts into practice the previously introduced technique. Initially, edges cost equals the distance between the centers of the linked areas. E_{inc} is the set of edge whose cost has already been increased (initially empty, line 4). Increasing a given edge cost is allowed only once (line 15). P_{ref} is the shortest path belonging to the solution flow F_{sol} (lines 5–6). Its length is used as a reference, and the algorithm will not search for a path longer than x times this length (lines 10–13), where x is the user-defined scattering factor. Before searching for a new alternative path, edges costs are modified (lines 15–18): the thinnest gate whose cost has not been modified yet is increased.

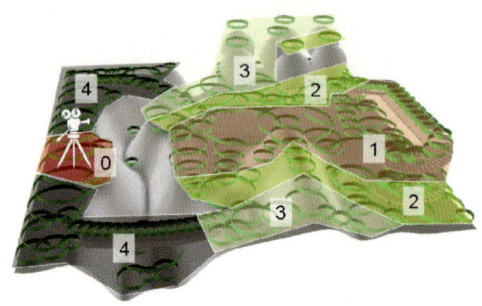

Fig. 5.13 Scalable simulation: distribution of the LoS values according to the point of view

The algorithm results in a set of paths joining A and B. All paths are different, and implicitly ordered from the shortest to the longest, as they are progressively discovered in this order.

Scalable Simulation

The previously dispatched population of pedestrians is brought to life by the crowd navigation simulator [PdHCM*06]. The simulator is designed to handle very large crowds up to tens of thousands of pedestrians in real time, on a desktop computer. Current power of such computers does not allow high-fidelity simulation for all pedestrians at the same time. As a result, the simulation must be scaled to distribute the available computation time so that the simulation remains believable in the surrounding area of the immersed spectator, while simplifications are done elsewhere.

To do so, the position and orientation of the spectator's look are taken into account each time step, and a level of simulation (LoS) is computed for each pedestrian according to their relative position. The LoS determines how precisely is executed by the navigation task:

- simulation update frequency,
- enabling collision avoidance between pedestrians or not,
- quality of steering.

In a large scene, most of the pedestrians are invisible to the spectator at a given time. For these pedestrians, the update will be done at low quality: at low frequencies and approximately.

In case of a huge virtual population, even the time required for computing LoS and simulating may compromise the real-time rates. Batched computations allow to push the limit back. A key-idea is to reuse the spatial partition of the space captured by Navigation Graphs. Indeed, LoS are computed for a whole navigable area and it affects to all the pedestrians contained in this area. The repartition of LoS values according to the point of view is illustrated in Fig. 5.13.

Algorithm 5.2 updates the simulation. Unlike other simulations, the loop first scans all the navigable areas captured in the Navigation Graph (V, line 2). A LoS is

5.4 Crowds Navigation

Algorithm 5.2: Simulation loop

Data: simulation initialized, Navigation Graph $\mathcal{NG}$, spectator's point of view PoV
Result: updated situation

1 **begin**
2   **forall the** *vertex* $V \in \mathcal{NG}$ **do**
3   LoS $\leftarrow$ ComputeLoS(V, PoV)
4   **if** *UpdateRequired(LoS,V::LastUpdateTime)* **then**
5   V::LastUpdateTime $\leftarrow$ Time
6   **forall the** *pedestrian* $P \in V$ **do**
7   Steering(P,LoS)
8   **if** *WayPointReached* **then**
9   **if** *EndOfPath* **then**
10   GoBackward
11   ChooseCurrentBestPath
12   **end**
13   ComputeNewWayPoint
14   MoveToNextVertex
15   **end**
16   **end**
17   **end**
18   **end**
19   UpdatePathsTravelTimes
20 **end**

---

computed for each area (line 3).[3] Updating is required or not according to the LoS value and the time at which the considered area was last updated (line 4). Updates are done at low rates (e.g., 1 Hz) for low-quality LoS values (far or invisible areas), whereas real-time rates are wanted in front of the spectator (25 Hz, high-quality LoS).

Now, pedestrians contained in V are considered individually (line 6). They are steered according to the LoS again: with or without collision avoidance [HM95, Rey99], smoothly ([Rey99] using only the seek behavior) or not (linear steering toward the way point). Way points are computed according to the followed path: a point is picked within each gate to cross. As a result, reaching a way point corresponds to a transition from a vertex to another for the considered pedestrian. The references to the pedestrians navigating inside each vertex are changed accordingly

---

[3] In some rare cases, an area may correspond to several LoS (e.g., because the area is very large), and each pedestrian is then considered individually. This case is not detailed here in the interest of readability.

Fig. 5.14 Way-point computing according to an individual parameter p

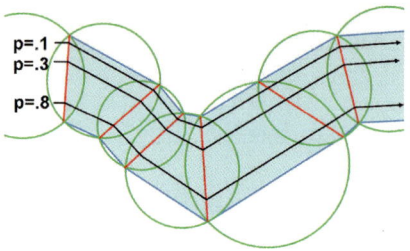

(lines 13–14). These references are crucial: they allow a fast selection of pedestrians navigating in a given area.

Way points are computed at each gate which must be crossed according to an individual parameter. This parameter ranges from 0 to 1: 0 corresponds to the left extremity of the gate, and 1 is the right extremity. For values between 0 and 1, the way point is moved from the left to the right of the gate accordingly, as shown in Fig. 5.14.

When the end of the path is reached, the pedestrian is at the extremity of the flow (see Sect. 5.4.3). He then goes back to the previous extremity, following any path of the set composing the flow (lines 9–12). Our solution chooses the path currently having the best travel time. Travel time is estimated by taking into account the distance and the population density along the path (line 19).

5.4.4 An Hybrid Architecture Based on Regions of Interest (ROI)

More recently, Treuille et al. [TCP06] proposed realistic motion planning for crowds. Their method produces a potential field that provides, for each pedestrian, the next suitable position in space (a waypoint) to avoid all obstacles. Compared to agent-based approaches, these techniques allow to simulate thousands of pedestrians in real time, and are also able to show emergent behaviors. However, they produced less believable results, because they require assumptions that prevent treating each pedestrian with individual characteristics. For instance, only a limited number of goals can be defined and assigned to groups of pedestrians. The resulting performance depends on the size of the grid cells and the number of groups.

We proposed [MYMT08] a hybrid architecture to handle the path planning of thousands of pedestrians in real time, while ensuring dynamic collision avoidance. The scalability of our approach allows to interactively create and distribute regions of varied interest, where motion planning is ruled by different algorithms. Practically, regions of high interest are governed by a long-term potential field-based approach, while other zones exploit a graph of the environment and short-term avoidance techniques. Our method also ensures pedestrian motion continuity when switching between motion planning algorithms. Tests and comparisons show that our architecture is able to realistically plan motion for many groups of characters, for a total of several thousands of people in real time, and in varied environments.

5.4 Crowds Navigation

Fig. 5.15 The three Regions of Interest

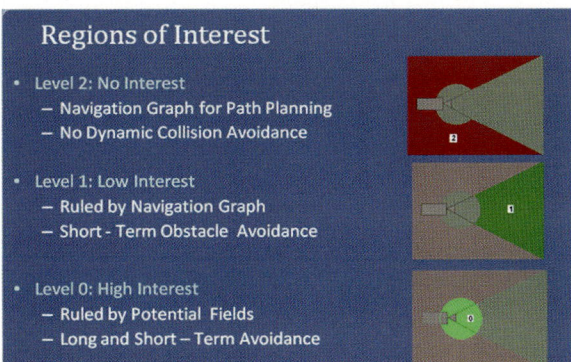

The goal of our architecture is to handle thousands of pedestrians in real time. We thus exploit the above mentioned vertex structure to divide the environment into regions ruled by different motion planning techniques. Regions of interest (ROI) can be defined in any number and anywhere in the walkable space with high-level parameters, modifiable at runtime.

By defining three different ROIs, we obtain a simple and flexible architecture for realistic results: ROI 0 is composed of vertices of high interest, ROI 1 regroups vertices of low interest, and ROI 2 contains all other vertices, of no interest.

For regions of no interest (ROI 2), path planning is ruled by the navigation graph. Pedestrians are linearly steered to the list of waypoints on their path edges. To use the minimal computation resources, obstacle avoidance is not handled.

Path planning in regions of low interest (ROI 1) is also ruled by the navigation graph. To steer pedestrians to their waypoints, an approach similar to Reynolds' is used [Rey99], and obstacles are avoided with an agent-based short-term algorithm. Although agent-based, this algorithm works at low level, and thus stays simple and efficient.

In the regions of high interest (ROI 0), path planning and obstacle avoidance are both ruled by a potential field-based algorithm, similarly to Treuille et al. [TCP06]. Figure 5.15 summarizes the situation.

This hybrid architecture allows realistic real-time crowd motion planning for thousands of pedestrians. Our approach is scalable; it is possible to divide the scene into regions and exploit different motion planning algorithms according to their level of interest. The architecture flexibility allows the user to determine the performance he wishes and to select and distribute the regions of interest (ROI) accordingly. In our implementation, we employ an accurate potential field-based method for pedestrians in ROI 0. A simple and efficient short-term avoidance algorithm is exploited in both ROI 0 and 1, thus ensuring no noticeable transition at region borders. Results show that it is possible to simulate over 10,000 characters in real time, while defining many more groups than in a purely potential field-based approach. Realism is further demonstrated with observable emergent behaviors, like lane formations, and panic escape. Figure 5.16 shows a crowd moving using the hybrid path planning algorithm.

Fig. 5.16 Shows a crowd moving using the hybrid path planning algorithm

Fig. 5.17 Panic escape

As an example, we have a scenario using a city pedestrian area with several surrounding streets and buildings. There are 5,000 pedestrians and some cars on the roads, as illustrated in Fig. 5.17. Each cell of the grid covers a 3×3 m^2 area. Since the user attention is mainly drawn by the threatening cars, a region of high interest (ROI 0) is set around each of them. Moreover, to make pedestrians flee potential collisions, a high discomfort and speed increase are set in front of the cars, as in [TCP06]. As a result, pedestrians close to a car are always in a region of high interest, and thus ruled by a potential field. In front of cars particularly, the pedestrians flee the zone of danger, demonstrating an emergent panic behavior. The remaining visible environment is classified as a region of low interest (ROI 1), so that pedestrians still take care to avoid each other, while the zone outside the view frustum is set as of no interest (ROI 2). The resulting fps varies between 15 and 30, depending on the number of visible cars (1 to 3), and the size of their surrounding ROI 0 (10 to 15 m radius).

There are some limitations to our architecture. Firstly, in too crowded narrow environments, severe bottlenecks may appear, making the use of our potential field-based approach a waste of computational time. However, it is possible to enforce a low level of interest in these regions, e.g., ruled by a short-term avoidance algorithm. Another limitation is our group-based approach: we are constrained to assign general goals for groups of pedestrians. One goal per pedestrian would be too prohibitive for real-time applications. Yet, we note that our architecture is able to handle many more groups than previous potential field-based methods. This is mainly due to our massive reduction of the number of cells in which the potential is actually computed, and implies the possibility to refine the grid for more accurate results.

An interesting lead for future work is to merge other avoidance algorithms in the architecture to obtain better results in crowded situations where the space is narrow. Algorithms simulating each pedestrian individually, with respective characteristics, should be investigated and possibly merged with our ROI architecture. Also, techniques to make the pedestrian animation perfectly synchronized with its motion should be explored. Another aspect of crowds that arouses our interest is the simulation of small groups of people. Indeed, in real life, it is rare to observe people walking alone, and flocking behaviors are necessary to obtain realistic results.

5.5 A Collision Avoidance Method Based on the Space Colonization Algorithm

The crowd modeling method proposed in this section is based on the space colonization algorithm, which was originally proposed to model leaf venation patterns [RFL*05]. Variants of this algorithm make it possible to generate branching or reticulate patterns. Here we review the branching venation model, which more directly applies to crowd animation.

The venation model simulates three processes within an iterative loop: leaf blade growth, the placement of markers of free space, and the addition of new veins. The markers correspond to sources of the plant hormone auxin, which, according to a biological hypothesis [ASLU03], emerge in the growing leaf regions not penetrated by veins. A set of markers S interacts with the vein pattern, which consists of a set of points V called *vein nodes*. This pattern is extended iteratively toward the markers of free space. The markers that are approached by the advancing veins are gradually removed, since the space around them is no longer free. As the leaf grows, additional markers of free space are added in the space between existing veins and markers. This process continues until the growth stops, and there are no markers left.

The interplay between markers of free space and vein nodes is at the heart of the space colonization algorithm. During each iteration, a vein node is influenced by all the markers closer to it than any other vein node. Thus, veins compete for markers, and thus space, as they grow. There may be several markers that influence a single vein node v: this set of points is denoted by $S(v)$. If $S(v)$ is not empty, a new vein node v' will be created and attached to v by an edge representing a vein segment. The node v' is positioned at a distance D from v, in the direction defined as the average of the normalized vectors toward all the markers $s \in S(v)$. Thus, $v' = v + D\hat{n}$, where

$$\hat{n} = \frac{n}{\|n\|} \quad \text{and} \quad n = \sum_{s \in S(v)} \frac{s - v}{\|s - v\|}. \tag{5.6}$$

The distance D serves as the basic unit of distance in the model and provides control over the resolution of the resulting structure. Once the new nodes have been added to V, a check is performed to test which, if any, of the markers of free space should be removed due to the proximity of veins that have grown toward these points.

The space colonization algorithm has subsequently been adapted to model trees [RLP07]. Beyond the extension to 3D structures, the algorithm for trees introduced the notion of the radius of influence, which limits the distance from which markers of free space can attract tree nodes. Furthermore, the set of marker points is usually predefined at the beginning of simulation and no new markers are added afterwards, since, in contrast to the expanding leaf blade, the space in which a tree grows remains fixed.

5.5.1 The Crowd Model: Biocrowds

The proposed method for crowd modeling is based on the space colonization algorithm. In its original applications to biological patterning, veins or tree branches could be regarded as paths created by vein or branch tips as they penetrated free space. In crowd simulation, these growing tips are identified with moving agents. Interestingly, an analogous relation between paths and motions can be observed in the development and applications of ideas related to particle systems. While some applications focused on the motion of particles (e.g., simulations of fire and fireworks), others emphasized their paths (e.g., simulation of grass and trees) [Ree83, RB85].

The proposed approach preserves many characteristics of the original space colonization algorithm and its extension to trees. The key new elements, underlying the adaptation of the space colonization algorithm to crowd simulation, are listed below.

1. *Persistence of markers.* In contrast to the sources of auxin, which are permanently removed when reached by veins, the markers in crowd simulations are claimed by each agent temporarily, upon entering the agent's personal space, and are released when the agent moves away. The released markers can subsequently be used by other agents.
2. *Goal seeking.* The development of veins is guided locally by the presence of auxin sources in the proximity of a vein. In contrast, the motion of people is also influenced by the intention of each individual to reach a goal.
3. *Speed adjustment.* In the original space colonization algorithm, veins grow at a constant rate. On the other hand, agents vary their speed according to the available space in our crowd model.

5.5 A Collision Avoidance Method

Input

The input to our method consists of a few parameters, namely:

- Specification of the scene in which the agents will move (e.g. obstacles).
- The number and initial positions of agents.
- The position of goals, which can be distributed by individuals or groups, depending on the application.
- The density of markers μ, that basically controls the number of markers that will be created.
- The radius R of the agents' perception field (the maximum distance from which an agent can perceive markers).
- The maximum speed s_{max} of agents.

It is important to notice that the first three parameters are crucial to define the simulation itself, regardless of the crowd simulation algorithm: obstacles, goals and location of agents. The remaining parameters (μ, R and s_{max}) can be adjusted to obtain different simulation results, but a default set values is adequate for a variety of environments, as analyzed in Sect. 5.5.2.

Initialization

In the initialization step, the virtual world is populated with markers of free space. These markers are placed randomly using the dart-throwing algorithm [Coo86] over the portions of space in which the agents are allowed to move. The walkable regions are specified by placing markers, for example using an interactive "spraying tool" (see Sect. 5.5.2). Obstacles to be avoided are left without markers. Indeed, any shape format can be used as obstacle. The optimal density of markers represents a compromise between the shape of trajectories (densely distributed markers yield smother trajectories, which are more consistent with the minimum effort hypothesis), and computation time (which increases with the marker numbers). Experimental results pertinent to the choice of marker density are discussed in Sect. 5.5.2.

Computation of the Motion Direction

The motion of each agent I is computed iteratively. At each simulation step, the position $p(t)$ and the goal vector $g(t)$ pointing to the agent's goal are updated synchronously.[4] Furthermore, the set S containing all the markers within the agent's personal space is computed. This space consists of all points closer to agent I than any other agent (this represents a Voronoi region associated with agent I, which also reside in the perception field of agent I (Fig. 5.18).

---

[4]For clarity, the time index t will be omitted from now on, unless necessary.

Fig. 5.18 Personal space (*shaded regions*) and markers (*dots*) associated with five sample agents (*squares*). The markers captured by each agent are shown in the same color as the agent

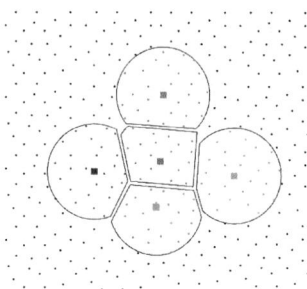

Let us consider the set of N markers $S = \{a_1, a_2, \ldots, a_N\}$ associated with agent I. In order to compute the next move of this agent, we first find the set S' of orientation vectors from this agent to all the markers in S:

$$S' = \{d_1, d_2, \ldots, d_N\}, \quad d_k = a_k - p. \tag{5.7}$$

In the simulation of vein development, the orientation vectors were normalized and simply averaged to define the direction of vein growth (Eq. (5.6)). However, in the simulation of the agents' motion we also need to take their goal vectors into account. To this end, we weight each orientation vector according to the degree to which it is aligned with the agent's goal. Specifically, the *tentative motion vector* m is computed as

$$m = \sum_{k=1}^{N} w_k d_k, \tag{5.8}$$

where coefficients w_k are the weights, calculated using the equation

$$w_k = \frac{f(g, d_k)}{\sum_{l=1}^{N} f(g, d_l)}. \tag{5.9}$$

To determine the function f, let us first assume that all markers a_k affecting agent I are at the same distance $\|d_k\|$ from this agent. The function f should then: (i) reach maximum when the (non-directed) angle θ between the goal and orientation vector is equal to $0°$; (ii) reach minimum when $\theta = 180°$; and (iii) decrease monotonically as θ increases from 0 to $180°$. If the distances $\|d_k\|$ differ, the markers further from the agent should have relatively smaller weights, to prevent them from dominating the computation of the tentative motion vector m.

A possible choice for f that satisfies these assumptions is

$$f(g, d_k) = \frac{1 + \cos \theta}{1 + \|d_k\|} = \frac{1}{1 + \|d_k\|} \left(1 + \frac{\langle g, d_k \rangle}{\|g\| \|d_k\|} \right), \tag{5.10}$$

where $\langle \cdot, \cdot \rangle$ denotes the inner product. If markers claimed by an agent are continuously and uniformly distributed in its personal space and within the agent's perception field, this choice of f will guarantee that the tentative motion vector m will point in the direction of the agent's goal. Obviously, for other marker distributions (e.g. when the user inserts obstacles) or when the perception field of an agent does

5.5 A Collision Avoidance Method

not lie in the interior of its personal space (e.g. when there are neighbors at a short distance), the agent's direction may deviate somewhat from the goal.

Computation of the Velocity Vector

It is also possible to show that (i) the position of agent I, displaced by vector m, remains within the current personal space of agent I, and (ii) the magnitude of vector m increases with the size of this space. Taken together, these properties make vector m a good candidate for specifying next-step movement of the agent, guaranteeing a collision-free trajectory and capturing the increase of speed in larger spaces. However, in calculating the actual displacement, we have to also consider the maximum speed (displacement per simulation step) $s_{\max}$ of the agent. Consequently, we calculate the actual displacement v as

$$v = s \frac{m}{\|m\|}, \quad \text{where } s = \min\{\|m\|, s_{\max}\}. \tag{5.11}$$

Equation (5.11) implies that if $\|m\| > s_{\max}$, the speed of the agent is limited by $s_{\max}$. Otherwise, the speed is given by $\|m\|$. It is important to notice that, if the radius R of the perception field is too small, the magnitude of the direction vector calculated in Eq. (5.8) will always be smaller than $s_{\max}$, making it impossible for an agent to achieve its maximum speed.

As a special case, note that the weights defined by Eq. (5.9) do not satisfy the normalizing condition $w_1 + \cdots + w_N = 1$ when the denominator is zero. This occurs when the personal space of the agent includes no markers, or when all the markers are in the direction exactly opposite to the goal ($\theta = 180°$). In these cases, we set $m = 0$, indicating that agent I should not move in a given simulation step (which makes sense, since traveling toward the markers in S would move the agent away from its goal).

Elimination of Collision Between Finite-Sized Agents

As discussed before, the motion of the agents is collision free, irrespective of the density of the crowd or markers, since their personal spaces are always non-intersecting. Furthermore, in any simulation step, not only the positions, but also the trajectories of the agents do not intersect, which appears to enhance the realism of motion. However, these observations only apply to infinitesimally small agents, and agents occupying a finite space may theoretically collide (if they approach from opposite sides the same point on an edge of a Voronoi polygon). We could generate a guaranteed collision-free motion in this case as well, by assuring that in each time step, each agent I maintains a minimum distance (based on the radius of each agent) from the edges of its current Voronoi region. We did not implement this extension, which would increase the computation time, because in our simulations using the basic algorithm we could not notice any collisions.

Fig. 5.19 Line segments connect agents and corresponding markers in 2D visualization

5.5.2 Experimental Results

In this section we present several examples that illustrate various features of the proposed crowd simulation method. In particular, we show that different aspects of the crowd dynamics outlined in Sect. 2.1 are emergent properties of our model. It is important to mention that, unless otherwise indicated, all results were obtained using the same set of parameters, regardless of the density of simulated crowds. The density of markers was set to 15 markers/m^2, and the personal space R surrounding each agent had radius of 1.25 m. Since every person in real life has their own preferred maximum speed, the individual maximum speed s_{max}^i for each virtual agent I_i was drawn at random within the interval 0.9 m/s to 1.5 m/s (0.03 to 0.05 meters per time step of 1/30 s). The default simulated environment was a square of dimensions 50 × 50 m.

We used two methods to visualize simulation results. In 2D visualizations, agents are shown as moving dots associated with line segments, and these lines point to the markers influencing each agent. An example of such a visualization is given in Fig. 5.19. It reveals that, in this case, the agents in the center of the crowd have fewer markers available to them, and therefore a more limited range of movements than the agents near the boundaries. In 3D visualizations, agents are represented as articulated virtual humans. An example of such a visualization is shown in Fig. 5.20, where 50 agents originate at the bottom left corner of the scene and move toward the flag at the opposite corner. This animation also illustrates the possibility of specifying a goal for a group of agents.

Impact of the Density of Markers

In order to properly set parameters for further experiments, we analyzed the impact of the density of markers on the trajectory of agents and the computational efficiency of simulations. According to the least effort hypothesis, the ideal trajectory in the simplest case of a single agent is a straight line between its initial position and the goal. Figure 5.21 shows the average and standard deviation (vertical line segments) of the angular variation of the agent's direction for several densities of

5.5 A Collision Avoidance Method

Fig. 5.20 Example of goal seeking behavior. Virtual agents start at the *bottom left corner* and reach the goal at the *opposite corner* of the scene

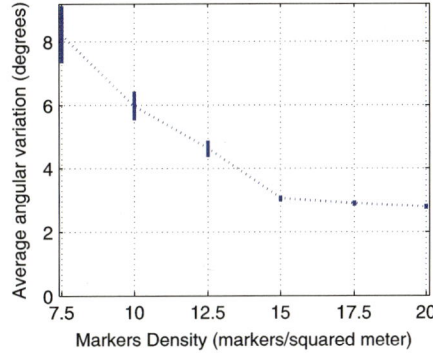

Fig. 5.21 Average variation of the agents' direction per simulation step as a function of the density of markers. *Vertical bars* indicate standard error

markers. As it can be observed, the average angular variation (as well as the standard deviation) decreases rapidly for marker densities increasing from 7.5 to 15 per m^2. The decrease is slower for marker densities exceeding 15 per m^2.

We also analyzed the relation between the density of markers and simulation time. The results were obtained for markers distributed over a square of dimension 80×80 m^2 at four different densities. As shown in Fig. 5.22, the simulation speed decreases with the number of markers, as expected.

Based on the results shown in Figs. 5.21 and 5.22, we used 15 markers per m^2 in all subsequent experiments. This value represents a compromise between computational time (simulation of 800 agents can be performed in real-time, 30 frames per second) trajectory smoothness (increases in marker density above 15 markers per m^2 do not reduce the angular variation significantly).

It is interesting to notice that a continuum distribution of markers into Voronoi polygons could be easily formulated, just replacing the summations in Eqs. (5.8) and (5.9) by integrals. However, such integrals would have to be solved numerically, which would lead to the discrete formulation proposed in this work (and higher densities of markers would correspond to a more accurate numerical solution).

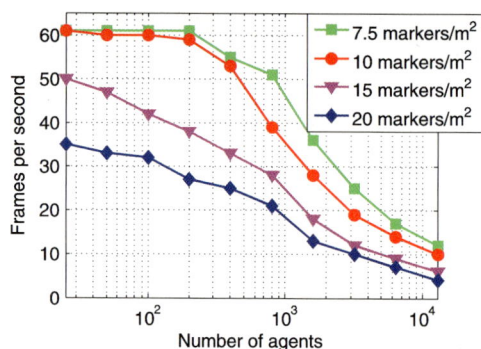

Fig. 5.22 Simulation speed as a function of the number of agents, evaluated for 4 different densities of markers. All standard deviations were less than 1 and thus are not shown. These results were obtained using Intel(R) Core^{TM} 2 Duo T7500 2.2 GHz (Mobile Technology) processor with 3 GB 667 MHz Shared Dual Channel DDR2 memory and 128 MB NVIDIA(R) GeForce(R) 8400M GS video card

The Shape of Trajectories

The smoothness of the trajectories depend not only on the density of markers, but also on the density of agents. In fact, when two groups of people move through the same space in opposite directions, people at the front of their group have to change direction to a larger extent than people who walk behind, to avoid frontal collisions with the members of the other group [Sti00]. This behavior is consistent with the least effort hypothesis, applied to each individual agent. To verify whether the same behavior emerges in our simulations, we considered two groups of agents moving in opposite directions (Fig. 5.23). We then selected two agents from the same group, one at front and the other in the middle of the group. Their trajectories are highlighted in blue and red, respectively, in Fig. 5.23. The red trajectory appears smoother than the blue one, and this observation is confirmed quantitatively: the average change (in absolute value) of the direction of the agent at the front (mean 19.19°, standard deviation 13.69° per simulation step) is larger than that of the agent in the middle (mean 15.11°, standard deviation 12.99°). For sakes of comparison, an isolated agent moving in the same field of markers would change its direction with average 3.86° and standard deviation 4.64°. Thus, as expected, a follower in a crowd changes its direction to a larger extent than an isolated agent.

Minimization of effort leads to a spontaneous formation of lanes, or chains of people who walk behind each other (cf. Sect. 2.1). Such lanes also readily emerge in our simulations, as it can be observed in Fig. 5.24. Once again, these results were obtained for two groups of agents moving in opposite directions.

Collision Avoidance

A very important behavior is collision avoidance within the crowd. While our algorithm guarantees collision-free motion, it is nevertheless interesting to evaluate it in

5.5 A Collision Avoidance Method

Fig. 5.23 Impact of the position in a crowd on the smoothness of trajectories. The *highlighted* agents are members of the *dark grey* group, which moves from the *bottom right* to the *top left corner* of the scene. Another group, shown in *light grey*, moves in the opposite direction. Due to the competition for space, the *blue trajectory*, generated by the agent near the front of its group, is less smooth than the *red trajectory*, generated by an agent in the middle

Fig. 5.24 Formation of lanes (indicated by *circles* and *squares*) in two groups of 50 people moving in opposite directions

the simulations. To this end, we considered four groups, each with 50 agents, which originated at the corners of a square scene and moved toward the opposite corners. These groups create a dense crowd of people moving in different directions near the center of the scene. Figure 5.25 shows four frames from the resulting simulation. While the set of markers allocated to each agent decreased near the center, these sets do not interpenetrate. For each agent, the next step will thus be collision free. Collision avoidance is also clearly seen in a 3D visualization of the same simulation (Fig. 5.26).

As the density of crowd increases, the number of markers associated with each agent decrease, suggesting that the agents' speed is reduced as a function of crowd density. This reduction is the essence of the "speed reduction effect." To analyze its emergence in our simulations, we performed a series of experiments with different

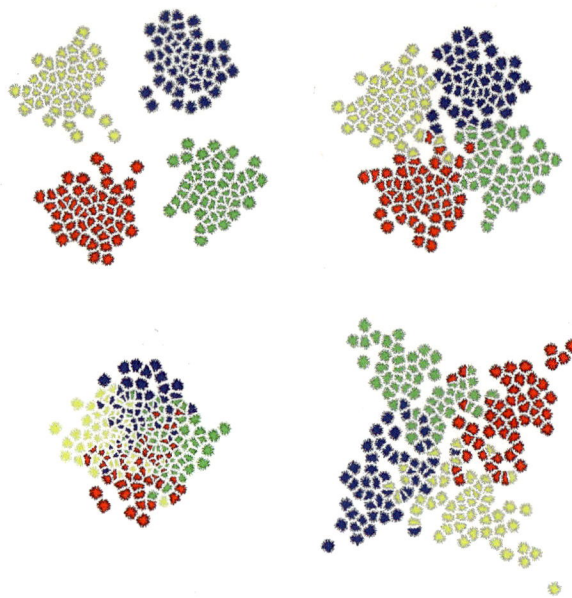

Fig. 5.25 2D visualization of the collision-avoidance behavior. Four groups cross each other in the center of the scene

Fig. 5.26 3D visualization of the collision-avoidance behavior

groups and numbers of agents moving in a corridor of dimensions 10 m × 40 m. The maximum desired speed of all agents was fixed at $s_{max} = 1.2$ m/s. In the first two experiments, one group of 25 or 50 agents moved from one end of the corridor to the other. In the remaining experiments, two groups of 25, 50, 100, 200 and 400 agents moved in opposite directions. Each experiment was repeated 20 times for different randomized configurations of marker points and initial positions of the agents. The average speeds of agents realized in these experiments are shown in Table 5.2. As expected, in the absence of flow in the opposite direction (the first two experiments), the realized speed is almost equal to the maximum speed allowed for the agents (1.2 m/s). In the simulations with groups of agents moving in opposite

5.5 A Collision Avoidance Method

Table 5.2 Speed Reduction effect: reduction of realized speed as a function of the number of agents. Maximum agent speed in each case is $s_{max} = 1.2$ m/s

	Number of agents (number of groups)						
	25 (1)	50 (1)	50 (2)	100 (2)	200 (2)	400 (2)	800 (2)
Mean realized speed (m/s)	1.19	1.19	1.17	1.16	1.14	1.11	1.09
Standard deviation (m/s)	0.0006	0.0006	0.0021	0.0045	0.0096	0.0206	0.0319

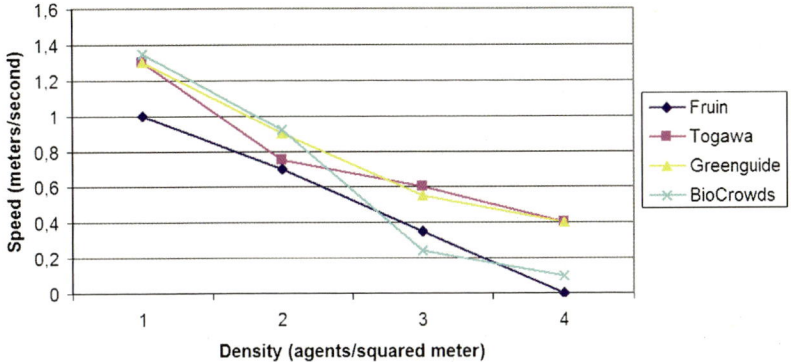

Fig. 5.27 Mean agent speed as a function of local crowd density. Plots labeled Green guide, Fruin, and Purple guide represent measured data from real life, while plot labeled BioCrowds describes emergent results of our method. In these simulations, we assumed that the maximum velocity of agents was 1.2 m/s

directions, the realized speeds were progressively smaller as the number of agents increased.

These results can be expressed in terms of the global density of agents. For instance, in the last experiment (last column in Table 5.2) there are on average 2 agents per m² (800 agents/400 m²). However, global density is not a very informative measure of crowding, since it may vary spatially. In our simulations, the groups crossed each other near the center of the corridor, forming a high-density area there, while other areas were relatively empty. To take these differences into account, we divided the corridor into cells of dimensions 1 m × 1 m, and computed the number and mean velocity of agents in each cell. The results are shown in Fig. 5.27, which compares the distribution of speeds generated using our method (here labeled BioCrowds) with the average speeds reported for various densities of real crowds [Fru71, Dep97, Hea93]. It can be observed, the emergent speeds of crowds simulated using our method are consistent with the measured data.

The Stopping Effects

Virtual agents move when they have available markers in their perception fields and personal spaces. It is the essence of competition for space strategy in which

Fig. 5.28 Bottleneck effect: *Ellipses* highlight the regions where agents stop due to the environment

Fig. 5.29 Arc formation: Agents have the same goal (e.g. location of a door—*black square*) and stop forming an arc

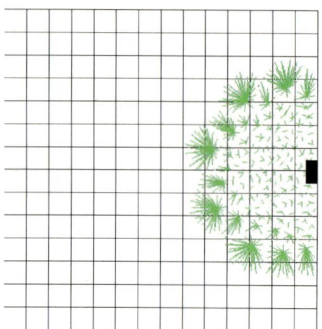

agents fight for space and, then, move accordingly. However, when there are no markers available, stopping effects can happen, as it can also happen in real life. Two stopping effects are illustrated in this section: (i) Bottleneck effect and (ii) Arc formation. The first one describes the increase of density (and reduction of speed) that happens in environment presenting bottleneck due to walls (see Fig. 5.28). In this figure, ellipses and squares are used to show the bottleneck effect, respectively to measure density and speed before and after the bottleneck in the environment as well as in the middle of the corridor. The higher density in regions defined by ellipses (before the bottleneck) is 4 persons/m^2, with average speed of 0.31 m/s and standard deviation 0.056. On the other hand, higher density measured in regions after the bottleneck present a density of 2 persons/m^2, with average speed of 1.18 m/s and standard deviation 0.03. Finally, in the middle of the corridor (illustrated as a square in Fig. 5.28) the greater observed density is equal to 3 persons/m^2, with average speed 0.99 m/s and standard deviation 0.004.

The second behavior was firstly proposed by Helbing et al. [HFV00], and it describes the phenomena that occurs when people stop due to an exit door, including stopping effect and also the emerging geometrical arc formation (see Fig. 5.29).

Interactive Crowd Control

The motion of agents can be interactively controlled by interactively spraying or erasing markers. Figure 5.30 shows a screenshot of our prototype system that implements such interaction. Agents tend to follow paths with higher density of markers, so that local control can be achieved by increasing the number of markers along preferred paths. When markers are removed, agents immediately adjust their paths as shown in Fig. 5.31.

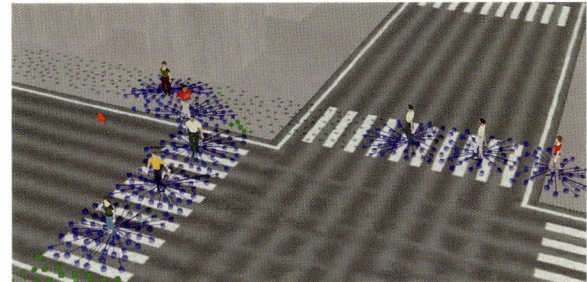

Fig. 5.30 Prototype system for crowd simulation with interactive control. The user "sprays" markers (*green dots*) on the floor. The distribution of markers directs the agents

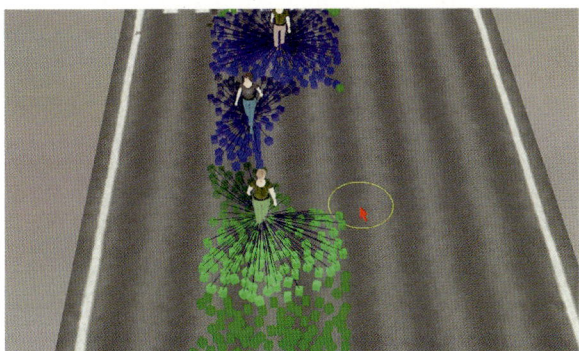

Fig. 5.31 Removing markers in the environment affect the virtual humans' trajectories (the first and second agents are influenced by the new configuration of markers). The *yellow circle* represents the marker eraser, and it has been used to narrow down the region where the agents can walk

Fig. 5.32 Example of gaze behaviors for virtual crowd characters

5.6 Gaze Behaviors for Virtual Crowd Characters

We believe that an important aspect which can greatly enhance crowd simulation realism (see Fig. 5.32) is for the characters to be aware of their environment, other characters and/or a user. This can partly be achieved with the navigation and path planning algorithms already presented in this Chapter. In this Section, we propose a method [GT09] integrated in the crowd simulation pipeline, to obtain more advanced behaviors than what navigation can provide. To add attentional behaviors to crowds, we are confronted to two issues. The first one is to detect the points of interest for characters to look at. The second one is to edit the character motions for them to perform the gaze behavior.

5.6.1 Simulation of Attentional Behaviors

Attention Models

The synthesis of human vision and perception is a complex problem which has been tackled in many different ways. Models of synthetic vision based on memory have been developed for the navigation of characters [RMTT90, NRTMT95, KJL99, PO02].

Other proposed models relied on bottom-up, stimulus-driven rules [HJ99, CKB99] and saliency maps [ID03, POS03, MC02, KHT05]. Similarly, much work has been conducted in the simulation of visual attention and gaze in Embodied Conversational Agents [PPB*05, EN06, LM07]. On a different note, [LBB02] described an eye movement model based on saccade empirical models and statistical models of eye-tracking data, and [LT06] proposed a head-neck model based on biomechanics. All these methods give very convincing results but are prohibitive in terms of computational times or not applicable crowd simulations.

The attentional behaviors should be added to the walking character motion in a specific Gaze module. The first step is to define the interest points, i.e. the points in space which we consider interesting and which therefore attract the characters' attention. We use several different methods to do this depending on the result we want to obtain:

- The interest points can be defined as regions in space which have been described as interesting. In this case, they will be static.
- They can be defined as characters evolving in space. All characters may then potentially attract the attention of other characters as long as they are in their field of view. In this case, we have dynamic constraints, since the characters move around.
- They can be defined as a user if we track a user interacting with the system.
- A coupled head- and eye-tracking setup allows us to define the position of the user in the 3D space as depicted in Fig. 5.33. Characters may then look at the user.

The second step to obtain the desired attentional behaviors consists in computing the displacement map which allows for the current character posture to achieve the gaze posture, i.e. to satisfy the gaze constraints. Once the displacement map has been computed, it is dispatched to the various joints composing the eyes, head, and spine in order for each to contribute to the final posture. Finally, this displacement is propagated in time in order for the looking or looking away motions to be smooth, natural, and human-like.

5.6 Gaze Behaviors for Virtual Crowd Characters

Fig. 5.33 A user is tracked in a CAVE environment. His position and orientation is used to interact with the characters walking in the virtual environment

Fig. 5.34 Interest point for a character

5.6.2 Gaze Behaviors for Crowds

Interest Points

The first step is to define where and when each character should look (Fig. 5.34). As mentioned in Sect. 5.5.1, the method to do this varies depending on the setup and the results we want to obtain.

The first method is to use the meta-information present in the environment model. This meta-information allows to describe the various environmental elements as "interesting" to look at. If this is the case, they will attract character attention. Characters will perform the gaze behavior in proximity of these elements and as long as they are in their field of view. These types of interest points are always at the same position in the scene; they are static elements.

The second method we use to define interest points is by assigning them to other characters in the scene. We may assign different levels of interest to different characters. In this way, some of them will attract attention more than others. As for the environmental elements, characters will attract the attention of other characters when in their proximity and as long as they remain in their field of view. These types of interest points are moving entities; they are therefore dynamic.

Finally, the third type of interest point is the user. A person using our system may be tracked using a coupled head- and eye-tracker. In this way, we can track the user position and gaze in the crowd engine 3D space. In this case, the user will be the interest point. Moreover, since we can track the user's gaze, the user's interest points (where he looks at) may become interest points for the characters in the environment. They will thus seem to unconsciously imitate the user. They will seem to try and find out what the user is looking at.

5.6.3 Automatic Interest Point Detection

The first step in our method consists of automatically detecting the interest points from the entity trajectories. We define an interest point *IP* as an entity E which should be attended to by a given character C. More formally, *IP* is defined as:

$$IP(t) = [p_t, t_a, t_d, [t_b, t_e]] \quad \text{where } p_t \in \mathbb{R}^3 \tag{5.12}$$

where p_t is *IP*'s position in space at time t. t_a is its activation duration, t_d its deactivation duration, and $[t_b, t_e]$ represents its lifespan. The purpose of t_a is to define the amount of time it will take for the looking motion to be executed. Conversely, t_d defines the amount of time for C to look away from *IP*. It is to be noted that in the case where the *IP* is replaced by another, the deactivation is skipped and replaced by the activation to go from the first *IP* to the second. Another important factor in gaze behaviors is that we do not look at things indefinitely. We can either lose interest or find something else more interesting to look at. It is the duration for which an entity E is an *IP*. For each character C and at each time t, we define the level of interest other entities have by assigning them a score S(t) computed through a scoring function. The entity E which obtains the highest score *Smax*(t) becomes the *IP* that should be attended to by C at time t as long as it fulfills two conditions. *Smax*(t) first has to be above an attention threshold. This defines the percentage of time C will be attentive to other entities. Second, E should obtain *Smax*(t) for a minimal amount of time $[t_b, t_e]$ which we have empirically set to 1/3 s. Previous studies such as Neisser's [Ulr67] explain that human attention is captured by substantial differences in one or more simple visual attributes. Simple visual attributes are features such as color, orientation, size, and motion [WH04]. Additionally, Yantis and Jonides [YJ90] underlined that abrupt visual onsets equally attract human attention. These studies have motivated our choice of four different criteria as components to our scoring function:

- Proximity: closer objects or people seem larger and attract attention more easily than those far away. Moreover, those which are closer occlude those which are further away.
- Relative speed: a person will be more prone to set his/her attention on something moving fast than moving slowly relative to his/her own velocity.
- Relative orientation: we are more attentive to objects coming towards us than moving away from us. Moreover, something coming towards us seems to become larger.

Fig. 5.35 Periphery vision

- Periphery: we are very sensitive to movements occurring in the peripheral vision. More specifically, to objects or people entering the field of view (Fig. 5.35).

To decide where a given character will look at a given time we evaluate all entities in terms of these criteria. As depicted in Fig. 5.36, we evaluate a set of parameters for each of these entities: the distance $d_{c_e}(t)$, the relative speed $r_s(t)$ defined by forward differentiation as $\|d_e(t) - d_c(t)\|$, the orientation in the field of view $\alpha(t)$, and the relative direction $\beta(t)$. Similarly to Sung et al. [SGC04], we then combine these parameters to create more complex scoring functions: S_p for proximity, S_s for speed, S_o for orientation, and S_{p_e} for periphery.

5.6.4 Motion Adaptation

In order to obtain convincing results, we then have to adapt the character motion in order for them to look at the interest points. Since the characters and the interest points may be dynamic, we have to compute the joint displacements to be applied to the base motion at each time step.

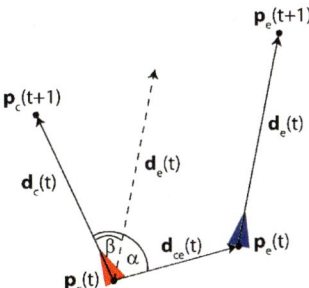

Fig. 5.36 Schematical representation of the parameters used for the elementary scoring $p_c(t)$ is the character position at time t, $p_e(t)$ is the entity position at time t, α is the entity orientation in the character's field of view, and β is the angle between the character and the entity forward directions

The skeletons we use are composed of 86 joints. Our method adjusts 10 of them: 5 spinal cord joints, 2 cervical joints, 1 head joint and 2 eye joints, in order for the characters to align their gaze to the interest points. By considering only this subset of the full skeleton, we greatly reduce the complexity of our algorithm. This allows us to have very small computational times and thus to animate a large number of characters.

Our method consists of two distinct phases. The first one computes the displacement maps to be applied to the various joints in order to satisfy the gaze constraints poral resolution. This allows to propagate the displacement maps over an automatically defined number of frames onto the original motion. We thus ensure a smooth and continuous final movement.

Spatial Resolution

The purpose of the spatial resolution is to find a displacement map that modifies the initial motion in order to satisfy a given gaze constraint. At each timestep, and for each deformable mesh in the crowd, if there is an active constraint, we launch an iterative loop starting with the bottom of the kinematic chain (lumbar verterbrae) and ending with the top of the kinematic chain (the eyes). At each iteration, we calculate the total remaining rotation to be done by the average eyes position (global eye) to satisfy the constraint. However, since the eyes are not the only joints to adjust, we dispatch this rotation to the other recruited joints.

To determine the contribution of each joint to the complete rotation we take inspiration from the work of [BUT04]. The authors proposed a set of formulae to define the angle proportions to be assigned to the spine joints depending on the type of rotation to be done (pitch, yaw or roll). We use the formula they propose for the linearly increasing rotation distribution around the vertical axis. In our model, the rotations around the sagittal and frontal axes are very small in comparison to those in the vertical axis. We therefore keep the same formula for all types of rotations:

$$c_i = (-i - n)(2/n(n-1)) \quad i = 1, \ldots, 9 \tag{5.13}$$

where n is total number of joints through which to iterate and i is the joint index with i = 1 the lowest lumbar vertebra and i = 9 the global eye. At each step, c_i determines the percentage of remaining rotation to be assigned to joint i. The total rotation to be done by each joint for the character to satisfy the constraint may then by calculated by spherical linear interpolation (slerp) using these contribution values.

The remaining rotation to be done by each eye joint is then computed in order for them to converge on the interest point. Moreover, for interest points in the 30° composing the central foveal area, only the eye joints are recruited. For the farther on each side composing the central vision area, only the eye, head, and cervical joints are recruited. Small movements therefore do not recruit the heavier joints.

Fig. 5.37 Awareness

Temporal Resolution

The time it takes to look at something or someone depends, amongst other things, on where it is placed in the field of view. It will take less time to perform the gaze movement to look at something just in front than at something in the periphery.

When initiating a gaze movement, we therefore define how long it will take to perform it. We first define the upper and lower bounds for the movement duration. The lower bound is set to 0, which corresponds to no movement, i.e. the character already facing the interest point. The upper bound is set to 2 seconds, which corresponds to a 180° movement. We then simply interpolate between the two to obtain the duration of the gaze movement.

Moreover, this duration is different if considering the eye joints, the head and cervical joints, or the joints composing the remainder of the spine. The duration for the head to move is 2 times smaller than for the spine. Similarly, the duration for the eyes to converge is 5 times smaller than for the head. In this way, we allow for the lighter joints to move more rapidly than the others. The eyes therefore converge on the interest point well before any of the other joints attain their final posture. Our final movement therefore allows for the eyes to converge on the interest point and then recenter with respect to the head as the remainder of the joints move to satisfy the constraint.

As previously mentioned, some of the gaze constraints may be dynamic, i.e. in the case where the constraint is either another moving character or the system user. We therefore recompute the displacement map to satisfy the constraint at each timestep. We can assume that the constraint's position from one frame to the next one does not change much. We therefore recompute the rotation to be done at each frame but maintain the total contribution c_i to apply which we calculated before the initiation of the gaze motion. However, we reset the contributions to 0 if the gaze constraint changes. More specifically, when the current constraint location is farther than a predetermined threshold from the constraint location at the previous frame. The newly calculated rotations to be performed by the joints to attain the new constraint's position are then distributed over the appropriate number of frames.

Finally, if the gaze behavior is deactivated, either because the character has been looking at a point of interest for too long or if there are no more interest points, the character will look back in front of him.

The added gaze motions strongly increase the human-like behaviors of crowd characters. By adding this functionality to the crowd simulation engine, we obtain characters which seem to be aware of their environment and of other characters, as depicted in Fig. 5.37.

5.7 Final Remarks

This chapter presented a review of methods of behavioral animation and also discussed some specific solutions described in crowd literature. Such methods have a large importance in the context of crowd simulation where users should be focused on more high-level situations.

References

[AMTT12] ALLEN B., MAGNENAT-THALMANN N., THALMANN D.: Politeness improves interactivity in dense crowds. *Computer Animation and Virtual Worlds* (2012), doi:10.1002/cav.1472.

[ASLU03] ALONI R., SCHWALM K., LANGHANS M., ULLRICH C. I.: Gradual shifts in sites of free auxin-production during leaf-primordium development and their role in vascular differentiation and leaf morphogenesis in *Arabidopsis. Planta 216*, 5 (2003), 841–853.

[BBM05] BRAUN A., BODMAN B. J., MUSSE S. R.: Simulating virtual crowds in emergency situations. In *Proceedings of ACM Symposium on Virtual Reality Software and Technology—VRST 2005* (Monterey, California, USA, 2005), ACM, New York.

[BdSM04] BARROS L. M., DA SILVA A. T., MUSSE S. R.: Petrosim: An architecture to manage virtual crowds in panic situations. In *Proceedings of the 17th International Conference on Computer Animation and Social Agents (CASA 2004)* (Geneva, Switzerland, 2004), vol. 1, pp. 111–120.

[BH97] BROGAN D., HODGINS J.: Group behaviors for systems with significant dynamics. *Autonomous Robots 4* (1997), 137–153.

[BMB03] BRAUN A., MUSSE S., BODMANN L. O. B.: Modeling individual behaviors in crowd simulation. In *Computer Animation and Social Agents* (New Jersey, USA, May 2003), pp. 143–148.

[BO05] BERG J., OVERMARS M.: Prioritized motion planning for multiple robots. In *IEEE/RSJ International Conference on Intelligent Robots and Systems (IROS'05)* (2005), pp. 2217–2222.

[BUT04] BOULIC R., ULICNY B., THALMANN D.: Versatile walk engine. *Journal of Game Development 1*, 1 (2004), 29–52.

[Cha87] CHAZELLE B.: Approximation and decomposition of shapes. In *Algorithmic and Geometric Aspects of Robotics* (1987), pp. 145–185.

[CKB99] CHOPRA-KHULLAR S., BADLER N. I.: Where to look? Automating attending behaviors of virtual human characters. In *Proceedings of the Third Annual Conference on Autonomous Agents, AGENTS'99* (New York, NY, USA, 1999), ACM New York, pp. 16–23.

References

[Coo86] COOK L. R.: Stochastic sampling in computer graphics. *ACM Transactions on Graphics 5*, 1 (1986), 51–72.

[Dep97] DEPARTMENT OF NATIONAL HERITAGE: *Guide to Safety at Sports Grounds (The Green Guide)*, 4 edn. HMSO, London, 1997.

[DHOO05] DOBBYN S., HAMILL J., O'CONOR K., O'SULLIVAN C.: Geopostors: A real-time geometry/impostor crowd rendering system. In *SI3D'05: Proceedings of the 2005 Symposium on Interactive 3D Graphics and Games* (New York, NY, USA, 2005), ACM, New York, pp. 95–102.

[Dij59] DIJKSTRA E. W.: A note on two problems in connexion with graphs. *Numerische Mathematik 1* (1959), 269–271.

[EN06] GU E., BADLER N.: Visual attention and eye gaze during multiparty conversations with distractors. In *Proceedings of the 6th International Conference on Intelligent Virtual Agents* (2006), Lecture Notes in Computer Science, vol. 4133, Springer, Heidelberg, pp. 193–204.

[For97] FORTUNE S. J.: Voronoi diagrams and Delaunay triangulations. In *Handbook of Discrete and Computational Geometry* (1997), pp. 377–388.

[Fru71] FRUIN J. J.: *Pedestrian and Planning Design*. Metropolitan Association of Urban Designers and Environmental Planners, New York, 1971.

[Fru87] FRUIN J. J.: *Pedestrian Planning and Design*, revised edn. Elevator World, Inc., Mobile, 1987.

[GG93] GALEA E. R., GALPARSORO J. M. P.: A brief description of the exodus evacuation model. In *Proceedings of the 18th International Conference on Fire Safety* (1993).

[GT09] GRILLON H., THALMANN D.: Simulating gaze attention behaviors for crowds. *Computer Animation and Virtual Worlds 20*, 23 (June 2009), 111–119.

[Hea93] HEALTH AND SAFETY EXECUTIVE: *Guide to Health, Safety and Welfare at Pop Concerts and Similar Events (The Purple Guide)*, 1st edn. HMSO, London, 1993.

[HFV00] HELBING D., FARKAS I., VICSEK T.: Simulating dynamical features of escape panic. *Nature 407* (2000), 487–490.

[HJ99] HILL R. W. JR.: Modeling perceptual attention in virtual humans. In *Proc. of the 8th Conference on Computes Generated Faces and Behavioral Representation* (Orlando, FL, May 1999).

[HM95] HELBING D., MOLNAR P.: Social force model for pedestrian dynamics. *Physcal Review E 51* (1995), 4282–4286.

[ID03] ITTI L., DHAVALE N.: Realistic avatar eye and head animation using a neurobiological model of visual attention. In *Proc. SPIE* (2003), SPIE, Bellingham, pp. 64–78.

[KFN98] KISKO T. M., FRANCIS R. L., NOBEL C. R.: *EVACNET4 User's Guide*. University of Florida, 1998.

[Kha86] KHATIB O.: Real-time obstacle avoidance for manipulators and mobile robots. *International Journal of Robotics Research 5*, 1 (1986), 90–98.

[KHT05] KIM Y., HILL R. W., TRAUM D. R.: A computational model of dynamic perceptual attention for virtual humans, 2005.

[KJL99] KUFFNER J. J. JR., LATOMBE J.-C.: Fast synthetic vision, memory, and learning models for virtual humans. In *Proceedings of the Computer Animation, CA'99* (Washington, DC, USA, 1999), IEEE Computer Society, Los Alamitos, pp. 118–127.

[KL00] KUFFNER J., LAVALLE S.: RRT-connect: An efficient approach to single-query path planning. In *Proceedings of IEEE International Conference on Robotics and Automation (ICRA'00)* (2000).

[KO04] KAMPHUIS A., OVERMARS M.: Finding paths for coherent groups using clearance. In *SCA'04: Proceedings of the ACM SIGGRAPH/Eurographics Symposium on Computer Animation* (2004), pp. 19–28.

[KSLO96] KAVRAKI L., SVESTKA P., LATOMBE J., OVERMARS M.: *Probabilistic Roadmaps for Path Planning in High-Dimensional Configuration Spaces*. Tech-

nical Report 12, Stanford, CA, USA, 1996.
[Kuf04a] KUFFNER J.: Efficient optimal search of Euclidean-cost grids and lattices. In *IEEE/RSJ International Conference on Intelligent Robots and Systems (IROS'04)* (2004).
[Kuf04b] KUFFNER J. J.: Effective sampling and distance metrics for 3D rigid body path planning. In *Proceedings IEEE International Conference on Robotics & Automation* (2004).
[Lat91] LATOMBE J.-C.: *Robot Motion Planning*. Kluwer Academic, Boston, 1991.
[Lau98] LAUMOND J.-P.: *Robot Motion Planning and Control*. Springer, Berlin, 1998.
[Lav06] LAVALLE S. M.: *Planning Algorithms*. Cambridge University Press, Cambridge, 2006.
[LBB02] LEE S. P., BADLER J. B., BADLER N. I.: Eyes alive. *ACM Transactions on Graphics 21*, 3 (July 2002), 637–644.
[LD04] LAMARCHE F., DONIKIAN S.: Crowds of virtual humans: A new approach for real time navigation in complex and structured environments. *Computer Graphics Forum 23*, 3 (September 2004), 509–518.
[LK05] LAU M., KUFFNER J. J.: Behavior planning for character animation. In *Proceedings of the Eurographics/ACM SIGGRAPH Symposium on Computer Animation* (2005).
[LK06] LAU M., KUFFNER J. J.: Precomputed search trees: Planning for interactive goal-driven animation. In *Proceedings of the Eurographics/ACM SIGGRAPH Symposium on Computer Animation* (2006).
[LM07] LANCE B., MARSELLA S. C.: Emotionally expressive head and body movement during gaze shifts. In *Proceedings of the 7th International Conference on Intelligent Virtual Agents, IVA'07* (2007), Springer, Berlin, pp. 72–85.
[LP83] LOZANO-PÉREZ T.: Spatial planning: A configuration space approach. *IEEE Transactions on Computing C-32*, 2 (1983), 108–120.
[LT06] LEE S.-H., TERZOPOULOS D.: Heads up!: Biomechanical modeling and neuromuscular control of the neck. *ACM Transactions on Graphics 25*, 3 (July 2006), 1188–1198.
[MC02] MARCHAND E., COURTY N.: Controlling a camera in a virtual environment. *The Visual Computer 18*, 1 (2002), 1–19.
[MT01] MUSSE S. R., THALMANN D.: A hierarchical model for real time simulation of virtual human crowds. *IEEE Transactions on Visualization and Computer Graphics 7*, 2 (April–June 2001), 152–164.
[MYMT08] MORINI F., YERSIN B., MAÏM J., THALMANN D.: Real-time scalable motion planning for crowds. *The Visual Computer 24* (2008), 859–870.
[NRTMT95] NOSER H., RENAULT O., THALMANN D., MAGNENAT-THALMANN N.: Navigation for digital actors based on synthetic vision, memory and learning. *Computers and Graphics 19* (1995), 7–19.
[OY82] O'DUNLAING C., YAP C. K.: A retraction method for planning the motion of a disc. *Journal of Algorithms 6* (1982), 104–111.
[PdHCM*06] PETTRÉ J., DE HERAS CIECHOMSKI P., MAÏM J., YERSIN B., LAUMOND J.-P., THALMANN D.: Real-time navigating crowds: scalable simulation and rendering: Research articles. *Computer Animation and Virtual Worlds 17*, 3-4 (2006), 445–455.
[PLT05] PETTRÉ J., LAUMOND J. P., THALMANN D.: A navigation graph for real-time crowd animation on multilayered and uneven terrain. In *First International Workshop on Crowd Simulation (V-CROWDS'05)* (2005), pp. 81–89.
[PO02] PETERS C., O'SULLIVAN C.: Synthetic vision and memory for autonomous virtual humans. *Computer Graphics Forum 4*, 21 (2002), 743–752.
[POS03] PETERS C., O'SULLIVAN C.: Bottom-up visual attention for virtual human animation. In *Proceedings of the 16th International Conference on Computer Animation*

and Social Agents (CASA 2003) (Washington, DC, USA, 2003), IEEE Computer Society, Los Alamitos, pp. 111–117.

[PPB*05] PETERS C., PELACHAUD C., BEVACQUA E., MANCINI M., POGGI I.: A model of attention and interest using Gaze behavior. In *Intelligent Virtual Agents* (2005), Lecture Notes in Computer Science, vol. 3661, Springer, London, pp. 229–240.

[RB85] REEVES W. T., BLAU R.: Approximate and probabilistic algorithms for shading and rendering structured particle systems. In *SIGGRAPH'85: Proceedings of the 12th Annual Conference on Computer Graphics and Interactive Techniques* (New York, NY, USA, 1985), ACM, New York, pp. 313–322.

[Ree83] REEVES W. T.: Particle systems—A technique for modeling a class of fuzzy objects. *ACM Transactions on Graphics 2*, 2 (1983), 91–108.

[Rey87] REYNOLDS C. W.: Flocks, herds and schools: A distributed behavioral model. In *Proceedings of the Annual Conference on Computer Graphics and Interactive Techniques (SIGGRAPH'87)* (New York, NY, USA, 1987), ACM, New York, pp. 25–34.

[Rey99] REYNOLDS C. W.: Steering behaviors for autonomous characters. In *Game Developers Conference* (San Jose, California, USA, 1999), pp. 763–782.

[RFL*05] RUNIONS A., FUHRER M., LANE B., FEDERL P., ROLLAND-LAGAN A.-G., PRUSINKIEWICZ P.: Modeling and visualization of leaf venation patterns. *ACM Transactions on Graphics 24*, 3 (2005), 702–711.

[RLP07] RUNIONS A., LANE B., PRUSINKIEWICZ P.: Modeling trees with a space colonization algorithm. In *Proceedings of the Eurographics Workshop on Natural Phenomena* (Aire-la-Ville, Switzerland, September 2007), Ebert D., Mérillou S. (Eds.), Eurographics Association, Geneve, pp. 63–70.

[RMTT90] RENAULT O., MAGNENAT-THALMANN N., THALMANN D.: A vision-based approach to behavioural animation. *The Journal of Visualization and Computer Animation 1*, 1 (1990), 18–21.

[SA05] SANTOS G., AGUIRRE B. E.: Critical review of emergency evacuation simulation models. In *Proceedings of the Workshop on Building Occupant Movement During Fire Emergencies* (2005), pp. 25–27.

[SGC04] SUNG M., GLEICHER M., CHENNEY S.: Scalable behaviors for crowd simulation. *Computer Graphics Forum 3*, 23 (2004), 519–528.

[SKG05] SUNG M., KOVAR L., GLEICHER M.: Fast and accurate goal-directed motion synthesis for crowds. In *Proceedings of the 2005 ACM SIGGRAPH/Eurographics Symposium on Computer Animation, SCA'05* (New York, NY, USA, 2005), ACM, New York, pp. 291–300.

[SL02] SÁNCHEZ G., LATOMBE J. C.: Using a PRM planner to compare centralized and decoupled planning for multi-robots systems. In *Proceedings of IEEE International Conference on Robotics and Automation (ICRA'02)* (2002), pp. 2112–2119.

[SLN00] SIMÉON T., LAUMOND J.-P., NISSOUX C.: Visibility based probabilistic roadmaps for motion planning. *Advanced Robotics 14*, 6 (2000), 477–493.

[Sof] SOFTWARE M.: http://www.massivesoftware.com.

[ST05] SHAO W., TERZOPOULOS D.: Autonomous pedestrians. In *SCA'05: Proceedings of the ACM SIGGRAPH/Eurographics Symposium on Computer Animation* (2005), pp. 19–28.

[Sti00] STILL G.: *Crowd Dynamics*. PhD thesis, Warwick University, 2000.

[TCP06] TREUILLE A., COOPER S., POPOVIĆ Z.: Continuum crowds. *ACM Transactions on Graphics 25*, 3 (July 2006), 1160–1168.

[Tec] TECHNOLOGY A.: A technical summary of the aea egress code. AEA Technology, Warrington, UK.

[TLC02a] TECCHIA F., LOSCOS C., CHRYSANTHOU Y.: Image-based crowd rendering. *IEEE Computer Graphics and Applications 22*, 2 (March–April 2002), 36–43.

[TM94] THOMPSON P. A., MARCHANT E. W.: Simulex: Developing new techniques for modelling evacuation. In *Proceedings of the Fourth International Symposium on Fire Safety Science* (1994).

[TT94] TU X., TERZOPOULOS D.: Artificial fishes: Physics, locomotion, perception, behavior. In *Computer Graphics (ACM SIGGRAPH'94 Conference Proceedings)* (Orlando, USA, July 1994), vol. 28, ACM, New York, pp. 43–50.

[Ulr67] NEISSER U.: *Cognitive Psychology*. Appleton-Century-Crofts, New York, 1967.

[UT02] ULICNY B., THALMANN D.: Towards interactive real-time crowd behavior simulation. *Computer Graphics Forum 21*, 4 (Dec. 2002), 767–775.

[WH04] WOLFE J. M., HOROWITZ T. S.: What attributes guide the deployment of visual attention and how do they do it? *Nature Reviews Neuroscience 5*, 6 (2004), 495–501.

[YJ90] YANTIS S., JONIDES J.: Abrupt visual onsets and selective attention: Voluntary versus automatic allocation. *Journal of Experimental Psychology: Human Perception and Performance 16*, 1 (1990), 121–134.

Chapter 6
Relating Real Crowds with Virtual Crowds

6.1 Introduction

This chapter describes some reflections concerning the challenge of capturing information from real crowds to relate it with virtual crowds. Three parts are discussed here: (i) a study undertaken on the motion and behavior of real crowds, where the goal is to identify some patterns of the behaviors of real people to be used subsequently in virtual crowds, (ii) discussion of a few sociological crowd aspects, and (iii) computer vision methods as automatic ways to capture information from real life to guide virtual crowds.

6.2 Studying the Motion of Real Groups of People

In this section, we present a simple and empirical way to observe real crowds, and to use such observation for crowd simulation. We do not employ computer vision algorithms (as it will be presented later) to capture semantic information from videos, but only a visual process, trying to select information from the crowd structure. This process is important for defining which and how the observed information can be used to simulate realistic behaviors in virtual crowds. The observed information in the real crowd relies on two aspects: crowd characteristics and crowd events, as discussed in the next subsections.

6.2.1 Crowd Characteristics

Characteristics of the crowd can include: crowd space (if all the space is occupied, if the individuals are close to each other, regions where there is some action, regions where people walk are examples of crowd space questions), crowd size (number of groups and individuals within each group), crowd density (relation between space

Fig. 6.1 Group acting on the train station. The *drawing* in the figure shows the action location

Fig. 6.2 Real crowd scene representing directions of movement (*arrows*) and interest locations (*circle*) for crowds

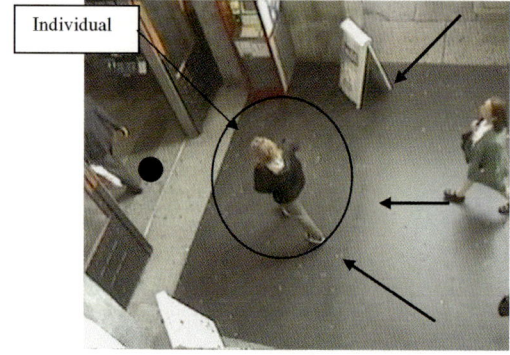

Fig. 6.3 Grouping formation observed in a filmed sequence

and crowd sizes), crowd structure (considering the grouping of individuals), and crowd basic behaviors (walk, grasp, look at some location, apply a posture).

Concerning the crowd space, some data are identified:

- Space to apply actions (location and size of space). For example, Fig. 6.1 shows a space to apply action identified in a video sequence.
- Space to walk (location and size of space), as shown in Fig. 6.2.
- The way groups walk (speed, respecting the group formation, occupying all the walking space), as shown in Fig. 6.3.

6.2 Studying the Motion of Real Groups of People

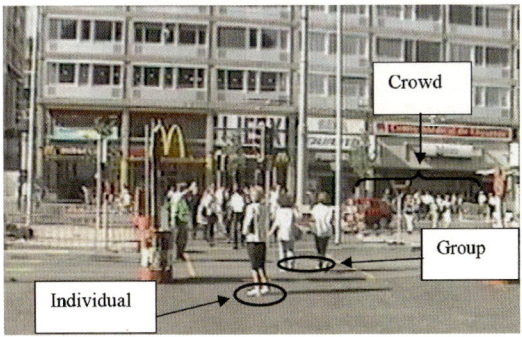

Fig. 6.4 Complex scene of crowds where different entities (crowd, groups, and individuals) can be recognized

In order to describe the crowd size, observations are made to identify the grouping existent in the filmed sequences as well as the number of members in each group. For instance, in the filmed sequence of Fig. 6.3 (only shown one picture), approximately 40 persons were observed during some time, whereas the groups are formed by approximately two persons.

The relationship between the number of individuals and the occupied space represents the crowd density. The concept of high density, meaning when people feel that the space is crowded, can be subjective and dependent on other parameters. For instance, people in a football stadium normally expect to find a lot of people. Then, the feeling of a crowded environment can only appear when the people cannot move due to the proximity of other individuals. However, let us imagine people in a restaurant or any other place where they do not expect to find a crowd. If some event occurs in this environment, even if people can still have a normal unimpeded walking motion, they can present the feeling of being in a crowded environment. As this concept is subjective, we can use an informal (but more objective) definition, which does not consider the feeling of people but really the physical space concerned with each one. For example, a crowded environment occurs when each person has less than two square meters of personal space. Then, depending on the space and the crowd size, an environment can be crowded or not.

Concerning the structure of crowds, three entities are observed in the real filmed sequences (Figs. 6.2 and 6.4) and can be used to define a model of virtual crowds: the whole crowd, groups, and individuals. These entities are recognized as a function of their position, grouping, and/or their function in the scene. Thus, the crowd is considered as the whole structure of people in the scene which can be subdivided in groups (or not), depending on the different actions and motion occurrence. A group is recognized when it takes a different intention from the others, where intention deals with a different motion, velocities, or behavior. For example, let us consider a crowd situated in a theater. If a group of people stand up and start to clap, we automatically recognize it as a group, which arises from the crowd. Also, when we observe pedestrians on the street, we can identify some families or groups which walk together because they have a relationship (know each other, are friends, etc.) or only because they are going in the same direction (see Fig. 6.3). The third

Algorithm 6.1: Example of information to be captured from real crowd sequences

```
 1  begin
 2      CROWD CHARACTERISTICS
 3      Size: 60 persons
 4      Density = NO-CROWDED
 5      Entities: CROWD and 3 GROUPS formed by approximately 5 persons
 6      Basic behaviors: walking to different interest locations: LEFT, BACK and
        FRONT in the real crowd space and waiting (sited or not)
 7      CROWD EVENTS
 8      WHEN: Time = 5,2 min
 9      WHAT: Event = Doors are opened
10      REACTION: People enter the train
11      WHERE: Location of doors in the real space
12      WHO: Group on gate 3
13  end
```

entity observed in our examples is the individual, which is recognized in the same way as groups.

The basic behavior of crowds defines what the crowd is doing, e.g., walking, watching something, applying some posture, etc. We have focused our analysis basically on four types of basic behaviors: action, motion, attention, and interaction. However, depending on the basic behavior, some other parameters can be required. For instance, if the crowd is walking (*motion behavior*), the locations where the crowd is going can be recognized as "interest locations" or "goals" of the crowd, and if the crowd is watching a show (*attention behavior*), an "interesting point" can exist (e.g., the stage of a theater). The *action behavior* implies doing something, like clapping, for instance. And the *interaction behavior* can include interaction with persons or with objects. Figs. 6.1, 6.3, 6.2, 6.4 show some information observed in filmed sequences, such as direction of movement, interest locations, action locations, grouping of individuals, etc.

6.2.2 Crowd Events

Crowd events describe both temporal and spatial information associated when something occurs. For instance, some groups of the crowd, which were walking and waiting, enter a train when they perceive the sign of open doors. The associated information describes the time and location in which the event happened in the real space. An example of information observed in real group interaction is presented in pseudo-code (Algorithm 6.1).

Each time something occurs in the observed crowd, crowd events specified in Algorithm 6.1 can be described to be simulated in virtual space. These data are then used to simulate virtual crowds, as will be discussed next.

6.2.3 Parameters for Simulating Virtual Crowds Using Real Crowd Information

Based on information observed in real crowds, we have defined some parameters than can be handled to simulate virtual crowds. In this case, the virtual crowd can mimic the crowd structure and events observed in real crowds.

Some examples of parameters to be used to simulate virtual crowds are:

- Crowd structure
- Basic behaviors
- Crowd events and associated reactions

Crowd structure concerns the information about the number of individuals existing in the crowd as well as in the groups. The basic behaviors describe the action or motion associated with the crowd at the beginning of the simulation. Afterwards, events can be triggered, which can generate reactions to be achieved by groups of the crowd. Pseudo-code in Algorithm 6.2 presents an example of information used to simulate virtual crowds according to the information observed in real crowds and described in Algorithm 6.1.

While crowd structure deals with quantitative parameters of the people, crowd events are related to what occurred with the crowd during the simulation (for virtual crowds) or during the observation period (for real crowds). For instance, in Algorithm 6.2, the crowd is formed by 100 agents divided in 4 groups. Three groups each contained 3 to 6 agents, and the fourth group contained the rest of the agents. The basic behaviors of agents relate to walk in the defined space or to stay seated in the action areas. The event named ⟨Event1⟩ will be generated at a specified time (5.2 minutes of simulation). Virtual people to be affected are defined in ⟨ALL_PEOPLE_IN_THE_GATE3⟩, where gate 3 is recognized as a specific region inside the train station, from where all agents inside it react to ⟨Event1⟩.

Nevertheless, there are other events that can be modeled to simulate events generated in real crowds. Table 6.1 presents some other possibilities of existent behaviors in virtual crowds.

The next subsections present some images and information taken from real crowds and the respective simulation using virtual crowds.

6.2.4 Simulating Real Scenes

To exemplify the relationship between virtual and real crowds, we chose two filmed sequences to be simulated. One sequence deals with a group of people passing

Algorithm 6.2: Virtual crowd event generated using real crowd observations

```
1  begin
2      CROWD STRUCTURE
3      NUMBER_PEOPLE: 100
4      Density = NO-CROWDED
5      GOALS_CROWD:
6      LEFT LOCATION ( X Y Z )RIGHT LOCATION ( X Y Z ) (Related to the
       crowd space)
7      ACTION_LOCATION SIT ( X Y Z )
8      REGION GATE_3 (X Y Z) (X Y Z)
9      NUMBER_GROUPS: 3
10     BASIC BEHAVIORS
11     GROUP_1NB_PEOPLE: [3,6] (Group contains from 3 to 6 individuals)
12     BASIC_BEHAVIOUR: WALK from LEFT to RIGHT
13     GROUP_2NB_PEOPLE: [3,6]
14     BASIC_BEHAVIOUR: SITED
15     GROUP_3NB_PEOPLE: [3,6]
16     BASIC_BEHAVIOUR: WALK from LEFT to RIGHT
17     CROWD EVENTS
18     Event_1:
19     WHEN: Time = 5,2 min
20     WHO: ALL PEOPLE IN REGION OF GATE 3
21     Reaction Event_1:
22     ACTION: ENTER THE TRAIN THROUGH THE CLOSEST DOOR
23 end
```

through a door, and the other with a crowd entering a train in a station. Filmed sequences were shot in the train and metro station in Lausanne, Switzerland.

First Sequence: People Passing Through a Door

For the first sequence, we filmed for about 10 minutes, approximately 40 people passing through a door to go in or come out from the gates in the train station. Some variables were recognized:

1. The maximum number of people on the screen was 7.
2. There were different ways of walking as well as different speeds.
3. At the most two agents form a group in this crowd. In addition, no event is triggered during the sequence.
4. The directions of movement and objects to avoid (as well as regions to walk) were identified and are shown in Fig. 6.5.

6.2 Studying the Motion of Real Groups of People

Table 6.1 Association between real and virtual crowd events

Real Crowd Events	Virtual Crowd Behaviors
Group appears	Split of the biggest group or merging of two smaller groups
Group disappears	Merging of groups
Group moves toward specific direction	Walking toward specific direction (FRONT, BACK, RIGHT, LEFT, FRONT_RIGHT, ...)
Group acts	Play an animated keyframe sequence (clapping, dancing, boohooing, etc.)
Group occupies all the space	Adaptability of the group in order to occupy all the space
Group walks in line trying to have the same trajectory	There is no adaptability behavior
Family walks together in similar speeds	Flocking behavior
Groups are attracted to a specific location	Attraction behavior

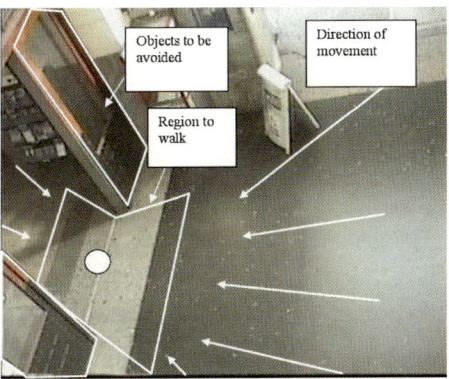

Fig. 6.5 Spatial information came from the real crowd observation

First, we have modeled the environment in order to represent the characteristics of the real space. Then, different goals and initial positions were distributed to the crowd as well as the constraints of movement, e.g., the regions where walking is possible and the objects to be avoided. Figure 6.6 shows the Open Inventor graphical interface *(Open Inventor, 1984)* we have used to specify the geometrical information.

From the behavioral point of view, we applied only the seek goal behavior to provide crowds which follow the programmed movement specified using the graphical interface. Moreover, different ways of walking and different speeds (which are randomly distributed among the groups and individuals) were used to provide a more heterogeneous population. As there were no events occurring in the real crowd sequence, no events were generated for the virtual crowds. Figure 6.7 shows a screenshot of simulation using ViCrowd [MT01].

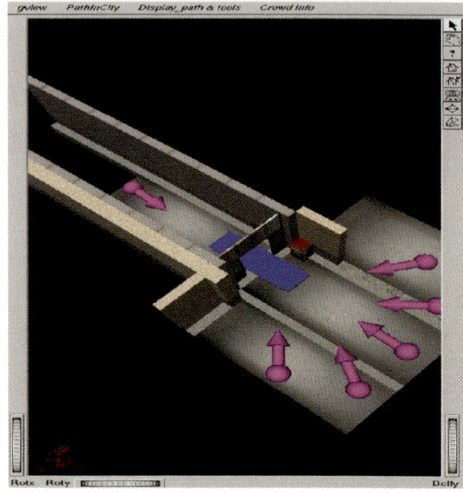

Fig. 6.6 Open Inventor interface to specify interest points, regions to walk, and goals of crowd

Fig. 6.7 Image of virtual crowd simulation

Second Sequence: People Waiting and Entering the Train

While the first sequence used only the programmed movement because there were no events occurring, the second sequence used events and reactions in order to program the reaction of people when the train arrived. Each individual should react based on the distance from the nearest door, as normally occurs in real life. The images in Figs. 6.1 and 6.8 present the real space as well as the crowd goals.

From a geometrical point of view, the regions where agents can walk or wait (stand up or sit) are also defined, as well as the doors where the crowd can enter the train. Figure 6.9 shows the graphical interface used to specify these geometrical attributes.

6.3 Sociological Aspects

Fig. 6.8 Real space: region to walk and train doors. People walking toward their goals

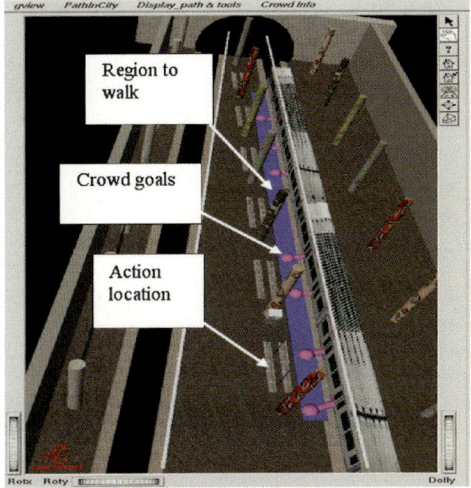

Fig. 6.9 Interface to specify interest points and regions where autonomous crowd should walk

In the simulation, virtual agents arrived and were positioned in the region as shown in Fig. 6.9. When the train arrived in the gate, a crowd event was generated: agents in this gate move to the nearest door and enter the train. Also, other agents continue to arrive, after activation of the event. Figure 6.10 shows some images of this simulation.

6.3 Sociological Aspects

In order to provide some sociological behaviors that can be included in crowd models, we can also study some effects investigated by sociologists and psychologists related to a mass of people. For instance, the distance kept by each individual (called *personal space* by sociologists) has the meaning of isolating him/her from other people as well maintaining relationship with them [Jef98]. In crowd models, the

Fig. 6.10 Crowd waiting for the metro and entering the metro

distance that separates individuals and groups is important in order to apply the collision avoidance behaviors as well as the communication.

Due to crowd requirements, we have focused only on a few sociological aspects found in the literature. They are subdivided into three parts: individual aspects, group aspects, and sociological effects, which arise as a function of people interaction.

Individual Aspects:

- The *individual space* treated in this section is dependent on the density. It should be maintained in order to establish a group membership as well as to avoid collision with another individual (privacy) [Jef98].
- *Communication between individuals* (who do not use media peripherals) can be applied between agents that are close to each other. To communicate, individuals use all the information they know: their intentions, knowledge, and memory of past experiences, among others [Bel95].

Group Aspects:

- *Social conventions* observed relate to the behavioral rules defined in the society to be simulated, as the social hierarchy where individuals follow group tendency. Yet, the past events that have been saved in the group memory can be used to define social conventions [Jef98].
- People can *group* and *desegregate* as a function of personal or group interest as well as the relationship with members of groups [Man85].
- One *leader* is someone who tries to influence or guide others. A crowd may need to be guided by one or more leaders [Bel95].

Sociological Effects:

- These effect arise from the interaction between groups and individuals. Some parameters are evaluated and can generate changes of groups and individual behaviors [Rol81].

- *Polarization* occurs within a crowd when two or more groups adopt divergent attitudes, opinions, or behavior and they may argue or fight even if they do not know each other [Bel95].
- *Changing of group structure*. For example, a football match is a situation in which a group structure exists. When the players are children, they do not obey the group structure existent in the social convention to play football, but they run in mass to touch the ball [Man85].
- *Domination* happens when one or more leaders in a crowd influence the others [McC89].
- *Adding* is the name given to the influence established by others and applied to the group [Bel95].
- *Loss of individualities* happens when individuals assume crowd or group behaviors, and act according to these behaviors [Bel95].
- When people feel interested in someone/something, people can be *attracted*. Also, people can feel *repulsion* and try to stay away from some person or object [Man85].

Basically, we consider these sociological aspects to change individual goals and allow agents to change groups. Some of these effects can be perceived only as emergent behaviors, for instance when individualities are lost and a group tries to follow their leader.

6.4 Computer Vision for Crowds

A challenging problem in crowd simulation is how to generate the motion of virtual agents based on real-life scenarios. For that purpose, it is necessary to obtain the trajectories of actual people in real observed scenarios, and feed them to the crowd simulator. For example, some authors [ALA*01, BJ03] presented an approach for crowd simulation based on empirical observation of real-life situations. However, it is clear that to observe real life and manually extract information is a time-consuming task that requires large amounts of human interaction.

A cheap and noninvasive technique for people tracking can be achieved by using cameras combined with computer vision algorithms. Such algorithms can be used to obtain the global motion of denser crowds [BV99], or extract the individual trajectory of each filmed person [WADP97, SG99, HHD00, KB03, CGPP03, NTWH04, CC06, FV06, PTM06]. In fact, there are several methods for people tracking reported in the literature, but tracking simultaneously a large number of people (in particular, crowds) is still a challenge in the computer vision community.

6.4.1 A Brief Overview on People Tracking

A large variety of methods have been proposed in the past years for people tracking, employing a variety of approaches. Tracking can be performed using one or more cameras, which can be color or monochromatic. By far, the most common approach is to use a single static camera (color or monochromatic), and the first step of tracking algorithms is typically background removal (also called background subtraction) [WADP97, SG99, MJD*00, HHD00, EDHD02, CMC02, CGPP03, NTWH04, XLLY05, WTLW05, TLH05, CC06, FV06, JJM06, ZvdH06]. In a few words, this step consists of obtaining a mathematical model of the background, which is compared to each frame of the video sequence. Then, pixels with sufficient discrepancy are considered foreground pixels, and sets of connected pixels are usually called *blobs*.

One problem inherent to background subtraction is the undesired detection of shadows (or highlights) as foreground objects. Indeed, shadows may connect isolated people in a scene, generating a single blob and probably compromising the performance of the tracking algorithm. Several algorithms have been proposed for shadow identification and removal, some of them exploring the expected chromatic invariance in shadowed regions (assuming that color cameras are employed) [MJD*00, EDHD02, KB03, CGPP03, GFK03, SB05], and others using some kind of property based on luminance only (grayscale cameras) [CMC02, XLLY05, WTLW05, TLH05, JJM06]. In general, methods relying on chromatic information achieve more accurate detection of shadows, but at a higher computational cost. On the other hand, algorithms that use only luminance are more generic (they can be applied to monochromatic video sequences), and tend to be faster.

Another desired characteristic for background removal is adaptation to changes in the background. The background is usually not static in time (there are variations due to illumination changes, objects that are dropped or removed from the scene, etc.), and the background removal should adapt accordingly. Although there are several methods for background adaptation, the general form may be expressed as:

$$B(t + \Delta t) = f\big(B(t), I(t + \Delta t)\big) \qquad (6.1)$$

where $B(t)$ is the background model at time t, $B(t + \Delta t)$ is the updated background model at time $t + \Delta t$, and f is a function that depends on the previous background model $B(t)$ and the current image $I(t + \Delta t)$ that was acquired by the camera.

For object tracking itself, there are also several different approaches. Some of them are briefly described below (for a more comprehensive review on people tracking, the reader may refer to the survey papers [WS03, WHT03, VV05, MaVK06].

In the W4 system [HHD00], the vertical projections of foreground blobs are used to estimate the position of the head. Isolated body parts are then detected through a curvature analysis of the shape, and a grayscale textural appearance model is combined with shape information to relate each person in consecutive frames.

Pai and collaborators [PTL*04] proposed an algorithm for pedestrian tracking focused on traffic applications. After background subtraction with shadow removal, a dynamical graph matching approach is employed to track individual persons. The correlation metric is the Kullback–Leibler distance of color histograms, quantized into 16 or 64 levels for each color channel. The *walking rhythm*, which relates to the periodicity of human motion, is also included to discriminate humans from other objects (such as vehicles). Adam et al. [ARS06] used *integral histograms* and the

Earth's Moving Distance (EMD) to perform the matching between two histograms. The integral histogram is based on multiple rectangular regions, and it is useful to match only portions of the regions (that happens frequently in partial occlusions). It should be noted that the approach proposed in [ARS06] does not rely on background subtraction, and requires a manual initialization of the template to be tracked.

In [KB03], tracking is performed by combining a motion model, shape, and color features. The motion model is implemented using Kalman filters, assuming that the acceleration of the object's centroid is modeled as white noise. The shape is roughly characterized by the dimensions of the bounding box, and color information is introduced by matching color histograms.

Cheng and Chen [CC06] proposed a tracking algorithm that relies on wavelet coefficients of the input video sequence. The authors claim that several "fake motions" (such as moving branches and leaves) can be detected in high-frequency wavelet coefficients, and then distinguished from the motion of actual objects. For identifying and tracking actual moving objects, each blob is characterized by shape and color features (such as height and width of bounding box, mean and standard deviation in each color channel), which are stored in a feature vector and compared to each foreground blob.

In [YLPL05], a tracking algorithm focused on long-term occlusions was presented. After background removal, the authors check for splitting or merging of blobs, detecting possible occlusions. Then, color information is used to characterize each blob, and the Kullback–Leibler distance is employed for histogram matching.

It is important to note that this section presented just a brief overview of people tracking in video sequences, focusing on approaches based on static cameras. There are several other methods for people/object tracking, such as methods based on optical flow (using the KLT tracker [LK81, ST94], or SIFT [Low04]), among others. A more comprehensive overview on tracking can be found in the survey papers [WS03, WHT03, VV05, MaVK06].

6.5 An Approach for Crowd Simulation Using Computer Vision

This section presents an approach for crowd simulation based on information from real life captured automatically using computer vision algorithms. This method is focused on the motion of virtual agents (preferred directions, speeds, etc.), and does not deal with individual actions (sitting, grabbing, pointing, etc.). A brief summary of this method is provided below.

1. Use computer vision algorithms to track the trajectory of each filmed individual.
2. Group coherent trajectories into "motion clusters," based on the main direction of each trajectory.
3. Compute an extrapolated velocity field for each motion cluster.
4. Apply a crowd simulator that uses the extrapolated velocity fields to guide virtual humans.

Next, each of these steps is described in more detail.

6.5.1 Using Computer Vision for People Tracking

As described in Sect. 6.4.1, there are several methods based on computer vision for tracking individual persons in filmed video sequences, such as [EDHD02, CGPP03, NTWH04, TLH05, CC06, PTM06]. However, most algorithms for people tracking are focused on surveillance applications, where an oblique (or almost lateral) view of the scene is required (to recognize faces). Such camera setups often result in occlusions, and mapping from image pixels to world coordinates may not be accurate (due to camera projection). Since the main goal is to extract trajectories for each individual in world coordinates, it is advisable to use a camera setup that provides a normal view with respect to the ground (thus reducing perspective problems and occlusions). In fact, the mapping from pixel coordinates (x, y) to world coordinates (u, v) in such camera setups is trivial (assuming planar projective mapping):

$$u = ax, \qquad v = by \tag{6.2}$$

where a and b are related to the focal length of the camera (and distance from the ground). Radial distortion close to image boundaries can also be corrected when necessary [Dav05], but we do not consider such distortion for our purposes. Also, Eq. (6.2) indicates that persons have the same dimensions at all positions, indicating that an area thresholding technique may be used for people detection.

A common approach for object tracking for static cameras is to apply background subtraction techniques, which isolate foreground objects from static background pixels. There are several algorithms for background subtraction reported in the literature, such as [HHD00, EDHD02, CMC02, CGPP03, NTWH04, XLLY05, WTLW05, TLH05, CC06, JJM06, FV06]. In particular, shadows usually produce spurious foreground pixels that may influence the tracking algorithm. Some background subtraction algorithms already include some kind of treatment for shadows [CMC02, EDHD02, CGPP03, XLLY05, WTLW05, TLH05, JJM06], and a subset is suited for monochromatic video sequences (which are more generic and faster to process), such as [CMC02, XLLY05, WTLW05, TLH05, JJM06]. Results presented in this section were generated using the algorithm described in [JJM06], due to its simplicity, speed, and adaptation to illumination changes (including shadows and highlights).

After obtaining foreground pixels, it is necessary to determine the set of connected pixels (or *blob*) that relates to each individual to be tracked. It is important to note that the expected longitudinal projection of a person in oblique-lateral views is explored by several tracking algorithms, such as [HHD00, EDHD02, CC06, FV06]. However, such hypothesis clearly does not apply for top-view cameras, requiring a different strategy for people tracking. In fact, the projection of a person in a top-view camera setup is roughly elliptic. Furthermore, the person's head is a relatively invariant feature in such camera setups, indicating that tracking can be performed through template matching.

When a new blob is detected in the scene, a threshold is used to discard blobs with small area. The center of the person's head is expected to be at the center of the blob (innermost position). To find the template T that corresponds approximately

6.5 An Approach for Crowd Simulation Using Computer Vision

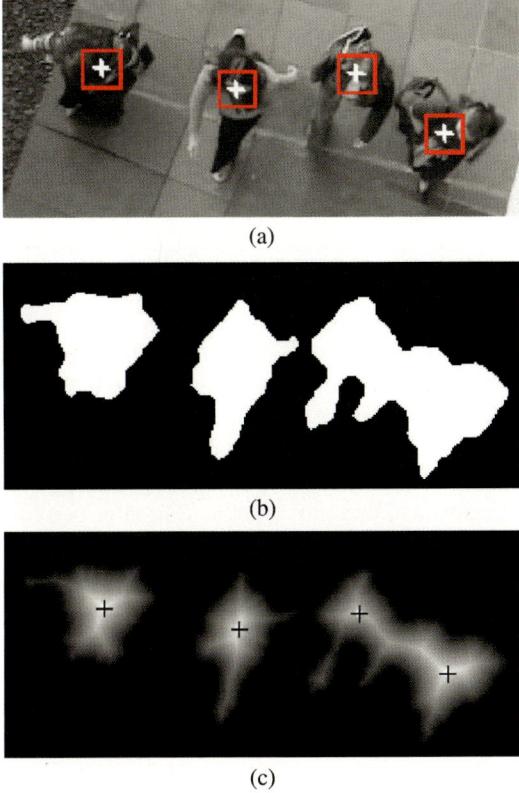

Fig. 6.11 (a) Frame of a video sequence, with detected center heads and correlation templates. (b) Result of background subtraction. (c) Distance transform and its maxima, which are used to detect head centers

with the head, the Distance Transform (DT) is applied to the negative of each foreground blob (i.e., the blob exterior is considered the foreground object). The global maximum of the DT corresponds to the center of the largest circle that can be inscribed in the blob, and it provides an estimate of the person's head center.

If the blob area exceeds a certain threshold (in this analysis, we used three times the minimum area value), then such a blob is probably related to two or more connected persons, as in the rightmost blob in Fig. 6.11(b). In this case, not only the global maximum of the DT is analyzed, but also the local maxima with largest values. If the distance between the global maximum and a certain local maximum is larger than the diameter of the template (so that templates do not overlap), such local maximum is also considered a head center, as shown in the rightmost blob of Fig. 6.11(c). Figure 6.11(a) illustrates the corresponding frame, along with head centers and correlation templates. It is important to note that the procedure for detecting individual templates belonging to the same blob may fail when people enter the scene forming a compact cluster, which generates a blob without a recognizable geometry. In such cases, individual persons will only be detected when the cluster breaks apart.

The next step is to identify template T in the following frame. Although there are several correlation metrics designed for matching a small template within a larger image, Martin and Crowley [MC95] indicated that the Sum of Squared Differences (SSD) provides a more stable result than other correlation metrics in generic applications, leading us to use the SSD as the correlation metric. It should be noticed that more generic object tracking methods (such as the covariance tracking described in [PTM06]) can be used instead of the SSD, but with additional computational cost.

Although the head is a good choice for the correlation template, head tilts and illumination changes may vary the gray levels within the template. Also, the procedure for selecting the initial template may not detect exactly the center of the head. To cope with such situations, T is updated every N frames (a recommended choice is $N = 5$ for sequences acquired at 15 FPS).

As a result of our tracking procedure, we can determine the trajectory (and hence the velocity) of each person captured by the camera. Extracted trajectories can be used directly in some simulators (e.g., [BJ03, MH04]), but other simulators require a vector field that provides the desired velocity for each person at each point of the image (e.g., [HM97, HFV00, BMB03, Che04]). Such extrapolated vector field can be computed using all trajectories extracted automatically using computer vision. However, people walking in opposite directions may generate a null extrapolated velocity field at some positions, which would cause the virtual agent to stop. A better approach is to group trajectories into "coherent" clusters, and compute an extrapolated velocity field for each of these clusters. A possible approach for generating such clusters is described next.

6.5.2 Clustering of Coherent Trajectories

The definition of coherent (or similar) trajectories is very application dependent. For instance, Junejo et al. [JJS04] used envelope boundaries, velocity, and curvature information as features to group similar trajectories. Makris and Ellis [ME05] also used envelope boundaries to determine main routes from filmed video sequences. In both approaches, the spatial distance between trajectories is an important feature in the clustering procedure. For purposes of virtual human simulation, we believe that coherent trajectories are those having approximately the same displacement vectors (e.g., two trajectories going from left to right are coherent, regardless of their mean speed and the distance between them). For automatic classification and grouping of coherent trajectories, it is necessary to extract relevant features and then apply an unsupervised clustering technique, as explained next.

Let $(x(s), y(s))$, $s \in [0, 1]$, denote a trajectory reparametrized by arc length (normalized to unity), so that $(x(0), y(0))$ is the start point and $(x(1), y(1))$ is the end point of the trajectory. Each trajectory is then characterized by a set of N displacement vectors $\mathbf{d}_i = (\Delta x_i, \Delta y_i)$ computed at equidistant arc lengths:

$$\mathbf{d}_i = \left(x(t_{i+1}) - x(t_i), y(t_{i+1}) - y(t_i) \right) \qquad (6.3)$$

6.5 An Approach for Crowd Simulation Using Computer Vision

where $t_i = i/N$, for $i = 0, \ldots, N-1$. Then, each trajectory j is represented by a $2N$-dimensional feature vector $\mathbf{f}_j$, obtained by combining the N displacement vectors associated with the trajectory:

$$\mathbf{f}_j = (\Delta x_0, \Delta y_0, \Delta x_1, \Delta y_1, \ldots, \Delta x_{N-1}, \Delta y_{N-1}) \qquad (6.4)$$

Coherent trajectories tend to produce similar feature vectors $\mathbf{f}$. Hence, a set of coherent trajectories is expected to produce a cluster in the $2N$-dimensional space, which is modeled as a Gaussian probability distribution characterized by its mean vector and covariance matrix. Since each cluster relates to a different Gaussian function, the overall distribution considering all feature vectors $\mathbf{f}_j$ is a mixture of Gaussians. The number of Gaussians in the mixture (which corresponds to the number of clusters), as well as the distribution parameters of each individual distribution can be obtained automatically using the unsupervised clustering algorithm described in [FJ02].

The number N of displacement vectors used to assemble $\mathbf{f}_j$ is chosen based on how structured the flow of people is. For relatively simple trajectories, small values of N can capture the essence of the trajectories. On the other hand, more complicated trajectories (with many turns) are better characterized using larger values of N. In general, public spaces (such as sidewalks, parks, center towns, among others) tend to present main flow directions, and $N = 1$ or $N = 2$ is usually enough to identify different clusters. It should be noted that, as N increases, the dimension of the feature vectors increases, and a larger number of samples is needed for a reliable estimation of the Gaussian distributions. At the same time, unstructured motion (e.g., football players in a match, or kids playing) requires larger values of N to summarize the desired trajectories, and a very large number of samples would be needed for the clustering algorithm. Hence, the proposed method is, in general, not suited to unstructured motion.

An example of automatic clustering of similar trajectories is illustrated in Fig. 6.12. It shows a portion of a corridor, where people move from top to bottom or bottom to top. All the trajectories of people going up were correctly grouped together (shown in red), as well as trajectories of people coming down (shown in green).

6.5.3 Generation of Extrapolated Velocity Fields

After grouping similar trajectories into clusters, it is necessary to generate a velocity field for each cluster that provides the instantaneous velocity for each virtual agent at each position in the viewing field of the camera. There are different approaches to obtain dense vector fields from sparse ones, varying from traditional interpolation/extrapolation techniques, such as nearest neighbor, linear, cubic, and splines [Wat92], to more sophisticated methods, such as gradient vector fields [XP98]. However, in most scenarios there are no tracked trajectories at image

Fig. 6.12 Result of trajectory clustering

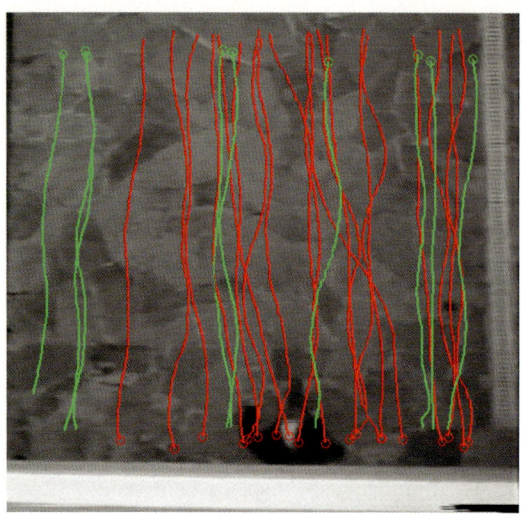

borders, indicating that extrapolation techniques should be used instead of interpolation. In fact, interpolation by nearest neighbor can be easily extended for extrapolation, and it does not propagate the error in the extrapolated regions as much as other interpolation techniques (such as linear or cubic), because it is basically a piecewise-constant function. Another possible way to generate the full vector field is to use radial-basis-like functions [DR02], but all results presented in this section were generated using nearest-neighbor interpolation/extrapolation.

An example of velocity field is shown in Fig. 6.13, which illustrates the extrapolated velocity fields related to the two clusters shown in Fig. 6.12. In fact, this example illustrates two "layers" of velocity fields, where each layer relates to a different cluster of coherent trajectories.

6.5.4 Simulation Based on Real Data

The final step of the approach is to feed the extrapolated velocity fields into a crowd simulator. As explained before, there are several existing crowd simulators that accept/require as input the desired velocity for each agent at each time step, such as [HM97, Rey99, HFV00, BMB03, Che04]. In this book, we show some simulation results using the physically based approach proposed in [HFV00], but other simulators could have been used instead.

In a few words, this model is based on a particle system where each particle i of mass m_i has a predefined velocity $\mathbf{v}_i^g$ (goal velocity, typically pointing toward exits of the virtual environment) to which it tends to adapt its instantaneous velocity $\mathbf{v}_i$ within a certain time interval τ_i. Simultaneously, each particle i tries to keep a velocity-dependent distance from other entities j and walls w, controlled by in-

Fig. 6.13 Extrapolated velocity fields for the two trajectory clusters shown in Fig. 6.12

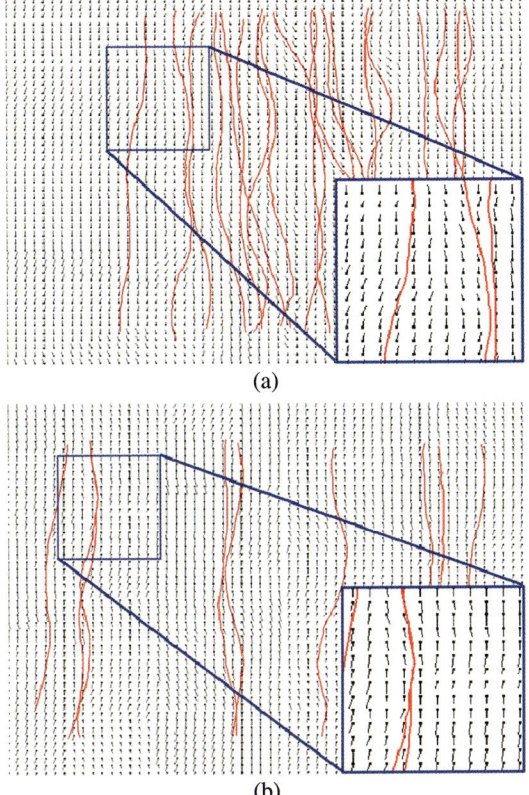

teraction forces $\mathbf{f}_{ij}$ and $\mathbf{f}_{iw}$, respectively. The change of velocity in time t for each particle i is given by the following dynamical equation:

$$m_i \frac{d\mathbf{v}_i}{dt} = m_i \frac{\mathbf{v}_i^g - \mathbf{v}_i(t)}{\tau_i} + \sum_{j \neq i} \mathbf{f}_{ij} + \sum_w \mathbf{f}_{iw} \quad (6.5)$$

When the simulation is initialized, each new agent is related to only one layer of velocity fields (such assignment is proportional to the number of real people related to each layer in the filmed video sequence). Then, the desired velocity $\mathbf{v}_i^g$ of agent i is obtained from its layer of extrapolated velocity fields $\mathbf{v}^{\text{tracked}}$ at the agent's current position, and Eq. (6.5) is used to perform the simulation. It should be noted that, although each agent is associated with only one layer of velocity field, it can "see" all agents in all layers (and also information about the virtual environment such as walls and obstacles, which are accessible for all agents in all layers). Moreover, the radial repulsion force introduced by agents and obstacles in Helbing's model (see Eq. (6.5)) guarantees collision-free trajectories. Hence, agents tend to follow main directions provided by the velocity fields, and at the same time they avoid collisions with obstacles and other agents.

Fig. 6.14 Different layers of velocity fields for the *T-intersection* scenario

It is important to note that, in denser crowds, the movement of each person includes not only his/her desired paths, but also a great amount of interactions with the environment and other people (in the sense of collision avoidance), as noted in [HBJW05]. Hence, it is suggested to film the environment with a smaller number of people (nondense crowds) to capture more accurately the intentions of each person. The simulation can be performed with a larger number of agents, and the expected interactions among people in the dense simulated crowd are taken into account by using Eq. (6.5). On the other hand, if we have footage of a dense crowd (which contains the inherent interactions among people), it is not easy to simulate the same scenario with a smaller number of agents without "undoing" the registered interactions.

6.5.5 Some Examples

To illustrate the approach described in this section, we used filmed video sequences of a T-shaped region. This scenario presents diversity of trajectories; resulting in four trajectory clusters (layers), as illustrated with different colors in Fig. 6.14 (circles indicate starting points of each trajectory).

This scenario presents particular characteristics that make people move with different speeds depending on the region in which they are walking. In particular, there is a set of stairs (region B in Fig. 6.15(a)) that connects two roughly flat plateaus (for camera calibration and simulation purposes we considered that the region is planar, since the difference of the plane heights is small compared to the height of the camera). In fact, Table 6.2 indicates that filmed people clearly slow down when climbing up or down the stairs when compared to flat regions (A and C in Fig. 6.15(a)).

We simulated this environment with approximately the same number of people as in the filmed video sequence (a snapshot is presented in Fig. 6.15(b)). As shown in Table 6.2, the simulated experiment yielded results similar to the filmed sequence, and virtual humans also kept the tendency of reducing their speed in the region of the stairs. It should be emphasized that velocity fields used in this simulation were obtained in a fully automatic way (from people tracking to automatic clustering).

Fig. 6.15 (a) Regions used for quantitative validation. (b) Snapshot of simulation with a small number of agents. (c) Snapshot of simulation with a large number of agents

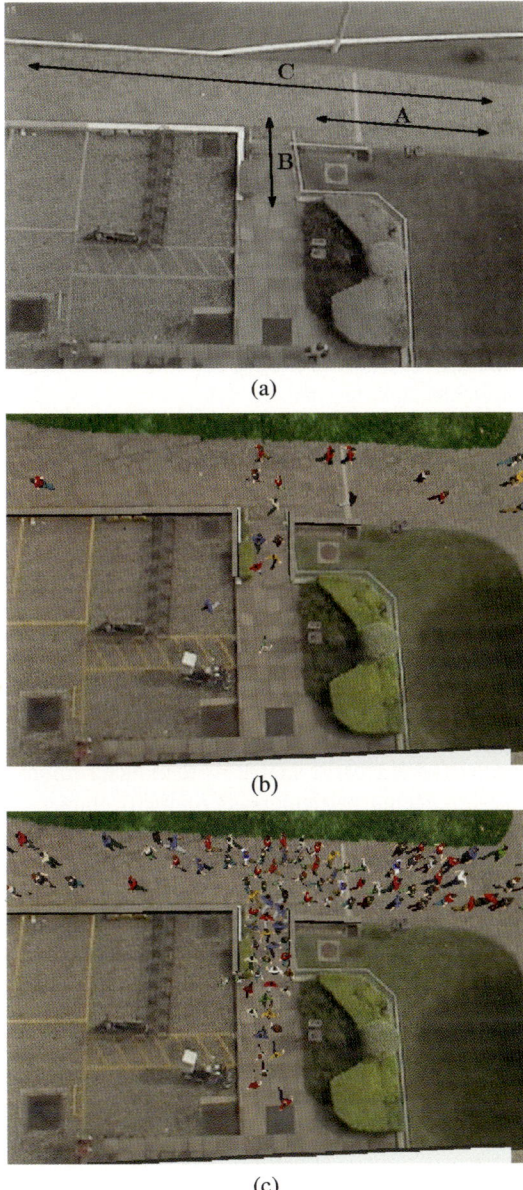

We also analyzed the influence of increasing the number of simulated agents, using the velocity fields obtained with a smaller number of people. Such experiments can be useful to predict the flow of people in public spaces during special occasions (e.g., a shopping mall near Christmas). We extrapolated the number of people for the *T-intersection* scenario from 20 to 150 agents, as illustrated in Fig. 6.15(c). Average

Table 6.2 Quantitative metrics for evaluating the *T-intersection* scenario with 20 agents

Region	Dir.	Video (speed) Mean	std	Simulation (speed) Mean	std
A	→	0.96 m/s	0.17 m/s	0.84 m/s	0.26 m/s
	←	1.00 m/s	0.19 m/s	0.91 m/s	0.21 m/s
B	↓	0.52 m/s	0.33 m/s	0.48 m/s	0.30 m/s
	↑	0.53 m/s	0.29 m/s	0.58 m/s	0.29 m/s
C	→	1.03 m/s	0.20 m/s	0.89 m/s	0.27 m/s
	←	1.06 m/s	0.20 m/s	0.99 m/s	0.23 m/s

Table 6.3 Quantitative metrics for evaluating the *T-intersection* scenario with 150 agents

Region	Dir.	Simulation (speed) Mean	std
A	→	0.81 m/s	0.26 m/s
	←	0.90 m/s	0.28 m/s
B	↓	0.35 m/s	0.31 m/s
	↑	0.31 m/s	0.27 m/s
C	→	0.78 m/s	0.33 m/s
	←	0.85 m/s	0.34 m/s

speeds in regions A, B, and C for this experiment are shown in Table 6.3. As expected, such average speeds were reduced compared with the experiment performed with 20 agents, particularly in region B. In fact, this crowded scenario produces traffic jams, which can be observed more evidently in regions with spatial constraints, such as the relatively narrow stairway. It is important to observe that all crowds in this scenario (filmed, simulated with same number of agents as filmed sequence and extrapolating number of agents) present similar characteristics (spatial formation, decreasing velocities as a function of stairs and corridors).

6.6 Final Remarks

This chapter presented different approaches for using real-life data to improve the realism of crowd simulation. Some of the methods described in the chapter require a visual inspection of the filmed (real) scene, and a manual calibration of parameters in the simulated scenario. However, there is a great potential for using computer vision algorithms to automatically extract information from filmed video sequences. Although this brief review focused on people tracking, several other aspects can be tackled using computer vision, such as tracking of individual body parts (for vision-based motion capture, for instance), detection of events [ORP00, GX03, DCXL06], and others. Reviews on vision-based analysis of human dynamics can be found in [WS03, WHT03, VV05, MaVK06].

References

[ALA*01] ASHIDA K., LEE S., ALLBECK J., SUN H., BADLER N., METAXAS D.: Pedestrians: Creating agent behaviors through statistical analysis of observation data. In *Proceedings of IEEE Computer Animation* (Seoul, Korea, 2001), pp. 84–92.

[ARS06] ADAM A., RIVLIN E., SHIMSHONI I.: Robust fragments-based tracking using the integral histogram. In *CVPR'06: Proceedings of the 2006 IEEE Computer Society Conference on Computer Vision and Pattern Recognition* (Washington, DC, USA, 2006), IEEE Computer Society, Los Alamitos, pp. 798–805.

[Bel95] BENESCH H.: *Atlas de la Psicologie*. Livre de Poche, Paris, 1995.

[BJ03] BROGAN D. C., JOHNSON N. L.: Realistic human walking paths. In *Proceedings of Computer Animation and Social Agents 2003* (2003), IEEE Computer Society, Los Alamitos, pp. 94–101.

[BMB03] BRAUN A., MUSSE S., BODMANN L. O. B.: Modeling individual behaviors in crowd simulation. In *Computer Animation and Social Agents* (New Jersey, USA, May 2003), pp. 143–148.

[BV99] BOGHOSSIAN A. B., VELASTIN S. A.: Motion-based machine vision techniques for the management of large crowds. In *IEEE International Conference on Electronics, Circuits and Systems* (1999), vol. 2, pp. 961–964.

[CC06] CHENG F., CHEN Y.: Real time multiple objects tracking and identification based on discrete wavelet transform. *Pattern Recognition 39*, 6 (June 2006), 1126–1139.

[CGPP03] CUCCHIARA R., GRANA C., PICCARDI M., PRATI A.: Detecting moving objects, ghosts, and shadows in video streams. *IEEE Transactions on Pattern Analysis and Machine Intelligence 25*, 10 (October 2003), 1337–1342.

[Che04] CHENNEY S.: Flow tiles. In *Proc. ACM SIGGRAPH/Eurographics Symposium on Computer Animation (SCA'04)* (2004), pp. 233–245.

[CMC02] CHIEN S.-Y., MA S.-Y., CHEN L.-G.: Efficient moving object segmentation algorithm using background registration technique. *IEEE Transactions on Circuits and Systems for Video Technology 12*, 7 (2002), 577–586.

[Dav05] DAVIES E.: *Machine Vision: Theory, Algorithms, Practicalities*, 3rd edn. Morgan Kaufmann, San Mateo, 2005.

[DCXL06] DU Y., CHEN G., XU W., LI Y.: Recognizing interaction activities using dynamic Bayesian network. In *IEEE International Conference on Pattern Recognition* (August 2006), vol. 1, pp. 618–621.

[DR02] DODU F., RABUT C.: Vectorial interpolation using radial-basis-like functions. *Computers & Mathematics with Applications 43*, 3–5 (February–March 2002), 393–411.

[EDHD02] ELGAMMAL A., DURAISWAMI R., HARWOOD D., DAVIS L.: Background and foreground modeling using nonparametric kernel density estimation for visual surveillance. *Proceedings of the IEEE 90*, 7 (2002), 1151–1163.

[FJ02] FIGUEIREDO M. A. T., JAIN A. K.: Unsupervised learning of finite mixture models. *IEEE Transactions on Pattern Analysis and Machine Intelligence 24*, 3 (March 2002), 381–396.

[FV06] FUENTES L., VELASTIN S.: People tracking in surveillance applications. *Image and Vision Computing 24*, 11 (November 2006), 1165–1171.

[GFK03] GREST D., FRAHM J.-M., KOCH R.: A color similarity measure for robust shadow removal in real time. In *Vision, Modeling and Visualization* (2003), pp. 253–260.

[GX03] GONG S., XIANG T.: Recognition of group activities using dynamic probabilistic networks. In *IEEE International Conference on Computer Vision* (Washington, DC, USA, 2003), IEEE Computer Society, Los Alamitos, p. 742.

[HBJW05] HELBING D., BUZNA L., JOHANSSON A., WERNER T.: Self-organized pedestrian crowd dynamics: Experiments, simulations, and design solutions. *Transportation Science 39*, 1 (Feb. 2005), 1–24.

[HFV00] HELBING D., FARKAS I., VICSEK T.: Simulating dynamical features of escape panic. *Nature 407* (2000), 487–490.

[HHD00] HARITAOGLU I., HARWOOD D., DAVIS L.: W4: Real-time surveillance of people and their activities. *IEEE Transactions on Pattern Analysis and Machine Intelligence 22*, 8 (August 2000), 809–830.

[HM97] HELBING D., MOLNAR P.: Self-organization phenomena in pedestrian crowds. In *Self-Organization of Complex Structures: From Individual to Collective Dynamics* (1997), Gordon & Breach, London, pp. 569–577.

[Jef98] JEFFREY P.: *Emerging Social Conventions: Personal Space and Privacy in Shared Virtual Worlds*. Technical Report: CS 27-430 Project, 1998.

[JJM06] JACQUES J. C. S. JR., JUNG C. R., MUSSE S. R.: A background subtraction model adapted to illumination changes. In *IEEE International Conference on Image Processing* (2006), IEEE Press, New York, pp. 1817–1820.

[JJS04] JUNEJO I., JAVED O., SHAH M.: Multi feature path modeling for video surveillance. In *IEEE International Conference on Pattern Recognition* (2004), vol. II, pp. 716–719.

[KB03] KAEWTRAKULPONG P., BOWDEN R.: A real time adaptive visual surveillance system for tracking low-resolution colour targets in dynamically changing scenes. *Image and Vision Computing 21*, 9 (September 2003), 913–929.

[LK81] LUCAS B., KANADE T.: An iterative image registration technique with an application to stereo vision. In *Proceedings of International Joint Conference on Artificial Intelligence* (1981), pp. 674–679.

[Low04] LOWE D. G.: Distinctive image features from scale-invariant keypoints. *International Journal of Computer Vision 60*, 2 (2004), 91–110.

[Man85] MANNONI P.: *La Psychologie Collective*. Presses Universitaires de France, Paris, 1985.

[MaVK06] MOESLUND T. B., HILTON A., KRUGER V.: A survey of advances in vision-based human motion capture and analysis. *Computer Vision and Image Understanding 104*, 1 (October 2006), 90–126.

[MC95] MARTIN J., CROWLEY J. L.: Comparison of correlation techniques. In *Conference on Intelligent Autonomous Systems* (Karsluhe, Germany, March 1995).

[McC89] MCCLELLAND J. S.: *The Crowd and the Mob*. Cambridge University Press, Cambridge, 1989.

[ME05] MAKRIS D., ELLIS T.: Learning semantic scene models from observing activity in visual surveillance. *IEEE Transactions on Systems, Man, and Cybernetics B 35*, 3 (June 2005), 397–408.

[MH04] METOYER R., HODGINS J.: Reactive pedestrian navigation from examples. *The Visual Computer 10*, 20 (2004), 635–649.

[MJD*00] MCKENNA S., JABRI S., DURIC Z., ROSENFELD A., WECHSLER H.: Tracking groups of people. *Computer Vision and Image Understanding 80*, 1 (October 2000), 42–56.

[MT01] MUSSE S. R., THALMANN D.: A hierarchical model for real time simulation of virtual human crowds. *IEEE Transactions on Visualization and Computer Graphics 7*, 2 (April–June 2001), 152–164.

[NTWH04] NING H., TAN T., WANG L., HU W.: People tracking based on motion model and motion constraints with automatic initialization. *Pattern Recognition 37*, 7 (July 2004), 1423–1440.

[ORP00] OLIVER N., ROSARIO B., PENTLAND A.: A Bayesian computer vision system for modeling human interactions. *IEEE Transactions on Pattern Analysis and Machine Intelligence 22*, 8 (August 2000), 831–843.

[PTL*04] PAI C.-J., TYAN H.-R., LIANG Y.-M., LIAO H.-Y. M., CHEN S.-W.: Pedestrian detection and tracking at crossroads. *Pattern Recognition 37*, 5 (2004), 1025–1034.

[PTM06] PORIKLI F., TUZEL O., MEER P.: Covariance tracking using model update based on Lie algebra. In *IEEE Computer Vision and Pattern Recognition* (2006), vol. I, pp. 728–735.

References

[Rey99] REYNOLDS C. W.: Steering behaviors for autonomous characters. In *Game Developers Conference* (San Jose, California, USA, 1999), pp. 763–782.

[Rol81] ROLOFF M. E.: *Interpersonal Communication—The Social Exchange Approach*. SAGE Publications, London, 1981.

[SB05] SHOUSHTARIAN B., BEZ H. E.: A practical adaptive approach for dynamic background subtraction using an invariant colour model and object tracking. *Pattern Recognition Letters 26*, 1 (2005), 91–99.

[SG99] STAUFFER C., GRIMSON W.: Adaptive background mixture models for real-time tracking. In *IEEE Computer Vision and Pattern Recognition* (1999), vol. II, pp. 246–252.

[ST94] SHI J., TOMASI C.: Good features to track. In *IEEE Conference on Computer Vision and Pattern Recognition (CVPR'94)* (Seattle, June 1994).

[TLH05] TIAN Y., LU M., HAMPAPUR A.: Robust and efficient foreground analysis for real-time video surveillance. In *IEEE Computer Vision and Pattern Recognition* (2005), vol. I, pp. 1182–1187.

[VV05] VALERA M., VELASTIN S.: Intelligent distributed surveillance systems: A review. *IEE Vision, Image and Signal Processing 152*, 2 (April 2005), 192–204.

[WADP97] WREN C., AZARBAYEJANI A., DARRELL T., PENTLAND A.: Pfinder: Real-time tracking of the human body. *IEEE Transactions on Pattern Analysis and Machine Intelligence 19*, 7 (July 1997), 780–785.

[Wat92] WATSON D. E.: *Contouring: A Guide to the Analysis and Display of Spatial Data*. Pergamon, Tarrytown, 1992.

[WHT03] WANG L., HU W., TAN T.: Recent developments in human motion analysis. *Pattern Recognition 36* (2003), 585–601.

[WS03] WANG J. J., SINGH S.: Video analysis of human dynamics: A survey. *Real-Time Imaging 9*, 5 (2003), 321–346.

[WTLW05] WANG Y., TAN T., LOE K., WU J.: A probabilistic approach for foreground and shadow segmentation in monocular image sequences. *Pattern Recognition 38*, 11 (November 2005), 1937–1946.

[XLLY05] XU D., LI X., LIU Z., YUAN Y.: Cast shadow detection in video segmentation. *Pattern Recognition Letters 26*, 1 (2005), 5–26.

[XP98] XU C., PRINCE J.: Snakes, shapes, and gradient vector flow. *IEEE Transactions on Image Processing 7*, 3 (March 1998), 359–369.

[YLPL05] YANG T., LI S. Z., PAN Q., LI J.: Real-time multiple objects tracking with occlusion handling in dynamic scenes. In *IEEE Computer Vision and Pattern Recognition* (2005), pp. 970–975.

[ZvdH06] ZIVKOVIC Z., VAN DER HEIJDEN F.: Efficient adaptive density estimation per image pixel for the task of background subtraction. *Pattern Recognition Letters 27*, 7 (May 2006), 773–780.

Chapter 7
Crowd Rendering

7.1 Introduction

In this chapter, we focus on the technical aspect of real-time crowd simulation, and how an efficient architecture can be developed. But first, it is important to identify the main goals to achieve. We need:

- Quantity: real-time simulation of thousands of characters,
- Quality: state-of-the-art virtual humans,
- Efficiency: storage and real-time management of massive crowd data,
- Versatility: adaptation to diversified environments and situations.

The main problem when dealing with thousands of characters is the quantity of information that needs to be processed for each one of them. Such a task is very demanding, even for modern processors. Naive approaches, where virtual humans are processed one after another, in no specific order, provoke costly state switches for both the CPU and GPU. For an efficient use of the available computing power, and to approach hardware peak performance, data flowing through the same path need to be grouped. We thus present an architecture able to handle, early in its pipeline, the sorting of virtual human related data into grouped slots. We show results of thousands of simulated characters. As for the quality, we display state-of-the-art virtual humans where the user attention is focused. Characters capable of facial and hand animation are simulated in the vicinity of the camera to improve believability, while farther, less expensive representations are used. Concerning efficiency of storage and data management, we mainly employ a database to store all the virtual human-related data. Finally, the presented architecture is versatile enough to be stressed in very different scenarios, e.g., in confined environments like an auditorium or a classroom, and also in large-scale environments like a crowded fun fair or city.

In this chapter, we first introduce in Sect. 7.2 how the virtual humans can be represented, along with their different levels of detail, depending on their distance and eccentricity to the camera. Then, in Sect. 7.3, we fully detail our architecture pipeline, and how the virtual human related data are sorted in order to be processed faster. In Sect. 7.4, we introduce the motion kit, a data structure specifically developed for managing the different levels of detail at the animation stage. The storage and management of unchanging data with a dedicated database is developed in Sect. 7.5. In Sect. 7.6, we introduce a shadow mapping algorithm applied to a crowd. Finally, in Sect. 7.7, we introduced crowd patches.

7.2 Virtual Human Representations

In an ideal world, graphic cards are able, at each frame, to render an infinite number of triangles with an arbitrary complex shading on them. To visualize crowds of virtual humans, we would simply use thousands of very detailed meshes, e.g., capable of hand and facial animation. Unfortunately, in spite of the recent programmable graphics hardware advances, we are still compelled to stick to a limited triangle budget per frame. This budget is spent wisely to be able to display dense crowds without too much perceptible degradations. The concept of levels of detail (LOD), extensively treated in the literature (see [LRC*02]), is exploited to meet our real-time constraints. We specifically discuss levels of detail for virtual humans composing a crowd: depending on the location of the camera, a character is rendered with a specific representation, resulting from the compromise of rendering cost and quality. In this Section, we first introduce the data structure we use to create and simulate virtual humans: the human template. Then, we describe the three levels of detail a human template uses: the deformable mesh, rigid mesh, and finally the impostor.

7.2.1 Human Template

A type of human such as a woman, man, or child is described as a human template, which consists of:

- A skeleton, composed of joints, representing articulations,
- A set of meshes, all representing the same virtual human, but with a decreasing number of triangles,
- Several appearance sets, used to vary its appearance (see Chap. 3),
- A set of animation sequences which it can play.

Each rendered virtual human is derived from a human template, i.e., it is an instance of a human template. In order for all the instances of the same human template to look different, we use several appearance sets, which us allow to vary the texture applied to the instances, as well as modulate the colors of the texture.

7.2.2 Deformable Mesh

A deformable mesh is a representation of a human template composed of triangles. It is enveloping a skeleton of 78 joints, used for animation: when the skeleton moves,

7.2 Virtual Human Representations

the vertices of the mesh follow smoothly its joint movements, similarly to our skin. We call such an animation a skeletal animation. Each vertex of the mesh is influenced by one or a few joints. Thus, at every keyframe of an animation sequence, a vertex is deformed by the weighted transformation of the joints influencing it, as follows:

$$v(t) = \sum_{i=1}^{n} X_i^t X_i^{-ref} v^{ref} \qquad (7.1)$$

where $v(t)$ is the deformed vertex at time t, X_i^t is the global transform of joint i at time t, X_i^{-ref} is the inverse global transform of the joint in the reference position, and v^{ref} is the vertex in its reference position. This technique, first described by Magnenat-Thalmann et al. [MTLT88], is known as skeletal subspace deformation, or skinning [Lan98].

The skinning can be efficiently performed by the GPU: the deformable mesh sends the joint transformations of its skeleton to the GPU, which takes care of moving each vertex according to its joint influences. However, it is important to take into account the limitations of today's graphic cards, which can store only up to 256 atomic values, i.e., 256 vectors of 4 floating points. The joint transformations of a skeleton can be sent to the GPU as 4×4 matrices, i.e., four atomic values. This way, the maximum number of joints a skeleton can have reaches

$$\frac{256}{4} = 64 \qquad (7.2)$$

When wishing to perform hand and facial animation, 64 bones are not sufficient. Our solution is to send each joint transformation to the GPU as a unit quaternion [Sho85] and a translation, i.e., two atomic values. This allows doubling the number of joints possible to send. Note that one usually does not wish to use all the atomic structures of a GPU exclusively for the joints of a skeleton, since it usually is exploited to process other data.

Although rendering deformable meshes is costly, due to the expensive vertex skinning and joint transmission, it would be a great quality drop to do without them:

- They are the most flexible representation to animate, allowing even for facial and hand animation (if using a sufficiently detailed skeleton).
- Such animation sequences, called skeletal animations, are cheap to store: for each keyframe, only the transformation of deforming joints, i.e., those moved in the animation, need to be kept. Thus, a tremendous quantity of those animations can be exploited in the simulation, increasing crowd movement variety.
- Procedural and composited animations are suited for this representation, e.g., idle motions can be generated on-the-fly [EGMT06].
- Blending is also possible for smooth transitions between different skeletal animations.

Unfortunately, the cost of using deformable meshes as the sole representation of virtual humans in a crowd is too prohibitive. We therefore use them in a limited number and only at the fore-front of the camera. Note that before switching to rigid meshes, we use several deformable meshes, keeping the same animation algorithm, but with a decreasing number of triangles.

Skilled designers are required to model skinned and textured deformable meshes. But once finished, they are automatically used as the raw material to derive all subsequent representations: the rigid meshes and the impostors.

7.2.3 Rigid Mesh

A rigid mesh is a precomputed geometric posture of a deformable mesh, thus sharing the very same appearance. A rigid animation sequence is always inspired from an original skeletal animation, and from an external point of view, both look alike. However, the process to create them is different. To compute a keyframe of a rigid animation, the corresponding keyframe for the skeletal animation is retrieved. It provides a skeleton posture (or joint transformations). Then, as a preprocessing step, each vertex is deformed on the CPU, in opposition to a skeletal animation, where the vertex deformation is achieved online, and on the GPU. Once the rigid mesh is deformed, it is stored as a keyframe, in a table of vertices, normals (3D points), and texture coordinates (2D points). This process is repeated for each keyframe of a rigid animation. At runtime, a rigid animation is simply played as the succession of several postures or keyframes. There are several advantages in using such a rigid mesh representation:

- It is much faster to display, because the skeleton deformation and vertex skinning stages are already done and stored in keyframes.
- The communication between the CPU and the GPU is kept to a minimum, since no joint transformation needs to be sent.
- It looks exactly the same as the skeletal animation used to generate it.

The gain in speed brought by this new representation is considerable. It is possible to display about 10 times more rigid meshes than deformable meshes. However, the rigid meshes need to be displayed farther from the camera than deformable meshes, because they allow for neither procedural animations nor blending, and no composited, facial, or hand animation is possible.

7.2.4 Impostor

Impostors are the less detailed representation, and extensively exploited in the domain of crowd rendering [TLC02b, DHOO05]. An impostor represents a virtual human with only two textured triangles, forming a quad, which is enough to give the wanted illusion at long range from the camera. Similarly to a rigid animation, an impostor animation is a succession of postures, or keyframes, inspired from an original skeletal animation. The main difference with a rigid animation is that it is only a 2D image of the posture that is kept for each keyframe, instead of the whole geometry. Creating an impostor animation is complex and time consuming. Thus, its construction is achieved in a preprocessing step, and the result is then stored into a database in a binary format (see Sect. 7.5), similarly to a rigid animation. We detail here how each keyframe of an impostor animation is developed. The first step when generating such a keyframe for a human template is to create two textures, or atlas:

- A normal map, storing in its texels the 3D normals as RGB components. This normal map is necessary to apply the correct shading to the virtual humans rendered as impostors. Indeed, if the normals were not saved, a terrible shading would be applied to the virtual human, since it is represented with only two triangles. Switching from a rigid mesh to an impostor would thus lead to awful popping artifacts.
- A UV map, storing in its texels the 2D texture coordinates as RG components. This information is also very important, because it allows one to apply correctly a texture to each texel of an impostor. Otherwise, we would need to generate an atlas for every texture of a human template.

Since impostors are only 2D quads, we need to store normals and texture coordinates from several points of view, so that, at runtime, when the camera moves, we can display the correct keyframe from the correct camera view point. In summary, each texture described above holds a single mesh posture for several points of view. This is why we also call such textures atlas. We illustrate in Fig. 7.1 a 1024 × 1024 atlas for a particular keyframe. The top of the atlas is used to store the UV map, and its bottom the normal map.

The main advantage of impostors is that they are very efficient, since only two triangles per virtual human are displayed. Thus, they constitute the biggest part of the crowd. However, their rendering quality is poor, and thus they cannot be exploited close to the camera. Moreover, the storage of an impostor animation is very costly, due to the high number of textures that need to be saved.

We summarize in Table 7.1 and Fig. 7.2 the performance and animation storage for each virtual human representation. Observe that each step down the representation hierarchy allows one to increase by an order of magnitude the number of displayable characters. Also note that the faster the display of a representation is, the bigger the animation storage. Moreover, rigid meshes and impostors are stored in GPU memory, which is usually much smaller than CPU memory. Figure 7.3 summarizes the shared resources inside a human template.

7.3 Architecture Pipeline

Modeling a varied crowd of virtual humans, individual by individual, mesh by mesh, and texture by texture, would be extremely time consuming and would also require an army of dedicated skilled designers. Moreover, it would pose an evident storage problem. We adopt a different strategy to model such a crowd, and concentrate our

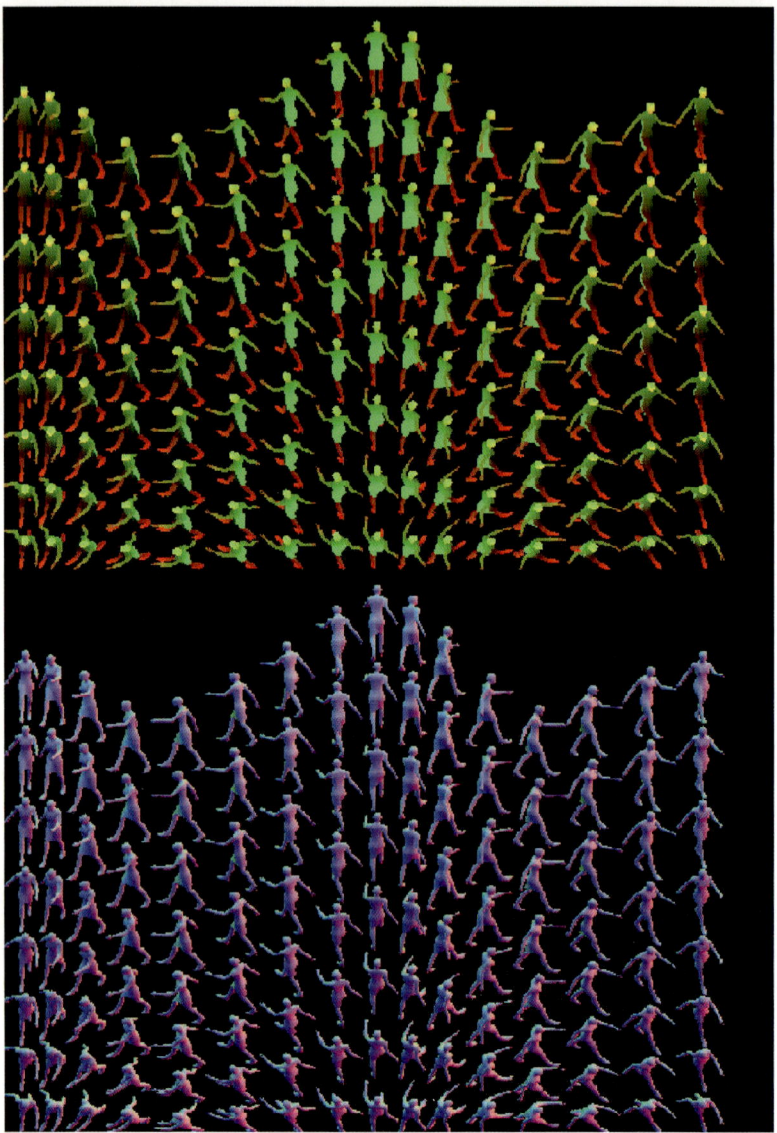

Fig. 7.1 A 1024 × 1024 atlas storing the UV map (*above*) and the normal map (*below*) of a virtual human performing a keyframe of an animation from several points of view

efforts on creating only a few human templates. From this reduced set, we then instantiate thousands of different characters. We use different techniques to obtain variety each time a character is instantiated from a human template. More details on the specific variety methods can be found in Chap. 3.

7.3 Architecture Pipeline

Table 7.1 Storage space in [Mb] for 1 second of an animation clip of (a) deformable meshes, (b) rigid meshes, and (c) impostors

	Max Displayable Number @30 Hz	Animation Frequency [Hz]	Animation Sequence Storage [Mb/s]	Memory Location
(a) Deformable Meshes	$\tilde{2}00$	25	$\tilde{0}.03$	CPU
(b) Rigid Meshes	$\tilde{2}000$	20	$\tilde{0}.3$	GPU
(c) Impostors	$\tilde{2}0000$	10	$\tilde{1}5$	GPU

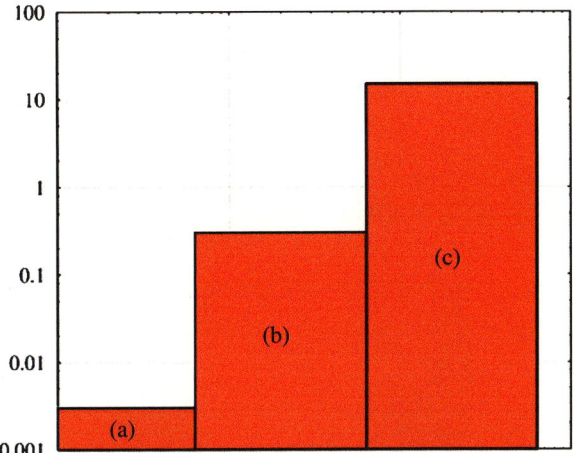

Fig. 7.2 Storage space in [Mb] for 1 second of an animation clip of (**a**) a deformable mesh, (**b**) a rigid mesh, and (**c**) an impostor

In this section, we describe the main stages of the architecture pipeline along with the data flowing through them. Figure 7.4 depicts the different stages: at each frame, data are flowing sequentially through each one of them, beginning from the top, down to the bottom. Simulating a crowd of virtual humans is an extremely demanding task, even for modern processors. An architecture sustaining thousands of realistic characters needs to be "hardware-friendly." Indeed, simple approaches, i.e., treating virtual humans in no particular order, "as they come," tend to produce too many state switches for both the CPU and GPU. A more efficient use of the available computing power is recommended, in order to get closer to hardware peak performance. Data flowing through the same path of the pipeline need to be grouped. As a consequence, at the beginning of each new frame, care is taken to batch data together into predefined slots. More details may be found in [MYTP09].

7.3.1 Human Data Structures

Virtual human instances are shared in several data structures, and a unique identifier is associated with each one of them. Our crowd data structure is mainly composed of two arrays: an array of body entities and an array of brain entities. The unique

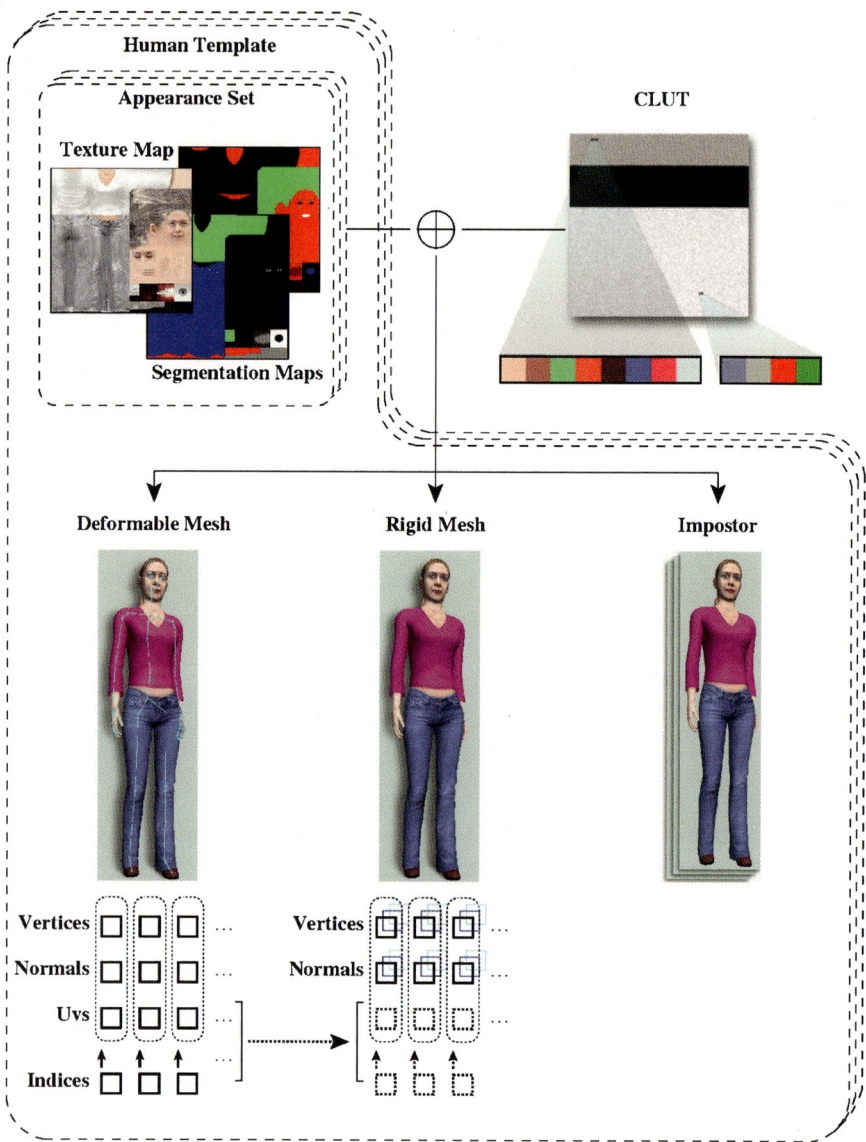

Fig. 7.3 Shared resources between representations inside a human template

identifier of each virtual human is used to index these arrays and retrieve specific data, which is distributed in a body and brain entity. Body data consist of all the parameters used at every frame, like the position and orientation of the virtual human. Brain data are more related to behavior parameters, and are less regularly exploited. By separating these parameters from the body entity, we tighten the storage of very often used data. Indeed, such a regrouping improves performance: in a recent work

7.3 Architecture Pipeline

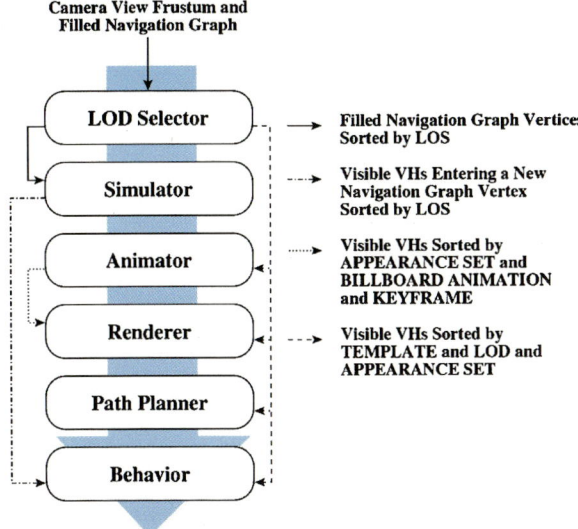

Fig. 7.4 Crowd architecture pipeline

[PdHCM*06], while experimenting on different steering methods, we observed that with a very large number of characters (tens of thousands), the performance of the different methods was about the same. Memory latency to jump from an instance to the other was the bottleneck when dealing with large crowds.

7.3.2 Pipeline Stages

In this section, we first provide a short reminder on navigation graphs (see Sect. 5.4.3). Then, we detail the stages of the pipeline illustrated in Fig. 7.4.

For a given scene, a navigation graph is provided and used to steer virtual humans along predefined paths. The graph is composed of a set of vertices, represented in the scene as vertical cylinders where no collision with the environment can occur. Two vertices can be connected by an edge, represented as a gate between two overlapping cylinders (see Fig. 7.5 on the bottom right). When several cylinders overlap, their consecutive gates delimit a corridor. In the scene, a path to follow is defined as a sequence of gates to reach one after the other, i.e., simple subgoals for the chosen steering method. A navigation graph with apparent vertices and gates is pictured in Fig. 7.5 on the bottom right. During simulation, each vertex keeps a list of the ids of virtual humans currently traveling through it. Here follows a detailed description of each pipeline stage.

The LOD Selector is the first stage of the pipeline. It receives as input a navigation graph filled with virtual human ids and the camera view frustum. The role of the LOD Selector entity is to categorize graph vertices, i.e., to score each of them for

Fig. 7.5 *Top left*: virtual humans navigating in a complex environment. *Top right*: similar image with apparent levels of detail. *In red*: the rigid meshes; *in green*: the impostors. *Bottom left*: dense crowd in a large environment. *Bottom right*: virtual humans steering along a path sustained by a navigation graph structure (in *green* and *white*). Overlapping vertices form gates (*in red*). Consecutive gates on the path form corridors (*in black*)

further processing. We have two different scores to attribute to each vertex: a level of detail (LOD) and a level of simulation (LOS). They are both determined by finding the distance from the vertex to the camera and its eccentricity from the middle of the screen. The LOD score is used to choose the appropriate virtual human representation inside the vertex, and the LOS score allows one to choose the suitable collision avoidance algorithm, along with the frequency of the simulation. Indeed, the structure of the navigation graph already allows one to avoid collisions between the characters and the environment and is also used to decompose a complex goal into simple reachable subgoals. However, without further treatment, virtual humans navigate independently of each other, without attempting to avoid interpenetrations. The resulting effect tends to look like a simulation of awkward "ghosts." Thus, it is important to provide a robust collision handling method for at least virtual humans in the vicinity of the camera. Farther away, characters use an approximate but less costly method.

The LOD Selector uses the navigation graph as a hierarchical structure to avoid testing individually each character. The processing of data is achieved as follows: first, each vertex of the graph is tested against the camera view frustum, i.e., frustum culled. Empty vertices are not even scored, nor further held in the process for the

7.3 Architecture Pipeline

Algorithm 7.1: Process the rendering list

```
1  begin
2      for each human template: do
3          apply human template common data operations, e.g., get its skeleton
4          for For each LOD: do
5              apply LOD common data operations, e.g., enable LOD specific
                 shader program
6              for For each appearance set: do
7                  apply appearance set common data operations, e.g., bind it
8                  for For each virtual human id: do
9                      get body or brain structure from the id
10                     apply operations on it
11                 end
12             end
13         end
14     end
15 end
```

current frame; indeed, there is no interest to keep them in the subsequent stages of the pipeline. On the other hand, vertices filled with at least one character and outside the camera view are kept, but they are not assigned any LOD score, since they are outside the view frustum, and thus, their virtual humans are not displayed. As for their LOS score, they get the lowest one. Indeed, even if they are not in the camera field, virtual humans contained in these vertices need a minimal simulation to sporadically move along their path. Without care, when they quit the camera field, they immediately stop moving, and thus, when the camera changes its point of view, packages of stagnant characters suddenly move again, causing a disturbing effect for the user. Finally, the vertices that are filled and visible are assigned a LOS score, and then are further investigated to sort their embedded virtual humans by human template, LOD, and appearance set.

At the end of this first stage, we obtain two lists. The first one contains all virtual human ids, sorted by human template, by LOD, and finally by appearance set. The second list contains occupied vertices, sorted by LOS. Obtaining such lists takes some time. However, it is very useful to group data and process through the next stages of the pipeline. We illustrate in the pseudo-code in Algorithm 7.1 how the first list is typically used in the next stages of the pipeline.

The second stage is the Simulator, which uses the second list to iterate through all LOS slots and obtain the corresponding filled vertices. At this stage, virtual humans are considered as individual 3D points. Each of them knows the next subgoal to reach, i.e., the next gate to attain. Depending on the LOS, the proper steering method is then applied. Virtual humans detected as crossing a gate get a new subgoal and are assigned to special slots used later by the Behavior stage. Note that

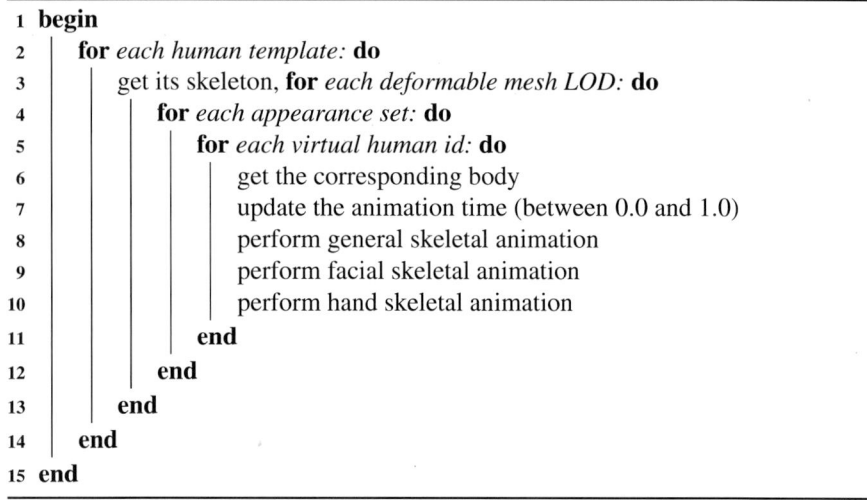

Algorithm 7.2: Process the deformable meshes

1 **begin**
2   **for** *each human template:* **do**
3   get its skeleton, **for** *each deformable mesh LOD:* **do**
4   **for** *each appearance set:* **do**
5   **for** *each virtual human id:* **do**
6   get the corresponding body
7   update the animation time (between 0.0 and 1.0)
8   perform general skeletal animation
9   perform facial skeletal animation
10   perform hand skeletal animation
11   **end**
12   **end**
13   **end**
14   **end**
15 **end**

collision avoidance between pedestrians is not performed at this stage, but later in the pipeline.

The Animator is responsible for the animation of the characters, whichever representation they are using. The slots of visible virtual humans, sorted by human template, LOD, and appearance set in the LOD Selection phase, are the main data structure used in this stage. In Algorithm 7.2 is described the specific tasks that are achieved for the deformable meshes.

Since the virtual humans are also sorted by LOD, we can iterate over the deformable meshes without having to check that they actually are deformable. Performing a skeletal animation, whether it is for the face, the hands, or all the joints of a virtual human, can be summarized in four steps. First, the correct keyframe, depending on the animation time, is retrieved. Note that at this step, it is possible to perform a blending operation between two animations. The final keyframe used is then the interpolation of the ones retrieved from each animation. The second step is to duplicate the original skeleton relative joint matrices in a cache. Then, in the cache, the matrices of the joints modified by the keyframe are overwritten. Finally, all the relative matrices (including those not overwritten) are concatenated to obtain world transforms, and each of them is post-multiplied by the inversed world matrices of the skeleton. Note that optional animations, like the facial animation, are usually performed only for the best deformable mesh LOD, i.e., the most detailed mesh, at the forefront.

For the rigid meshes, the role of the Animator is much reduced, since all the deformations are precomputed (Algorithm 7.3) (see Sect. 7.2).

Note that we do not iterate over all LOD slots, since we are only concerned with the rigid meshes. Once again, the sorting achieved in the LOD Selection stage

7.3 Architecture Pipeline

Algorithm 7.3: Process the rigid meshes

```
1  begin
2      for each human template: do
3          for each rigid mesh LOD: do
4              for each appearance set: do
5                  for each virtual human id: do
6                      get the corresponding body
7                      update the animation time (between 0.0 and 1.0)
8                  end
9              end
10         end
11     end
12 end
```

ensures that we are exclusively iterating over rigid meshes, without cumbersome tests.

Finally, for the impostors, since a keyframe of an impostor animation is only represented by two texture atlases, no specific deformation needs to be achieved. However, we assign the animator a special job: to update a new list of virtual human ids, specifically sorted to suit a fast rendering of impostors. Indeed, at initialization, and for each human template, a special list of virtual human ids is created, sorted by appearance set, impostor animation, and keyframe. The first task achieved by the Animator is to reset the impostor specific list in order to refill it accordingly to the current state of the simulation. Then, to refill this list, an iteration is performed over the current up-to-date list, the one sorted by human template, LOD, and appearance set (updated in the LOD Selection stage) (see Algorithm 7.4).

In this way, the impostor specific list is updated every time the data pass through the Animator stage, and is thus ready to be exploited at the next stage, the Renderer.

The Renderer represents the phase where draw calls are issued to the GPU to display the crowd. Rendering shadows is a two-pass algorithm, and achieved in this stage: first, deformable and rigid meshes are sequentially rendered from the point of view of the sun, i.e., the main directional light. Then, they are consecutively rendered from the point of view of the camera. To diminish state change overhead, the number of draw calls is minimized, thanks to our slots of visible humans sorted by human template, LOD, and appearance set. In the pseudo-code in Algorithm 7.5, we show the second pass in the deformable mesh rendering process.

This second pass is preceded by another pass, used to compute the shadows. Note that in this first pass, the process is quite similar, although data useless for shadow computation are not sent, e.g., normal and texture parameters. In this rendering phase, one can see the full power of the sorted lists: all the instances of the same deformable mesh have the same vertices, normals, and texture coordinates. Thus, these coordinates need to be bound only once per deformable mesh LOD.

Algorithm 7.4: Process the impostors

```
1  begin
2      for each human template: do
3          get its impostor animations
4          for the only impostor LOD: do
5              for each appearance set AS: do
6                  for each virtual human id: do
7                      get the corresponding body
8                      update the animation time (between 0.0 and 1.0)
9                      get body's current impostor animation id a
10                     get body's current impostor keyframe id k
11                     put virtual human id in special
12                     list[AS][a][k]
13                 end
14             end
15         end
16     end
17 end
```

Algorithm 7.5: Render the deformable meshes

```
1  begin
2      for each human template: do
3          for each deformable mesh LOD: do
4              bind vertex, normal, and texture buffer
5              send to the GPU the joint ids influencing each vertex
6              send to the GPU their corresponding weights
7              for each appearance set: do
8                  send to the GPU texture specular parameters
9                  bind texture and segmentation maps
10                 for each virtual human id: do
11                     get the corresponding body
12                     send the joint orientations from cache
13                     send the joint translations from cache
14                 end
15             end
16         end
17     end
18 end
```

7.3 Architecture Pipeline

Algorithm 7.6: Render the rigid meshes

```
1  begin
2    for each human template: do
3      for the only rigid mesh LOD: do
4        bind texture coordinate buffer
5        bind indices buffer
6        for each appearance set: do
7          send to the GPU texture specular parameters
8          bind texture and segmentation maps
9          for each virtual human id: do
10           get the corresponding body
11           get the correct rigid animation keyframe
12           bind its vertex and normal buffer
13         end
14       end
15     end
16   end
17 end
```

The same applies for the appearance sets: even though they are used by several virtual humans, each one needs to be sent only once to the GPU. Note that each joint transformation is sent to the GPU as two vectors of four floating points, retrieved from the cache filled in the Animation phase.

For the rigid meshes, the process is quite different, since all the vertex deformations have been achieved in a preprocessing step. We develop here the second pass in pseudo-code shown in Algorithm 7.6.

In the rendering phase of the rigid meshes, only the texture coordinates and indices can be bound at the LOD level, in opposition to the deformable meshes, where all mesh data are bound at this level. The reason is obvious: for a deformable mesh, all the components representing its mesh information (vertices, normals, etc.) are the same for all instances. It is only later, on the GPU, that the mesh is deformed to fit the skeleton posture of each individual. For a rigid mesh, its texture coordinates, along with its indices (to access the buffers), remain the same for all of their instances. However, since the vertices and normals are displaced in a preprocess and stored in the keyframes of a rigid animation, it is only at the individual level, where we know the animation played, that their binding can be achieved. Note that since the vertices sent to the GPU are already deformed, there is no specific work to be achieved in the vertex shader. Concerning the shadow computation phase, i.e., the first pass, the pseudo-code is the same, but without sending useless data, like normal and texture information.

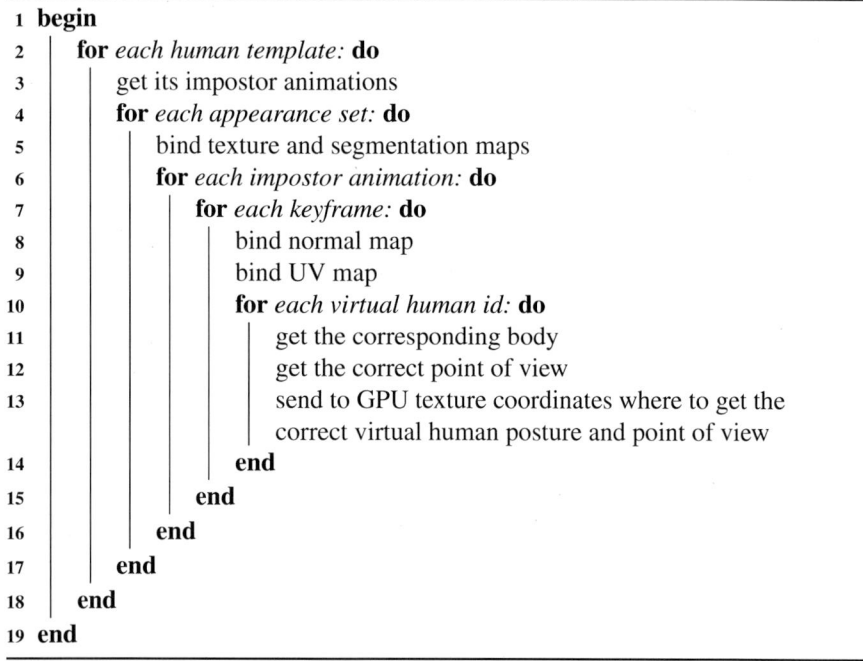

Rendering impostors is fast, thanks to the virtual human id list sorted by human template, appearance set, animation, and keyframe, that is updated at the Animation phase. Algorithm 7.7 provides the corresponding pseudo-code.

The Path Planner is performing the collision avoidance between virtual humans. It is at the Simulator stage that subgoals are set several frames ahead, and that the followed directions are interpolated by steering methods. The Path Planner cares only for collision avoidance, and runs at a lower frequency than the other presented stages. Note that we put this stage and the next one, the Behavior, after the Renderer, because the GPU is rendering in parallel. So, instead of waiting for the frame to finish being rendered, we concurrently use the CPU.

The Behavior is the phase exploiting the slots of virtual humans reaching new navigation graph vertices. All along the entire pipeline, virtual humans cannot change their current animation or steering, because it would invalidate our various sorted slots. This last stage is thus the only one which is allowed to change the steering and current animation sequence of virtual humans. It is always achieved at the end of the pipeline, one frame ahead. Basically, each time a character is entering a new graph vertex (detected at the Simulator phase), we apply a probability to change the steering and/or animation. For instance, a character entering a new vertex with a walk animation clip has a probability to start playing another animation sequence, e.g., an idle one.

7.4 Motion Kits

7.4.1 Data Structure

We introduce three levels of representation for the virtual humans: the deformable meshes, the rigid meshes, and the impostors. When playing an animation sequence, a virtual human is treated differently depending on its current distance and eccentricity to the camera, i.e., the current level of detail it uses. For clarity purpose, we recall giving an animation clip a different name depending on which level of detail it applies to (see Sect. 7.2). An animation clip intended for a deformable mesh is a skeletal animation, one for a rigid mesh is a rigid animation, and an animation clip for an impostor is an impostor animation.

We have already shown that the main advantage of using less detailed representations is the speed of rendering. However, for the memory, the cost of storing an animation sequence for a deformable, a rigid mesh, or an impostor is growing (see Table 7.1). From this, it is obvious that the number of animation sequences stored must be limited for the less detailed representations. It is also true that we want to keep as many skeletal animation clips as possible for the deformable meshes, first, because their storage requirement is reasonable, and second, for variety purpose. Indeed, deformable meshes are at the forefront, close to the camera, and several virtual humans playing the same animation clip are immediately noticed.

The issue arising then is the switching from a level of representation to another. For instance, what should happen if a deformable mesh performing a walk cycle reaches the limit at which it switches to the rigid mesh representation? If a rigid animation with the same walk cycle (same speed) has been precomputed, switching is done smoothly. However, if the only rigid animation available is a fast run cycle, the virtual human will "pop" from a representation to the other, greatly disturbing the user. We therefore need each skeletal animation to be linked to a reassembling rigid animation, and similarly to an impostor animation. For this reason, we need a motion kit data structure. A motion kit holds several items:

- A name, identifying what sort of animation it represents, e.g., walk_1.5ms,
- Its duration,
- Its type, determined by four identifiers: action, subaction, left arm action, and right arm action,
- A link to a skeletal animation,
- A link to a rigid animation,
- A link to an impostor animation.

Each virtual human knows only the current motion kit it uses. Then, at the Animator stage, depending on the distance of the virtual human to the camera, the correct animation clip is used. Note that there is always a 1:1 relation between the motion kits and the skeletal animations, i.e., a motion kit is useless if there is not an exact corresponding skeletal animation. As for the rigid and impostor animations,

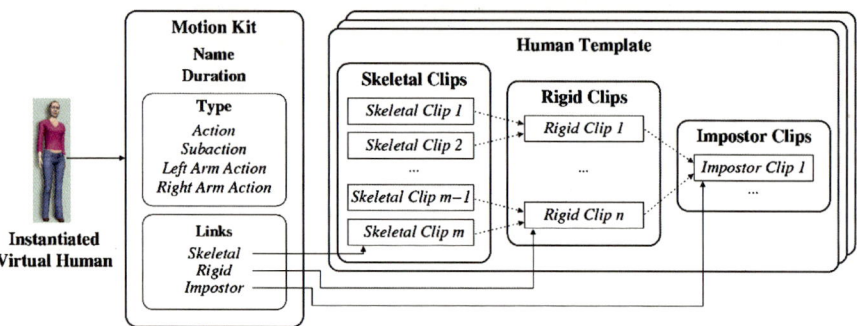

Fig. 7.6 Example of motion kit structure. In the *center*, a motion kit with its links identifying the corresponding animations to use for all human templates. On the *left*, a virtual human instantiated from a human template point to the motion kit it currently uses

their number is much smaller than for skeletal animations, and thus, several motion kits may point to the same rigid or impostor animation. For instance, imagine a virtual human using a motion kit representing a walk cycle at 1.7 m/s. The motion kit has the exact skeletal animation needed for a deformable mesh (same speed). If the virtual human is a rigid mesh, the motion kit may point to a rigid animation at 1.5 m/s, which is the closest one available. And finally, the motion kit also points to the impostor animation with the closest speed. The presented data structure is very useful to easily pass from a representation to another. In Fig. 7.6, we show a schema representing a motion kit and its links to different animation clips. All the motion kits and the animations are stored in a database, along with the links joining them (see Sect. 7.5).

One may wonder what the four identifiers are for. They are used as categories to sort the motion kits. With such a classification, it is easy to randomly choose a motion kit for a virtual human, given certain constraints. First, the action type describes the general kind of movement represented by the motion kit. It is defined as either:

- *stand*: for all animations where the virtual human is standing on its feet,
- *sit*: for all animations where the virtual human is sitting,
- *walk*: for all walk cycles, or
- *run*: for all run cycles.

The second identifier is the subaction type, which more restrains the kind of activity of the motion kit. Its list is nonexhaustive, but it contains descriptors such as talk, dance, idle, etc. We have also added a special subaction called none, which is used when a motion kit does not fit in any of the other subaction types. Let us note that some action/subaction couples are likely to contain no motion kit at all. For instance, a motion kit categorized as a sit action and a dance subaction is not likely to exist. The third and fourth identifiers: left and right arm actions are used to add some specific animation to the arms of the virtual humans. For instance, a virtual human can walk with the left hand in its pocket and the right hand holding a

7.4 Motion Kits

Fig. 7.7 A virtual human using a motion kit with identifiers: walk, none, cell phone, pocket

cell phone. For now, we have three categories that are common to both identifiers: none, pocket, and cell phone. However, this list can be extended to other possible arm actions, such as holding an umbrella, pulling a caster suitcase, or scratching one's head.

When one needs a varied crowd, it is simple for each virtual human to ask randomly for one of all the motion kits available. If the need is more specific, like a crowd following a path, it is easy to choose only the adequate walk/run motion kits, thanks to the identifiers.

7.4.2 Architecture

In our architecture, the motion kits are stored in a four-dimensional table:
 Table [action id] [subaction id] [left arm action id] [right arm action id]
For each combination of the four identifiers, a list of motion kits corresponding to the given criteria is stored. As previously mentioned, not all combinations are possible, and thus, some lists are empty. In Fig. 7.7, a virtual human is playing a skeletal animation, linked to a motion kit with the following identifiers: walk, none, cell phone, pocket.

In our architecture, an animation (whatever its level of detail) is dependent on the human template playing it: for a deformable mesh, a skeletal animation sequence specifies how its skeleton is moved, which causes the vertices of the mesh to get deformed on the GPU. Since each human template has its own skeleton, it is impossible to share such an animation with other human templates. Indeed, it is easy to imagine the difference there is between a child and an adult skeleton. For a rigid animation, it is the already deformed vertices and normals that are sent to the GPU, thus such an animation is specific to a mesh, and can only be performed by a virtual human having this particular set of vertices, i.e., issued from the same human template. Finally, an impostor animation clip is stored as a sequence of pictures of the virtual human. It is possible to modify the texture and color used for the instances of the same human template, but it seems obvious that such animation pictures cannot be shared by different human templates. This specificity is reflected in our architecture, where three lists of skeletal, rigid, and impostor animations are stored for each human template.

It follows that each motion kit should also be human template-dependent, since it has a physical link to the corresponding animation triplet. However, this way of managing the data is far from optimal, because usually, an animation (whatever its level of detail) is always available for all the existing human templates. It means that, for instance, if a template possesses an animation imitating a monkey, all other human templates are likely to have it. Thus, making the information contained in a motion kit human template-dependent would be redundant. We introduce two simple rules that allow us to keep a motion kit independent from a human template:

1. For any motion kit, all human templates have the corresponding animations.
2. For all animations of all human templates, there is a corresponding motion kit.

We now explain how, thanks to these assertions, we can keep a motion kit independent from the human templates and still know to which animation triplet it should link. First, note that each human template contains among other things:

- the list of skeletal animations,
- the list of rigid animations,
- the list of impostor animations.

Now, following the two rules mentioned above, all human templates contain the same number of skeletal animations, the same number of rigid animations, and the same number of impostor animations. If we manage to sort similarly these animation lists for all human templates, we can link the motion kits with them by using their index in the lists. We show a simple example in Fig. 7.6, where a structure representing the human templates is depicted: each human template contains a list of skeletal, rigid, and impostor animations. On the left of the image, a motion kit is represented, with all its parameters. In particular, it possesses three links that indicate where the corresponding animations can be found for all human templates. These links are represented with arrows in the figure, but in reality, they are simply indices that can be used to index each of the three animation lists for all human templates.

With this technique, we are able to treat all motion kits independently from the human templates using them. The only constraint is to respect rules (1) and (2).

7.5 Database Management

As detailed in Chap. 4, we use the locomotion engine described by Glardon et al. [GBT04] to generate varied locomotion cycles. Although this engine is fast enough to generate a walk or run cycle in real time, it cannot keep up that rhythm with thousands of virtual humans. When this problem first occurred, the idea of precomputing a series of locomotion cycles and storing them in a database came up. Since then, this system has proved very useful for storing other unchanging data. The main tables that can be found in the database are the following:

- Skeletal animations,
- Rigid animations,
- Impostor animations,
- Motion kits,
- Human templates, and
- Accessories.

In this section, we detail the advantages and drawbacks of using such a database, and what kind of information we can safely store there.

As previously mentioned, all the skeletal, rigid and impostor animations can neither be generated online, nor at the initialization phase of the application, because the user would have to wait during an important amount of time. This is why the database is used. With it, the only work that needs to be done at initialization is to load the animations, so that they are ready when needed at runtime. Although this loading phase may look time-consuming, it is quite fast, since all the animation data are serialized into a binary format. Within the database, the animation tables have four important fields:[1] unique id, motion kit id, template id, and serialized data. For each animation entry A, its motion kit id is later used to create the necessary links (see previous section), while its template id is needed to find to which human template A belongs. It also allows one to restrain the number of animations to load to the strict minimum, i.e., only those needed for the human templates used in the application. It is mainly the serialized data that allow distinguishing a skeletal from a rigid or an impostor animation. For a skeletal animation, we mainly serialize all the information concerning the orientation of each joint for each keyframe. With a rigid animation, for each keyframe, a set of already deformed vertices and normals are saved. Finally, for an impostor animation, two series of images of the human template are kept (the normal and the UV map) for several keyframes and points of view.

Another table in the database is used to store the motion kits. It is important to note that since they are mainly composed of simple data, like integers and strings (see Sect. 7.4), they are not serialized in the database. Instead, each of their elements is introduced as a specific field: unique id, name, duration, speed, four identifiers (action id, subaction id, left arm action id, right arm action id), and two special motion kit ids (rigid motion kit id, impostor motion kit id). When loading a motion kit M from the database, its basic information, i.e., speed, name, etc., is directly

---

[1] By field, understand a column in the database that allows for table requests with conditions.

extracted to be saved in our application. Each of the two special motion kit ids is an index referring to another motion kit. This reference is necessary to complete the linking between M and its corresponding rigid and impostor animations.

We have introduced in the database a table in order to store unchanging data on the human templates. Indeed, we have some human templates already designed and ready to be used in the crowd application. This table has the following fields: unique id, name, skeleton hierarchy, and skeleton posture. The skeleton hierarchy is a string summarizing the skeleton features, i.e., all the joint names, ids, and parent. When loading a human template, this string is used to create its skeleton hierarchy. The skeleton posture is a string giving the default posture of a skeleton: with the previous field, the joints and their parents are identified, but they are not placed. In this specific field, we get for each joint its default position and orientation, relative to its parent.

Finally, the database possesses two tables dedicated to accessories. Let us recall that an accessory is a mesh used to add variety and believability to the appearance of the virtual humans. For instance, it can be a hat, a pair of glasses, a bag, etc. In the first table, we store the elements specific to an accessory, independently from the human template wearing it: unique id, name, type, serialized data. In the serialized data is stored all the vertices, normal and texture information to make an accessory displayable. The second table is necessary to share information between the accessories and the human templates. The displacement of a specific accessory relative to a joint is different for each human template. This displacement is stored as a matrix. So, in this second table, we employ a field template id and a field accessory id to know exactly where the field matrix must be used. Thus, for each accessory/human template couple, corresponds an entry within this table. Note that we also store there the joint to which the accessory needs to be attached. This is because in some special cases, they may differ from a skeleton to another. For instance, when we attach a backpack to a child template, the joint used is a vertebra that is lower than the one for an adult template.

Using a database to store serialized information has proven to be very useful, because it greatly accelerates the initialization time of the application. The main problem is its size, which increases each time a new element is introduced into it. However, with real-time constraints, we allow ourselves to have a sufficiently large database to obtain varied crowds, within reasonable limits.

7.6 Shadows

Illumination ambiances are set from three directional lights, whose direction and diffuse and ambient colors are prealably (or interactively) defined by the designer. The light coming from the sun is the only one provoking shadows. As we lack a real-time global illumination system, the two other lights are present to provide enough freedom for the designer to give a realistic look to the scene. This configuration has given us satisfaction as we mainly work on outdoor scenes. See the top-left and bottom-left panels of Fig. 7.5 for results.

7.6 Shadows

Virtual humans cast shadows on the environment and, reciprocally, the environment casts shadows on them. This is achieved using a shadow mapping algorithm [Wil78] implemented on the GPU. At each frame, virtual humans are rendered twice:

- The first pass is from the directional light view perspective, i.e., the sun. The resulting z-buffer values are stored in the shadow map.
- The second pass is from the camera view perspective. Each pixel is transformed into light perspective space and its z value is compared with the one stored in the shadow map. Thus, it is possible to know if the current pixel is in shadow or not.

So, we need to render twice the number of virtual humans really present. Though with modern graphics hardware, rendering to a z-only framebuffer is twice as fast as rendering to a complete framebuffer, one expects a certain drop in the frame rate. Moreover, standard shadow mapping suffers from important aliasing artifacts located at shadow borders. Indeed, the resolution of the shadow map is finite, and the bigger the scene, the more aliasing artifacts appear. To alleviate this limitation, different strategies are used:

- Dynamically constrain the shadow map resolution to visible characters, and
- Combine percentage closer filtering [RSC78] with stochastic sampling [Coo86], to obtain fake soft shadows [Ura06].

We now further describe how to dynamically constrain the shadow map resolution to visible characters. A directional light, as its name indicates, is defined only by a direction. Rendering from a directional light implies using an orthographic projection, i.e., its frustum is a box, as depicted in Fig. 7.8(top).

An axis-aligned bounding box (AABB) is a box whose faces have normals that coincide with the basis axes [AMH02]. They are very compact to store; only its two extreme points are necessary to determine the whole box. AABB are often used as bounding volumes, e.g., in a first pass of a collision detection algorithm, to efficiently eliminate simple cases.

A directional light necessarily has an orthographic frustum aligned along its own axes. So, we can consider this frustum as an AABB. The idea is, at each frame, to compute the box englobing all the visible virtual humans, so that it is as tight as possible. Indeed, using an AABB as small as possible allows one to have a less stretched shadow map. At each frame, we compute this AABB in a four-step algorithm:

1. The crowd AABB is computed in world coordinates, using visible navigation graph vertices. By default, the AABB height is set to 2 meters, in order to bound the characters at their full height.
2. The light space axes are defined, based on the light normalized direction L_z:

$$L_x = normalize\big((0, 1, 0)^T\big)^{L_z} \qquad (7.3)$$

$$L_y = normalize\big(L_z^{L_x}\big) \qquad (7.4)$$

3. The directional light coordinate system is defined as the 3×3 matrix $M_l = [L_x, L_y, L_z]$.

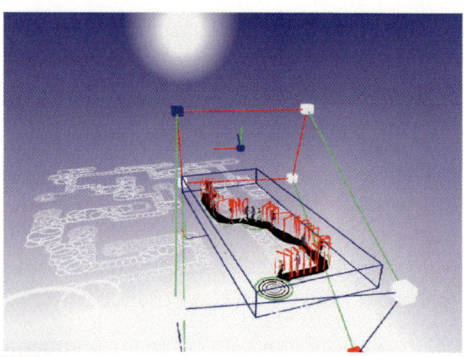

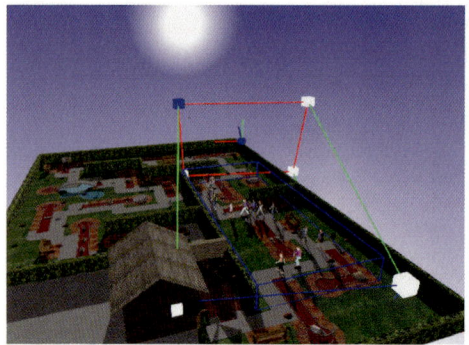

Fig. 7.8 Shadowed scene with apparent directional light frustum

4. The eight points composing the AABB (in world coordinates) are multiplied by M_l^{-1}, i.e., the transpose of M_l. This operation expresses these points in our light coordinate system.

Note that remultiplying the obtained points by M_l would express the crowd AABB back into world coordinates. In Fig. 7.8(bottom) are illustrated the shadows obtained with this algorithm.

7.7 Crowd Patches

7.7.1 Introduction

We break classical crowd simulation limitations on the environment dimensions: instead of pre-computing a global simulation dedicated to the whole environment, we independently pre-compute the simulation of small areas, called crowd patches [YMPT09] (see Figs. 7.9 and 7.10). To create virtual populations, the crowd patches are interconnected to infinity from the spectator's point of view. We also break limitations on the usual durations of pre-computed motions: by adapting our local simulation technique, we provide periodic trajectories that can be replayed seamlessly

7.7 Crowd Patches

Fig. 7.9 *Left*: A predefined city environment where patches are computed offline. *Right*: The same image with apparent patch borders and trajectories

(a)　　　　　　　　　　　　(b)

Fig. 7.10 *Left*: A procedurally computed pedestrian street, where patches are generated at run–time. *Right*: The same image revealing the patch borders and their trajectories

and endlessly in loops over time. Our technique is based on a set of patch templates, having specific constraints on the patch content, e.g., the type of obstacles in the patch, the human trajectories there, etc. A large variety of different patches can be generated out of a same template, and then be assembled according to designers directives. Patches can be pre-computed to populate the empty areas of an existing virtual environment, or generated online with the scene model. In the latter case, some of the patches also contain large obstacles such as the buildings of a virtual city.

7.7.2 Patches and Patterns

Patches

Patches are geometrical areas with convex polygonal shapes. They may contain static and dynamic objects. Static objects are simple obstacles which geometry is fully contained inside the patch.

Larger obstacles, such as buildings, are handled differently. Dynamic objects are animated: they are moving in time according to a trajectory $\tau(t)$. In this context, we want all dynamic objects to have a periodic motion in order to be seamlessly repeated in time. We note π this period and we define the patch periodicity condition for each dynamic object:

$$\tau(0) = \tau(\pi) \tag{7.5}$$

Two categories of dynamic objects may be distinguished: endogenous and exogenous objects. The trajectory of endogenous objects remains inside the geometrical limits of the patch for the whole period. The point's trajectory is fully contained in the patch and respects the periodicity condition (7.5). If the animation is looped with a period τ, the point appears to be moving endlessly inside the patch. Note that static objects can be considered as endogenous objects, with no animation. Exogenous objects have a trajectory $\tau(t)$ that goes out of the patch borders at some time, and thus, does not meet the periodicity condition (7.5). In order to enforce this condition, we impose the presence of another instance of the same exogenous object whose trajectory is $\tau(t)$. As the two objects are of the same type, i.e., they have an identical kinematics model, their trajectories can be directly compared. Different cases are then to be distinguished and are discussed in [YMPT09].

Patterns

The role of patterns is to register the limit conditions of exogenous object trajectories to allow the connection of patches. A pattern is defined for each face of a polygonal patch. As a result, patterns fully delimit patches. They are two-dimensional: a space dimension with length l, and a time dimension with duration (period) π. Patterns identify limit conditions for exogenous object trajectories.

We build environments and their population by assembling patches. Thus, two adjacent patches have at least one common face. They also share identical limit conditions for exogenous objects trajectories. Indeed, when an exogenous object goes from one patch to an adjacent one, it first follows the trajectory contained by the first patch, and then switches to the one described by the second patch. These two trajectories have to be at least continuous C0 to ensure a seamless transition from the first patch to the second one. The patterns between the two adjacent patches allow to share these limit conditions.

7.7.3 Creating Patches

The patch is first geometrically defined by assembling a set of patterns, which also provide a set of input and output points for exogenous objects. Then, static and endogenous objects are added to the patch. Finally, exogenous object trajectories are computed for walking humans, so that they respect limit conditions imposed by patterns, while avoiding object collisions.

7.7 Crowd Patches

Patterns Assembly

Our method for creating patches first starts by defining their shape. From the definitions of Sect. 7.7.2, one understands that patches are delimited by patterns: each face of the convex polygonal shape of patches is defined by one pattern. As a result, patches are created by assembling patterns. Two conditions have to be respected when assembling patterns to create a patch. First, all patterns must have a common period π which will be the patch's period too. Second, the sum of inputs defined by the set of patterns composing the patch must match the number of outputs. Indeed, each exogenous object entering the patch must, sooner or later, leave it.

Static Objects and Endogenous Trajectories

The second step is either to define ourselves, or get the online information on all the static and endogenous objects contained in the patch. Static objects have their geometry fully contained in the patch. Endogenous objects are animated and have a cyclic motion with period π. In the case of a patch built in a virtual shopping street, static obstacles are trash cans, trees, public benches, streetlights, signboards, etc. Endogenous objects can be humans talking, sitting, watching shop windows, etc. They can also represent animated objects or animals, such as a merry-go-round, or dogs. Note that once defined, static and endogenous objects are no longer modified. We respectively consider them as static and moving obstacles in the next step, which consists in automatically computing exogenous trajectories.

Exogenous Trajectories: Case of Walking Humans

Computing trajectories of exogenous objects (Fig. 7.11) is more complex than previous steps: the limit conditions of patterns must be ensured, and collision avoidance with static objects, endogenous objects (whose animations are now fixed), and other exogenous objects, must be achieved. We propose a method to automatically compute exogenous trajectories of walking humans. We consider the evolution of their global position only; a trajectory is thus modeled as a moving 2D point. Computing exogenous trajectories for walking humans is done in 3 steps.

1. *Initialization of Trajectories.* We initialize exogenous trajectories by connecting each input to an output, as defined by patterns. We thus obtain initial limit conditions for the trajectories, and count as many trajectories as the total number of inputs (or outputs) defined for the patch. Inputs and outputs are connected at random, with the sole constraint that we avoid connecting inputs and outputs of the same pattern. This way, walking humans pass through the pattern rather than head back.
2. *Velocity Adaptation.* Inputs and outputs being arbitrarily connected, the resulting trajectories may be infeasible for walking humans. The key-idea to address this issue is to split the trajectory into two trajectories passing by a new way-point.

Fig. 7.11 Exogenous trajectories

In other words, instead of having one pedestrian joining the considered input and output points, we obtain two humans: one going from the input point to pw, while the second one heads from pw towards the output point. These two humans have an identical position pw at different times: at $t = \pi$ for the first human, and at $t = 0$ for the second one, thus ensuring condition (7.5).

3. *Collision Avoidance.* Trajectories may result in collisions between objects, static or dynamic. We consider static and endogenous objects unmodifiable, and refine exogenous object motions to avoid collisions. To reach this goal, we use a particle-based method that, at each time step, steers exogenous objects from a set of forces.

7.7.4 Creating Worlds

Assembly of Patches

We distinguish two major ways of using crowd patches (see Fig. 7.12) for creating and/or populating virtual environments: a bottom-up, or a top-down technique. The bottom-up approach starts from an empty scene. A first patch is created, and then, iteratively, new adjacent patches are progressively added. A top-down approach starts

7.7 Crowd Patches

Fig. 7.12 Assembly of patches

from a geometrical model of the environment. The obstacle-free parts of the environment are decomposed into polygonal cells that are used as a blueprint for creating patches. This technique perfectly fits the case of virtual cities where large buildings are already present, and streets have to be populated by patches.

Patch Templates

The content of a patch is dependent on its precise location in the environment, and on the considered environment itself. Let us take the example of a shopping pedestrian zone. The corresponding patches should then contain static obstacles such as benches, trees or flowerpots. Endogenous objects can be people standing in front of shop windows, talking together, sitting on benches, while exogenous objects are simply walking humans. Designers want to have a certain control over the environment content, but accurately defining the objects in each patch is too time consuming. A solution is then to automatically generate patches from given templates. A patch template groups patches meeting a set of constraints on their objects and patterns. In order to associate geographic zones with desired templates, designers provide a template map. The map defines which template to use at any point of the environment. When a patch of a given template is created, some static and endogenous objects are randomly selected among the allowed set to compose its content. Designers also need to control the flow of walking humans going through patches, which implicitly defines the overall distribution of people in an environment. This is possible by constraining the pattern types to use. Pattern Types Controlling walking humans in our method is achieved by defining specific pattern types. These types allow to choose the specific distribution of input and out-put points in space, or time. We give here some examples of usage for specific distributions.

1. *Empty Patterns.* Environments are likely to contain large obstacles, such as buildings. In order to avoid collisions between exogenous walking humans and these obstacles, patterns delimiting them are empty of inputs or outputs.
2. *One-way Patterns.* One-way patterns are exclusively composed of inputs or outputs. When correctly combined in a patch, they allow to simulate, for example, one-way flows of walking humans.
3. *Specific I=O Space Distribution.* It is possible to limit the range of input and output positions in space on a given pattern. This allows to simulate the presence of a narrow passage, such as a door, between two patches for instance, or to simulate crowded streets of walking humans forming lanes.
4. *Specific I=O Time Distribution.* Users may want pedestrians to enter or exit patches irregularly in time. For instance, at zebra crossings, pedestrians leave sidewalks when the walk sign is green, and have to reach the opposite sidewalk before the light switches to red.

7.7.5 Applications and Results

In this Section, we illustrate the concept of crowd patches with an application consisting in procedurally generating a potentially infinite pedestrian using a bottom-up approach. Several steps have to be followed in a pre-process. First of all, we design a library of static obstacles: streetlights, trash cans, trees, city maps, benches, etc. These static objects are illustrated in Fig. 7.13(left). Secondly, endogenous objects, like humans talking together, playing children, or seated people, are created (Fig. 7.13(center)). In a third step, the required pattern types are identified: an endless street requires among others, empty patterns for building borders, and specific I/O space distributions to simulate lane formations in highly crowded portions of the street. Various pattern examples are illustrated on the right of Fig. 7.13. Similarly to pattern types, patch templates are identified according to the sort of environment to generate online. A first non-exhaustive set of patches for each template is created too, using the pattern library. Some of these patches are shown in the bottom of Fig. 7.13. Finally, to further vary the patch content, we also define an additional set of grounds, or textures that can be applied on a patch: cobblestones, grass, asphalt, etc. At run-time, patches are introduced in the scene wherever the camera is looking. Specific patches are first looked for in the existing library. If no patch matches the requirements, it is generated on the fly. If the patch generation requires a specific pattern that has not yet been created, it is also created online. A second important step at run-time is to update each pedestrian on its trajectory. When a human

7.7 Crowd Patches

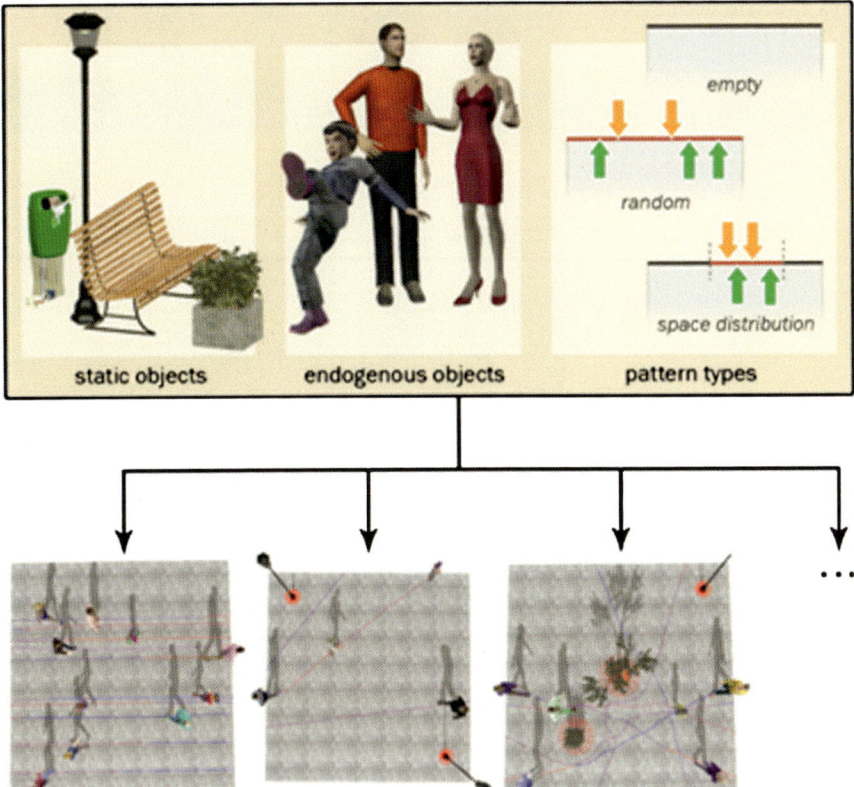

Fig. 7.13 To build a lively pedestrian street, we use (*left*) static obstacle, (*center*) endogenous obstacle, and (*right*) specific patterns. (*Bottom*) From these sets, we fist define several patch templates. Finally, each template is instantiated to result in a variety of patches

reaches a patch border, we seamlessly make it move to the neighbor patch. To efficiently achieve this, each trajectory possesses a parameter pointing to the neighbor trajectory that should be followed next.

Results

The performance tests and the video have all been performed on a desktop PC with a dual core 2.4 GHz, 2 GB of RAM, and an Nvidia Geforce 8800 GTX. We have instantiated 6 different human templates, rendered with a level-of-detail approach, ranging from about 6,000 to 1,000 triangles. They are animated with a motion capture database. Shadows are computed on the environment and the humans. In our implementation, the computation of a patch takes approximately 60 ms. This number fits perfectly to real-time procedurally generated environments, given that a first non-exhaustive library of patches has been pre-computed. The infinite street envi-

Fig. 7.14 The infinite street

ronment has been built with one template patch, and a total amount of 10 patterns only, of empty, space constrained, and random types. The patterns all have a period of 10 s and an 8 m length. The average number of visible patches in front of the camera is 500, 75% of which are buildings with 2 entrances where people come in and out. The remaining visible patches represent the street and its crossings. There are approximately 750 visible walking humans at all times (exogenous objects), 30 idle humans representing endogenous objects, and 80 static objects, such as benches, or streetlights. On average, we obtain 30 frames per second, including the rendering of the humans and the environment. The frame rate is relatively constant over the whole progression on the street, since the number of patches and humans which are computed and displayed remains the same. Figure 7.14 illustrates an infinite street generated using this method.

7.8 Final Remarks

In this chapter we focused on aspects of real-time crowd simulation, discussing attributes such as the quantity of agents that could be rendered, the quality of resulting rendering, the efficiency of methods concerning crowd data, and the versatility and adaptation of methods.

References

[AMH02] AKENINE-MOLLER T., HAINES E.: *Real-Time Rendering*. AK Peters, Wellesley, 2002.

[Coo86] COOK L. R.: Stochastic sampling in computer graphics. *ACM Transactions on Graphics 5*, 1 (1986), 51–72.

References

[DHOO05] DOBBYN S., HAMILL J., O'CONOR K., O'SULLIVAN C.: Geopostors: A real-time geometry/impostor crowd rendering system. In *SI3D'05: Proceedings of the 2005 Symposium on Interactive 3D Graphics and Games* (New York, NY, USA, 2005), ACM, New York, pp. 95–102.

[EGMT06] EGGES A. D., GIACOMO T. D., MAGNENAT-THALMANN N.: Synthesis of realistic idle motion for interactive characters. In *Game Programming Gems 6* (2006).

[GBT04] GLARDON P., BOULIC R., THALMANN D.: Pca-based walking engine using motion capture data. In *Proc. Computer Graphics International* (2004), pp. 292–298.

[Lan98] LANDER J.: Skin them bones: Game programming for the web generation. *Game Developer Magazine 5* (1998), 11–16.

[LRC*02] LUEBKE D., REDDY M., COHEN J., VARSHNEY A., WATSON B., HUEBNER R.: *Level of Detail for 3D Graphics*. Morgan Kaufmann, San Mateo, 2002.

[MTLT88] MAGNENAT-THALMANN N., LAPERRIÈRE R., THALMANN D.: Joint-dependent local deformations for hand animation and object grasping. In *Proceedings on Graphics Interface'88* (1988), Canadian Information Processing Society, Toronto, pp. 26–33.

[MYTP09] MAÏM J., YERSIN B., THALMANN D., PETTRÉ J.: Yaq: An architecture for real-time navigation and rendering of varied crowds. *IEEE Computer Graphics and Applications 29*, 4 (July 2009), 44–53.

[PdHCM*06] PETTRÉ J., DE HERAS CIECHOMSKI P., MAÏM J., YERSIN B., LAUMOND J.-P., THALMANN D.: Real-time navigating crowds: scalable simulation and rendering: Research articles. *Computer Animation and Virtual Worlds 17*, 3–4 (2006), 445–455.

[RSC78] REEVES W. T., SALESIN D. H., COOK R. L.: Rendering antialiased shadows with depth maps. In *Proceedings of ACM SIGGRAPH* (New York, NY, USA, 1978), ACM, New York, pp. 283–291.

[Sho85] SHOEMAKE K.: Animating rotation with quaternion curves. In *Proceedings of ACM SIGGRAPH* (New York, NY, USA, 1985), ACM, New York, pp. 245–254.

[TLC02b] TECCHIA F., LOSCOS C., CHRYSANTHOU Y.: Visualizing crowds in real-time. *Computer Graphics Forum 21*, 4 (December 2002), 753–765.

[Ura06] URALSKY Y.: Efficient soft-edged shadows using pixel shader branching. In *GPU Gems 2* (2006).

[Wil78] WILLIAMS L.: Casting curved shadows on curved surfaces. In *Proceedings of ACM SIGGRAPH* (New York, NY, USA, 1978), ACM, New York.

[YMPT09] YERSIN B., MAÏM J., PETTRÉ J., THALMANN D.: Crowd patches: Populating large-scale virtual environments for real-time applications. In *Proceedings of the 2009 Symposium on Interactive 3D Graphics and Games, I3D'09* (New York, NY, USA, 2009), ACM, New York, pp. 207–214.

Chapter 8
Populated Environments

8.1 Introduction

The construction of huge and complex urban environments useful for real-time virtual human simulations has been regarded to be a major endeavor. The main challenges arise in the modeling, management, and visualization of large amounts of data and compound semantically rich environments so as to perform real-time crowd simulation.

The modeling of realistic populated environments requires the acquisition and processing of different sources of data, and design of complex systems to create a terrain to describe geographic relief, landing algorithms to subdivide regions into lots, and fulfill these lots with buildings, houses, parks, lakes, or other different city artifacts. Besides, a realistic virtual human simulation requires a powerful data structure to store and retrieve data efficiently. It is desirable to tackle collision avoidance and detection, finding the shortest path between two interest points and so on. The huge amount of objects impose restrictions on real-time rendering and visualization, requiring development techniques to process these tasks efficiently.

Traditional methods for modeling virtual cities based on manual reconstruction have provided high-quality results, but require an enormous amount of time and operator expertise. In the context of automatic or semiautomatic methods for generating virtual cities, two main approaches have been distinguished: reconstruction [For99, DEC03, TSSS03] and parametric [PM01, YBH*02, dSJM06] based methods.

The first category looks for virtual remake real environments, which requires different sources of data, since global information is provided by aerial photos and 2D maps, including local information of building geometry, and appearance (texture) is provided by photography and laser profiler data. Reconstruction techniques are used in cultural heritage projects to recover architectural information of historically important places [ZKB*01, DEC03]. This type of application is concerned with architectural aspects and high fidelity in the reproduction of real environments.

Parametric methods are not necessarily concerned with the reproduction of the real world, but normally they intend to construct cities according to population aspects. For example, Parish and Müller [PM01] have used sociostatistical and geographical information to construct virtual cities. However, the major part of these works does not deal with virtual human simulation in generated environments, consequently they do not treat some specific problems. For instance, virtual people should evolve in the virtual environment, being able to enter the buildings from the sidewalks, walk in parks and pedestrian zones, perceive the semantics of the environment, and behave in a way similar to real life.

Another proposal to fill in this gap provides tools for automatic city generation and virtual human simulation [dSJM06]. As a consequence, a framework where different levels of details about the environment have been provided, e.g., city maps, pictures, textures, and shape of buildings, can be useful to generate a realistic virtual representation. On the other hand, if the user just knows information about the population distribution in the space and a map of the real city, the framework can also generate a virtual city with less compromise with real life. In addition, in every case, the virtual city can be easily populated by virtual humans, from sociostatistical data and constraints.

The simulation of virtual humans has been discussed in the context of complex and structured environments. However, the city construction is not sufficient for virtual human simulation, as semantic information is needed to perform realistic virtual human simulation. Some of these environments have been created with semantic information to allow their exploration by realistic virtual humans [FBT99], and cars [TD00]. A navigation technique has been developed over structured environment with representation scheme, path planning, and collision avoidance components [LD04].

Concerning complex environment design, some authors have proposed the use of pattern systems to make uniform building constructions [AIS77], and theories to explain the complexity of large spaces, such as urban environments [Hil96]. The latter takes into account pedestrian flow and human behavior in virtual environments. Recent works concentrate on methods for automatic modeling of architecture, with distinction for Instant Architecture [WWSR03].

Other research groups have concentrated their efforts to achieve real-time simulation and visualization optimization [TC00, DHOO05]. When large amounts of data must be managed, processed, and, more importantly, rendered and displayed in real time, some techniques are required to achieve this objective.

8.2 Terrain Modeling

Terrain modeling has become integral to virtual city modeling as land-use planning and engineering. A terrain can be defined as the surface features of an area of land. For computational purposes it is required to define a precise mathematical model.

Definition 8.1 A real *terrain* can be described by a continuous function $f : \Re^2 \to \Re$, $z = f(x, y)$, where x, y are plane coordinates and z represents correspondent

8.2 Terrain Modeling

Fig. 8.1 A terrain mesh

elevation values. Thus, the terrain model can be defined by triangulated function of $f\colon H(f) = \{(x, y, f)\}$, as illustrated in Fig. 8.1.

The computer processing of square-grid arrays of terrain heights, digital elevation models (DEMs), has revolutionized the discipline's two chief functions of topographic analysis and display. Geographic information system (GIS) technology further enables terrain-modeling results to be combined with nontopographic data. A digital terrain model should be stored and managed in a compact way. The digital terrain is laid out in a grid of vertices with a fixed distance between, with $2^n + 1$ vertices in width and depth, and $n > 1$. If vertices are equally spaced, the mesh has $2n$ quadrilaterals with 2 triangles in each one.

In Fig. 8.2, terrain elevations are extracted from a grayscale image (a), where each pixel value represents terrain elevation. The texture images contribute to terrain appearance. Two different textures have been used to give realistic terrain appearance: common terrain texture (b) is used to give a general appearance of terrain, and

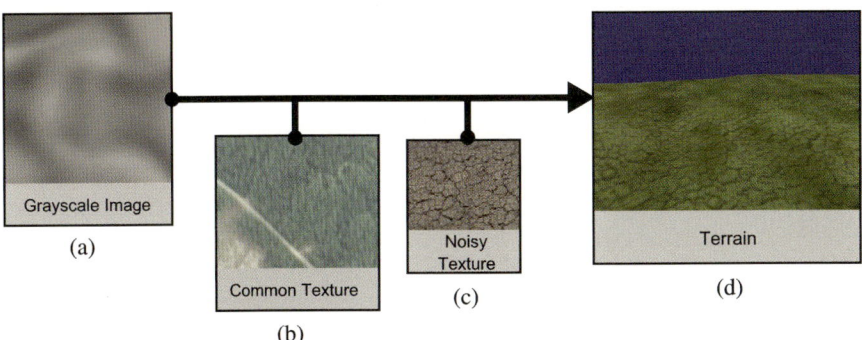

Fig. 8.2 Terrain extraction from 2D images and texture

a noisy texture (c), which is a small image bump-mapped, is used to give realism to the generated terrain (d).

The terrain mesh [dBSvKO00] is obtained by the triangulation of terrain elevations. For instance, data models can easily provide elevation value z for any (x, y) valid pair. In general, other system components can retrieve information from terrain. Then, virtual human component uses this information for virtual human animation on the relief, while city simulation uses it for building placement.

De Floriani and Magillo deal with the problem of modeling large-size terrain [DFM02]. They perform a comparison between two multiresolution terrain models, based on regular and irregular grids. This problem affects directly memory usage, and rendering and visualization processing, because level-of-detail algorithms are implemented through fast storage and retrieval of information about terrain and its appearance, too.

8.2.1 Plants and Lakes

Different approaches have been considered to generate realistic model of plants, with special attention to L-systems and to visual representation through graphic impostors. The basic idea about L-systems is to define complex objects by successively replacing parts of a simple object using a set of rewriting rules or productions [PHMH95]. This approach produces very realistic plant architectures. However, when real-time simulation is required, the most common approach is based on impostor, i.e., image-based representation (impostor) are used instead of complex geometric models.

A third approach combines geometric detailed and impostor representation rendering techniques to support interactive frame rate in high visual quality [DHOO05]. Artifacts close to the camera are represented by 3D models, for example, modeled through L-systems, whereas distant artifacts are swapped by their image-based representations. Boulanger et al. [BPB06] propose a new method to the rendering of realistic grass fields in real time with dynamic lighting, shadows, antialiasing, animation and density management. It uses per-pixel lighting, grass density maps, and three levels of detail: geometry, vertical, and horizontal slices, with smooth transitions between them. They claim worst-case 20 fps, common-case 80 fps or better on an NVidia 7800 GTX. Rendering realistic water is one of the most difficult and time-consuming tasks in computer graphics. It requires a correct illumination as will as an accurate water surface deformation model [PA01]. Interactive techniques for physics-based simulation and realistic rendering of rivers using Smoothed Particle Hydrodynamics have been developed by Kipfer and Westermann [KW06]. They describe the design and implementation of a grid-less data structure to efficiently determine particles in close proximity and to resolve particle collisions. Besides, an efficient method to extract and display the fluid free surface from elongated particle structures as they are generated in particle-based fluid simulation is presented. The implementation of surface extraction can be realized on the GPU, saving simulation time.

8.2.2 Sky and Clouds

The sky modeling adds more realism to city modeling, mainly when combined with clouds and meteorological phenomena, through different rendering schemes. As in plants and lakes modeling, creating realistic sky and clouds is a huge task and demands heavy computational power. Schpok et al. [SSEH03] have developed an interactive system to model, animate, and render visually volumetric clouds using graphics hardware. It is recommended to be used in interactive systems or exported for higher quality offline rendering. However, it is restricted to real-time systems due its low performance.

A method for fast simulation of cloud dynamics on graphics hardware promises to be applicable in real-time simulations without sacrificing interactivity [HBSL03]. Clouds are modeled using partial differential equations that model fluid flow, water condensation and evaporation. An optimized implementation using programmable floating point fragment processors is performed on the GPU.

For virtual human simulation, sky and clouds modeling are useful for achieving high-quality visual scenes. However, methods for simulating these natural phenomena are time-consuming and spend a large amount of memory and CPU. Instead, "fake" models fulfill all requirements to achieve visual quality under real-time constraints. Nowadays procedural approaches have been considered for generating water, clouds, fire, and other natural phenomena [EMP*02]. Besides, implementations of these techniques on the GPUs make them very attractive.

8.3 Generation of Virtual Environments

Considering the game titles released in the last decade, it is remarkable the increase in visual complexity of Virtual Environments (VE) used as scenarios. Huge cities can be found in games like the GTA franchise,[1] Assassin's Creed[2] and Left 4 Dead.[3] Beyond cities, it can be necessary to create whole worlds, as in the case of Massively Multiplayer Online Game (MMOG), represented by World of Warcraft[4] and Perfect World.[5] In this sense, the cost and time to develop a game is also increased.

The creation of a VE requires a background in diverse areas of expertise. Because of this, it is necessary to allocate a team of professionals to create, maintain and re-use large VE. Some of the main problems faced when developing interactive virtual environments are described by [OCS03] as the non-extensibility, limited interoperability, poor scalability, monolithic architecture, among others.

---

[1] http://www.rockstargames.com/IV.
[2] http://assassinscreed.us.ubi.com.
[3] http://www.l4d.com.
[4] http://www.worldofwarcraft.com.
[5] http://www.perfectworld.com.

A possible solution to these problems is the use of procedural generation techniques [EMP*02], which allows the creation of VE content just by setting input parameters. It can generate terrains, buildings, characters, items, weapons, quests and even stories adding a broad range of elements, but in a controlled way. A perfect example to illustrate the potential uses of procedural contents generation is the game Spore.[6] In such game, procedural techniques are used to create characters, vehicles, and buildings [CIQ*07], textures [DGH*07] and planets [CGG*07]. Even the music is created using this kind of technique. There are some academic and commercial solutions that provide the creation of buildings with great realism. Nevertheless, there are few studies that focus on the generation of buildings interiors as furthers discussed.

The process of creating large virtual cities can spend considerable time and resources to be finalized. Parish and Müller [PM01] propose a model that allows to generate a three-dimensional city from socio-statistical and geographical maps. The method builds the road network using an extended L-Systems. After creating the streets, the system extracts the information about blocks. Through a subdivision process, lots are created. In every lot a building is built, generated by another module based on L-Systems. With this information the system generates the three-dimensional geometric model of the city, and textures are added in order to provide greater realism to the final model.

A method to generate procedural 'pseudo infinite' virtual cities in real-time is proposed by Greuter et al. [GPSL03]. The area of the city is mapped into a grid defined by a given granularity and a global seed. Each grid's cell has a local seed that can be used to create building generation parameters. A print foot is produced by combining randomly generated polygons in an iterative process. The building geometries are extruded from a set of floor plans. To optimize the rendering, a view *frustrum* is implemented to determine the visibility of virtual world objects before generation. Thus, only visible elements are generated. Although generation of the environment, the appearance of the buildings can be improved. In this context, Müller et al. [MWH*06] propose a shape grammar called CGA Shapes, focused on the generation of buildings with high visual quality and geometric details. Using some rules, the user can describe geometric shapes and specify the interactions between hierarchical groups in order to create a geometrically complex object. In addition, the user can interact dynamically in all stages of creation.

The techniques presented previously are focused on the external appearance of buildings, without concerning about their interior. Martin [Mar06] introduces an algorithm to create floor plans of houses. The process consists of three main phases. In the first step of the procedure, a graph is created to represent the basic structure of a house. This graph contains the connections between different rooms and ensure that every room of house is accessible. The next step is the placement phase and distributes the rooms over the footprint. At last, the rooms are expanded to their proper size using a Monte Carlo method to choose which room to grow or shrink next.

---

[6]http://www.spore.com.

An approach to generate virtual building interiors in real-time is presented by Harn et al. [HBW06]. The interiors are created using eleven rules that work like a guideline to the generation process. Buildings created by this technique are divided into regions connected by portals. Only the visible parts of the building are generated, thus avoiding the use of memory and processing. When a region is no longer visible, the structure is removed from memory. The generation process also provides a persistent environment. All changes made in a given region, are stored in a record that is accessed through a hash map when necessary.

Horna et al. [HDMB07] propose a method to generate 3D constructions from two-dimensional architectural plans. Additional information can be aggregated to the two-dimensional plans in order to support the creation of three-dimensional model. It is possible to construct of several floors using the same architectural plan.

A rule-based layout approach is proposed by Tutenel et al. [TBSD09]. The method allows to solve the layout and also to distribute objects in the scene at the same time. From an initial layout, the algorithm finds the possible locations of a new object based on a given set of rules. The relationships among objects can be specified either explicitly as implicitly. The method uses hierarchical blocks in the solving process, so if a set of elements are solved, they are treated as single block.

Besides the definition of appearance and geometry of objects, it is also necessary to specify their features and functionalities. Semantic information can be used to enrich the environment of games and simulations. This can be done by specifying features of a given actor or object, such as functionality, physical or psychological attributes and behaviors. Tutenel et al. [TBSK08] list three levels of semantic specification: object semantics, object relationships and world semantics. These levels can be used for creation and simulation of environments. For example, information such as the climate of a region can be used to define the kind of vegetation as well as the weight an object has can be used to decide if a agent can carry it or not.

8.4 A Model for Floor Plans Creation

A common drawback in procedural generation of environments is when some component is not accessible from any other component. For instance, in a virtual city, one related problem is the generation of buildings that are not accessible from the streets. Concerning internal structure of buildings, a similar problem happens when one room is not connected with any other. As far as we know, neither of the proposed procedural models to generate floor plans can solve such type of situation. Our proposed method treats this problem by adding corridors into the generated floor plan, as similarly occurs in real life.

Our method for generation of floor plans is based on Squarified Treemaps, proposed by Bruls et al. [BHvW00]. Treemap [JS91] is an efficient and compact form to organize and to visualize elements of hierarchical structures of information, for instance, directory structures, organization structures, family trees, among others. In general, treemaps subdivide an area into small pieces to represent the importance

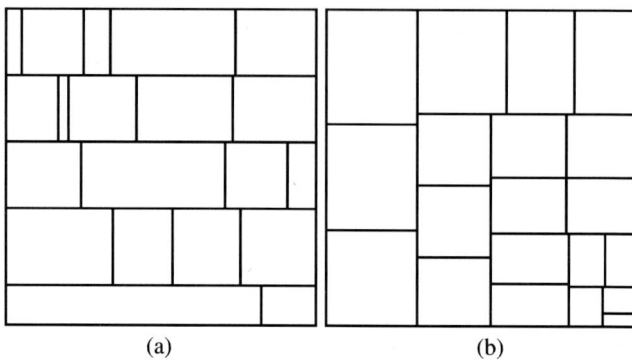

Fig. 8.3 Original treemap (**a**) and squarified treemap (**b**)

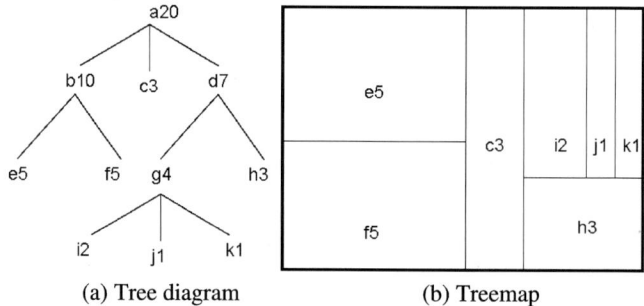

Fig. 8.4 Tree diagram (**a**) and related treemap (**b**)

of each part in the hierarchy. The main difference between treemaps and squarified treemaps is how the subdivision is performed. In squarified treemaps, authors propose a subdivision method which takes into account the aspect ratio of generated regions, intended to approach to 1. Figure 8.3 shows on the left the result of original treemap method, while on the right squarified treemap is illustrated. Next section discusses both models.

8.4.1 Treemaps and Squarified Treemaps

The original treemaps [JS91] uses a tree structure to define how information should be used to subdivide the space. Figure 8.4 shows an example. Let us consider that each node in the tree (Fig. 8.4a) has an associated size (e.g. in Fig. 8.4 the name of node is a and size is 20). The treemap is built using recursive subdivision of an initial rectangle (see Fig. 8.4b). The direction of subdivision alternates per level (horizontally and vertically). Consequently, the initial rectangle is subdivided in small rectangles. Further details about treemaps can be found in [JS91].

8.4 A Model for Floor Plans Creation

Fig. 8.5 Example of treemap subdivision generating rectangles with aspect ratio different from 1

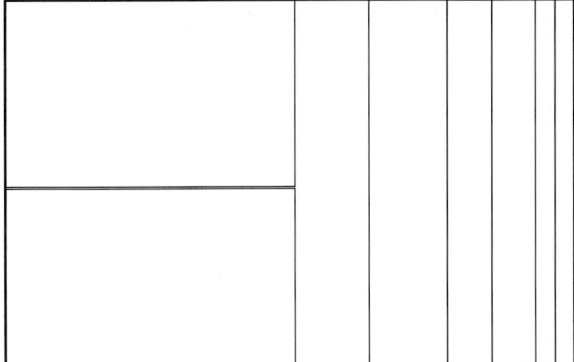

This method can originate figures like the one illustrated in Fig. 8.5. In such case it is possible to see that aspect ratios of generated rectangles is very different from 1. Consequently, this approach does not support the problem we want to deal in this Chapter.

Squarified treemaps were proposed by Bruls et al. [BHvW00] and has the main goal of maintaining the aspect ratios of generated rectangles, defined as $\max(\frac{height}{width}, \frac{width}{height})$, approach to 1 as possible. The method is implemented using recursive programming and aims to generate rectangles based on a pre-defined and sorted list containing their desired areas (from larger to smaller areas). Then, the aspect ratio of region to be subdivided is considered in order to take a decision about to proceed in horizontal or vertical way. Also, aspect ratio of generated regions in a specific step t are compared to step $t+1$, being possible to ignore later computing regions in $t+1$ and reconsider data from step t. Figure 8.6 illustrates the generation process of squarified treemaps presented by Bruls et al. [BHvW00]. We discuss this example in this Section since the understanding of our model is very dependent of squarified treemap method.

The list of rectangles areas to be considered in example of Fig. 8.6 are: 6, 6, 4, 3, 2, 2, 1. In step 1, the method generates a rectangle with aspect ratio $= \frac{8}{3}$ in vertical subdivision. So, in step 2 the horizontal subdivision is tested, generating 2 rectangles with aspect ratio $= \frac{3}{2}$ which approaches of 1. In step 3, next rectangle is generated presenting aspect ratio $= \frac{4}{1}$. Last step is ignored and step 4 is computed based on rectangles computed in step 2. The algorithm (described in details in [BHvW00]) presents rectangles which aspect ratios approach to 1. In our point of view, this method is more adequate to provide generation of floor plans than original treemaps, due to the fact that rooms in real houses present aspect ratios not very different from 1. However, other problems can arise as discussed in next sections.

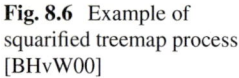

Fig. 8.6 Example of squarified treemap process [BHvW00]

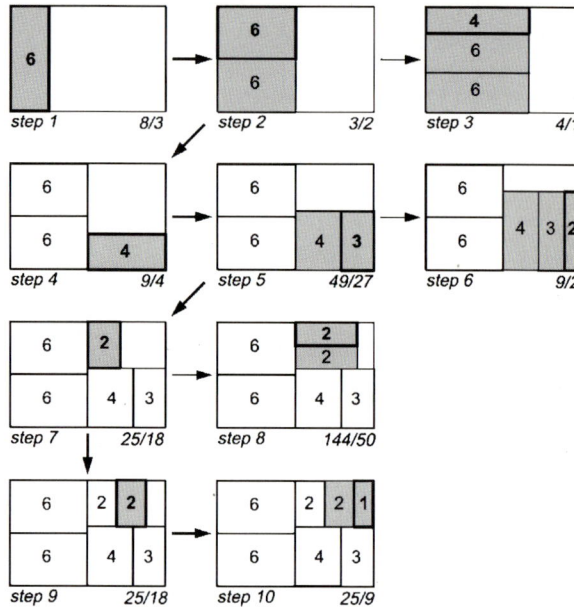

8.4.2 The Proposed Model

The pipeline of the proposed model to build floor plans is presented in the Fig. 8.7. The process begins with the definition of construction parameters and layout constraints.

In order to create a floor plan, some parameters such as height, length and width of the building are required. It is also necessary to know the list of desired dimensions for each room and their functionalities. The functionality specifies how a particular area of residence should be used. There are three distinct possibilities: the social area, service area and private area. The social area can include the living room, the dining room and the toilet. In the service area we can have the kitchen, the

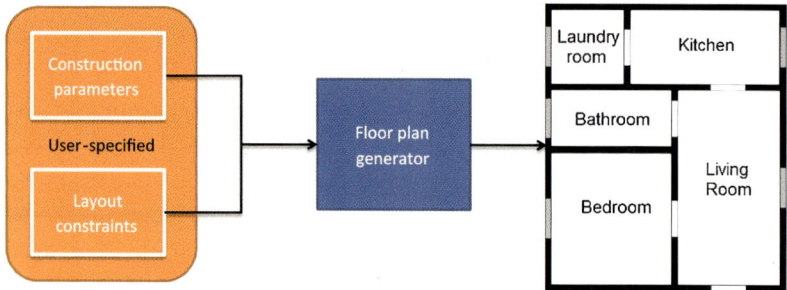

Fig. 8.7 The generation process of floor plans. Construction parameters and layout constraints are provided by the user as input to floor plan generator

8.4 A Model for Floor Plans Creation

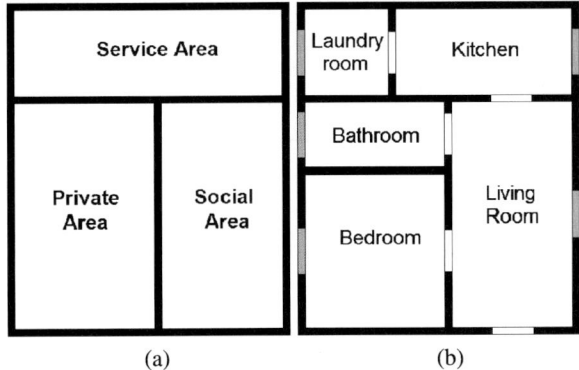

Fig. 8.8 Dividing the total space of the house in three main areas (**a**): private, social and service area. Example floor plan generated by the model (**b**)

pantry and the laundry room. At last, the private area can embrace the bedroom, the master bedroom, the intimate bathroom and a possible secondary room that can be used in different ways, e.g. as a library. This list is not fixed and can be customized by the user. This categorization is made to group the common areas.

The division of the residence area occurs in two different steps. At first, we compute the area of each one of three parts of the building (i.e. social, service and private) and firstly apply the squarified treemap in order to define three regions where rooms will be generated. This process generates an initial layout, containing three rectangles, each one for a specific area of the building (see Fig. 8.8a).

After obtaining the positions of the polygon that represents a specific area, each polygon serves as input to squarified treemap algorithm in order to generate the geometry of each room. It is important to notice that we use original squarified treemap to generate each room in the building. Figure 8.8b shows the generated rooms.

After the rooms subdivision, two steps are required in order to finalize the floor plan generation. Firstly, connections among rooms should be created. Secondly, rooms that are not accessible should be solved, since our environments should be used for character animation. These two steps are further discussed in next sections.

Including Connections Among the Rooms

With all the rooms generated as previously described, connections (doors) should be created among them. These connections are created using as criteria the functionalities of each room, i.e. some rooms are normally not connected, e.g. the kitchen and the bedroom. All the possible connections are presented in Table 8.1, which has been modeled based on a previous analysis of various floor plans available commercially. In this table, we consider the entry door of the floor plan as a connection between outside and two possible rooms: kitchen and living room. However, it is important to note that another set of connections can be defined by a user, in order to represent another style of architecture.

Geometrically, the door is created on the edge shared by two rooms that keep a possible connection. For instance, it is possible to have connection between the

Table 8.1 Possible connections among rooms

	outside	kitchen	pantry	laundry room	living room	dining room	toilet	bedroom	master bedroom	bathroom	secondary room
outside		X			X						
kitchen	X		X	X	X	X					
pantry		X		X							
laundry room		X	X								
living room	X	X					X	X	X	X	X
dining room		X					X	X	X	X	X
toilet					X	X					
bedroom					X	X				X	
master bedroom					X	X				X	
bathroom					X	X		X	X		X
secondary room					X	X				X	

kitchen and the living room, where a door can be created. The size of the doors is pre-defined and their center on the edge is randomly defined. Similar process happens with windows generation. However, they should be placed on the external edges. Figure 8.8b illustrates a generated floor plan, containing windows (dark rectangles) and doors (white rectangles).

After connections among rooms are processed, a connectivity graph is automatically created (Fig. 8.9), which represent the links among the rooms. It allows checking if there is any room that is not accessible. Also, buildings and houses created with our method can be used to provide environment for characters simulation. The graph always starts from outside and follows all possible connections form accessed room.

If any room is not present in the graph, it is necessary to include corridors. This situation can occur when there are not possible connections among neighbor rooms (rooms which share edges). This process will be described in next section.

Including Corridors on the Floor Plans

The generation process of corridors is necessary in order to maintain the coherence of generated environment and provide valid space for characters navigation. Firstly, the rooms without access from the living room are selected. These rooms are flagged with a X, as illustrated in Fig. 8.10a. The main idea is to find candidates edges shared by non-connected rooms in order to be used to create the corridor.

The corridor must connect the living room (marked with a L in Fig. 8.10a) with all X rooms. The proposed solution uses the internal walls of the building to generate a kind of circulation "backbone" of the space, i.e. the most probable region to

8.4 A Model for Floor Plans Creation

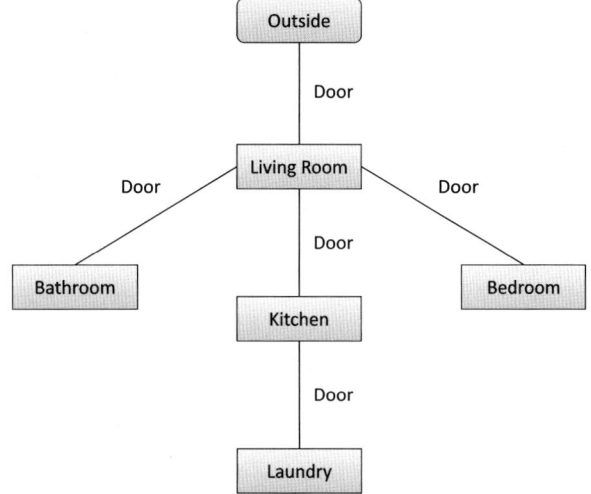

Fig. 8.9 Connectivity graph for a generated floor plan

generate the corridor in the floor plan. The algorithm is very simple and has three main steps. Firstly, all external walls are removed, since corridors are avoided in the boundary of the floor plan (Fig. 8.10b).

Secondly, we remove all internal segments (representing walls) that belong to the living room (Fig. 8.10c). The remaining segments (described through their vertices) are used as input to a graph creation. Vertices are related to nodes and segments describe the edges in the graph (Fig. 8.10c). In order to deal with the graph, we use A* algorithm [HNR68], which is a very known algorithm widely used in pathfinding and graph traversal, the process of efficiently traversable path between points, called nodes. In our case, the graph is explored to find the shortest path that connect all rooms without connectivity with the living room. A room is considered as connected if the graph traverse at least one of its edges. Finally the shortest path is chosen to create the corridor (Fig. 8.10d).

After the "backbone" generation, meaning select the set of edges candidates to be used to generate the corridor, we should generate it geometrically. So, the corridor

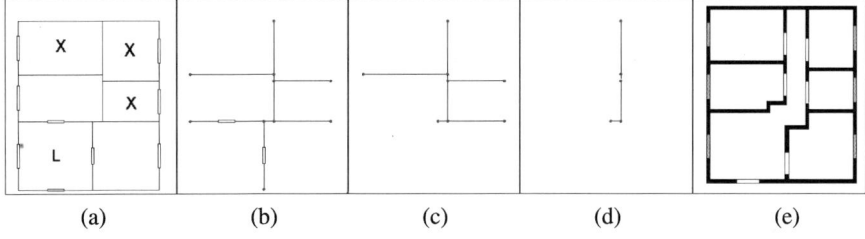

Fig. 8.10 Steps of a corridor creation. (**a**) Original floor plan with rooms without connectivity flagged with an X and the living room is marked with L. (**b**) Floor plan after external edges removed. (**c**) Internal walls that not belong to living room. (**d**) The shortest path linking all rooms without connectivity to the living room

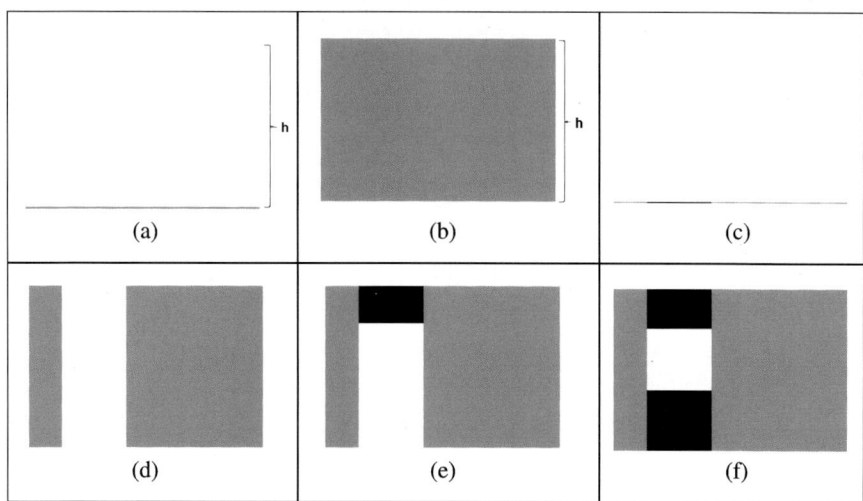

Fig. 8.11 Generation process of a 3D wall. Edge representing a wall in the floor plan (**a**) and the extrusion result using a given height h (**b**). Generation of wall with a door (**c**) and the extrusion result (**d**). Creation of doorways (**e**) and windows (**f**)

is initially composed by a set of edges/segments. These segments must pass through a process of 2D extrusion to generate rectangles allowing agents walk inside the house. Indeed, the size of corridor is increased perpendicularly to edges direction. However, this process can cause an overlap between the corridor and some rooms, reducing their areas. If the final area of any room is smaller than allowed, the floor plan undergoes a global readjustment process to correct this, as shown in Eq. (8.1)

$$area_{house} = area_{private} + area_{social} + area_{service} + area_{corridor}. \quad (8.1)$$

3D House Generation

After obtaining the final floor plan, an extrusion process to generate a three-dimensional representation of the house is applied. Initially, each 2D wall represented on the floor plan (Fig. 8.11a) is extruded to a given height H defined by the user (Fig. 8.11b). Referred walls can have doors (between two rooms) (Figs. 8.11c and 8.11d) and windows (in external edges), that should be properly modeled. To generate the doorways, it is needed to know their heights. This information is used to create a block at the top of the doorway (Fig. 8.11e). This block must have the same thickness of walls. In the generation of windows, a similar process is done. In the space reserved for the window are positioned two blocks, one on the top and another on the bottom (Fig. 8.11f). The lower block has a predetermined height specified by the user. The height of the upper block is defined as the sum of the height of the window and the height of the lower block. The last step of process is to add an appropriate type of window to each room, according to its functionality,

8.4 A Model for Floor Plans Creation

Fig. 8.12 Three-dimensional model of a generated floor plan

from a set of models. A three-dimensional view of a 2D floor plan (Fig. 8.8b) is presented in Fig. 8.12.

8.4.3 Results

In this section we discuss some obtained results using our prototype. In the following floor plans, we explicitly present the parameters used and show the geometric and semantic information generated. In addition, the connectivity graph is showed for each house or building.

Figure 8.13a shows a floor plan generated using our model. The list of rooms and their respective areas are: living room (27 m^2), two bedrooms (13 m^2 and 14 m^2), secondary room (8 m^2), bathroom (10 m^2), kitchen (11 m^2), and laundry (7 m^2). The dimensions of house are 9 meters wide, 10 meters long and 3 meters high. The corresponding connectivity graph can be seen in Fig. 8.13b. Both the bathroom and the secondary room do not have connection with any other room. This situation is corrected by adding a corridor (Fig. 8.14a). The new connectivity graph is shown in Fig. 8.14b. All rooms are now connected, being accessible from outside or from any other internal room.

Another case study is illustrated in Fig. 8.15a. This house has 84 squared meters (12 m long × 7 m wide × 3.1 m high). The list of rooms and their respective areas are: living room (22 m^2), two bedrooms (both with 14 m^2), a secondary room used as home office (12 m^2), bathroom (10 m^2), and kitchen (12 m^2). To this specific configuration was generated a connectivity graph that can be seen in Fig. 8.15b. Both bedrooms and the bathroom are not accessible from any other room. The solution is presented in Fig. 8.16a. Using the corridor, the new connectivity graph looks like presented in Fig. 8.16b. A generated 2D floor plan can be saved to disk and used

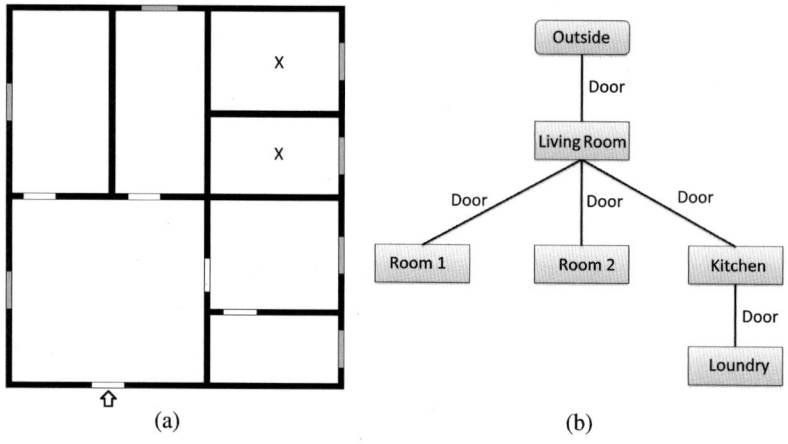

Fig. 8.13 Example of floor plan (**a**) containing 2 non-connected rooms (labeled with X) and its respective connectivity graph (**b**)

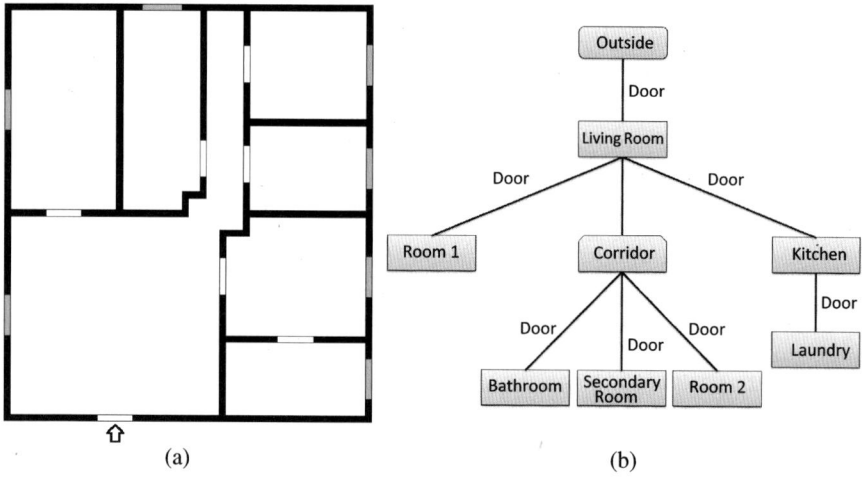

Fig. 8.14 Example of floor plan of Fig. 8.13 (**a**) containing corridors and all rooms are connected to the living room and its respective connectivity graph (**b**)

as input to a home design software. Figure 8.17 shows the result of same floor plan when adding some 2D furniture.

In addition, we compared floor plan of Fig. 8.17 with an available real floor plan. As can be seen in Fig. 8.18, such real floor plan could generate exactly the same connectivity graph (see Fig. 8.16b). Furthermore, the total dimension of real plan is 94 m^2, while virtual plan has 84 m^2 and generates similar size of the rooms.

In Fig. 8.19 we can observe a 3D model of floor plan visualized with textures.

8.4 A Model for Floor Plans Creation

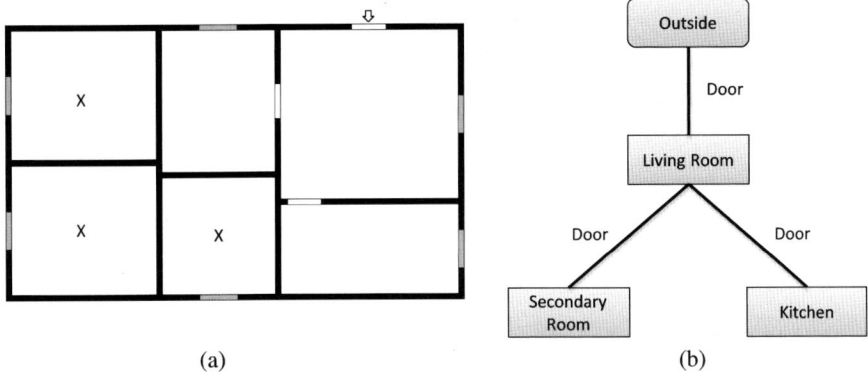

Fig. 8.15 Example of floor plan (**a**) containing 3 non-connected rooms (labeled with *X*) and its respective connectivity graph (**b**)

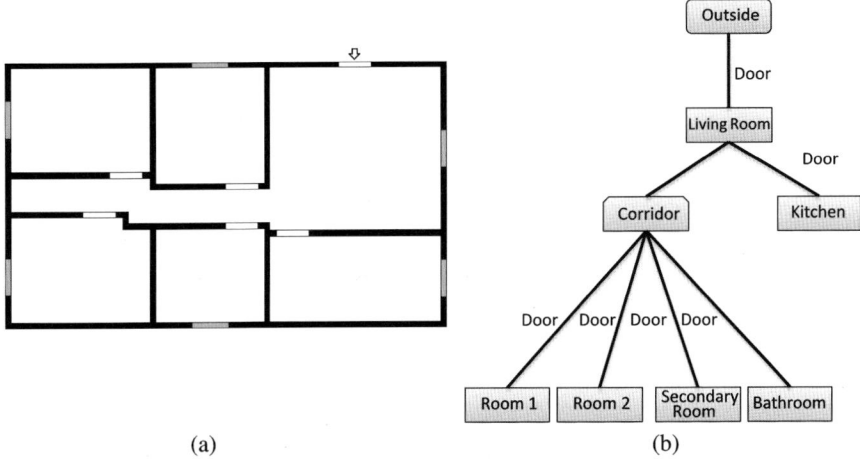

Fig. 8.16 Example of floor plan of Fig. 8.15 (**a**) containing corridors and all rooms are connected to the living room and its respective connectivity graph (**b**)

It is important to note that for these results we determine parameters values in order to provide specific floor plans, and even compare with available house, existent in real life. However, one can imagine to have our method integrated into a game engine, and generating different floor plans, in a dynamic way. For instance, using aleatory functions and intervals for areas and random number of rooms, our method is able to generate different floor plans automatically. So, during the game, the player can visit different buildings and having always different floor plans, without previous modeling. We compared a generated floor plan with a available commercially house in order to compare possible connection graph and generated rooms. Moreover, another contribution of our work is to generate the connection graph which

Fig. 8.17 Our floor plan and included furnitures

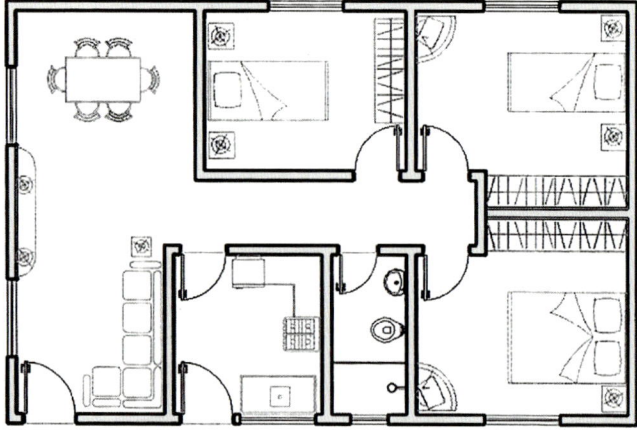

Fig. 8.18 Real floor plan

determines the navigation graph in the environment. Corridors could be created to solve problems of non-connected rooms.

8.5 Informed Environment

Populated environments must offer assistance to virtual human walk, avoiding obstacles, and access to services distributed through the city. This requires that environments offer necessary semantic information for virtual human decision-making to achieve these basic actions. This kind of environment is called Informed Environment, see [FBT99]. Some of these semantically rich environments allow their exploration by realistic virtual humans [FBT99], and cars [TD00] during simu-

8.5 Informed Environment

Fig. 8.19 Tridimensional model of floor plan illustrated in Fig. 8.8b

lations. A navigation technique has been developed over structured environments with representation scheme, path planning, and collision avoidance components [LD04]. Ontology-based methods have been successful employed on Informed Environments [PVM05].

The method for creating the Informed Environment proposed by Farenc et al. [FBT99] provides information for the recognition of places, location, and exploration of interesting objects. The method is based on environment decomposition, linked to geographic information, and hierarchically stored. The environment entities composed by different kinds of objects are represented by graphical objects with semantic information associated. The Informed Environment is compounded by these entities and allows different levels of simulations.

The management of this scene is achieved by subdividing the scene into some structured regions. These regions can be subdivided into subregions or grouped, depending on the level of information required. Each level has pertinent information. Object naming scheme allows one to associate the information to an object, requiring the designer to assign a name to each type of object, e.g., street, block, junction, sidewalk, and so on.

Ontologies are explicit specifications of concepts related to a knowledge domain. Their use allows interoperability among different systems and they can help the integration of different aspects in various kinds of simulation systems. In this case, it is a powerful tool for describing the environment and the crowd to be simulated, allowing the specification of the activity of urban environments to be done in a semantically organized way.

This means that the organization of the data is clear to the user and it can be easily adapted and expanded. Figure 8.20 presents the basic model. Tables 8.2, 8.3, 8.4, 8.5 show the main attributes for some of the components of the environment.

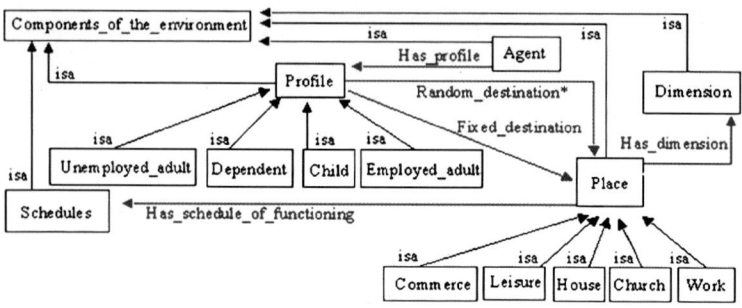

Fig. 8.20 Environment ontology

Table 8.2 Profile properties

Name	String	
Identifier	Integer	
Fixed Destination	Instance	Place
Random Destination	Instance*	Place

Table 8.3 Schedule properties

Opening time	String
Closing time	String
Average time of permanence	String
Entering time interval	String

Table 8.4 Dimension properties

X	Integer
Y	Integer
Dimension-X	Integer
Dimension-Y	Integer

Table 8.5 Place properties

Name	String	
Capacity	Integer	
Identifier	Integer	
Has Dimension	Instance	Dimension
Has schedule of functioning	Instance*	Schedules

Below we give an overview of the model, its main components, attributes defined in parentheses ( ) and subclasses in brackets [ ]:

- *Agent* (has profile)
  A specific profile is assigned to each agent.
- *Profile* (fixed destination, random destination)

8.5 Informed Environment

[employed and unemployed adult, child, dependent]

Each profile will define their main activities, which correspond to their usual (fixed) and eventual (random) destinations at certain times in the environment.

- *Place* (has name, has capacity, has dimension, has schedule of functioning) [leisure, house, commerce, church, workplace]
- *Place* refers to the agent destination according to their profiles. *Places* have capacity (number of allowed agents), and relations with schedule and dimension, the classes listed below.
- *Schedule* (opening time, closing time, time of permanence, entering interval)
- *Dimension* (coordinates X, Y, size)

On the basis of this model, the activity of the population of the environment is defined. Children, for instance, will have as their fixed destination the school at a certain time with a determined time of permanence; at other times, they have random destinations in the environment. Besides children, the current model includes employed adults with fixed and random destination, unemployed adults with random destinations only, and dependents that only move when accompanied by an adult. By modeling the environment on the basis of this model we can generate a simulation that reflects more realistically the population activity in the environment. However, to achieve fast retrieval of information, we have structured different abstraction data into different levels, through a multilevel data model. Then, only required information is processed during the simulation.

8.5.1 Data Model

An important requirement in city modeling is the ability to access, render, animate, and display huge sets of heterogeneous geometric objects and allowing insertion of semantic information. A multilevel representation scheme to address theses challenges has been developed [dSJM06]. All framework input data and spatial models retrieved from repositories are tackled in different levels of abstraction. Figure 8.21 illustrates the data model into different levels.

The relationship between different levels allows information to be retrieved and efficiently used, with low overhead. Each level provides information for upper level and allows to access lower levels. For instance, virtual humans and buildings need information about terrain and topo mesh, which must be retrieved in levels 0 and 1, respectively.

The terrain is represented by a triangulated planar mesh in level-0. It is described by geometry and attributes (textures) (see Sect. 8.2). Level-1 stores the topo mesh representation (see Sect. 8.5.2). For example, each vertex of topo mesh retrieves its geometric elevation value into the lower level (terrain).

The topo mesh (level-1) represents a coarse grain division of the city, where edges abstract streets and sidewalks, bounded by vertices which represent street crossings and faces the blocks. Then, each entity in level-1 is refined in level-2. For instance, each edge (level-1) points to a mesh (level-2), which describes sidewalks and streets

Fig. 8.21 Data model into levels 0, 1, 2, and 3

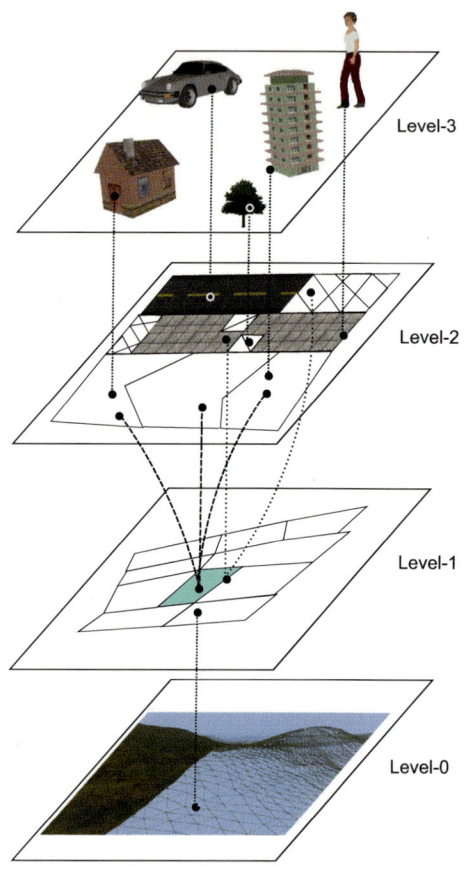

(including appearance attributes). Vertices into level-1 points to a mesh (level-2), which describe street crossing and traffic sign information. Faces in level-1 point to a list of polygons (level-2), which represent lots, generated through the allotment algorithm (Sect. 8.7). A block without allotment has a null pointer, i.e., no references to upper level.

Level-3 holds the spatial objects imported from repositories, as buildings, human models, sign plates, plants, cars, and others. The position and orientation of these objects are given in lower level (level-1 and level-2, respectively). For instance, each lot defines building orientation, making its exit to the sidewalk direction.

This hierarchical structure allows to achieve efficient visualization of city and queries for simulation. Each level can provide a proper representation for rendering, with geometry and appearance attributes (mainly textures) of stored objects. In addition, scene nodes are encoded with levels-of-detail capabilities (details in Sect. 8.9). Besides, path planning algorithms can improve the running time of any shortest path, by performing a coarse query in level-1, and finally refining it into level-2. Finally, the selection of spatial objects has improved significantly the com-

8.5 Informed Environment

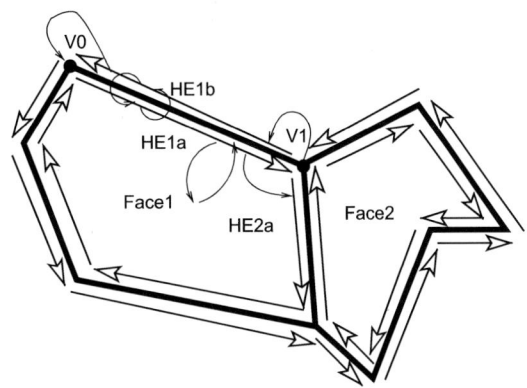

Fig. 8.22 Data structure diagram: *biggest arrows* represent half-edges and *smallest* ones represent pointers in data structure

putational time during the rendering process, because objects stored in one level can be processed without interference of objects in another level.

8.5.2 Topo Mesh

The amount of information processed, stored, rendered, and visualized in a huge populated virtual city is enormous. Polygon meshes usually employ a list of unrelated polygons, which are described by a list of vertices and a list of faces. The vertices represent street corners, faces the blocks, and edges the borders between two blocks. However, more information is required in order to simulate the virtual population. For instance, if a virtual human needs to move from one place to another, information about the (best or shortest) path to be followed is required.

This operation is time-consuming if the system only provides a list of polygons. A planar-embedding polygonal mesh, constructed by preprocessing the polygon list, helps to solve the path query problems because it creates and maintains adjacency relationship among polygons. This structure is called a planar topological mesh (or topo mesh), and it represents the first level in the multilevel data model. Details about the data model are presented in Sect. 8.5.1, where levels are also described.

Definition 8.2 *Topological mesh (topo mesh)* is a combinatorial structure embedded in an $\Re^2$ plane. It supplies the ability to maintain subdivisions of the plane induced by collections of curves. In this case, these curves are straight segments, bounded by a pair of vertices. The mesh subdivides the plane into interconnected vertices, edges, and faces.

The topo mesh is a half-edge-like data structure [Wei85]. It stores half-edges instead of edges. A half-edge is a direct edge, useful to capture the face orientation. This structure is convenient for modeling convex or nonconvex orientable 2D manifolds, as illustrated in Fig. 8.22.

Fig. 8.23 An extraction of simple polygons from 2D maps

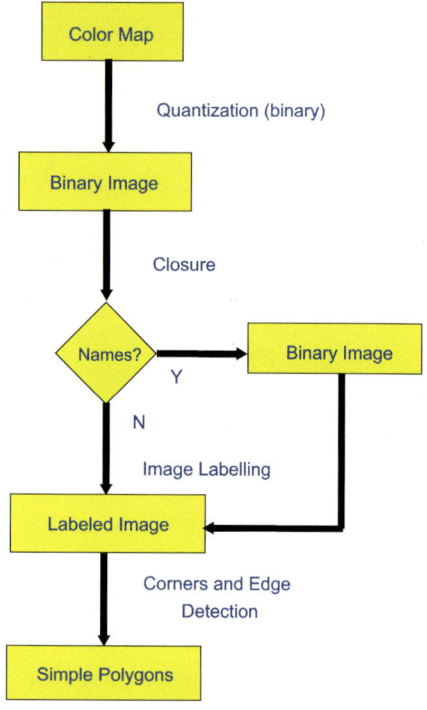

Each face is bounded by circular linked list of half-edges. The list can be oriented either clockwise or counterclockwise around the face. Once an orientation has been chosen, it must be maintained to all remaining faces in the mesh. Each half-edge in a list has a pointer to the next half-edge, the endpoint vertex, a face, and its pair (oppositely oriented adjacent half-edge). Each vertex holds its position in $\Re^3$, and has a pointer to half-edge. Finally, each face has a pointer to one half-edge. The most adjacent queries are stored directly in the data structure primitives. For instance, an adjacent face is obtained when the common half-edge is found, its twin (opposite direction) and getting corresponding face. A half-edge or list of half-edges bordering one face is retrieved by a circular query around the face.

For our purpose, vertices, edges, and faces represent corners, streets, and blocks of a city, respectively. Half-edges codify street directions. The data structure maintains adjacency relationship between city elements, which allows one to implement queries efficiently, such as: which blocks use a corner? which streets bound a block? etc. Shortest path algorithms can be implemented efficiently through this data structure.

The topo mesh can be given, for example, by image segmentation combined with other image processing techniques, such as image quantization and labeling, as well as corners detection. Such processes identify and extract a list of simple polygons from 2D maps and images. Figure 8.23 illustrates the complete process.

A quantization is performed into the color image (map) to give a binary image. If maps contain street names, they are removed by morphological filtering. Streets and blocks are shown in different levels, then the image is labeled to identify connected components, and the algorithm SUSAN is applied to identified corners and edges of each block [SB97]. As a result, a list of polygons, representing blocks of the city, is obtained.

This hierarchical model has been designed to support addition of user-defined semantic information, required for crowd simulations. Each entity in different levels provides one hotspot, which defines one template to receive this data structure. Then, at runtime data can be introduced and retrieved in an efficient way, making simulation more flexible and semantically rich. Ontologies have been aggregated in some simulations of normal life and panic (see next sections).

8.6 Building Modeling

Traditional methods for building modeling are based on manual design to construct new buildings or to reconstruct existing ones. They have provided high-quality results, but require an enormous amount of time and operator expertise. Recent works concentrate on methods for automatic modeling of architecture, with distinction for Instant Architecture [WWSR03]. Completely automatic approaches have succeeded in generating completely fictitious cities with low or medium realism.

Another approach provides a framework where different levels of details about the environment can be provided, e.g., city maps, pictures, textures, and shape of buildings can be useful to generate a realistic virtual representation. On the other hand, if the user just has information about the population distribution in the space and a map of the real city, the framework can also generate a virtual city with less compromise with real life. This kind of framework makes the building construction process more flexible, because some repetitive tasks can be performed in an automatic way, while details to achieve high visual quality to buildings can be performed through a manual process.

Concerning complex environment design, particularly building modeling, some authors have proposed the use of pattern systems to make uniform building constructions [AIS77], and theories to explain the complexity of large spaces, such as urban environments [Hil96]. The latter takes into account pedestrian flow and human behavior in virtual environments. These works supply information to chosen building modeling process.

8.7 Landing Algorithms

An interesting problem in city modeling is the automatic generation of lots. We present a solution that includes blocks subdivision, according to their boundary description, zone information, and population density. These parameters determine also the minimum and average area threshold as stop criterion, which can be provided textually. A very important constraint is concerned with the avoidance of creating lots without access to the street.

In fact, from the computational geometry point of view, we have a polygon partitioning problem with a set of restrictions. Considering block edges as input and average area as stop condition, we have a relatively simple partitioning problem. However, it can be a complex problem once we want to avoid internal, malformed, and too small polygons. We have made three assumptions in the proposed algorithm:

- Any polygon of partitioning must have at least one (or piece of) edge of original polygon boundary;
- Too small polygons are marked as not useful to build up; and
- Polygons with at least twice the area of specified threshold are repartitioned.

The first assumption is made so that all lots will be accessible from the street. It is reached by verifying if one of two split edges belongs to the original polygon or else if new polygons have edges from the original one. The second assumption aims to avoid undesirable size of polygons, i.e., it avoids construction in small areas, while the third assumption avoids too big ones. The pseudo-code of this algorithm is presented in Algorithm 8.1.

This algorithm returns a list of subdivided simple polygons (or the original polygon if it cannot be subdivided according to specified constraints). The partitioning algorithm is generic for simple polygons, and not restricted to convex ones. After the allotment process, the buildings can be inserted into the lots. Figure 8.24 shows the result of allotment algorithm.

We have implemented a variation of this algorithm, first partitioning polygons into convex subpolygons, then applying Algorithm 8.1. The convex partitioning is performed through optimal Greene Algorithm [Gre83] or an approximation of Hertel and Mehlhorn [HM83]. These preprocessings can be interesting when convex lots are required.

8.8 Ontology-Based Simulation

This section describes a virtual environment, which uses high level knowledge and reasoning capabilities, using ontology-based VR simulations. The agents could have different behaviors, since they can reason based on the knowledge they have about the world where they are inserted.

The VR environments that make use of knowledge representation models (e.g., ontology, informed environments) [FBT99, PVM05] to describe the agents (e.g., emotional states, personality, personal profile) and the environment (e.g., special places, functioning rules, place profile) allow us to obtain more complex and interesting behaviors in a multiagent system (MAS). It is important to preserve the agents' individuality, in order to increase the simulation realism, but at the same time we need to manage complex scenarios composed of a great number of agents.

8.8 Ontology-Based Simulation

Algorithm 8.1: Polygon partitioning

Input: (Polygon P, AverageArea AA)
Output: List of subdivided polygons
inlist ← P // current list of polygon
outlist ← void // output list of polygon
for all poly in *inlist* **do**
    bedge ← polybiggest−edge
    v_1 ← subdivide *bedge* at midpoint
    line ← trace perpendicular straight line
    vlist ← intersect (poly, *line*)
    vlist ← lexisort(vlist)
    v_2 ← internal−visible (vlist.prev(v_1) or vlist.next(v_1)))
    pedge ← make−edge(poly,v_1,v_2)
    $polygon_1$ ← partition(poly,v_1,v_2)
    $polygon_2$ ← partition(poly,v_2,v_1)
    if ($polygon_1$.area() < AA) && (!$polygon_1$.$is_i sland$()) **then**
        outlist ← $polygon_1$
    else
        inlist ← $polygon_1$
    end if
    if ($polygon_2$.area() < AA) && (!$polygon_2$.$is_i sland$()) **then**
        outlist ← $polygon_2$
    else
        inlist ← $polygon_2$
    end if
end for
return *outlist*

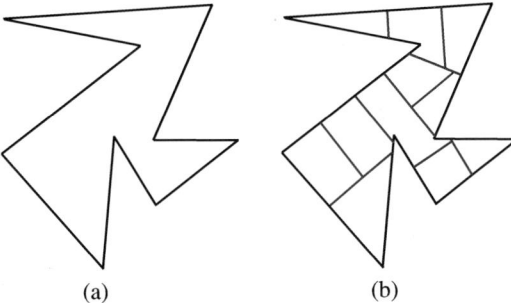

Fig. 8.24 Automatic allotment: (**a**) before and (**b**) after

In a complex MAS environment, the use of knowledge and automatic reasoning tools can make it possible to control and generate complex collective and individual behaviors.

For example, we can add information about the environment describing the opening hours of a store, or the security measures related to some flammable liquids (e.g., do not smoke near these objects, or create sparks). On the other hand, the agents can also use this knowledge, so they are able to decide where to go and how to act. In the above example, depending on whether the store is now open or closed, the agent will change his actions according to the present status of the environment (change the present destination), or also, if the agent wants to avoid some danger and needs to go to a place where flammable liquids are kept, the first action to be executed should be to extinguish his cigarette. This example explains some possible applications of the high-level reasoning, when associated with an informed VR environment.

In the next section we describe an example of application that makes use of an ontology-based VR simulation: Crowd Simulation in Normal Life Situations.

8.8.1 Using Ontology for Crowd Simulation in Normal Life Situations

Research on behavioral modeling has mainly focused on aspects of virtual human control in order to realistically populate virtual environments (VEs). Well known applications that require virtual populations are games development and simulation of urban environments. Some of the work in the area [MT01, BMB03, BdSM04] has focused on crowd simulation during hazardous events. Another approach is to deal with "normal behavior" of virtual people that occurs before such events in different moments of normal life. The goal of this section is to present UEM—An Urban Environment Model [PVM05], where knowledge and semantical information needed to realistically populate VEs are described by using an ontology that is associated with space and time of simulation, functionalities and normal occupation of space, etc. This is a novel approach through which a large number of virtual humans can populate an urban space by considering normal life situations. Using this model, semantical data is included in the virtual space considering normal life actions according to different agent profiles distributed in time and space, such as children going to school and adults going to work at usual times. Leisure and shopping activities are also considered. Agent profiles and their actions are also described using UEM.

Previous work has presented different ways of controlling virtual humans in order to improve their ability to evolve in an autonomous way in a VE. In such work, the main goal is to remove part of the complexity regarding some complex tasks processed by the agent and to transfer this information to the VE. As a consequence, a virtual agent can "ask" to the VE the position of a specific place, the best way to go to a location, the semantical information included into a place or a path, or other needed information to provide the agents' evolution in the VE.

In UEM, the agents are created on the basis of an ontology, which includes information of population profiles as well as information about the urban environment, in a way the knowledge about the general model of the VE can be represented and used

8.8 Ontology-Based Simulation

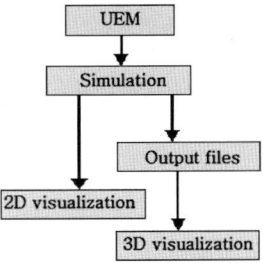

Fig. 8.25 Overview of the framework

as a basis for the simulation. People (virtual agents) can be created based on statistical data, if available, but also, fictitious information can be used. Agents move and behave in urban life according to the schedule that is related to their usual activities, as described in the ontologies. In this way, people move during "normal life" in a more realistic way, without a "random aspect," which is common in the major part of related work. For instance, at 10:00 AM, if a user wants to check what is happening in school, he or she will be able to see the students inside the school. Why is this similarity to normal life important in a simulation? For crowd simulation in panic situations, the location and the activity people are engaged in when the hazardous event occurs are very decisive in determining the perception and response of people. By considering this aspect, the simulation can be much more realistic. For example, the action response of people during the day or night can be different, and it can be simulated if we are able to model the normal life of people.

Besides presenting the details of the model, we present its integration into a crowd simulator whose main goal is to provide realistic and coherent population behavior in urban environments. The results show that urban environments can be populated in a more realistic way by using UEM, escaping from the usual impression we have in such a system that virtual people are walking in a random way by predefined paths in the virtual space. In the sequence, we describe the ontology associated with the VE.

8.8.2 Applying Ontology to VR Environment

This section describes a practical implementation of a VR simulation tool that uses ontology for crowd simulation in normal life situations. Figure 8.25 shows an overview of the framework.

8.8.3 The Prototype of UEM

UEM defines the ontology of the VE and the population configuration. The input information is processed in real time and provides information to be visualized in

Fig. 8.26 At 7:00 AM, people are at home

Fig. 8.27 At 7:25 AM, people populate the VR environment

2D, as shown in Fig. 8.25. Moreover, generated data are exported in a proprietary format as input to Player, which is a 3D viewer based on Cal3D library.[7] Player includes visualization of animated 3D lifelike humans.

Figure 8.26 shows a screenshot of the simulator, and 2D visualization. We can see on the bottom left of the image the time to be simulated (7:00 AM). At this time, the majority of agents are at home. People will then begin to apply their activities, as defined in the ontologies.

In Fig. 8.27 we can see agents on the street, populating the environment. Figures 8.28 and 8.29 illustrate the 3D visualization.

---

[7]http://cal3d.sourceforge.net.

8.8 Ontology-Based Simulation

Fig. 8.28 The 3D viewer

Fig. 8.29 The 3D viewer

For this simulation, we considered São José, a village located in the Brazilian state of Rio Grande do Norte. The village has around 600 inhabitants, and its main locations are two churches, a sports gymnasium (leisure), one school, three stores (commerce), and one industrial plant (workplace) in which 200 people work. This village was chosen due to the availability of information as it has been used as a case study for a system in a related project concerned with panic situations, PetroSim, which is briefly described below and fully presented in [BdSM04]. PetroSim was designed to help safety engineers to evaluate and improve safety plans and to help the training of people living in regions near dangerous installations (the village of São José is located near petroleum extraction installations). The simulation considers different agent psychological profiles (dependent, leader, or normal) and their behavior in danger situations.

Fig. 8.30 Locations of places

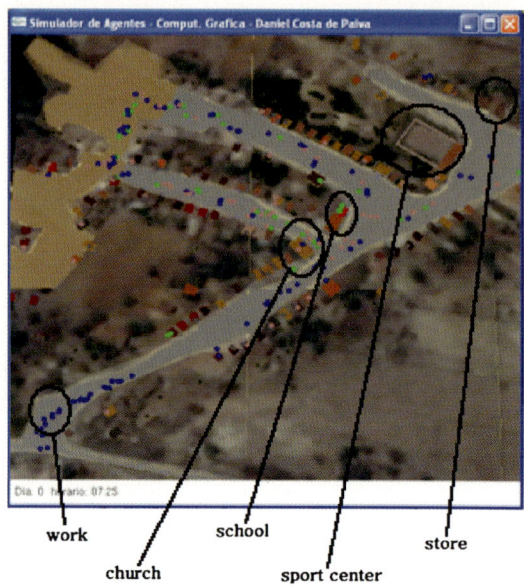

8.8.4 Simulation Results

For the simulation on the basis of UEM, the user determines the distribution of profiles and people in the houses, and the environment is populated at random. The people move in the environment and they stay for a determined time interval in the places where their presence is required (obligatory) according to their profile (children at school, etc.). The movement is guided by the A* algorithm (general search algorithm that is used to solve planning problems).

If the agent fails to reach its place at the regular time, it does not stay and goes back home or any other nonobligatory place. Agents go home after 10 PM. Locations of some places defined in the ontology are represented in Fig. 8.30.

The other images show the evolution of a specific simulation containing 250 people by using UEM. In Fig. 8.31, at 11:29 AM, one can observe students and employed adults at school and work locations, respectively. Figure 8.32 shows the time students leave school and go home.

The following graphs describe the spatial occupation of agents in São José Village, according to the simulation undertaken on the basis of our model. It is observed that employed adults (Fig. 8.33) spent more time at work, going to school after 7:00 PM (19:00) or adopting other behaviors (going to home, commerce, etc.).

Students (Fig. 8.34) stay at school until 12:00 AM, and then they adopt random behavior going to all possible places. After 10:00 PM (22:00) they are at home. On the other hand, unemployed adults stay mainly at home, but populate other places too, as shown in Fig. 8.35.

The system allows user interaction during the simulation. The interactivity is given by the visualization of the graph, the description of ontology into the space,

8.9 Real-Time Rendering and Visualization

Fig. 8.31 At 11:29 AM, students and employed adults are in school and work, respectively. We can observe some other people on the street

Fig. 8.32 At 12:05 PM, students leave school and go to their home or other places, as considered in the ontology

verification of profiles, etc. It is also possible to change specific place characteristics during the simulation, consequently changing the spatial occupation.

8.9 Real-Time Rendering and Visualization

The large amount of processed, rendered, and visualized data requires mechanisms to achieve performance for real-time simulation. For example, it must support frustum culling, occlusion culling, continuous (CLOD) and discrete (DLOD) levels of detail. A scenegraph can store scene objects in nodes which support levels of detail management, being CLOD for terrain and DLOD for other objects (like buildings,

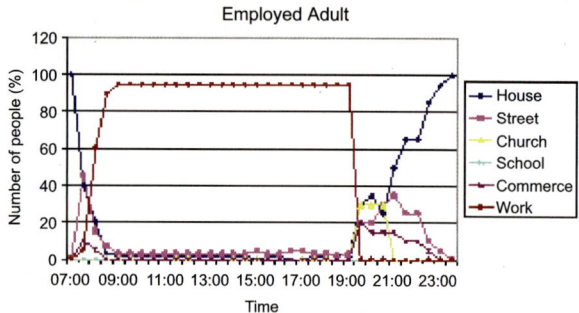

Fig. 8.33 Spatial occupation of employed adults

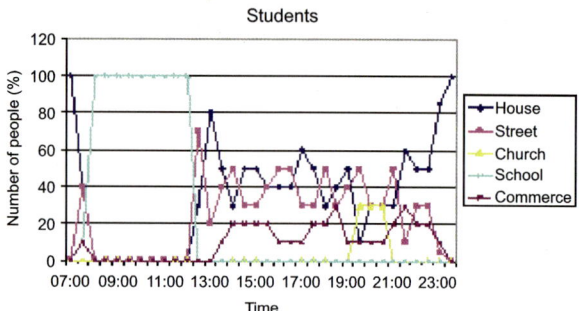

Fig. 8.34 Spatial occupation of students

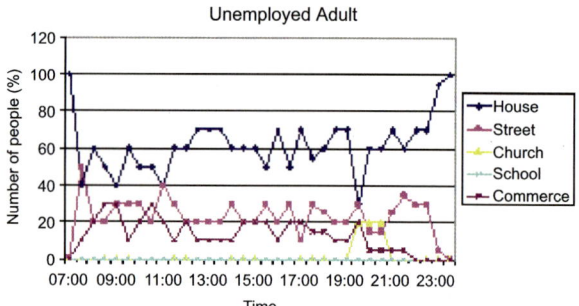

Fig. 8.35 Spatial occupation of unemployed adults

trees, and others), respectively. These city objects, except terrains and buildings, have been represented by impostors in different resolutions. They are switched at runtime according to proximity to camera.

Terrain LOD can performed by a LOD algorithm, as ChunkedLOD [Ulr05]. It is a view-dependent algorithm to aggregate primitives, achieving low CPU overhead and high triangle throughput. It requires a heavy preprocessing stage to generate high-detail meshes (chunks), stored in a tree structure. The chunk at the root of the tree is a low-detail representation, higher detail being added at leaves direction. When chunks are close to the camera, child nodes are reached and rendered. When chunks are far from the camera, parent nodes are selected to be rendered.

Low-resolution impostors are loaded and rendered when they are far from the camera, and they are changed by high-resolution version when they are close to (threshold) the camera. Only visible objects are rendered and displayed, while entities out of frustum are not considered (paged off to disk). Indeed, the entire scene can be saved into a database for further simulation.

8.10 Implementation Aspects

Some libraries and toolkits can support the development of city generation, useful for crowd simulation. One framework has been designed and implemented to support fast prototyping of these applications [dSJM06]. The code has been written in C++ language. It is designed with support of OpenSteer, Cal3D, OpenSceneGraph, and GDAL. The OpenSteer[8] library is the natural choice for steering behaviors, while the Cal3D library was chosen to produce the virtual character animation. An intermediate layer between Cal3D and steering was created due to the fact that the Cal3D library does not deal with the movement of the characters in the virtual world, but only with body animation. This layer controls automatically the animation of one character (movement of legs and arms) due to the trajectories processed in the OpenSteer library at each frame. To each animation keyframe, the displacement of the character from the previous position is computed and then the body animation is updated. For visualization, OpenSceneGraph[9] has been employed. Its synergy with Cal3D and GDAL[10] makes the visualization of animated human and geometric data of city relief easier.

8.11 Final Remarks

This chapter describes techniques employed to generate populated environments, useful for virtual human simulation, in particular real-time parametric generation of 3D virtual cities for behavioral simulations. We have focused on automatic and semiautomatic methods for city generation useful for crowd simulation, and real-time visualization. Hierarchical data structure gives support to fast management of heterogeneous and large amounts of data. Some tips about free software libraries to support human animation, behavior animation, and high-performance rendering are discussed.

---

[8] http://opensteer.sourceforge.net.
[9] http://www.openscenegraph.org.
[10] http://www.gdal.org.

References

[AIS77] ALEXANDER C., ISHIKAWA S., SILVERSTEIN M.: *A Pattern Language: Towns, Buildings Construction*. Oxford University Press, London, 1977.

[BdSM04] BARROS L. M., DA SILVA A. T., MUSSE S. R.: Petrosim: An architecture to manage virtual crowds in panic situations. In *Proceedings of the 17th International Conference on Computer Animation and Social Agents (CASA 2004)* (Geneva, Switzerland, 2004), vol. 1, pp. 111–120.

[BHvW00] BRULS M., HUIZING K., VAN WIJK J.: Squarified treemaps. In *Proceedings of the Joint Eurographics and IEEE TCVG Symposium on Visualization* (2000), pp. 33–42.

[BMB03] BRAUN A., MUSSE S., BODMANN L. O. B.: Modeling individual behaviors in crowd simulation. In *Computer Animation and Social Agents* (New Jersey, USA, May 2003), pp. 143–148.

[BPB06] BOULANGER K., PATTANAIK S., BOUATOUCH K.: Rendering grass terrains in real-time with dynamic lighting. In *SIGGRAPH'06* (2006), ACM, New York, p. 46.

[CGG*07] COMPTON K., GRIEVE J., GOLDMAN E., QUIGLEY O., STRATTON C., TODD E., WILLMOTT A.: Creating spherical worlds. In *SIGGRAPH'07: ACM SIGGRAPH 2007 Sketches* (New York, NY, USA, 2007), ACM, New York, p. 82.

[CIQ*07] CHOY L., INGRAM R., QUIGLEY O., SHARP B., WILLMOTT A.: Rigblocks: Player-deformable objects. In *SIGGRAPH'07: ACM SIGGRAPH 2007 Sketches* (New York, NY, USA, 2007), ACM, New York, p. 83.

[dBSvKO00] DE BERG M., SCHWARZKOPF O., VAN KREVELD M., OVERMARS M.: *Computational Geometry: Algorithms and Applications*, 2nd edn. Springer, Berlin, 2000.

[DEC03] DIKAIAKOU M., EFTHYMIOU A., CHRYSANTHOU Y.: Modelling the walled city of Nicosia. In *VAST 2003: Eurographics Workshop Proceedings*. (Brighton, United Kingdom, 5–7 Nov. 2003), Arnold D., Chalmers A., Niccolucci F. (Eds.), pp. 57–65.

[DGH*07] DEBRY D. G., GOFFIN H., HECKER C., QUIGLEY O., SHODHAN S., WILLMOTT A.: Player-driven procedural texturing. In *SIGGRAPH'07: ACM SIGGRAPH 2007 Sketches* (New York, NY, USA, 2007), ACM, New York, p. 81.

[DHOO05] DOBBYN S., HAMILL J., O'CONOR K., O'SULLIVAN C.: Geopostors: A real-time geometry/impostor crowd rendering system. In *SI3D'05: Proceedings of the 2005 Symposium on Interactive 3D Graphics and Games* (New York, NY, USA, 2005), ACM, New York, pp. 95–102.

[dSJM06] DA SILVEIRA-JR L. G., MUSSE S.: Real-time generation of populated virtual cities. In *VRST'06* (Limassol, Cyprus, 01–03 Nov. 2006), ACM, New York.

[EMP*02] EBERT D. S., MUSGRAVE F. K., PEACHEY D., PERLIN K., WORLEY S.: *Texturing & Modeling: A Procedural Approach*, 3rd edn. Morgan Kaufmann, San Mateo, 2002.

[FBT99] FARENC N., BOULIC R., THALMANN D.: An informed environment dedicated to the simulation of virtual humans in urban context. In *Eurographics'99* (Milano, Italy, 1999), Brunet P., Scopigno R. (Eds.), vol. 18, pp. 309–318.

[For99] FORSTNER W.: 3d-city models: Automatic and semiautomatic acquisition methods. In *Photogrametric Week'99* (1999), Fritsch D., Spiller R. (Eds.), pp. 291–303.

[GPSL03] GREUTER S., PARKER J., STEWART N., LEACH G.: Real-time procedural generation of 'pseudo infinite' cities. In *GRAPHITE'03: Proceedings of the 1st International Conference on Computer Graphics and Interactive Techniques in Australasia and South East Asia* (New York, NY, USA, 2003), ACM, New York, pp. 87–ff.

[Gre83] GREENE D.: The decomposition of polygons into convex parts. In *Computational Geometry* (1983), Advances in Computing Research, vol. 1, JAI Press, Greenwich, pp. 235–259.

[HBSL03] HARRIS M. J., BAXTER W. V., SCHEUERMANN T., LASTRA A.: Simulation of cloud dynamics on graphics hardware. In *HWWS'03: Proceedings of the ACM*

References

SIGGRAPH/EUROGRAPHICS Conference on Graphics Hardware (Aire-la-Ville, Switzerland, 2003), Eurographics Association, Geneve, pp. 92–101.

[HBW06] HAHN E., BOSE P., WHITEHEAD A.: Persistent realtime building interior generation. In *Sandbox'06: Proceedings of the 2006 ACM SIGGRAPH Symposium on Videogames* (New York, NY, USA, 2006), ACM, New York, pp. 179–186.

[HDMB07] HORNA S., DAMIAND G., MENEVEAUX D., BERTRAND Y.: Building 3d indoor scenes topology from 2d architectural plans. In *Conference on Computer Graphics Theory and Applications. GRAPP'2007* (Av. D.Manuel I, 27A 2esq. 2910-595 Setúbal—Portugal, March 2007).

[Hil96] HILLIER B.: *Space Is the Machine: A Configurational Theory of Architecture*. Cambridge University Press, Cambridge, 1996.

[HM83] HERTEL S., MEHLHORN K.: Fast triangulation of simple polygons. In *4th Internat. Conf. Found. Comput. Theory* (1983), Lecture Notes in Computer Science, vol. 158, pp. 207–218.

[HNR68] HART P., NILSSON N., RAPHAEL B.: A formal basis for the heuristic determination of minimum cost paths. *IEEE Transactions on Systems Science and Cybernetics* 4, 2 (July 1968), 100–107.

[JS91] JOHNSON B., SHNEIDERMAN B.: Tree-maps: A space-filling approach to the visualization of hierarchical information structures. In *VIS'91: Proceedings of the 2nd Conference on Visualization'91* (Los Alamitos, CA, USA, 1991), IEEE Computer Society, Los Alamitos, pp. 284–291.

[KW06] KIPFER P., WESTERMANN R.: Realistic and interactive simulation of rivers. In *Proceedings Graphics Interface 2006* (2006), Mann S., Gutwin C. (Eds.), Canadian Human–Computer Communications Society, Toronto, pp. 41–48.

[LD04] LAMARCHE F., DONIKIAN S.: Crowds of virtual humans: A new approach for real time navigation in complex and structured environments. *Computer Graphics Forum 23*, 3 (September 2004), 509–518.

[Mar06] MARTIN J.: Procedural house generation: A method for dynamically generating floor plans. In *Symposium on Interactive 3D Graphics and Games* (2006).

[MT01] MUSSE S. R., THALMANN D.: A hierarchical model for real time simulation of virtual human crowds. *IEEE Transactions on Visualization and Computer Graphics* 7, 2 (April–June 2001), 152–164.

[MWH*06] MÜLLER P., WONKA P., HAEGLER S., ULMER A., VAN GOOL L.: Procedural modeling of buildings. In *SIGGRAPH'06: ACM SIGGRAPH 2006 Papers* (New York, NY, USA, 2006), ACM, New York, pp. 614–623.

[OCS03] OLIVEIRA M., CROWCROFT J., SLATER M.: An innovative design approach to build virtual environment systems. In *EGVE'03: Proceedings of the Workshop on Virtual Environments 2003* (New York, NY, USA, 2003), ACM, New York, pp. 143–151.

[PA01] PREMOŽE S., ASHIKHMIN M.: Rendering natural waters. *Computer Graphics Forum 20* (2001), 189–200, doi:10.1111/1467-8659.00548.

[PHMH95] PRUSINKIEWICZ P., HAMMEL M., MECH R., HANAN J.: The artificial life of plants. In *Artificial Life for Graphics, Animation, and Virtual Reality* (1995), SIGGRAPH'95 Course Notes, vol. 7, pp. 1-1–1-38.

[PM01] PARISH Y. I. H., MÜLLER P.: Procedural modeling of cities. In *Computer Graphics Proc. (SIGGRAPH 2001)* (2001), pp. 301–308.

[PVM05] PAIVA D. C., VIEIRA R., MUSSE S. R.: Ontology-based crowd simulation for normal life situations. In *Proceedings of Computer Graphics International 2005* (Stony Brook, USA, 2005), IEEE Computer Society, Los Alamitos.

[SB97] SMITH S., BRADY J.: SUSAN—A new approach to low level image processing. *International Journal of Computer Vision 23*, 1 (May 1997), 45–78.

[SSEH03] SCHPOK J., SIMONS J., EBERT D. S., HANSEN C.: A real-time cloud modeling, rendering, and animation system. In *SCA'03: Proceedings of the 2003 ACM SIG-*

GRAPH/Eurographics Symposium on Computer Animation* (Aire-la-Ville, Switzerland, 2003), Eurographics Association, Geneve, pp. 160–166.

[TBSD09] TUTENEL T., BIDARRA R., SMELIK R. M., DE KRAKER K. J.: Rule-based layout solving and its application to procedural interior generation. In *Proceedings of CASA Workshop on 3D Advanced Media in Gaming and Simulation (3AMIGAS)* (Amsterdam, The Netherlands, 2009).

[TBSK08] TUTENEL T., BIDARRA R., SMELIK R. M., KRAKER K. J. D.: The role of semantics in games and simulations. *Computers in Entertainment 6*, 4 (2008), 1–35.

[TC00] TECCHIA F., CHRYSANTHOU Y.: Real-time rendering of densely populated urban environments. In *Eurographics Workshop on Rendering Techniques 2000* (London, UK, 2000), Springer, London, pp. 83–88.

[TD00] THOMAS G., DONIKIAN S.: Modeling virtual cities dedicated to behavioural animation. In *Eurographics'00* (Interlaken, Switzerland, 2000), Gross M., Hopgood F. (Eds.), vol. 19, pp. C71–C79.

[TSSS03] TAKASE Y., SHO N., SONE A., SHIMIYA K.: Automatic generation of 3d city models and related applications. *International Archives of the Photogrammetry, Remote Sensing and Spatial Information Sciences XXXIV*, 5 (2003), 113–120.

[Ulr05] ULRICH T.: Chunked lod: Rendering massive terrains using chunked level of detail control. http://www.vterrain.org/LOD/Papers/index.html, Nov. 2005 (last access).

[Wei85] WEILER K.: Edge-based data structures for solid modeling in curved-surface environments. *IEEE Computer Graphics and Applications 5*, 1 (Jan. 1985), 21–40.

[WWSR03] WONKA P., WIMMER M., SILLION F., RIBARSKY W.: Instant architecture. *ACM Transactions on Graphics 22*, 3 (2003), 669–677.

[YBH*02] YAP C., BIERMANN H., HERTZMAN A., LI C., MEYER J., PAO H., PAXIA T.: A different Manhattan project: Automatic statistical model generation. In *IS&T SPIE Symposium on Electronic Imaging* (San Jose, CA, USA, Jan. 2002).

[ZKB*01] ZACH C., KLAUS A., BAUER J., KARNER K., GRABNER M.: Modeling and visualizing the cultural heritage data set of Graz. In *Conference on Virtual Reality, Archeology, and Cultural Heritage* (New York, NY, USA, 2001), ACM, New York, pp. 219–226.

Chapter 9
Applications: Case Studies

9.1 Introduction

This chapter presents some applications that have dealt with virtual crowds. We are concerned with three applications. First, crowd simulation in the context of virtual heritage is considered. Second, we describe an interface built to guide crowds in real time. Finally, some examples of virtual crowds in safety systems are presented.

9.2 Crowd Simulation for Virtual Heritage

Virtual heritage reconstructions usually focus on creating visual representations of monuments or buildings, such as cathedrals, with virtual humans playing only a minor role. Usually there is a single "tour guide" [DeL99, FLKB01], or virtual humans are more artifacts than living beings such as Xian terra-cotta warriors [MTPM97, ZZ99] or Egyptian mummies [ABF*99].

In the real world, however, most of the reconstructed places are, or have been, populated by smaller or larger numbers of people—worshippers prayed in cathedrals, druids performed their ceremonies in Stonehenge, gladiators battled in the Colosseum in front of spectator crowds.

Although early virtual heritage works have been criticized for their lack of visual realism [Add00], nowadays advances in computer hardware and sophisticated 3D modeling packages allow one to create compelling visualizations of static objects. Yet, while photorealistic architecture reconstructions can be impressive, most of the times they lack dynamic elements such as virtual humans or animals.

In this section, we will study several cases of crowds in ancient times.

Fig. 9.1 Crowd performing praying in the Sokullu mosque

9.2.1 Virtual Population of Worshippers Performing Morning Namaz Prayer Inside a Virtual Mosque

In this section, we aim to increase the realism of the reconstructed edifices by re-creating life inside architectural models. This work was done in the context of the CAHRISMA project, which aims to create Hybrid Architectural Heritage, where not only visual, but also acoustical aspects of the heritage are reconstructed. We integrated a virtual crowd simulation [UT01] into a real-time photorealistic simulation of complex heritage edifices [PLFMT01]. We simulated a crowd of virtual humans able to move and interact within a virtual environment. We created a virtual population of worshippers performing morning Namaz prayer inside a virtual mosque (see Fig. 9.1). We used a rule behavior system allowing flexible representation of a complex scenario relatively easily adaptable to different edifices or different numbers of persons.

System Design

The crowd simulation was built as a part of the VHD++ development framework [PPM*03]. The VHD++ framework provides components, which allow, for example, loading and displaying of VRML models, animating H-Anim compatible humanoid models, or 3D sound playback. The application is constructed as a particular set of these software components, working on a particular set of data.

The crowd component is responsible for the generation of behaviors of virtual humans. It allows one to initialize a population of virtual human agents and then generates in real time sequences of actions, such as playing of a prerecorded body or facial animation keyframed sequence, walking to a particular location using walking motion model, or playing a sound.

The behavior of the agents is computed by a combination of rules and finite state machines: on the higher level, rules select behaviors appropriate for the state of the simulation; and on the lower level, finite state machines generate sequences of actions. The state of the agent is constituted by an arbitrary number of attributes. Events provide a means of communication between agents, perception of the environment, and interaction with objects and the user. An important part of the system is a model of the environment containing, for example, semantic information about the space, such as location of doors, or areas accessible for walking and praying. More detailed description of the employed behavior model can be found in [UT02].

The crowd module allows construction of scenarios defined by a set of behavioral rules, such as a crowd of worshippers coming to the mosque and performing the religious ceremony.

Scenario Creation

In this case study, the goal was to enhance the realism of reconstructed Sinan mosques by adding realistic animated virtual humans to architectural models. The scenario of a morning Namaz prayer was selected as a representation of a typical activity taking place in simulated mosques.

The reconstruction of the scenario was based on video and audio recordings of the actual ceremony. As the first step, a structured transcription of the ritual was created, serving as a further guide for the creation of behavioral rules and the selection of motion sequences and sound clips to be recorded.

VRML models of virtual humans have been created with the 3D Studio Max modeling package using a custom plug-in for creating H-Anim compatible hierarchies. As there is a fixed number of polygons possible to be displayed for a particular frame update rate, the polygon count was the constraining factor for creation of human models. The fixed number of polygons had to be divided between the model of the scene and the models of the humans. Human models of different complexities were chosen with more complex ones, with around 3000 polygons, for persons with specific roles in the ceremony, such as imam or muezzin, and less complex ones, with around 1000 polygons, for the rest of worshippers. The higher polygon count of "more significant" human models is mainly due to the higher complexity of their facial area, as these models have roles requiring them to perform facial animations. Sounds have been extracted from the audio recording of the ceremony, and corresponding FAP facial animations have been created.

Motion sequences of various parts of the ceremony have been produced by a motion capture of a person performing Namaz prayer. For a convincing scenario, crowds should not look too uniform as to motion: a higher level of variety is needed as explained in Chap. 3. Because it would not be feasible to record all motions for every human, a single motion captured animation clip was reused for multiple virtual humans, and the illusion of variety was created by a rule system.

The rule system has two main roles: first, it is responsible for orchestration of the scenario; and second, it helps with creating the variety by generating slightly different commands for the different agents, even while they are executing the same set of rules. Tools for achieving variety are: differences in the durations of the actions;

Fig. 9.2 Crowd enters Sokullu mosque

slightly shifted starts of the actions; and the selection of the animations corresponding to the particular action randomly from a set of similar animations. Most rules are shared by all the agents; some agents with specific roles, such as imam or muezzin, have additional, role-specific, rules. Sharing a significant number of rules by many agents proved to be important for the development and manageability of the simulation, as eventual changes in the scenario did not have to be propagated to many places in the rule set, leaving less space for errors and speeding up the development.

Behavioral rules in conjunction with the model of the environment provide a flexible way of representing complex behaviors. One of the requirements of the CAHRISMA project was that several mosques would be reconstructed. Each mosque, however, is different, with a different size and a different layout of the building. Thus, even while on the higher level of description, the scenario of a morning Namaz is the same for each mosque, lower-level details, such as the exact location and exact timing of the actions, are different.

To construct these multiple similar scenarios by a linear script would require unnecessary repetitive work prone to errors. The rule system has the advantage over the simpler script of specifying behavior on the level of logical units instead of absolute actions with absolute timings. For example, the synchronization of worshippers performing different steps of the praying sequence (as required by the ceremony) is done by interagent communication via events. Each person is announcing the end of the current step; a designated leader then observes when everybody finishes the current step, and gives a command to proceed with the next one. Such representation of the behavior is independent of the number of involved persons, or a particular length of the animation clip.

Further flexibility comes from the use of the environmental model: the rules operate on semantic information about the scene rather than on absolute coordinates of the locations. For example, one of the rules states that before starting praying, the agent has to pass through the door of the mosque, and then to arrive to the area designated for praying (see Fig. 9.2). This rule is equally valid for any of the mosques, as the model of the environment supplies the correct absolute coordinates of the door and the praying place.

9.2.2 *Virtual Roman Audience in the Aphrodisias Odeon*

In this section, we will discuss the system implementation and data design necessary for creating a crowd of virtual actors in the Roman Odeon of Aphrodisias. We use the techniques described in Chap. 3 to create a crowd that is varied in animation and appearance using a few template actors while having large variety means we reduce the work of designers. Using scenario scripts we bring life to the audience which is following a play on stage. The work was realized as part of the EU project ERATO—identification Evaluation and Revival of the Acoustical heritage of ancient Theaters and Odea.

We summarize a method that creates a believable crowd of digital actors listening to a play on stage. With the transition to programmable graphics hardware even on laptops the system is able to run a crowd with smooth animations and transitional updates in real time.

Crowd Engine Resume

The crowd engine used for this application has been described in Chap. 7. It renders at least 1000 digital actors in real time. It is responsible for updating the animation and for rendering the spectators. The input needed per template is two or three meshes with decreasing level of detail, and four or more different textures that have different clothing styles and color key areas described in their alpha channels [dHCSMT05, dHSMT05]. Given these data the crowd engine can start rendering the humans, but still we need scripting and scenarios as well as audio to make the experience complete. In collaboration with the Danish Technical University (DTU), we defined camera placements for audio recordings that have the characteristics of that specific listening location. This process is called auralization, described in [NRC04], and relies on a sound wave ray tracing.

Variety comes through textures and modifiable color areas. These areas are defined by the artist in each texture for each color area such as the dress, jewels, and hair. Each of these areas can then be modified individually and their color ranges are described in an HSB space as detailed in Chap. 3. Examples of this variety can be seen in Fig. 9.3, where there are four different templates visible: two for the patricians and noblemen. The nobles have four textures per template and the patricians have eight and using the color variety on each such texture we get a greater effect of variety. This means we work very little on creating variety and spend more time on scenario authoring and tuning.

To be able to have smooth animation transitioning and updates we have all animation clips stored as quaternions and interpolate the key frames using spherical linear interpolation for each individual in the crowd for each animation that is active. To further smooth the interpolation when transitioning we use a cosine function to weight which animation clip is more important.

With the use of programmable graphics hardware we deform the mesh in the vertex shader and light it with Phong shading and apply the color variety at fragment level. This was already described in Chap. 7.

Fig. 9.3 Audience applauding the entrance of the senator

High-Fidelity Actors

The high level of variety in a crowd reenforces the believability and reliability of the simulation. The crowd engine can render up to 1000 virtual characters including the odeon environment with interactive frame rates. To emphasize the importance of special characters, the system is extended for rendering and animating virtual characters using different code paths. Based on requirements, we can use a fast and low resource usage path or a more detailed path for more realistic rendering. When rendering a crowd simulation, it is impossible to give as much detail and attention to every virtual character, than with systems that are displaying only a few characters at the same time.

Experience has shown that if the crowd can use basic behaviors with a good sensation of presence, special characters that attract the attention of end-users need to be more detailed. Thus, special characters, such as senators, have their own alternate code path. They shared the same DNA in terms of functionalities than the lighter model. High-fidelity actors represent virtual characters that have an influence on the scenario. From a content creation point of view, designers are allowed to increase the complexity by creating more detailed 3D meshes or by taking advantage of more advanced vertex and fragment shaders. From an animation perspective, the high-fidelity actors need to be compliant with the H-Anim 1.1 standard.[1] This opens to a wide range of additional techniques including the benefit of extending the animation bank with hundreds of motion capture clips and inverse kinematics as featured in Fig. 9.4.

---

[1] http://www.h-anim.org.

Fig. 9.4 A senator (high-fidelity actor) making his entrance in the odeon

Scenario Authoring

Since the beginning of the project, the focus has always been on creating a graphical pipeline that could be applied to many different scenarios and cultural heritage settings. The goals were to overcome the development costs involved in creating unique individual characters. We come to a solution promoting variety, code, and content reuse by allowing to prototype quickly different scenarios, through the use of customizable meshes, textures, colorings, behaviors, and scenarios. Using the techniques described in Chap. 3, different digital actor templates were developed that cover different social classes as depicted in Fig. 9.5. Variety in colors and clothes were based on information collected by archaeologists.

Audience Placement

An important part of a scenario is the distribution of the audience in the odeon. A plan of the distribution was created according to historical sources. Figure 9.6 shows on the left side the plan of the audience distribution according to social class—starting from the center there are places for nobles, patricians, and plebeians. On the right side of the figure is the distribution of 3D humans in the actual model of the Aphrodisias odeon according to the plan.

In order to facilitate positioning of digital actors, we created a grid of valid positions in the theater following the distribution of the seats. Then, we used the creation brush [UdHCT04] with the restriction of operating only on this grid, instead of free picking. Using the grid, humans can be positioned without regard to collisions, for example, if two humans happen to materialize very close to each other. The correct position and orientation of the audience is thus automatic. The same scene will have a certain expected behavior when you interact with it, in much the same way a in a paint program, where pixel positions are placed in a grid.

Fig. 9.5 The different social classes represented in our simulation. Note the difference in *color range* for clothes

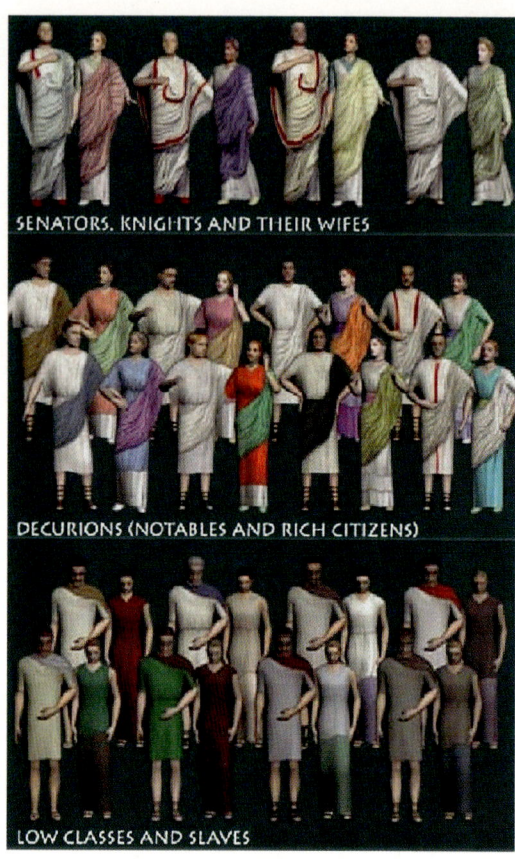

Fig. 9.6 *Left*: 2D distribution plan. *Right*: audience distributed in odeon

Fig. 9.7 Crowd of virtual Romans simulated in a reconstructed part of Pompeii

9.2.3 Populating Ancient Pompeii with Crowds of Virtual Romans

In this Section, we detail the process, based on archeological data, of simulating the city of Pompeii [MHY*07]. Pompeii was a Roman city, destroyed and completely buried during a catastrophic eruption of the volcano Mount Vesuvius. We have revived its glorious past by using a 3D model of its previous appearance and populated it with crowds of virtual Romans. The project was developed in the framework of EPOCH [EPO] is a network composed of about a hundred European cultural institutions whose goal is to improve the use of Information and Communication Technology for Cultural Heritage. Figure 9.7 illustrates the populated virtual city. We introduce an automatic process that reads the city semantics and consequently induces special behaviors in the crowd of virtual Romans, depending on their location in the city. We have empirically defined each behavior as a series of scripted actions.

The main goal of our work was to simulate in real time a crowd of virtual Romans exhibiting realistic behaviors in a reconstructed district of ancient Pompeii. In an offline process, the city is first automatically reconstructed and exported into two different representations: a high-resolution model for rendering purpose, a low-resolution model labeled with semantic data. A second important stage achieved in a preprocess is the extraction of the semantics to be used during the real-time crowd simulation.

There are several buildings in the city model where virtual Romans can enter freely. Some of them are labelled as shops and bakeries, and the characters entering them acquire related accessories, e.g., oil amphoras or bread. These accessories are directly attached to a joint of the virtual character's skeleton, and follow its movements when deformed. We can attach accessories to various joints, depending on their nature. In Pompeii, this variety is illustrated with the amphoras: rich people

Table 9.1 Summary of semantics and associated behaviors

Geometry semantics	Behavior	Actions
shop	get amphora	walk inside, get out with amphora.
bakery	get bread	walk inside, get out with bread.
young	rich	only rich people go there
old	poor	only poor people go there.
door	look at	slow down, look through it
window	look at	slow down, look through it
	stop look at	accelerate, stop looking

get out of shops with an amphora in their hand, while slaves get out of shops carrying them on their heads.

The idea of rich and poor districts is based on age maps that were provided by archeologists taking part in the EPOCH project. These maps show the age of buildings in the city. Although we do not yet have the building textures to visually express this kind of differences, we have decided to install the rich Roman templates in the most recent districts, while poor people have been established in old buildings. From this, virtual characters know where they belong and while most parts of the city are accessible for everybody, some districts are restricted to a certain class of people: rich Romans in young areas and slaves in poor zones.

Semantics to Behavior

We know that each semantic label corresponds to a specific behavior. For instance, the window and door semantics trigger a "look at" behavior that makes virtual Romans slow down and look through the window (see Table 9.1). To keep our crowd engine as generic as possible, each graph vertex triggering a special behavior also receives a series of variables used later on for parameterization. Let us again consider the "look at" example. Each graph vertex associated to this behavior should make Romans look through the window or the door. In order to know exactly where Romans have to look, each of these graph vertices also receives a target point, computed as the center of the window/door quad.

In our Pompeii scenario, only the "look at" semantics requires extra parameters. Since a graph vertex may be close to several windows or doors at the same time, we make sure to save a set of target points (one per door/window) as its behavior parameters. When a virtual Roman crosses such a graph vertex, he chooses among the target points the closest one facing him. For other semantics, no parameter is required. However, the engine has been developed to accept variables in any number.

Finally, this process outputs a script describing which behaviors apply to which vertices and with which parameters. This script is later used at the initialization of the crowd simulation to assign behaviors to graph vertices.

Fig. 9.8 Crowds of virtual Romans in a street of Ancient Pompeii

Long Term vs Short Term Behaviors

There are many behaviors that can be triggered when a virtual Roman passes over a graph vertex. Some of them are permanent, i.e., once they are triggered for a Roman, they are kept until the end of the simulation, while others are temporary: once the Roman leaves their area, the behaviors are stopped. For instance, a Roman entering a bakery acquires some bread and will keep it when leaving the bakery until the end of the simulation. However, a Roman passing close to a window will slow down to look through it until he is too far away and then resume his faster walk.

The permanent behaviors are not complex to manage. Once triggered, they modify parameters within the Roman data that will never be set back to their previous value. For temporary behaviors however, it is important to detect when a Roman leaves an area with a specific behavior, and set his modified parameters back to normal values.

Results

Seven human templates have been exploited to create the simulation: a couple of nobles (one male and one female), a couple of plebeians, another couple of patricians and finally, a legionary. These seven templates are instantiated several hundred times to generate large crowds. To ensure a varied and appealing result, per body part color variety techniques are exploited. The simulation of the crowd in the city has been achieved with an Intel core duo 2.4 GHz 2 Gb RAM and a Nvidia Geforce 8800 GTX 768 Mb RAM. The crowd engine is mainly implemented in C++, but to ease the definition of behavior actions, we use the Lua scripting language. One of its main advantages is the fast test/fix cycles while programming behavior functions. The city part used for the simulation (illustrated in Fig. 9.8) is composed of about 700,000 triangles and 12 Mb of compressed textures.

For the crowds, combining the different LOD, it is possible to simulate in this environment 4,000 Romans, i.e., about 600,000 triangles and 88 Mb of compressed textures, with real-time performance (30 fps in average).

Fig. 9.9 The Immersive Room in the Institute for Media Innovation, Nanyang Technological University, Singapore

9.3 Immersion in a Crowd

In this Section, we present an interactive multi-agent system [WDMTT12], which allows the user to interact with the virtual characters dynamically in immersive environments. This work concentrates on two issues of interactive multi-agent system. The first one is the real-time dynamic path planning for autonomous agents. The second one is the design of the interaction between user's avatar and agents based on gesture recognition. The simulation system is developed based on the Immersive 3D Display System (by EON Reality) at the Institute for Media Innovation in Nanyang Technological University in Singapore. The users in the immersive system are surrounded by a concave screen of 320 degree (3m8m, 5 channels), which can display graphics of 20 megapixels in stereoscopic 3D (see Fig. 9.9). This immersive system also provides other peripheral devices, like head tracking system and audio system, to enhance the interaction between the users and virtual environments. Microsoft Kinect Sensor is integrated in the system for motion capture. EON Studio is used as the rendering engine.

The structure of the interactive multi-agent system is specially designed for the dynamic interacting with individual or groups of agents. Currently, this system can only support single-user input. The user's motion is captured with the Kinect Sensor, and then processed by the module of gesture recognition. Finally, the affected agents react to the user's avatar according to its gesture. The simulation process includes the following steps or modules, path planning, steering, collision avoidance, keyframe animation for agent and skeletal animation for avatar. The rendering of virtual human characters and environment is automatically taken care of by the rendering engine. Other technical issues are covered by the immersive system solution, e.g. stereoscopic 3D display, head tracking, multi-channel blending, etc.

To provide the user with a natural interface to interact with the virtual environment, gesture recognition is integrated into the system. The template-based method is adopted. To perform the template-based gesture recognition, a library of template gesture has to be built first. The template gestures are recorded in a pre-process. At runtime, new gesture data read from Kinect Sensor are standardized and then compared with the gestures in the template library. A gesture is

9.4 Crowdbrush

Table 9.2 Interaction design based on gesture recognition

Interaction	Gesture	Description
Walk	Left knee up -> left knee down -> right knee up -> right knee down ... (mark time)	Walk forward in the virtual environment, Turn left or right to control the direction; Change the stride frequency to control the walking speed
Pick	Left/right hand wave -> left/right hand point	Pick one character to interact with
Direct	Left/right hand sweep left/right	Direct the selected character or a whole group of agents to the direction indicated
Gather	Both hands up	Make the agents gather around the avatar
Disperse	Left hand sweep left and right hand sweep right	Disperse the agents
Lead	Left/right hand up while walking	Make the agents follow the avatar
Stop	Both hands push forward	Prevent the agents that is in front of and approaching the avatar from moving forward

represented by a sequence of points. To compare two gestures is to compare the points array of the new gesture with that of the target gesture. A match will be found if the result of Golden Section Search [FO04] reaches a given threshold value. Once a predefined gesture is detected, the corresponding response process will be started. A new goal will be set for each of the affected agents and the path planner will find a route to the goal. For example, when the avatar raises both hands, this gesture will be captured and detected by the gesture recognition module. Then the response process of gathering will be started. The cells around the position of the avatar will be set as the new goals for the agents. The interactions between the avatar and the virtual environment are defined as follows (Table 9.2). Figure 9.10 shows three scenarios demonstrating the interaction behaviors, including directing the agents to a specific orientation (Fig. 9.10a), making agents gather around the avatar (Fig. 9.10b), and leading agents to move (Fig. 9.10c).

9.4 Crowdbrush

The idea of Crowdbrush [UdHCT04] is simple: the designer manipulates virtual tools, working in a 2D screen space, with a mouse and a keyboard. These tools then affect the corresponding objects in a 3D world space, as shown in Fig. 9.11. Different tools have different visualizations and produce different effects on the scene including creation and deletion of crowd members, modifying their appearances, triggering of various animations, or setting high-level behavioral parameters.

Fig. 9.10 a. Directing the agents to a specific orientation, **b.** making the agents gather around the avatar, **c.** leading agents to move

(a)

(b)

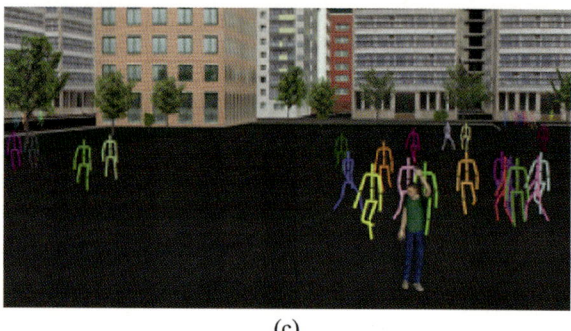

(c)

Briefly, experiments were made with a fully 3D interface, where tools existed in a 3D world space. Nevertheless, it appeared to be not very practical, at least not when using standard input devices operating in 2D as a mouse or a trackball. The usability of a 3D interface could be improved with some truly 3D input devices such as a spaceball, a 3D mouse, or magnetic sensors. However, it would limit the number of potential users as such devices are not common.

Figure 9.12 shows an overview of the system design. The user controls the application using a mouse and a keyboard. The mouse moves the visual representation of the brush tool (an icon of a spray can is used) on the screen, with the mouse but-

9.4 Crowdbrush

Fig. 9.11 Crowdbrush used on the Roman crowd of the Aphrodisias Odeon

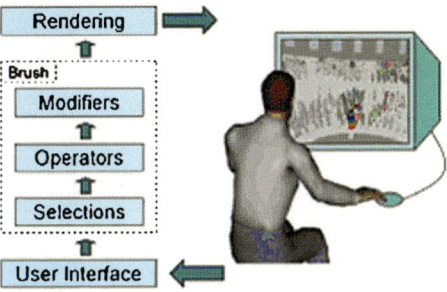

Fig. 9.12 Overview of the system design

tons triggering different actions. The keyboard selects different tools and switches between "navigate" and "paint" modes. In the "navigate" mode, the mouse controls position and orientation of the camera. In the "paint" mode, the camera control is suspended and different areas on screen are selected depending on triggered actions. These areas are then further processed by the brush according to their particular configurations, explained in the next section.

9.4.1 Brushes

Brushes are tools with a visual representation that affects crowd members in different manners. For example, a brush can create new individuals in the scene, or it can change their appearances or behaviors. Selected visualizations of brushes intuitively hint at their specific function. For example, the creation brush has an icon of a human, the orientation brush has an icon of a compass, the deletion brush has an icon of a crossed over human, and so on, as in Fig. 9.13.

A brush is processed in three stages. First, a selection of the affected area in 2D screen space is performed according to a triggered action, with subsequent picking of entities in the 3D world space. Then, the operator modifies the manner of ex-

Fig. 9.13 Laughter Crowdbrush used on the Roman crowd of the Aphrodisias Odeon

Fig. 9.14 Creation brush with random operator

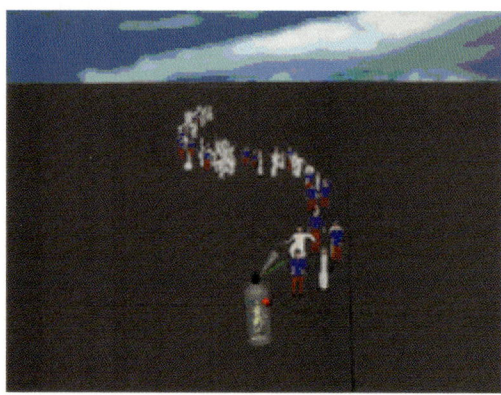

ecution of the brush in the selected area. Finally, the brush changes the values of the modifiers for the affected individuals, or in the case of the creation brush, new population members are created.

1. *Selections* are defined in screenspace. A selection can be a single point at the location of a cursor, or an area around a cursor. If the selection is a single point, picking in the 3D world is performed by computing the intersection of a line segment with the scene. If the selection is an area, picking is performed on a random sample of points from that area, following a "spray" metaphor. The size of the selected area in world space, changes with the level of zoom into the 3D scene. This provides an intuitive control of focus: if one wants to work on a large part of the crowd, zoom-out of the 3D view is performed; if focus is on a smaller group or individual, zoom-in is performed.
2. *Operators* define how selections are affected. For example, a stroke of the creation brush with the random operator creates a random mix of entities (see Fig. 9.14); a stroke of the uniform color brush sets colors of affected individuals to the same value, as shown in Fig. 9.15.

Fig. 9.15 Color brush with uniform operator

3. *Modificators* are nonsharable properties, giving uniqueness to every individual of the crowd. Modifiers encapsulate low-level features influencing both appearance and animations of virtual humans. Spatial configuration is qualified by modificators of position and orientation. Appearance is influenced by modifiers of color, texture, material, and scale. Execution of actions is determined by animation selection, shift, and speed modifiers. High-level features can use a combination of several low-level features accessed through their modifiers. For example, a particular emotional state sets animations from a predefined set with some specific speed, or clothing style selects a set of appropriate textures and colors for different body parts.

Scenario Management

To elaborate the different scenarios which can feature more than a few hundred distinct digital actors, we need to provide tools and scripting capabilities to unleash the potential for simulation designers. Our system offers different levels of interaction for offline and online simulation adjustments. Therefore, our applications are able to parse scenario configuration files written in the scripting language Python.[2] Most of our use-case scenarios were based on reconstructing life in ancient theaters. Table 9.3 describes the sequence and user interactions of a complete scenario.

Scripting

To control the simulation events, our software architecture is responsible for maintenance, consistent simulation, and interactive scenario states controlled by Python scripts at runtime. Our system relies on microthreads for spreading the workflow

---

[2] http://www.python.org.

Table 9.3 Sequence and user interactions of a complete scenario

Part	Description	User control	Interface	3.2.1 Action	3.2.2 Elements
1.0 Introduction (sequence)	Audience idle - > senators entering - ... sit - > people stand up and salute - > **when sequence is over, go to Part 2.0**	> predefined camera animation	= no interface	Script (trigger at the same time): - Senators entering + crowd reacting - synchronized sound (clapping) - synchronized camera path	# *scenarioPart1.0.py* # *Part1.0_intro.wav* # *eratoVP_intro.path* = **all synchronized (duration 50 s)**
2.0 Selection (interactive loop)	User chooses what he wants to see Audience idle = loop	> control the camera - choose cameras > choose simulation > quit	= 4 buttons (1 per camera) = 3 - theater play = > **go to 3.1** - music = > **go to 3.2** - spray = > **go to 4.0** = 1 button (x)	- Switch to selected camera & corresp. sound (current time) - Switch to selected scenario & sound (start time), for current camera - quit app.	# *scenarioPart2.0.py* # loop sound: *Part2.0_idle*.wav* # 4 cameras: *eratoVP_crowd*.path*
3.1 Theater Play (sequence)	User hears actors playing on stage - > Audience is reacting to the play: - > **when sequence is over, go back to 2.0**	*Idem 2.0*	*Idem 2.0*	*Idem 2.0*	# *scenarioPart3.1.py* # 4 sounds: *Part3.1_CreonCrowd*.wav* 4 sounds: *Part3.1_CreonStage*.wav* = **synchronized with script (1 min 45 s)** # 4 cameras: *eratoVP_crowd*.path*
3.2 Music (sequence)	User hears music played on stage - > audience listening, - > at the end applauses - > **when sequence is over, go back to 2.0**	*Idem 2.0*	*Idem 2.0*	*Idem 2.0*	# *scenarioPart3.2.py* # 4 sounds: *Part3.2_musicCrowd*.wav* 4 sounds: *Part3.2_musicStage*.wav* = **synchronized with script (1 min 02 s)** # 4 cameras: *eratoVP_crowd*.path*

9.4 Crowdbrush

Algorithm 9.1: Extract of a script sequence

```
1  begin
2      import time
3      #music has started: people listen
4      for i in range(len(agents)) do
5          agentName = agents[i]simulationService.setCurrentState(agentName
           ,"State_ListenMStart")
6      end
7      while time.time()-val < 45 do
8          #wait for the completion of the music score.vhdYIELD
9      end
10     #concert finished: applause
11     for i in range(len(agents)) do
12         agentName = agents[i]simulationService.setCurrentState(agentName
           ,"State_PositiveStart")
13     end
14     while time.time()-val < 57 do
15         vhdYIELD #back to idle for i in range(len(agents))
16         agentName = agents[i]simulationService.setCurrentState(agentName
           ,"State_IdleStart")
17     end
18 end
```

and script execution over several frames. This offers the ability to describe complete sequences of events as Python scripts. Algorithm 9.1 is an extract of a script sequence which affects behaviors of digital actors dynamically.

In effect, virtual characters are associated with animation banks which define sets of animations connected to human emotions such as being positive, negative, laughing, crying. Theses emotions are represented as distinct states within an HFSM system where states are defined using Lua metatables [Ier03].

Results

To conclude, Fig. 9.16 illustrates the different widgets available at runtime by our system. The application provides different sets of widgets for end-users and for designers to interact with the crowds in real time. To illustrate the simulation complexity, our most complete use-case scenario uses around 800 virtual humans, including two high-fidelity actors representing two Roman senators and eight different humans template. The animation library is composed of 750 unique animations. All of these assets are directly manipulated by simulation events relying on more than 50 Python scripts similarly to [PSO*05].

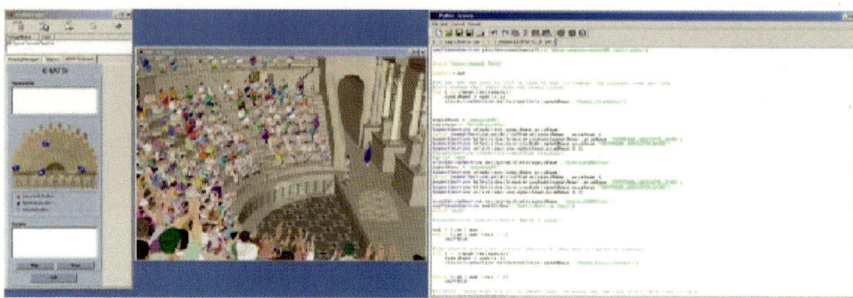

Fig. 9.16 On the *left* is the widget to interact with the scenario allowing are to choose predefined viewpoints and scenarios. In the *middle* is the 3D view and on the *right* the Python console, where designers can write scripts at runtime

9.5 Safety Systems

This section aims to present some applications of crowd simulation in safety systems. It describes an experience performed in a four-stage building, where we simulated a crowd evacuation, and compared results with a real simulated evacuation experiment with real people. The main goal was to validate the simulation and analyze results of the crowd simulator. In such an experiment the simulator proposed by [BBM05] was used.

Indeed, validating a model like the proposed one in comparison to real situations is still a considerable challenge. First, there is not much available data about real-life crowd experiments. Second, there do not exist obvious criteria that may be cast into a metric and indicate to what degree the simulator reproduces real data. Nevertheless, we believe that the present model already has sufficient generality which allows one to calibrate the parameter sets.

We present in this section a preliminary comparison of our simulations with a real building evacuation. This drill took place in a four-story building, where 191 people were distributed mainly in classrooms on the third floor and computer labs on the fourth floor. Due to safety questions, the drill was announced one week before, and people were instructed to abandon the building at the very moment they heard the global alarm. In this evacuation, we estimated the number of people in each room in order to reproduce it in simulations. We filmed the movement of people at several points in the building, in order to estimate velocities of people, regions of traffic jams, and time of evacuation.

Before this drill, we reproduced the building structure and the distribution of people on the simulator. In order to simulate a 3D structure on a 2D simulator, we planified the stairs and estimated a reduction of velocity of 50% in such regions. The maximum speed v_m^0 was set to 1.3 m/s, since people were instructed to exit calmly. A global alarm system was simulated, so that agents start evacuating at the same time. Altruism levels A and mobility levels M were set to 0.95 with a standard deviation of 0.05, since there were no disabled people in the building and everybody in the building was supposed to know very well the environment as well as how to

Table 9.4 Comparison between measured data on the drill and results of simulation. Velocities are measured in meters/second, densities in people/squared meter, and times in seconds

Criterion	Measure on Drill	Simulation Result
A	1.25 m/s	1.27 m/s
B	0.5 m/s	1.19 m/s
C	0.6 m/s	0.6 m/s
D	0.5 m/s	0.47 m/s
E	2.3 people/m^2	2.4 people/m^2
F	190 s	192 s

evacuate the building. Table 9.4 shows a comparison between measured data of the drill and results of computer simulation. The criteria used are

A: mean velocity in corridors without traffic jams
B: mean velocity in corridors with traffic jams
C: mean velocity on stairs without traffic jams
D: mean velocity on stairs with traffic jams
E: higher density
F: global evacuation time

The greater difference observed in Table 9.4, although a moderate variation only, was related to criterion B (mean velocity in corridors with traffic jams). This difference did not impact the global evacuation time (criterion F). We explained this difference to be a function of the spatial occupation, which was different in real and simulated situations. Indeed, in real life, people do not come as close together as the particles in the simulation, meaning that people observe the traffic jam and stop before sticking together. The opposite happens in the simulation. However, this different spatial occupation does not impact the global results for the simulated scenarios. Anyway, we are currently working to improve the model in order to imitate the spatial occupation observed in real life.

Another important observation reproduced with the simulator concerned the regions where traffic jams occurred. Figure 9.17 shows such regions where people had to reduce their velocities due to flows coming from several directions.

From the data of Table 9.4 and images of Fig. 9.17 one may conclude that the simulator achieved satisfactory performance. However, a more profound study considering other real data is planned, especially concerning the reaction of people to hazard events.

9.6 Olympic Stadium

Crowd Simulation techniques can be very useful in security applications which main goal is to simulate people behaviors in normal or specific situations, e.g. panic or hazard simulations. Some environments, as airports, train stations or stadiums can be simulated using this type of tool. In Brazil, a case of crowd simulation was tested

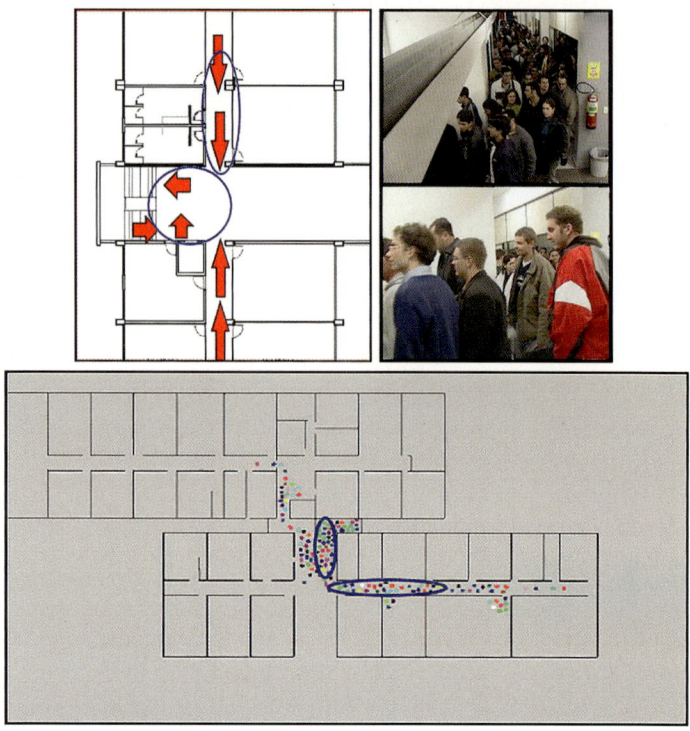

Fig. 9.17 Images showing the flow of people on the third floor (*left*), the traffic jam that occurred (*center*), and images of simulation (*right*)

in the *Estádio Olímpico Municipal João Havelange*, called *Stadium Rio* since 2010. The stadium was built for the *2007 Pan American Games* and actually can be considered the modernest stadium of the Latin America and the number five of the world.[3] The stadium, that is site of *Botafogo*[4] (a Brazilian soccer team), has capacity to 46 thousand people with project to increase 60 thousand aiming to attend the Olympic games in 2016.

With a partnership between Botafogo and PUCRS[5] we could provide a study of crowd behavior in the stadium. The simulations were performed using the tool *CrowdSim*, which was developed by VHLab[6] at PUCRS.

The main goal of simulations was to analyze the people behavior present in a soccer match at the stadium as well as to verify the time and comfort (density of people) they will adopt when moving in stadium. Firstly, we build a 3D model of

---

[3] http://www.bfr.com.br/stadium_rio/historia.asp.

[4] http://www.bfr.com.br.

[5] Pontifical Catholic University of Rio Grande do Sul—Brazil (http://pucrs.br).

[6] Virtual Humans Simulation Laboratory (http://www.inf.pucrs.br/vhlab/).

9.6 Olympic Stadium

Fig. 9.18 Three dimensional model of stadium

Fig. 9.19 Grandstands areas

Fig. 9.20 Grandstands areas

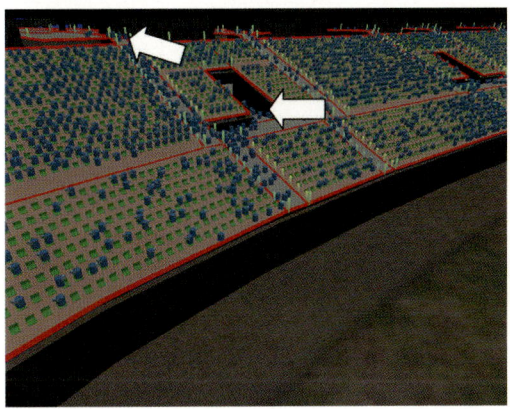

the stadium. Such model, illustrated in Fig. 9.18, was build take into account all the physical structure from the real stadium.

Another important aspect considered in this project was the correctly definition of the grandstands areas. In Fig. 9.19 it is possible to observe such areas (red) and the regions defined to allow free motion of pedestrians (blue). Considering this, when an event occurs, e.g. the end of a match, the pedestrians are able to leave their seats and find the best way to leave the stadium.

Follow, we show a simple example of a test case together with simulation output results. According with stadium features, we simulate the evacuation process and analyze the pedestrian flow in two specific exits, as presented in Fig. 9.20.

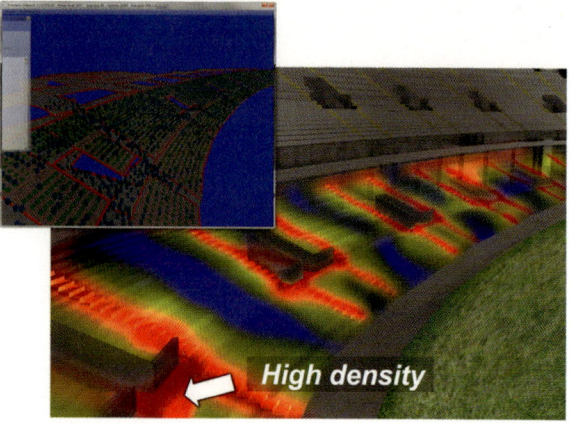

Fig. 9.21 Illustration of agents density based on *colors*. It is possible to observe after some time of simulation the regions where density of agents is high

After the simulation, it is possible to analyze data in a global way, considering all the stadium occupancy. With this data, a density map is provided illustrating different levels of density as presented in Fig. 9.21.

9.7 Final Remarks

This chapter presented a few examples of crowd simulation dealing with historical situations and very practical events.

References

[ABF*99] ATTARDI G., BETRÒ M., FORTE M., GORI R., GUIDAZZOLI A., IMBODEN S., MAL-LEGNI F.: 3d facial reconstruction and visualization of ancient Egyptian mummies using spiral ct data. In *Proc. ACM SIGGRAPH 1999* (1999).

[Add00] ADDISON A. C.: Emerging trends in virtual heritage. *IEEE Multimedia 2*, 7 (2000), 22–25.

[BBM05] BRAUN A., BODMAN B. J., MUSSE S. R.: Simulating virtual crowds in emergency situations. In *Proceedings of ACM Symposium on Virtual Reality Software and Technology—VRST 2005* (Monterey, California, USA, 2005), ACM, New York.

[DeL99] DELEON V. J.: Vrnd: Notre-dame cathedral: A globally accessible multi-user real-time virtual reconstruction. In *Proc. Virtual Systems and Multimedia 1999* (1999).

[dHCSMT05] DE HERAS CIECHOMSKI P., SCHERTENLEIB S., MAÏM J., THALMANN D.: Reviving the Roman Odeon of Aphrodisias: Dynamic animation and variety control of crowds in virtual heritage. In *Proc. of VSMM 2005* (2005).

[dHSMT05] DE HERAS P., SCHERTENLEIB S., MAÏM J., THALMANN D.: Real-time shader rendering for crowds in virtual heritage. In *Proc. 6th International Symposium on Virtual Reality, Archaeology and Cultural Heritage (VAST 05)* (2005).

[EPO] EPOCH: Excellence in processing open cultural heritage. http://www.epoch-net.org/.

References

[FLKB01] FRÖHLICH T., LUTZ B., KRESSE W., BEHR J.: The virtual cathedral of Siena. *Computer Graphik Topics 3* (2001), 24–26.
[FO04] GERALD C. F., WHEATLEY P. O.: Optimization. In *Applied Numerical Analysis* (2004), Addison Wesley, Reading.
[Ier03] IERUSALIMSCHY R.: *Programming in Lua*. Lablua, Rio de Janeiro, 2003.
[MHY*07] MAÏM J., HAEGLER S., YERSIN B., MÜLLER P., THALMANN D., GOOL L. J. V.: Populating ancient Pompeii with crowds of virtual Romans. In *VAST* (2007), Arnold D. B., Niccolucci F., Chalmers A. (Eds.), Eurographics Association, Geneve, pp. 109–116.
[MTPM97] MAGNENAT-THALMANN N., PANDZIC I. S., MOUSSALY J.-C.: The making of the terra-cotta Xian soldiers. *Digital Creativity 3*, 8 (1997), 66–73.
[NRC04] NIELSEN M. L., RINDEL J. H., CHRISTENSEN C. L.: Predicting the acoustics of ancient open-air theatres: The importance of calculation methods and geometrical details. In *Baltic-Nordic Acoustical Meeting* (2004).
[PLFMT01] PAPAGIANNAKIS G., L'HOSTE G., FONI A., MAGNENAT-THALMANN N.: Real-time photo realistic simulation of complex heritage edifices. In *Proc. Virtual Systems and Multimedia 2001* (2001), pp. 218–227.
[PPM*03] PONDER M., PAPAGIANNAKIS G., MOLET T., MAGNENAT-THALMANN N., THALMANN D.: Vhd++ development framework: Towards extendible, component based vr/ar simulation engine featuring advanced virtual character technologies. In *Proc. Computer Graphics International 2003* (2003), pp. 96–104.
[PSO*05] PAPAGIANNAKIS G., SCHERTENLEIB S., O'KENNEDY B., AREVALO-POIZAT M., MAGNENAT-THALMANN N., STODDART A., THALMANN D.: Mixing virtual and real scenes in the site of ancient Pompeii. *Computer Animation and Virtual Worlds 16* (2005), 11–24.
[UdHCT04] ULICNY B., DE HERAS CIECHOMSKI P., THALMANN D.: Crowdbrush: Interactive authoring of real-time crowd scenes. In *Proc. ACM SIGGRAPH/Eurographics Symposium on Computer Animation (SCA'04)* (2004), pp. 243–252.
[UT01] ULICNY B., THALMANN D.: Crowd simulation for interactive virtual environments and VR training systems. In *Proceedings of the Eurographic Workshop on Computer Animation and Simulation* (New York, NY, USA, 2001), Springer, New York, pp. 163–170.
[UT02] ULICNY B., THALMANN D.: Towards interactive real-time crowd behavior simulation. *Computer Graphics Forum 21*, 4 (Dec. 2002), 767–775.
[WDMTT12] WANG Y., DUBEY R., MAGNENAT-THALMANN N., THALMANN D.: Interacting with the virtual characters of multi-agent systems. In *Proc. Computer Graphics International* (2012).
[ZZ99] ZHENG J. Y., ZHANG Z. L.: Virtual recovery of excavated relics. *IEEE Computer Graphics and Applications 19*, 3 (1999), 6–11.

Book Contribution

Contributors to Chap. 1 (alphabetical order):
Soraia Raupp Musse and Daniel Thalmann

Contributors to Chap. 2 (alphabetical order):
Pablo de Heras Ciechomski, Soraia Raupp Musse, Daniel Thalmann and Branislav Ulicny

Contributors to Chap. 3 (alphabetical order):
Ronan Boulic, Adriana Braun, Henry Braun, Pablo de Heras Ciechomski, Leandro Dihl, Cláudio Rosito Jung, Júlio Cesar Jacques Júnior, Renato Keshet, Jonathan Maïm, Soraia Raupp Musse, André Tavares da Silva, Daniel Thalmann, Marcelo R. Thielo and Barbara Yersin

Contributors to Chap. 4 (alphabetical order):
Ronan Boulic, Pablo de Heras Ciechomski, Jonathan Maïm, Soraia Raupp Musse, André Tavares da Silva, Daniel Thalmann and Barbara Yersin

Contributors to Chap. 5 (alphabetical order):
Leandro Motta Barros, Alessandro de Lima Bicho, Helena Grillon, Cláudio Rosito Jung, Léo Pini Magalhães, Jonathan Maim, Soraia Raupp Musse, Marcelo Paravisi, Julien Pettré, Rafael Rodrigues, Daniel Thalmann and Barbara Yersin

Contributors to Chap. 6 (alphabetical order):
Cláudio Rosito Jung, Júlio Cesar Jacques Júnior, Soraia Raupp Musse and Daniel Thalmann

Contributors to Chap. 7 (alphabetical order):
Jonathan Maïm, Soraia Raupp Musse, Daniel Thalmann and Barbara Yersin

Contributors to Chap. 8 (alphabetical order):
Fernando Pinho Marson, Soraia Raupp Musse, Fernando Santos Osório, Daniel Paiva, Luiz Gonzaga da Silveira Júnior, Daniel Thalmann and Renata Vieira

Contributors to Chap. 9 (alphabetical order):
Adriana Braun, Vinicius Juranic Cassol, Pablo de Heras Ciechomski, Soraia Raupp Musse, Rafael Rodrigues, Daniel Thalmann and Branislav Ulicny

Index

A
AABB, 217, 218
Animation variety, 102
Ant system, 16
Anthropometric parameter, 35
Artificial life, 15, 16

B
Background subtraction, 180–183
Billboard, 21, 60, 81
Blob, 180–183
Boid, 13, 111, 112

C
Cal3D, 56, 258, 263
Cartoons, 22
Clustering, 11, 91, 184–186, 188
Coherent trajectory, 181, 184–186
Collision avoidance, 12, 14, 17, 19, 20, 114, 140, 141, 145, 152, 153, 188, 206, 210, 221, 222, 229, 278
Complex behavior, 4, 12, 13, 15, 16, 113, 270
Computer vision, 46, 179, 181, 182
Correlation metric, 180, 184
Crowd appearance, 57, 58
Crowd behaviors, 9, 18, 133, 175
Crowd characteristic, 169, 172
Crowd evacuation, 2, 9, 120, 286
Crowd event, 169, 172–175, 177
Crowdbrush, 24, 134, 279, 281, 282
Crowds navigation, 111, 126

D
Database management, 215
Deformable mesh, 196
Degrees of freedom, 33, 127, 128
Digital elevation model (DEM), 231
Digital terrain, 231
Distance transform, 183
Dynamic meshe, 21

E
Ectomorphy, 36, 39
Elastic deformation, 35
Ellipsoids, 32
Endomorphy, 36, 39
Entertainment application, 126, 131, 136
Environment modeling, 1, 16

F
Finite-state machine, 13, 14
Flock motion, 12
Foreground object, 180, 182, 183

G
Games, 23
GDAL, 263
Genotype, 34
Geometry baking, 21
Graphics processing units, 3, 20, 120
Group animation, 12–15
Group leader, 113

H
Human template, 57–59, 65, 68–74, 102, 196, 199, 200, 202, 205–210, 212–216, 226, 277

I
Impostor animations, 77, 198, 199, 207, 208, 210–212, 214–216
Impostors, 20, 21, 77, 196, 198, 199, 201, 204, 207, 211, 232, 262
Informed environment, 17, 246, 247
Instant architecture, 230, 253

K
Kinematic method, 82

L
L-systems, 232, 234
Landing algorithms, 253
Levels of autonomy, 11, 13, 113
Levels of detail, 14, 58, 67, 81, 195, 196, 204, 230, 232, 253, 261
Levels of simulation, 136, 247
Locomotion control, 99

M
Macroscopic analyse, 43, 46
Mesh variation, 37, 40
Mesomorphy, 36, 39, 43
Microscopic analyse, 43
Motion capture, 22, 23, 81, 82, 84, 87, 88, 226, 269, 272
Motion planning, 127–129
Motion retargeting, 95, 97
Muscles, 32, 36, 112

N
Navigation graph, 18, 137, 140, 141, 143, 203, 204, 246
Normal life situation, 123, 256, 257
Nurbs, 32

O
Ontology-based simulation, 254
OpenSceneGraph, 263
OpenSteer, 263

P
Particle, 9–11, 13, 146, 186, 187, 232, 287
People tracking, 179–182, 188, 190
Personification control, 99
Physically based method, 83, 84
Plants and lakes, 232
Point-based rendering, 21
Populated environment, 229–263
Principal component analysis (PCA), 35, 82, 87

R
Radial basis function, 84
Real crowd, 170, 173, 175
Real scene, 173
Real-time production, 22, 23
Rendering, 20, 71, 195, 207, 210, 217, 232, 261
Rigid animation, 76, 77, 198, 199, 209, 211, 212, 214, 215
Rigid mesh, 76, 81, 196, 198, 199, 201, 204, 206, 207, 209, 211, 212
Robot motion planning, 127, 129
Robotic, 15

S
Safety system, 267, 286
Scenario authoring, 24, 271, 273
Secondary character, 31, 34, 42
Shadow, 180, 182, 196, 207, 209, 216–218, 226, 232
Skeletal animation, 76, 197, 198, 206, 211–215, 278
Sky and cloud, 233
Sociological model, 10
Somatotype, 31, 35–41

T
Terrain modeling, 230
Textures, 21, 32–34, 42, 47, 48, 56–64, 69, 75, 196, 199, 207–210, 229–232, 234, 249, 250, 271, 276, 277, 283
Timewarping, 93, 95
Topo mesh, 249, 251, 252
Traffic simulation, 17
Training system, 1, 2, 15

V
Virtual heritage, 267
Virtual human skeleton, 101
Virtual mosque, 268
Virtual population, 134, 140, 218, 251, 256, 268
Virtual Roman audience, 271
Virtual world, 23, 134, 135, 147, 234, 263
Visual diversity, 32, 42

W
Walking model, 93

Printed by Printforce, the Netherlands